# Secret Jews

### THE COMPLEX IDENTITY OF CRYPTO-JEWS AND CRYPTO-JUDAISM

## Juan Marcos Bejarano Gutierrez

Yaron Publishing
GRAND PRAIRIE, TEXAS

Copyright © 2017 by Juan Marcos Bejarano Gutierrez.

All rights reserved. No part of this publication may be reproduced, distributed or transmitted in any form or by any means, including photocopying, recording, or other electronic or mechanical methods, without the prior written permission of the publisher, except in the case of brief quotations embodied in critical reviews and certain other noncommercial uses permitted by copyright law. For permission requests, write to the publisher, addressed "Attention: Permissions Coordinator," at the address below.

Juan Marcos Bejarano Gutierrez/Yaron Publishing
701 Forest Park Place
Grand Prairie, Tx 75052
www.cryptojewisheducation.com


Book Layout ©2017 BookDesignTemplates.com

Ordering Information:
Quantity sales. Special discounts are available on quantity purchases by corporations, associations, and others. For details, contact the "Special Sales Department" at the address above.

Secret Jews/ Juan Marcos Bejarano Gutierrez. —1st ed.
ISBN 978-1539620877
Cover image: Expulsión de los judíos de España (año de 1492) by Emilio Sala Francés (1850–1910).

# Contents

Introduction ................................................................. 6
The Rise of the Converso Problem .......................................... 17
Christian Attitudes Towards Conversos ..................................... 64
Jewish Attitudes Towards Apostates ....................................... 107
Types of Conversos ....................................................... 123
Skeptical Conversos ...................................................... 177
Jewish Attitudes Towards Conversos ....................................... 207
Modern Day Conversos ..................................................... 245
The Crypto-Jewish Controversy ............................................ 269
Conclusions .............................................................. 283
Glossary of Frequently Used Terms ........................................ 288
Bibliography ............................................................. 293
Index .................................................................... 305

*To Dr. Harvey P. Oshman*
"A good name is rather to be chosen than great riches, and loving favor rather than silver and gold."
Proverbs 22:1

## ACKNOWLEDGMENTS

I had the privilege of knowing Harvey P. Oshman for more than 22 years. Despite our difference in ages, he befriended me. He had a profound influence on me in many areas of my life.

He appreciated my passion for the study of Judaism in general as well as Crypto-Judaism. He provided me with a letter of recommendation when I applied to the Siegal College of Judaic Studies. He contributed financially to my Jewish education. He helped me in business. He was one of the two witnesses who signed the ketubah at my wedding.

These are just a few of the practical ways that Harvey impacted my life. But his effect on me went far beyond academics. We talked about theology, politics, and life in general. He chastised me when I needed it, even if I did not like it. I hope that I am a better man today because of it. His passing in 2016 was a terrible loss for all who knew him.

I will always remember him, and his memory will indeed be a blessing.

# Introduction

For Jews, life in the Iberian Peninsula was never quite as idyllic as is often portrayed. Jews residing there had experienced early Christian anti-Judaism in the fourth century and had undergone persecution, forced conversions, and expulsions under the Christianized Visigoths in the sixth and seventh centuries. The Islamic conquest of Spain in the eighth century improved Jewish life and created a period of stability and growth. Jewish life under Islamic rule, however, was not devoid of its trials and misfortunes as experienced under the Almovarids in the eleventh century and the Almohades in the twelfth century. Islamic fortunes eventually declined in the Iberian Peninsula. In the transition between Islamic and Christian rule, Jews flourished as an essential minority for the emerging Christian kingdoms now dominating the Peninsula.

In 1391, a new period in the history of the Jews of Spain began. Jewish communities throughout the Peninsula except those in the Kingdom of Portugal were attacked. The violence was stoked by long-held Christian anti-Judaism and popular discontent. The violence forever altered the position of Jews in the Iberian Peninsula. Thousands of Jews were murdered, and many more converted to Christianity under the direct threat of violence or to forestall it. The scope of the attacks in 1391 overshadowed all past trials as well as achievements and initiated a social and religious crisis that would last for more than a century.

The Jews who converted to Christianity were known as Conversos or New Christians in Christian literature and primarily as *anusim* (i.e. forced converts) in Jewish texts. According to the Spanish monarchs Ferdinand and Isabella, Judaizing by Conversos was the primary reason for their decision to order the expulsion of all unbaptized Jews in 1492 from their Iberian and overseas dominions. They argued that some unbaptized Jews had aided and abetted Conversos in Judaizing. The only way to resolve the problem was the absolute separation of the two groups. The accusation was, in fact, true. Their solution to the problem was brutal.

The descendants of Jews who had survived the mass conversions of 1391 were given a choice between exile and conversion. Further conversions were also brought about by the expulsion decrees issued by the Kingdom of Portugal in 1497 and the Kingdom of Navarre in 1498. Many exiles from the Kingdoms of Castile and Aragon had taken refuge in those domains in the wake of the original expulsion orders. Those Jews who converted to forgo exile faced challenges with an anti-Converso sentiment very much alive and well despite the drastic moves taken by the Spanish monarchs. Such actions had included the creation of the Spanish Inquisition in 1478, which was already firmly focused on Conversos continuing to observe Jewish practices. In the Kingdom of Portugal, no real choice between exile and baptism was presented. Thousands of Jews expecting to leave the Kingdom were forcibly baptized and forbidden to leave. Since these refugees had lived openly as Jews, their ability to preserve Jewish identity secretly was much stronger than had been the case for Conversos in Castile and Aragon. The latter had already experienced a century of severe conditions resulting in a weakened state of Jewish identity.

The real religious identity of Conversos has often been the source of debate among scholars. Yitzhak Baer and Haim Beinart argued that Conversos were one with the Jewish people. According to their position, the Jewish community recognized that the choice to convert had been made under duress and that Conversos, on the whole, were insincere in their attachment to Christianity. For Baer and Beinart, the Inquisitional documents correctly testified to the Jewish practices of Conversos. The initial Conversos, as well as their descendants, remained faithful to Judaism to the best of their ability. In contrast, Benzion Netanyahu argued vociferously that outside of the first onslaught of 1391, the subsequent generations of Conversos were, in fact, sincere converts to Christianity. The Inquisitional records were nothing short of a farce. According to Netanyahu, while the first generation may have converted due to the threat of death, their children and grandchildren were sincere Christians. Netanyahu argued that whatever Crypto-Jewish practices existed were mainly due to the resentment stirred by unjust Inquisitional tactics. Netanyahu maintained that the Inquisition was not religiously motivated to extirpate the heresy of Judaizing. While a hatred of Judaism had motivated previous sentiments against Jews, Old Christians were now driven by anti-Semitism to destroy the Conversos as a social and economic class regardless of what religious beliefs they sincerely held.

In contrast to Netanyahu's contentions, this study maintains that while there were certainly exceptions, most Conversos did retain essential elements of Jewish identity well beyond the years immediately following 1391. They did so despite challenging circumstances and the watchful eyes of local priests and bishops. Conversos had always been mindful that Old Christians (i.e. Christians prior to the violence of 1391 and effectively Gentile Christians) could rise violently against them as they had before. These concerns were proven to be correct several times throughout the fifteenth century in cities like Toledo, Ciudad Real, Córdoba, and in Lisbon in the early sixteenth century. That religious fervor did not solely motivate these outbreaks of violence was in due course admitted by the Christian populace. These persecutions were motivated in part by the resentment that many Old Christians felt towards Conversos because some had taken advantage of the new found social and economic opportunities open to them. In addition, recently converted Jews were suspected of continuing to practice Judaism secretly. Those who converted but observed Judaism clandestinely were known as Judaizers or *Marranos* meaning swine. The Old Christian population regarded Conversos and their descendants as Jews and treated them accordingly.

The insincerity of most of the conversions was also recognized by the Jewish community with which Conversos retained extensive connections. There were religious issues with regards to the status of these individuals in Jewish law. However, an expanded view of Jewish identity together with an appreciation for the nuances of Jewish law confirm that they remained a part of the Jewish people collectively. This was true regardless of whether or not their individual paths continued along the same accepted routes as their unbaptized brethren. While the majority of Conversos, not just the first generation, were insincere Catholics, the reality is much more complicated than the polar extremes depicted by either Yitzhak Baer or Benzion Netanyahu. The Jewish identity of the Conversos with respect to religious practice, belief, and theology lay along a broad spectrum reflective of their unique experiences. This applies also to the attitudes that Jews and Old Christians held toward Conversos.

To prove the assertion that most Conversos retained key elements of their Jewish identity, a series of chapters will lay out the case for their continued Jewish distinctiveness while also examining those who departed or deviated from it. This study will provide a conceptual overview rather than a strictly historical approach in the hope of offering a more easily understood discussion.

Chapter one, titled *The Rise of the Converso Problem*, will provide the historical context for the mass conversions of 1391. It will do so by providing a survey of important events in the history of Iberian Jewry from the Late Roman Period until the massacres of 1391. Under the rule of the Visigoths, Jews were forcibly converted. Many dissimulated in a manner eerily similar to the practices of the $15^{th}$ and $16^{th}$ century. The forced conversion of Jews to Islam by the Islamic sect known as the Almohades will also be discussed since dissimulation was similarly practiced during this era. The Castilian Civil War of the middle decades of the $14^{th}$ century will also be reviewed. Henry of Trastámara rebelled against his half-brother Peter I and introduced anti-Jewish sentiment as a powerful weapon of war. Henry's actions helped stir widespread resentment against Jews and set the stage for the approaching violence of 1391. A cursory study of the consequences and critical events following the massacres until the Expulsions at the end of the 15th century will also be included. Among these events will be the Tortosa Disputation, which saw the conversions of more Jews to Christianity.

The second chapter, titled *Christian Attitudes Towards Conversos*, will survey the range of Christian views towards Conversos during the 14th, 15th, and 16th centuries. The idea of supersessionism was critical to Christians' understanding of Jews. This idea that Christians had replaced the Jews as the chosen people of God was and remains a cornerstone of Christian thought. The continuing distinctiveness of Conversos evidenced in their ongoing relationships with Jewish family, cultural practices, and most important Jewish religious expressions challenged Christian notions regarding the boundaries between Jews and Christians rather than resolving them. The Christian concept concerning the irrevocable nature of baptism and most importantly, the problem of Judaizing among Conversos will also be considered.

An essential aspect of this discussion will be those Christian attitudes towards Jews which shaped the mindset of Christians during preceding centuries and influenced their views towards Conversos. The conversions of 1391 were initially met with enthusiasm by many Old Christians and even considered to be miraculous in nature. This excitement eventually turned to disdain as the reality of most Conversos' true attitude, towards Christianity became apparent. This viewpoint was matched by similar antipathy on the part of the Christian clergy towards Conversos. The minimal enthusiasm of the Conversos towards Christianity was motivated in part by the lack of Christian education given to Conversos in the years following the massacres of 1391. The fact that Conversos lacked Christian education only served to reinforce their identity as Jews and further distinguish them from an Old Christian community growing in its skepticism and contempt for them.

In some quarters, a measure of toleration for Converso Judaizing was given due to the need for the Crowns to balance their financial needs and their religious obligations. However, the supsupposed success of the conversions animated many, including the previously mentioned Geronimo de Santa Fe to drive more Jews towards embracing Christianity. The result was the Tortosa Disputation in 1412-1414. The perceived success of the debates by Christians notwithstanding, growing contempt for Converso economic success and accusations of Judaizing helped transform the perennial "Jewish Problem" into a new but equally devastating "Converso Problem." The tension boiled over into violence and resulted in the adoption of purity of blood laws to stem the rise of Conversos in public offices. Such laws proved insufficient for many Old Christians, and individuals such as Alonso de Espina called for the creation of a reinvigorated Inquisition to attack the "deadly cancer" of Judaizing at its source. Works such *El Alboraique* depicted Conversos as hideous beasts who were intent on the downfall of Christianity. Despite such rhetoric, many clerics defended Conversos and argued that discrimination against them was contrary to the Christian faith. Time and separation from Jews they argued were the ultimate guarantors of orthodoxy among Conversos. In the end, even the violent tactics of the Inquisition were deemed insufficient, and the expulsion of all the Jews of Castile and Aragon was proposed as the final solution to the Converso dilemma.

The third chapter, titled *Jewish Attitudes Towards Apostates*, will review the social and theological challenges that apostasy posed for Jews. While most Jews understood the circumstances they faced, Conversos had technically adopted a pagan religion. This fact impacted various aspects of Jewish identity including marriage and divorce, and the permissibility of food and wine prepared by apostates. How relapsed converts were accepted and treated in the Jewish community is another point of interest. Chapter six will expand on this topic by providing greater detail on concrete examples of interaction between Jews and Conversos.

The fourth chapter, titled *Types of Conversos*, relates the major categories of Conversos which existed and the motivations for their conversions. It will be demonstrated that most converts were not sincere in their conversions and did so only to escape violence, crippling poverty, or judicial punishment. Others did so to break free of the social and economic limitations Jews had increasingly endured as a religious minority under Christian rule. When the Edict of Expulsion was issued in Castile and Aragon, the various Jewish communities of these realms were still liable to repay their debts to the Spanish Crowns. The individual members of each community were taxed accordingly, and the weight of this burden caused some to contemplate conversion to escape their financial obligations. Other persons exhibited much more complex traits. Some such as Pedro de la Caballeria were quite adept at walking in both worlds. He falsified his Converso background and pretended to be of Old Christian ancestry. He even authored a work in defense of Christianity. Yet he was capable of participating in Jewish rites at his discretion and interacting intelligently on Jewish matters when he chose. Others, such as Guillem Ramon Splugues converted out of spite towards his family, later regretting the decision that forever tied him to Christianity. Splugues was a respected member of the Jewish community and a lay scholar. His involvement with Christian women led to friction with his family and a rash decision to convert. He remained committed to Judaism and even worked to convince others to embrace Jewish practices until the Inquisition arrested him.

Some were born as Conversos and maintained a sense of Jewish identity that was transmitted by their parents' generations after the massacres of 1391. Many of these individuals received assistance from friends and family in the Jewish community. As time passed, however, even the most sincere individuals intent on maintaining a sense of Jewish identity were stymied by the gradual decline of Judaic knowledge. Contact with other Jews even after the Expulsion was occasionally possible, but inquiring Conversos often gathered information regarding Judaism through the literature that the Inquisition itself had distributed to identify Judaizing practices. There were many Conversos who after generations strove to recapture their Jewish identity, but their understanding of Judaism was increasingly filtered through Catholic lenses. For many, the deterioration of their knowledge of Judaism slowly transformed their Jewish identity into a sum of anti-Christian beliefs. Jewish belief was the negation of and mockery of fundamental Christian dogmas.

Those who were able to escape the Iberian Peninsula and make their ways to openly Jewish communities underwent a process of return. The successful assimilation of individuals like Abraham Israel Pereyra and Isaac Orobio de Castro will be studied. Other Conversos who arrived did not adjust as quickly and struggled to accept the rabbinic norms that now defined Jewish life. Since they had rejected the authority of the Church, the tendency to question authority may have already been present making the path towards integration into Jewish life that much harder. Having survived the challenge of living a dissimulated Jewish life, they now encountered expectations that often differed from what they had envisioned.

There were some who gained a sophisticated knowledge of Jewish practices and theology even while still living outwardly as Catholics. Samuel Yahya was one such individual. He was born in Antwerp in 1576 and settled in Hamburg in 1605 when practicing Judaism openly was illegal. Samuel played a crucial role in the forming of the Hamburg Converso community. His Jewish education was very extensive as revealed in his sermons. He was conversant in Hebrew and quite impressively able to reference classical rabbinic commentaries as well as the Shulchan Aruch, and the Zohar, which he shared with his fellow Conversos. Another former Convero who mastered rabbinic texts was Abraham Miguel Cardozo. Born in Spain he and his brother Isaac fled the Peninsula and journeyed to Italy where they returned to Judaism. Cardozo was swept up in the frenzy of the Sabbatean messianic movement and became a principal theologian of it despite his never having met Sabbatai Zevi. Cardozo ultimately saw himself as a Messiah ben Joseph, the complimentary figure to Messiah ben David whose role was filled by Sabbatai Zevi. Cardozo's endorsement of Zevi and his own messianic claims were deeply rooted in his identity and experience as a Converso.

Some Jews had in fact converted sincerely to Christianity. Sadly, many of these individuals were not content to embrace their new faith quietly. Many of them rose to prominent positions in the Church. In these offices, they actively worked to ensure the social and economic isolation of the Jewish community. After their conversion, individuals like Solomon Ha-Levi and Joshua Lorqui successfully antagonized their former coreligionists. Despite their conversions, many of these people retained an odd measure of pride in their Jewish origins. Their Jewish backgrounds coupled with their Christian faith allowed them to claim that they most closely resembled the earliest followers of the Christian message. In this sense, even they retained a measure of Jewish identity that they sought to transmit to their progeny. Not all of these converts, however, were so enthusiastic about maintaining a claim to their Jewish backgrounds. Individuals like the great humanist Juan Luis Vives, who had witnessed multiple family members tried as Judaizers, saw themselves as wholly subsumed in the mystical body of Christ to the exclusion of any other identity.

The fifth chapter, titled *Skeptical Conversos* focuses on those Conversos who gave up on both religious traditions and endeavored to create a world where religious affiliations were no longer the determining factor in a person's life. The violence of 1391 had presented them with a choice of life or death. Their coerced adoption of Christianity and the anti-Converso sentiment that arose may have led them to conclude that all religious beliefs were pointless. These skeptically oriented Conversos were reported to search for false gospels, reject the immortality of the soul, involve themselves in philosophical discussions, and believe that salvation was available within various faith traditions. Generations later, other Conversos, who at least superficially, maintained allegiance to Catholicism, resurrected Academic and Pyrrhonian skepticism. They argued that ultimate knowledge was unachievable and human understanding was limited. Individuals like Francisco Sanchez and Michel de Montaigne as well as the biblical critic Isaac La Peyrère set the stage for the undermining of traditional religious beliefs. Their actions created the environment for Uriel da Costa and Baruch Spinoza in the 17$^{th}$ century who rejected the veracity of both Christianity and Judaism.

The sixth chapter, titled *Jewish Attitudes Towards Conversos,* will discuss the range of emotions and attitudes towards Conversos, which were held by unbaptized Jews. The continuing family bonds, which tied Jews and Conversos were an important factor in the relations between these two groups. Even those Jews not bound by blood were often supportive of Conversos and expressed this by providing them with kosher food, teaching them Hebrew, and giving them access to Jewish ritual items. They risked their fortunes and lives in doing so. They did so because they saw Conversos as continuing members of the Jewish people despite their conversions. Such sentiments were not limited to ordinary Jews. Rabbis were also supportive of Conversos trying to maintain their Jewish identity and worked to re-integrate them into the Jewish community. The venerable Isaac Abravanel held firmly to his belief that Conversos would play a crucial role in the future redemption of Israel and the nations even if their return to Judaism was not immediate. A century and a half after the Expulsion decrees, Rabbi Isaac Aboab from Amsterdam viewed Conversos as having a share in the World to Come regardless of their failures to live openly as Jews. Others, such as Rabbi Saul Levi Morteira of Amsterdam, were convinced that unless Conversos escaped the lands of idolatry to a place where they could worship openly as Jews, they were condemned to eternal punishment. Despite Rabbi Morteira's harsh stance, his view was predicated on the Jewish status of these individuals and a desire for them to fully rejoin the people of Israel.

The seventh chapter, titled *Modern Day Conversos,* will survey various accounts of modern Conversos ranging from Spain and

Portugal to Latin America, and the American Southwest. Hundreds if not thousands of individuals, from Hispanic backgrounds, have claimed Converso ancestry and have acted to reintegrate themselves into the Jewish community in some form or fashion. The subject of Conversos, therefore, is not merely a theoretical or historical subject, but a topic of increasing contemporary relevance and importance. The study of Crypto-Judaism has brought about the creation of some organizations, academic and others religiously focused, on assisting Hispanic individuals interested in Judaism or claiming to be the descendants of Conversos. There are controversies regarding their claims, but the number of persons interested in their Converso past is growing with the increasing availability of information and resources.

The last chapter, titled *The Crypto-Jewish Controversy*, discusses the scholarly debate over the veracity of Inquisitional records. The discussion is important since how the motivations of the Inquisition impacts how the subject of Crypto-Judaism is understood. A brief review of scholarship on the Inquisition and Crypto-Judaism is included.

Even after such extensive research, the material available for further study is truly expansive. Many areas of research remain open for further investigation. This book hopes to provide one small addition to the study of Conversos.

CHAPTER 1

# The Rise of the Converso Problem

An early testament to the presence of Jews in the Iberian Peninsula is a decree issued by the Council of Elvira in southern Spain circa 304 CE. The Christian Council was comprised of bishops and presbyters from the cities of Córdoba, Seville, Toledo, Saragossa, and various other towns populated by Jews. The council prohibited Christians from living or eating with Jews. It also barred Christians from allowing their daughters to marry Jews or pagans. Christians were also forbidden from asking Jews to bless their fields. The penalty for failing to comply with these rules was excommunication.

The Visigoths gained control over most of the Iberian Peninsula in the waning years of the Western Roman Empire. After 586 CE, Visigoth rule was increasingly characterized by anti-Jewish legislation.[1] In 551 CE, Athangild, one of many aspirants vying for the Visigoth throne requested support from the Eastern Roman Empire. The Byzantines supported his claim and also seized Córdoba, Granada, Cartagena, and the Balearic Islands in the process.[2]

---

[1] José Hinojosa Montalvo, "Los judíos en la España medieval: de la tolerancia a la expulsión." Lecture, Universidad de Alicante, 1998. https://goo.gl/mdB66Y

[2] Norman Roth, *Jews, Visigoths, and Muslims in Medieval Spain: Cooperation and Conflict* (Leiden: E.J. Brill, 1994), 7.

Furthermore, Byzantine anti-Judaism influenced the entire Visigoth kingdom. Byzantine rule in southern Spain eventually ended in 625 CE, but its religious and ideological power over the Visigoths persisted with a rather devastating impact on the Jewish community.

At the third ecclesiastical Council of Toledo in 589, King Reccared prohibited Jews from acquiring or owning Christian slaves. They were also barred from public office and banned from having intercourse with Christian women. The circumcision of either a slave or a Christian was punished with confiscation of property. The council also stipulated that children born of the intermarriage between a Jew and a Christian were to be baptized and reared as Christians. However, King Reccared was only partially successful in enforcing these laws. King Reccared resisted the attempts by Jews to rescind these decrees and earned praise from Pope Gregory I (540-604 CE) for his steadfastness.[3]

Successive church councils in Toledo were focused on preventing Jewish converts to Christianity from reverting to Judaism. Many of these Jews appear to have converted under duress and the weight of increasing anti-Jewish measures. Jewish converts were prohibited from associating with openly practicing Jews. The children of those suspected to have relapsed were seized and transferred to Christian families. Recent converts were also bound to sign a formal declaration that they had abandoned Jewish rituals and observances.[4]

In 613, King Sisebut demanded that all Jews residing in his domains convert. He commanded that all Jews were to either submit to baptism or leave within a year. According to Catholic sources, ninety thousand Jews converted to Christianity.[5] The Islamic

---

[3] Solomon Grazyel, "The Beginnings of Exclusion," The Jewish Quarterly Review, New Series, Vol. 61, No.1 (1970): 23.

[4] Cecil Roth, *A History of the Marranos* (Philadelphia : Jewish Publication Society, 1947), 9.

[5] Ibid., 7.

chronicler, Al-Razi, contends that all Iberian Jews converted to Christianity though later Church councils confirmed the continued existence of non-converted Jews in Spain.[6]

The forced conversions were severely criticized by the leading Spanish theologian of the day, St. Isidore of Seville. Despite his condemnation, during the fourth Toledo Council convened in 633, St. Isidore insisted that forced converts live a Christian life lest the Christian faith be considered worthless.[7] The fourth Toledo Council noted the ongoing Jewish practices of forced converts who were treated as blasphemers.[8] They lost their children and slaves if the latter had been circumcised.[9] Previously adopted laws, including forbidding contact between Jewish converts and unconverted Jews, were reiterated. Also, a convert to Christianity, whose sincerity was dubious, was excluded from giving testimony in a court of law.[10]

Following the death of King Sisebut in 621 CE, King Swinthila (circa 621-631) assumed the throne. According to Al-Razi, Jews from other territories settled in Spain during his reign. Swinthila was forced to relinquish his throne and was succeeded by Sisenand. King Sisenand ruled briefly from 631–636 CE.[11] Under Sisenand's reign, children of converted Jews were taken from their parents' custody and given to Christians or to monasteries to ensure they received a proper Christian education. Forced

---

[6] "And other Jews outside of the land of Spain came to settle [the places] which these [Jews of Spain] had left." Norman Roth, *Jews, Visigoths, and Muslims in Medieval Spain: Cooperation and Conflict* (Leiden: E.J. Brill, 1994), 13.

[7] Canon 57.

[8] Norman Roth, *Jews, Visigoths, and Muslims in Medieval Spain: Cooperation and Conflict* (Leiden: E.J. Brill, 1994), 31.

[9] The topic of *relapsi*, baptized Jews who reverted to Jewish practices, was discussed repeatedly in 506, 633, 638, 654, 655, 681, and 693 CE. Henriette-Rika Benveniste, "On the Language of Conversion: Visigothic Spain Revisited," Historein 6 (2006): 74, 79.

[10] Solomon Grazyel, "The Beginnings of Exclusion," The Jewish Quarterly Review, New Series, Vol. 61, No.1 (1970): 23–24.

[11] Bat- Sheva Albert, "Isidore of Seville: His Attitude towards Judaism and His Impact on Early Medieval Canon Law," The Jewish Quarterly Review, LXX, Nos 3-4 (1990): 216-217.

converts, known to practice Jewish ceremonies, were given away as slaves.¹² King Sisenand was succeeded by King Chintila, who reigned from 636–640 CE.

At the sixth Toledo council in 638 CE, Jews were forced to make a declaration known as the *Placitum*. The statement described all the Jewish observances, the Sabbath, holidays, and other practices from which they pledged to desist.¹³ Moreover, Jewish converts vowed to avoid contact with unbaptized Jews and not marry them.¹⁴ King Recesswinth (649-672 CE) outlawed all Jewish observances, including circumcision, the laws of *kashrut*, Jewish weddings, and banned Jews from appearing in court.

In 654 CE, another "declaration of faith" was presented by Jewish converts of Toledo to King Recesswinth. The document made reference to the fact that Jewish practices had been observed by Jews who had nominally converted to Christianity decades before under the reign of King Chintila or possibly as far back as under King Sisebut.¹⁵

Under the direction of King Erwig (circa 680-687), the twelfth Toledo Council decreed that any unconverted Jews still living throughout Visigoth territory were to convert. If they refused, their property was to be confiscated, and they would be expelled. King Erwig enacted harsh punishments for observing circumcision and reading anti-Christian writings. Egica, the son-in-law of King Erwig, succeeded him as king. King Egica confiscated all assets owned by Jews and declared all Jews, baptized or not, to be slaves

---

¹² Interestingly, St. Braulio, the Bishop of Saragossa, wrote to Pope Honorius I inquiring why baptized Jews were allowed to return to Judaism when they arrived in Rome. Bat- Sheva Albert, "Isidore of Seville: His Attitude towards Judaism and His Impact on Early Medieval Canon Law," The Jewish Quarterly Review, LXX, Nos 3-4 (1990): 214

¹³ Norman Roth, *Jews, Visigoths, and Muslims in Medieval Spain: Cooperation and Conflict* (Leiden: E.J. Brill, 1994), 23.

¹⁴ Ibid.

¹⁵ Paul Halsall, Jewish History Sourcebook: The Jews of Spain and the Visigothic Code, 654-681 CE. Retrieved 22 November 2012 from Fordham University: http://www.fordham.edu/halsall/jewish/jews-visigothic1.asp

offered to Christians as gifts. Jewish children over the age of seven were taken from their parents and also given away as slaves. The last Council of Toledo was convened in 694 CE. It decreed that the property of Jews was to be confiscated and that they were to be exiled from their homes and sold into slavery to prevent them from observing Judaism.[16]

## The Islamic Conquest of the Iberian Peninsula

The Islamic invasion of Spain in 711 radically changed the position of Jews throughout the Iberian Peninsula. The conquest was rapid, and the cities of Córdoba, Malaga, Granada, Seville, and Toledo were placed in charge of their Jewish residents as the Muslim armies moved northwards. The change in conditions was highly significant. Restrictions, which had previously affected the Jewish community, were finally lifted. Furthermore, some Jews served as advisors and guides to the advancing Muslim forces. Within the confines of Islamic law, Jews, as well as Christians, were religiously tolerated. As *dhimmis,* they were required to pay a tribute of one golden dinar per person and follow various restrictions for non-Muslims.

Under the rule of the Ommiad ruler, Abd al-Raḥman I (circa 731-788 CE), a prosperous kingdom was established with the city of Córdoba as its capital. During his reign, many Jews served the caliphate in critical positions. Jews enjoyed both stability and prosperity under the reigns of Abd al-Raḥman I and his son Al-Ḥakim. Under Islamic rule, Spain emerged as a refuge for the Jews oppressed in other parts of the world. The cities of Córdoba and Lucena in Spain flourished as centers of Jewish learning while the caliphate ruled most of the Peninsula from 756–1031.

---

[16] Solomon Grazyel, "The Beginnings of Exclusion," The Jewish Quarterly Review, New Series, Vol. 61, No.1 (1970): 25.

The unique conditions created under Islamic rule which lasted until the early 12th century CE is termed as *Convivencia*.[17] For some, the term connotes a near utopian society in which Jews, Christians, and Muslims lived and worked side by side in almost idyllic symbiosis.[18] There is no doubt that Iberian Jewry experienced a period of relative stability and success during this time, at least when compared to Jews living in Christian societies in Central or Eastern Europe. Under Islamic rule, Jews were not the dominant or sole minority community. In Christian lands, Jews—except for the occasional Christian heretical group —were the primary focus of attention for those looking to establish a homogenous religious and cultural society. Under Islam, Jews, various types of Christians, as well as Zoroastrians, and members of other religious faiths shared the spotlight as religious minorities.

But the extent of that success, beyond the ranks of the great Jewish poets, philosophers, and courtiers of roughly a two hundred years plus period, is likely overstated.[19] While there were positive interactions between the three communities, this does not suggest an entire state of harmony between them. Distrust, prejudice, and conflict were also part of the equation.[20]

From the 11th to the 13th century, some incidents of violence by Muslims towards Spanish and Moroccan Jews occurred. These include the Muslim massacre of the Jews of Fez in 1035 and an attack on the Jews of Granada in 1066. Moreover, around the year

---

[17] Ibid., xii.

[18] Norman Roth, *Conversos, Inquisition, and the Expulsion of the Jews from Spain* (Madison: University of Wisconsin, 1995), 9. There is something to be said for the unique circumstances of Jews within Spanish society. The Fuero de Cuenca relates: "If a Jew and a Christian contest something, they designate two neighboring townspeople, one Christian and one Jewish." Also, in the Fuero de Sepulveda, a Jew's testimony, was considered as a valid as a Christian's. Joseph Perez, *History of a Tragedy: The Expulsion of the Jews from Spain* (Chicago: University of Illinois Press, 1993), 123.

[19] Joaquim Carvalho ed., *Religion and Power in Europe: Conflict and Convergence* (Pisa: Edizioni Plus - Pisa University Press, 2007), 78.

[20] Joseph Perez, *History of a Tragedy: The Expulsion of the Jews from Spain* (Chicago: University of Illinois Press, 1993), xii. Elie Kedourie, *Spain and the Jews: The Sephardi Experience 1492 and After* (London: Thames and Hudson, 1992), 33.

1105, the Jews of Lucena were forcibly converted to Islam. Muslim authorities suppressed a Jewish revolt in Córdoba in 1117. The revolt was spurred by the belief that the Messiah was soon to be revealed. In 1127, Islamic authorities repressed another Jewish messianic revolt in Fez. Jews were forcibly converted in Spain between 1146 and 1163. Forced conversions of Jews in Morocco also occurred from 1164 to 1185. Violent atrocities continued to be committed against Jews as a new Muslim massacre took place in Marrakesh in 1232 followed by another in Fez in 1275.[21]

In those cases where Islamic persecution did break out, it was typically levied against all members of the *dhimmi* class. The violence erupted in a significant part because of "violations" or indiscretions by members of the class that were thought to impact the superior status of Muslims. Nevertheless, the clashes were largely different from the type of violence and discrimination faced by Jews in Christian lands. As Bernard Lewis notes, in Islamic society, antagonism against Jews was non-theological.[22]

## The Almoravides (1040–1147)

The conquests of King Alfonso VI of Castile caused Al-Mu'tamid, the last independent king of Andalusia, to summon help from King Yusuf ibn Tashfin of the growing Almoravid Empire in North Africa. The religious sect that ibn Tashfin commanded was known as the Almoravides. The battle of Zallaka resulted in an Almoravid victory and staved off further Christian conquest for the time being.[23] As a consequence, Yusuf ibn Tashfin gained supreme power on the Islamic side. The Almoravides were religious

---

[21] Allan Harris Cutler and Helen Elmquist Cutler, *The Jews as Ally of the Muslim: Medieval Roots of Anti-Semitism* (Notre Dame: University of Notre Dame, 1986), 259.

[22] Bernard Lewis, *The Jews of Islam* (Princeton: Princeton University Press, 1984), 85.

[23] The degree of Jewish integration in both Christian and Muslim camps is highlighted in part by the battle of Zallaka in October 1086. King Alfonso's army purportedly included 40,000 Jews. The battle purportedly was not initiated until after the Sabbath had ended. In addition to inquiring from his bishops, Alfonso also asked Jewish scholars and astrologers about their predictions for the battle.

zealots, and with their support, ibn Tashfin attempted to force the Jewish community of Lucena to convert to Islam.

During the rule of his son Ali (1106–43 CE), Islamic attitudes towards Jews were more positive. Some Jews were appointed collectors of royal taxes while others were allowed to serve in governmental positions, including those of "vizier" or "nasi." The communities of Seville, Granada, and Córdoba which had suffered previously were rebuilt.

## The Almohades (1121–1269)

The religious zealotry of the Almoravides was surpassed by Abdallah ibn Tumart in Morocco in 1112. Ibn Tumart established the new Islamic party known as the Almohades or the Muzmotas. He saw himself as a purist defender of Mohammed's original teachings relating to the unity of God. Following the death of Abdallah, Abd al-Mu'min assumed leadership and strove to eliminate the Almoravides as both political and religious rivals.

Abd al-Mu'min invaded southern Spain and overthrew the Almoravides. Córdoba was captured in 1148 while Seville, Lucena, Montilla, and other cities were taken within a year. The Almohades, as they had done in Africa, forced Jews to either convert to Islam or face death.[24] Abraham ibn Daud, the renowned Spanish Jewish chronicler, characterized the years of the Almohad con-

---

[24] An Egyptian Jew writing in the year 1148 relates that when Abd al-Mu'min, the successor of Ibn Tumart, subjugated Oran, he slaughtered the Almoravid garrison, killed the governor, and gibbeted his corpse. In Fez, he allegedly slaughtered 100,000 persons and another 150,000 in Marrakesh. He also executed the whole population of Tilimsen, with the exception of those Jews who converted to Islam. After subjugating Sijilmasa, a city that did not repel his attack, the Almohades attempted to force the Jewish residents to convert to Islam. Nothing came of the discussions for seven months. When the new governor took office, he gave the Jewish population an ultimatum: either conversion or death. Approximately, 150 Jews were put to death for their refusal to convert. The rest, led by a local rabbinic judge, accepted the "genial invitation" to adopt Islam. From the city Bejaia (Bougie) on the eastern Algerian coast to Gibraltar, no one professing "the name Jew…remains; he who was killed was killed, he who sinned [by converting to Islam] sinned." Herbert Davidson, *Moses Maimonides: The Man and His Works* (Oxford: Oxford University Press, 2005), 10.

quest as "years of calamity, evil decrees, and religious persecutions [shemad] [which] befell Israel." He also noted that there were some Jews who "were marked for leaving the faith at the threat of the sword…" Ibn Daud ascribed the following words to Ibn Tumart: "Come let us cut them off from being a nation so that the name of Israel may be no more in remembrance…he left them neither name nor remnant in his entire kingdom."[25]

The persecutions under the Almohades lasted for ten years. Regarding the harshness of the attacks, Maimonides stated,

> "You know, my brethren that on account of our sins God has cast us into the midst of this people, the nation of Ishmael, who persecute us severely, and who devise ways to harm us and to debase us. This is as the Exalted had warned us; 'Even our enemies themselves being judges' (Deuteronomy 32:31). No nation has ever done more harm to Israel. None has matched it in debasing, humiliating, and hating us." [26]

In 1160, the Muslim historian Ibn al-Athir stated that when the Almohades conquered "Ifriquiya," which likely refers to the area around Tunis, they compelled Jews and Christians to choose between Islam and death.[27] Some Jews apparently resisted the onslaught of the Almohades even though they proved unsuccessful.[28] Many Jews converted to Islam in a superficial

---

[25] Ibid., 11.

[26] Moses Ben Maimon, The Epistle to Yemen, Trans. Norman A. Stillman, *The Jews of Arab Lands: A History and Source Book* (Philadelphia: Jewish Publication Society, 1979), 241.

[27] Herbert Davidson, *Moses Maimonides: The Man and His Works* (Oxford: Oxford University Press, 2005), 15.

[28] Joseph Ibn Aqnin, a Moroccan Jewish writer in the 12th century, also provided a description of the actions taken under the Almohade regime. Ibn Aqnin relates that Jewish inheritances were confiscated; Jews were barred from engaging in trade, the Jewish ownership of slaves was banned, Jews were required to dress differently as to be easily identified, and their children were taken from them to be raised as Muslims. Ibn Aqnin notes that many of the descendants of those who did convert to Islam returned to Judaism in the second and third generations. Ibid., 13.

manner, while others fled to Castile, where King Alfonso VII received them openly, particularly in Toledo. Almohad power lasted until the Battle of Navas de Tolosa on July 16, 1212, when they were defeated. Islamic authority in the Iberian Peninsula declined rapidly. In a few years, they were driven back to the Kingdom of Granada, which remained largely intact until the end of the 15th century.

## Christian Hegemony

The steady Christian conquest of the Peninsula saw the relocation of Jews to Christian territory. This process was guaranteed, in part, by the legislation of King Ferdinand I of Leon in the 11th century, which offered Jews a haven. As a consequence of military successes against the Muslim *taifas* (i.e. city states), which rose after the demise of the Omayyad Caliphate, Christian kings found large swathes of conquered territory under inhabited. Many Muslims remained in these newly conquered territories. A Jewish presence helped resettle the land and offset potential concerns over Muslim fealty. Jewish linguistic and diplomatic skills served the Christian sovereigns well in the ongoing relationship, and at times, warfare with the Muslim Kingdom of Granada and the remaining independent city-states.

From the 13th to the 15th centuries, the Hispanic kingdoms of the Iberian Peninsula were home to the largest Jewish communities of the European continent. Jose Hinojosa Montalvo estimates that near the end of the 13th century, 100,000 Jews lived in Castile alone. By the latter part of the 14th century, the population had grown between 180,000 to 250,000. The most inhabited Jewish quarters, consisting of 3,000 or more people, were found in the cities of Toledo, Barcelona, Zaragoza, Valencia, Majorca, Seville, Córdoba, Tudela, Granada, and Lucena.[29]

---

[29] José Hinojosa Montalvo, "Los judíos en la España medieval: de la tolerancia a la expulsión." lecture, Universidad de Alicante, 1998. https://goo.gl/mdB66Y

Unfortunately, growing tension brought about by economic hardship and diseases increased the anti-Jewish sentiment already fostered by Christianity. Jews were depicted as heretics and subversive, unleashing attacks on various Jewish quarters. The island of Majorca off the eastern coast of the Peninsula was attacked in 1309, and in 1328 the Jewish communities of the Kingdom of Navarre were nearly exterminated.[30] In 1349 in Catalonia, with the advent of the *Black Death*, the bubonic and pneumonic plague, Jews were blamed for the onset of the catastrophe.[31]

## The Pinnacle of Jewish Life in Christian Castile

King Pedro I of Castile, the son and successor of King Alfonso XI, ruled between 1350 and 1369. He was positively inclined toward the Jews in his domains. Under his reign, Jews reached the peak of their influence in Christian Spain. From the start of his reign, Pedro gathered so many Jewish courtiers that his detractors mocked his court as a "Jewish" court. Inner rivalry in the royal family led to a series of bloody civil wars that devastated Castile along with its Jewish communities. Both parties to the civil war mulled the question of Jewish influence on the royal court. The supporters of Henry Trastamara, the aspiring usurper to the throne and Pedro's half-brother, accused Pedro of having been the son of a Jew, who was then substituted for the legitimate royal son. Trastamara secured the support of the nobility who regarded King Pedro I as too pro-Jewish.

On May 7th, 1355, Henry de Trastamara invaded a section of the Jewish quarter of Toledo. His forces attacked and murdered thousands of people. However, Henry de Trastamara and his followers were unable to take control of the central section of the Jewish quarter. Some Jews in that area had received reinforcements from certain Toledo noblemen and were able to defend them-

---

[30] Cecil Roth, *A History of the Marranos* (Philadelphia: Jewish Publication Society, 1947), 11.
[31] Natalie Oeltjen, "Crisis and Regeneration: The Conversos of Majorca, 1391 – 1416" (PhD diss., University of Toronto, 2012), 12.

selves. Five years later in 1360, Henry marched again through Castile with the assistance of King Pedro IV of Aragon. When the former reached Najera, he ordered the massacre of the Jews there. Those living in Miranda de Ebro were also attacked.

While King Pedro continued the war effort, Henry enlisted the services of mercenaries led by Bertrand du Guesclin—a Breton cavalier and French army commander. The mercenaries under Guesclin attacked Jews wherever they found them. In Briviesca, near the city of Burgos, 200 Jewish families were reportedly murdered. Henry was proclaimed King in Calahorra and entered Burgos on March 31$^{st}$, 1366. The new king levied a substantial tax on the Jews of Burgos. The Jews of Segovia and Avila also had their property seized. The Jews of Toledo had remained loyal to King Pedro and were also made to endure the burden of maintaining Henry's troops, and they were heavily fined. The deposed King Pedro requested aid from the Prince of Wales. Faced with these reinforcements, Henry was forced to escape, but his departure was short-lived as he returned to Castile with additional troops.

## The Massacres of 1366

The Jewish populations of Villa Diego, Aguilar, and other towns were attacked and destroyed by Henry's forces. The communities of Paredes and Palencia met with a similar fate. The residents of Valladolid, who pledged homage to Henry, plundered the Jews of their city. They destroyed their houses and synagogues and even shredded their Torah scrolls. 300 Jewish families from Jaen were also detained as prisoners and taken to Granada.

According to the contemporary writer, Samuel Zarza of Palencia, the distress reached its peak in Toledo. Henry laid siege to the city, and thousands died through starvation.[32] The civil war

---

[32] Singer, Isidore; Adler, Cyrus; (eds.) The Jewish Encyclopedia, "Spain." Last modified 1904. Accessed January 2, 2013. https://goo.gl/fuKwDe

ultimately ended when King Pedro was captured and beheaded by Henry and Bertrand Du Guesclin on March 14$^{th}$, 1369. Henry de Trastamara ascended the throne as King Henry II.

Once in power, King Henry II forged a policy towards Jews that mitigated the actions he had previously perpetrated against the Jewish community. The Jewish communities of Castile formed a historically significant group that filled some important roles for the crown and also provided extensive contributions to the royal exchequer. While amity with the king was the most active defense against violence, this very loyalty to the reigning monarch could be used against them by a usurper.

Regardless of his dislike for Jews, King Henry utilized their services. He employed wealthy Jews such as Samuel Abravanel and Joseph Pichon, among others, as financial councilors and tax-collectors. In 1371, the Cortes of Toro demanded that Jews be barred from royal palaces. They were not allowed to hold public office. Members of the Cortes argued that Jews should be forced to live apart from Christians, desist from wearing expensive clothes, not ride mules, wear distinctive badges, and cease from using Christian names. The King agreed to the last two demands. His agreement that Jews wear distinctive badges made him the first Castilian monarch to follow this directive previously established by Rome. He also agreed to a request made by the Cortes of Burgos in 1379 that Jews be prohibited from bearing or selling weapons. He did, however, allow Jews to retain the right to criminal jurisprudence. The trend towards limiting Jewish rights continued with the Cortes of Soria in 1380. The Cortes declared that rabbis and the heads of the Jewish quarters were forbidden under penalty of a fine, to impose the penalties of death, disfigurement, expulsion, or excommunication. However, Jews were allowed to select their judges in civil proceedings.[33]

In contrast to their kinsmen in the eastern part of the Peninsula, the Jews of Lisbon were left undisturbed by the violence that became characteristic of the Kingdom of Castile. The first significant violence against the Portuguese Jewish community erupted during the conflict between Dom Ferdinand of Portugal and Henry Trastamara II of Castile. In 1373, the Castilian army entered Lisbon. The invading army sacked the Jewish quarter in the area of Rua Nova, and several Jews were killed. Further harm against the Jews of Lisbon was brought about by the grand master of the Knights of St. Bennett of Aviz, who eventually succeeded Dom Ferdinand and was later crowned King John I.

## Ferrant Martinez and the Prelude to the Riots of 1391

The popular sentiment against the Jewish community, already stoked during the Castilian civil war, was increased by the malicious sermons of Ferrant Martinez of Seville. Martinez initially served as the Archdeacon of Ecija and vociferously called for the destruction of the twenty-three synagogues in Seville and the confinement of Jews to their quarter to prevent unnecessary contact with Christians.[34] The leaders of the Jewish community repeatedly tried to curtail his endeavors. Martinez promised his listeners that the royal court would not discipline any attack initiated by them.[35] He used this power to compel the magistrates of Alcalá de Guadeyra and Ecija among other cities to no longer tolerate Jews in their vicinity.

His activities were sufficiently troublesome to the Jewish community of Seville to appeal to King Henry II. The King

---

[33] E.H. Lindo, *The Jews of Spain and Portugal* (London: Longman, Brown, Green, & Longmans, 1848), 153-155, 162.

[34] Yitzhak Baer, *A History of the Jews in Christian Spain: Volume 2* (Philadelphia: Jewish Publication Society, 1961), 95.

[35] Ibid., 96.

ordered the Archdeacon not to intrude into the affairs of his subjects or incite the people against them. He was to abstain from deciding legal disputes between them. Jews in the area were granted permission to withdraw from the Archdeacon's jurisdiction. The Jewish community complained to King John I four years later regarding Martinez's continuing activities. King John I reproved Martinez on March 3rd, 1382 with little effect. This was followed up with a new edict on August 25th, 1383. This time, he castigated the Archdeacon and threatened severe punishment.

## The Public Trial of Ferrant Martinez

On February 11th, 1388, Martinez, and Judah Aben Abraham, a representative of the Jewish community of Seville, appeared before the *alcaldes mayores* Ferrant Gonzalez and Ruy Perez along with their respective witnesses. Abraham referred to the two royal edicts previously issued and demanded that the Archdeacon should desist once and for all from any arbitrary and unlawful acts against the community. Failure to do so would result in the community's immediate appeal before the King.

Despite this threat, Martinez pledged to continue to preach as he had previously. He argued that everything he had done was on the advice of the Archbishop and was motivated by his longing for the welfare of the Church and the king alike. Martinez claimed the Jewish community had offered him a bribe for adjudicating a significant case in their favor. The episcopal chapter intervened and sent two of its members to the king. They made it clear that the Archdeacon was overriding the authority of the Pope and that the safety of the Jewish community was being compromised. Through the likely influence of his wife Leonora, the king ruled that while Jews were under his protection and should not be mistreated, the Archdeacon's zeal was praiseworthy and that matters should not be further exacerbated.

## Ferrant Martinez Appointment as Vicar-General

The danger Ferrant Martinez posed was appreciated in 1388 by the Archbishop of Seville, Pedro Gomez Barroso. Barroso condemned Martinez as contemptuous and suspect of heresy. He convened a body of experts in canonical law and summoned Martinez to repudiate his previous actions. The latter was adamant and refused to recant. As a consequence, he was prohibited from performing any religious functions or deciding any case, on penalty of excommunication.

To add to the conflict, King John I of Castile died suddenly in an accident. He was succeeded by his adolescent son, Henry III, who was guided in part by a young stepmother. Ferrant Martinez was the confessor to the Queen Mother, Leonora.[36] Under the reign of the eleven-year-old King Henry III, Martinez's fortunes changed drastically. On July 7th, 1390 the Archbishop died, giving Ferrant room to maneuver even more freely. Ferrant became the Administrator of the Diocese, which gave him power over the local ecclesiastical council. In a dramatic turn of events, the archiepiscopal chapter chose Martinez as Vicar General. On December 8th, 1390, Ferrant Martinez called upon the clergy of his diocese to destroy all synagogues in their parishes and send to him all lamps, Hebrew books, and Torah scrolls. Martinez argued the synagogues were havens of the Devil. The clergy of Ecija and Alcalá de Guadeyra obeyed, and the synagogues of Soria and Santillana were damaged. The Jewish community of Seville appealed to the king. A few days later, the court responded by sending a letter to the archiepiscopal chapter holding it accountable for all reparations due to the Jewish community. This included an order to rebuild and repair any synagogues that had been damaged or destroyed. The king also gave orders that Martinez be removed from his post. Ferrant Martinez countered by arguing that an ecclesiastical official was subject to the Church and not to the king. The king, he argued,

---

[36] Cecil Roth, *A History of the Marranos* (Philadelphia: Jewish Publication Society, 1947), 12.

had no right to depose him from office, or require that he restore the damaged and destroyed synagogues.[37]

In early January 1391, prominent Jews assembling in Madrid received information that riots were on the verge of breaking out in Seville and Córdoba. Juan Alfonso de Guzman, Count of Niebla and governor of the city, and his relative, the Sheriff Mayor Alvar Perez de Guzman, ordered the arrest and public beating of two of the rioters' leaders. Instead of lowering tensions, several Jews were murdered and robbed. The Guzman brothers were threatened with death.[38]

On June 6th, 1391, mobs attacked the Jewish quarter of Seville. The chronicler Pedro López de Ayala reported that 4,000 Jews were killed. According to Rabbi Hasdai ibn Crescas, even Christian nobles joined in to reap plunder. Thousands of Jews converted to avoid death. From Seville, the onslaught spread to the surrounding cities and villages, including Alcalá de Guadeyra, Cazalla, Fregenal, Carmona, Ecija, and Santa Olalla. Many wanted to unleash similar violence against the Muslims living in their midst. The fear that retaliation would be brought against Christians in the Kingdom of Granada ended this desire.[39]

King Joan (John) of Aragon instructed his brother, Prince Marti, on July 3rd, to take the necessary measures to protect Jews since "some unbridled and incorrigible persons" were speaking against them. Rabble-rousers from Castile had arrived in the capital and exacerbated the situation.[40] By July 9th, the violence reached Valencia on the eastern side of the Peninsula. The mob was led by

---

[37] Mark D. Meyerson, *A Jewish Renaissance in Fifteenth-Century Spain* (Princeton: Princeton University Press, 2004), 23.

[38] Rica Amran Cohen, "Judíos y conversos en las crónicas de los Reyes de Castilla (desde finales del siglo XIV hasta la expulsión)," Espacio, Tiempo y Forma. Serie III. Historia medieval 9 (1996): 259.

[39] Kenneth R. Scholberg, "Minorities in Medieval Castilian Literature," Hispania, Vol. 37, No. 2 (1954): 203.

[40] Mark D. Meyerson, *A Jewish Renaissance in Fifteenth-Century Spain* (Princeton: Princeton University Press, 2004), 23.

approximately forty or fifty Christian youths. As they marched, they carried a blue banner with a white cross and several makeshift crosses made out of bamboo. They reached the Jewish quarter, "shouting that the Archdeacon of Castile is coming with his cross and that all the Jews should be baptized or die."[41] When the day ended, the Christian mob now comprised of "vagabonds and foreigners and people of lesser and poor condition...men of the Order Montesa and ...mendicants...knights...and mean of peerage and squires" had slaughtered several hundred Jews. The majority of the Jews of Valencia were forcibly baptized by the Friar Vicente Ferrer. The Jewish community of Valencia, which had once numbered 2,500, now numbered only 200 who had managed to escape the violence and coerced conversions.[42]

By the 16th of July, the violence spread to Córdoba where the entire Jewish quarter was destroyed, and the violence continued through Montoro, Andujar, Jaen, Ubeda, and Baeza in the heart of Andalusia. At least 2,000 Jews were killed. By June 20th, the attacks reached Toledo. Among those who perished, were the descendants of the famous Toledo Rabbi Asher ben Yehiel.[43] Murcia alone was spared, but the entire community of Ciudad Real was either slaughtered or converted. The communities of Huete and Cuenca survived but were not left unscathed by the violence. In Madrid, the news of the massacres reached the ears of its inhabitants and most, if not all Jews, were baptized in a preemptive move to avert violence.

The only community, which was left untouched in the region of Valencia, was Morvedre.[44] Within a week of the attack on the Jewish quarter of Valencia, a large number of people journeyed to

---

[41] Yitzhak Baer, *A History of the Jews in Christian Spain Volume 2* (Philadelphia: Jewish Publication Society, 1961), 100.

[42] Mark D. Meyerson, *A Jewish Renaissance in Fifteenth-Century Spain* (Princeton: Princeton University Press, 2004), 22.

[43] Yitzhak Baer, *A History of the Jews in Christian Spain Volume 2* (Philadelphia: Jewish Publication Society, 1961), 98.

[44] Ibid., 102.

Morvedre and rioted there. The quick action of the local bailiff, Bonafonat de Sant Feliu was critical, and the Jewish community was saved. They escaped the violence by moving into the local fortified castle. The actions of Sant Feliu were reinforced by various knightly families in the area who ensured that the local Jewish population was protected.[45] The violence in Valencia was reported throughout the kingdom, and the Jews in Alzira, Xativa, Castello, Borriana, and Lliria converted.

On July 16th, news of the rioting reached the King of Castile and his regents in the city of Segovia in the region of Old Castile and León. The king and his councilors were limited in their ability to stem the violence other than stressing to their councils the importance of saving the Jewish communities that were the official properties of the Crown. The ineffectual power of the Crown was demonstrated by the fact that even Segovia was not entirely free of the violence. In the northern reaches of Castile, in the Cuenca del Duero, many Jews converted while others fled the cities to escape the violence.[46] Seventy towns and cities in Castile had experienced violence.[47] The Kingdom of Portugal was spared the violence due to the diligent actions of its king.

## The Attack on the Community of Majorca

By August 2nd, the violence reached Palma, in Majorca. The riots coincided with civil rest. The mobs, who attacked the Jewish communities of Majorca, Girona, and Barcelona, and all parts of the Kingdom of Aragon, expressed their frustration with what were apparently massive debts to local Jewish moneylenders. Increased taxation was coupled with poor harvests, the outbreak of

---

[45] Mark D. Meyerson, *A Jewish Renaissance in Fifteenth-Century Spain* (Princeton: Princeton University Press, 2004), 24, 27.

[46] Natalie Oeltjen, "Crisis and Regeneration: The Conversos of Majorca, 1391 - 1416."(PhD diss., University of Toronto, 2012), 5, 23.

[47] Cecil Roth, *A History of the Marranos* (Philadelphia: Jewish Publication Society, 1947), 12.

disease, and for many, increased indebtedness to Jews.[48] According to Natalie Oeltjen, the concerns over baptism were secondary to the financial ones though the former were indeed supported by the clergy.

A group of peasants gathered outside the city of Majorca. Governor Francesc Sagarriga attempted to negotiate with the crowd, but he was attacked and wounded. The mob then proceeded to attack the royal castle at Bellver. They were unable to breach its walls. The crowd now turned its attention towards the Jewish quarter.

Several hundred Jews were killed, though the exact number is disputed.[49] Many Jews attempted to flee to North Africa while up to eight hundred Jews appear to have sought refuge in the royal castle. According to the historian Vicente Mut, the violence was primarily directed against Jews. Mut suggests that a Christian youth had died as a result of a confrontation with a young Jewish man. The Jew, merely trying to defend himself struggled with the man and killed him. The homes of Christian officials were then targeted since many of them were regarded as having protected Jews.[50] The violence continued, and the governor was still besieged in the palace. On the 27th of August, possibly four thousand armed peasants surrounded the city walls again and continued doing so for a week. The municipal judges gave in to various demands, which included the banning of corrupt officials from holding public office, a reform of the government to include greater representation of the peasants, the abolition of taxes, and the dismissal of all debts including those to Jews.[51]

---

[48] Ibid., 12.

[49] Natalie Oeltjen, "Crisis and Regeneration: The Conversos of Majorca, 1391 - 1416."(PhD diss., University of Toronto, 2012), 18.

[50] Cecil Roth, *A History of the Marranos* (Philadelphia: Jewish Publication Society, 1947), 20.

[51] Yitzhak Baer, *A History of the Jews in Christian Spain Volume 2* (Philadelphia: Jewish Publication Society, 1961), 102.

A rumor that the king had ordered the execution of those sent by the peasants to negotiate on their behalf sparked another rebellion. On October 2$^{nd}$, six to seven thousand armed men returned to the royal castle and besieged it. The mob issued a list of demands, which included that within eight days all the Jews who had sought refuge in the castle convert to Christianity or be killed.

The Jews agreed to the demand of conversion once the judges promised to pay 20,000 pounds of their collective debt. According to Oeltjen, the judges were desperate to convince Jews to convert so that the peasants would be placated. With few options, around October 21$^{st}$, the Jews in the castle converted.[52] In 1392, the island received a blanket amnesty for the attack on the Jewish quarter.

On Saturday, August 5$^{th}$, the violence spread to Barcelona. On the first day, approximately 100 Jews were killed while several others found protection in a local fort. On the following day, the masses invaded the Jewish quarter and began looting. The authorities tried to protect the Jews, but a mob attacked them and freed those who had been imprisoned. The citadel was stormed on the 8th, and more than 300 Jews were murdered, including the only son of the famed Rabbi Ḥasdai ibn Crescas. Many Jews submitted to baptism as a way to escape the violence as the riot continued in Barcelona until August 10$^{th}$. The Jewish quarter in Gerona was also attacked. While some fled, others were either killed or baptized.

On August 13$^{th}$, the last town to experience an onslaught of violence was Lerida. The Jews of this city attempted to find safety in Alcazar. Seventy-five Jews were killed, and the rest were baptized. In Lerida, the municipal authorities asked the king to send someone to deal with the situation. The officials related that several monks had asked permission to enter the Jewish quarter

---

[52] Natalie Oeltjen, "Crisis and Regeneration: The Conversos of Majorca, 1391 – 1416" (PhD diss., University of Toronto, 2012), 20-23.

with the purpose of preaching Christianity to Jews. The king denied their request.[53]

## The Aftermath

Howard Sachar estimates that as many as 30,000 Jews died in the violence of 1391.[54] Cecil Roth mentions the death toll may have been as high as 50,000.[55] The severity of the persecutions, which led to the forced conversions, is related by Reuven, the son of the Rabbi Nissim Gerundi and a survivor of the massacre. He claimed that 140,000 Jews converted.[56] Salo Wittmayer Baron characterized the violence as a "holy war" against Judaism. Approximately a third of the Jewish population of the kingdoms of Castile and Aragon may have been massacred; a third escaped their attackers by temporarily fleeing their homes, and another third possibly converted to Christianity.[57] Communities, which had existed for centuries, were decimated, and tens of thousands of Jews were slaughtered.[58] Perhaps up to two hundred thousand Jews were forced to convert as a means to save their lives and the lives of their families.[59]

Four years later, Ferrant Martinez was incarcerated in Seville in 1395 by the order of King Henry III but was rapidly released. Any concern which King Henry III felt over the destruction of the

---

[53] Yitzhak Baer, *A History of the Jews in Christian Spain: Volume 2* (Philadelphia: Jewish Publication Society, 1961), 108.

[54] Howard Sachar, *Farewell Espana: The World of the Sephardim Remembered* (New York: Vintage Books, 1995), 44-45.

[55] Cecil Roth, *the Spanish Inquisition*, (New York: W.W. Norton and Company, 1964), 22.

[56] David Nirenberg, "Mass conversion and Genealogical Mentalities: Jews and Christians in Fifteenth-Century Spain," *Past and Present*, No. 174 (2002): 9.

[57] Salo Wittmayer Baron, *A Social and the Religious History of the Jews: Volume XI* (Philadelphia: Jewish Publication Society, 1967), p.232. See also Kevin Ingram, "Secret lives, public lies: the conversos and socio-religious non-conformism in the Spanish Golden Age" (PhD diss., UC San Diego, 2006), 43-44.

[58] Cecil Roth, *A History of the Marranos* (Philadelphia: Jewish Publication Society, 1947), 12.

[59] Ibid., 13.

Jewish quarter of Seville was quickly forgotten. In 1396, he presented the Jewish quarter, including all its houses, lands, and synagogue buildings to two supporters. They were granted authority to sell, pledge as collateral, exchange, demolish, or otherwise administer this property according to their prerogative. The Jewish quarter was renamed the *Villa Nueva*. Its synagogues were converted into churches.

The remaining Jews continued to live in the old Jewish quarter and other areas. Due to the loss of tax revenue resulting from the decimation of the Jewish community, the city council granted permission to Jews to resume their traditional occupations. The situation remained precarious enough for the remaining Jews to hire 300 guards to protect them.

After the tragedy of 1391, hatred towards Jews continued to mount. The newly converted Jews known as *Conversos* were forbidden from sailing to Muslim lands.[60] Growing anti-Jewish legislation resulted in the emigration of many Jews from Castile and their relocation to the areas of Malaga, Almeria, and Granada where they were well received. The Jews of Córdoba were again attacked, and many of them murdered in 1406. King Henry III prohibited Jews from dressing like Christians. He also insisted on Jews wearing distinctive insignia. King Henry III died in 1406. In his will, Pablo de Santa Maria, the voluntary Jewish convert to Christianity was designated as executor of his will and protector of his son, John. The Regency was placed under the control of the Queen Mother Catalina and the *Infante* Fernando de Antequera.

Attempts to reestablish Jewish quarters, such as those in Barcelona or Valencia, were utter failures. The number of *Juderias* across the Kingdoms of Castile and Aragon in the 15$^{th}$ century was 216 and 35, respectively. Many of these were small and reflected the new reality of Jews having fled and abandoned the cities in favor

---

[60] Yitzhak Baer, *A History of the Jews in Christian Spain: Volume 2* (Philadelphia: Jewish Publication Society, 1961), 102.

of the countryside to prevent a population concentration, which had made them easier targets in previous years.

The theological challenges presented by the Conversos who continued to live alongside their Jewish compatriots were coupled with an economic transformation. The economic roles that Jews had typically filled were now increasingly occupied by Conversos. The hatred, which targeted Jews for usury and their roles as tax farmers, was steadily transferred to Conversos. Conversos were freed from the legal restrictions that had characterized their former status as Jews. These new opportunities included posts in public offices. As Converso prominence and services to the Crown grew, the relevance of the Jewish community lessened.

## Converso Impact on Christian and Jewish Communities

Among Jews, these individuals, who converted under coercion or threat, were known as *anusim*, i.e. forced ones. Those who converted wholeheartedly and typically independent of any persecution were known as *meshumadim*, meaning 'he who destroys.'[61] Many of those who did convert did observe Judaism clandestinely and were derogatorily called Judaizers or *Marranos* i.e. swine.[62] The term *Conversos* was also applied to their descendants

---

[61] The 15th century polemical work, titled El Alborayque, provides a definition of the term Converso: "Deos tales neophitos o conuersos judayzantes es el presente tratado, y por este vocabo conersos no se entiendad todos aquellos que descienden de la generacion delos judios:alos quales el vulgo impropriamente llama conuersos: mas entiend<n> se solame<n>te los judios q<ue> se co<n>uertiero<n> xp<ist>ianos los q<ua>les conuersos judayza<n>tes como fuessen conuertidos mas por fuerca q<ue> de buena voluntad. (Fols 1v-2r)." According to this statement, only those Jews who sincerely converted to Christianity should be deemed Conversos—not those who were converted by force. Dwayne E. Carpenter "From Al-Burak to Alboraycos: The Art of Transformation on the Eve of the Expulsion" in Jews and Conversos at the Time of the Expulsion, edited by Yom Tov Assis, Yosef Kaplan. (Jerusalem: The Zalman Shazar Center for Jewish History, 1999), 32. Also Kevin Ingram, "Secret lives, public lies: the conversos and socio-religious non-conformism in the Spanish Golden Age" (PhD diss., UC San Diego, 2006), 1.

[62] The term *Marrano* has often been used to designate Conversos who converted to Christianity for survival sake and continued to observe Jewish practices in some form. The exact origins of the term are disputed, however. The famous Spanish dictionary of 1611 authored by Sebastián de Covarrubias defined the term Marrano as "*Es el rezien*

who were not first generation converts but rather the descendants of practicing Jews (i.e. children, grandchildren, etc.) who had converted to Christianity in the late fourteenth and early fifteenth centuries.[63] This term was used in official correspondence.[64] By the middle of the sixteenth century, other terms were used to designate Conversos. These terms included *gente del linaje* (those of this lineage), *esta gente* (this people), *esta generacion* (this generation or this lineage), *esta raza* (this race), and *los de la nacion* (those of the

---

*convertido al christianismo, tenemos ruin concepto del por averse convertido fingidamente.*" "The recent convert to Christianity, of whom we have a despicable opinion for having feigned his conversion." Diego Velazquez, the author of the pamphlet *Defensio Statuti Toletani* stated "*Sed eos hispani marranos vocare solemus, qui ex iudaeis descendentes et baptizati ficti christiani.*" "We call those Spaniards, Marranos, who are descendants of Jews and were baptized fictitiously as Christians." See Sebastian de Covarrubias Horozco, "Tesoro de la Lengua Castellana o Española [1611]" (Madrid: Ed. Turner, 1979). In the present day, the Royal Spanish Academy's *Diccionario de la Lengua Espanola* relates that the term Marrano is derived from Arabic مُحَرَّم *muḥarram* i.e. forbidden or anathematized. A commonly held alternative view was that the term was derived from the New Testament phrase "maran atha" ("our Lord hath come"). Various unlikely origins for the term have also been suggested. These include the Hebrew *marit ayin* "the appearance of the eye," referring to the fact that the Marranos were superficially Christian but continued to practice Judaism. Other Hebrew phrases, including the phrase *mohoram attah* "you are excommunicated"; *mar anus-* forced convert and the Hebrew term *mumar* for "apostate" with the Spanish ending *ano* added. A secondary Arabic word, *mura'in* i.e. 'hypocrite' has also been suggested. Jewish Virtual Library, "Marranos, Conversos, and New Christians." Last modified 2012 – accessed November 24, 2012 https://goo.gl/WN2in9 For more information see JOSPIC-J Staff "A List of 134 Books Containing Marrano, Converso, Crypto Jew, Secret Jew, Hidden Jew, New Christian, or Anusim in the Title or Subtitle: Changes in Usage Over 86 Years" Journal of Spanish, Portuguese, and Italian Crypto Jews. Volume 3 (2011): 149–155. Salo Baron notes that it has also been suggested that the term may have originated from the form *barrano*. The term was a derivative of an Arabic noun meaning 'alien'. Salo Wittmayer Baron, *A Social and the Religious History of the Jews: Volume XIII* (Philadelphia: Jewish Publication Society, 1969), 336.

[63] Miriam Bodian states: "The group was self-perpetuating, since descendants continued to be regarded as conversos, or converts, for many generations. And the ranks of this group grew... [...] The status of Converso became, curiously, and inherited status- a fateful development." Miriam Bodian, "'Men of the Nation': The Shaping of Converso Identity in Early Modern Europe," Past and Present 143(1994): 48–76.

[64] In 1380, King John of Castile, as well as the Cortes of Soria banned the use of terms 'turncoats' and Marranos. Those who used it were subject to a penalty of 300 maravedis and fifteen days in prison. Salo Wittmayer Baron, *A Social and the Religious History of the Jews: Volume XIII* (Philadelphia: Jewish Publication Society, 1969), 66.

nation). As these terms reveal, an increasing emphasis was given to the perceived ethnic or racial characteristics of Conversos.[65]

The sheer number of those killed, as well as those who converted under duress, was so significant that few if any, Jews were unaffected. Close-knit families were often comprised of members who had managed to survive the massacres without converting and others who had acquiesced or been forced to convert. Continuing economic, cultural, and religious ties to Judaism characterized many, if not, most Conversos. The lack of extensive doctrinal education in Christianity, given to Conversos, only reinforced the reality that for most, conversion was an insincere act borne out of necessity.

Vicente Ferrer, who had participated in the onslaught of the Jewish communities in 1391 by eagerly accepting Jews at baptismal fonts was convinced that the path forward was to instruct the remaining Jews in the reality of the Christian faith. With what must have been nothing less than dramatic confrontations, Ferrer journeyed the countryside with a Torah scroll in one hand and a cross in the other, preaching Christianity to Jews.[66] His zeal was recognized by Pope Benedict XIII, who sought to appoint him as his confessor. However, Ferrer was driven by the goal of converting the remaining Jews.[67]

---

[65] Miriam Bodian, *Hebrews of the Portuguese Nation* (Bloomington: Indiana University Press, 1997), 11. Portuguese terms corresponding to the Castilian terms used included: *Cristãos Novos, gente da nação,* and *homens da nação.* Ibid., 12.

[66] Cecil Roth, *A History of the Marranos* (Philadelphia: Jewish Publication Society, 1947), 13. Four thousand Jews are said to have converted on a single day in Toledo. In the Bishopric of Segovia, the surviving Jewish remnants were further devastated. So successful was Vicente Ferrer and his assistant Geronimo de Santa Fe, that large numbers of Jews from the cities of Saragossa, Calatayud, Daroca, Fraga, and Barbastro converted. The communities Alcaniz, Caspe, Maella, Lerida, Tamarit, and Alcolea converted on mass. Within a short period of time, 35,000 Jews were reported to have converted.

[67] A description of Vicente Ferrer is provided in the *Cronica de Los Reyes Catolicos* authored by Hernando del Pulgar, the royal historiographer to Queen Isabella and King Ferdinand. "A Catholic saint, a male doctor of the Dominican Order, which desired at that time by preaching… by the Holy Law and Scripture to convert all Jews from Spain, and to end the inveterate and stench ridden synagogue." Rica Amran Cohen, "Judíos y

Ferrer rejected violence as a means of conversion, but his tactics were intimidating. With the violence of 1391 fresh in their minds, more Jews converted. This time, it had the official endorsement of the Castilian court. Rabbi Joseph ben Joshua ben Meir described Vicente Ferrer with the following statement:

> "He was unto them a Satan [adversary] and stirred up against them all the inhabitants of the country, and they arose to swallow them up alive, and slew many with the edge of the sword, and many they burned with fire, and many they turned away with the power of the sword from the LORD, the God of Israel. And they burned the books of the Law of our God, and trampled upon them the mire in the streets: and the mother they dashed in pieces upon her children in the day of the LORD's wrath..."[68]

## Vicente Ferrer's Assault on the Jewish Community

Ferrer traveled across Murcia, Lorca, Ocaña, Illescas, Valladolid, Tordesillas, Salamanca, and Zamora preaching. In July 1411, he reached Toledo where he took control of the chief synagogue, which he converted into the Church of Santa Maria la Blanca. He reportedly baptized more than 4,000 Jews in Toledo. The less violent nature of the intimidation provoking these conversions is in contrast to the conversions experienced in 1391. Jews were certainly aware of the violence that erupted in Córdoba in 1406. Many may have seen Ferrer's actions as a prelude to another wave of violence. Taking control of the synagogue must have certainly required a mob or armed force of some kind.

With the help of the Converso Pablo de Santa Maria, Ferrer pushed through legislation aimed at curtailing Jewish social,

---

conversos en las crónicas de los Reyes de Castilla (desde finales del siglo XIV hasta la expulsión)," Espacio, Tiempo y Forma. Serie III. Historia medieval 9 (1996): 269.
[68] Henry Charles Lea, "Ferrand Martinez and the Massacres of 1391," The American Historical Review, Vol. 1. No. 2 (1896): 218.

economic, and religious freedom. Several laws were enacted on January 1412 under the auspices of King John II. Furthermore, Jews were prohibited from practicing medicine and ordered to isolate themselves socially in designated Jewish quarters. Ferrer explained that, "Just as prostitutes should live apart, so should Jews."[69] Failing to comply within eight days of the decree would result in property loss. They were also banned from selling bread, wine, flour, and meat and from almost every economic activity. Holding public office and acting as money brokers were also forbidden. Regarding the intensity of the anti-Jewish legislation, Rabbi Solomon Alami wrote:

> "They barred us from commerce, agriculture, and crafts. They forced us to grow beards and hair long. Former palace dwellers were driven into wretched hovels and ill-lit huts. Instead of the rustle of silk, we were compelled to wear miserable clothing that only drew further contempt and revulsion upon us. Hunger looked everyone in the face, and children died at their mothers' breast from exposure and starvation."[70]

They were also restricted from eating and drinking with Christians or hiring them as servants. Practically all social interaction with Christians was prohibited.[71] Christian women, married or unmarried, were forbidden to enter the Jewish quarter, either by day or night. Even the ability to levy communal taxes was prohibited without royal permission. Markings of social rank, such as the title *Don*, were prohibited as was their ability to bear weapons. Men and women were also required to wear distinctive clothes consisting of long plain mantles of coarse material reaching the feet. Leaving the country to follow Jewish life unrestrained by

---

[69] Howard Sachar, *Farewell Espana: The World of the Sephardim Remembered* (New York: Vintage Books, 1995), 50.
[70] Ibid., 51.
[71] Ibid., 51.

Castilian rule, or even changing residences was prohibited and punishable by loss of property and even slavery.[72]

Ferrer's zeal was not limited to Castile. He continued undisturbed in Aragon. The *Infante* Fernando de Antequera, had recently ascended to the throne in part through the machinations of Ferrer. In 1407, King Henry III died leaving the throne of Castile to his young son. His wife and brother Fernando served as regents. In 1410, the King of Aragon also died, but without leaving a successor. Fernando vied for the throne of Aragon, and Vicente Ferrer's support was apparently essential to the former's goal of assuming the Aragonese crown. Perhaps with this in mind, he acted to implement a series of anti-Jewish laws in January 1412.[73] The same month Fernando received support for his goal and was to be installed as King of Aragon the following year. Ferrer's campaign of intimidation led many Jews to adopt Christianity in the cities of Saragossa, Daroco, and Calatayud. Other conversions occurred in Albacete, Astorga, Avila, Benevent, Burgos, Leon, Mayorga, Majorca, Palencia, Paredes, Toro, and Segovia. Vicente Ferrer's attempt to extend his campaign into Portuguese territory was abruptly halted by King John I of Portugal.[74]

## The Tortosa Disputation

The new laws adopted at Ayllon changed the relationship with the Jewish communities of Castile. The goal was to apply sufficient pressure for Jews to convert to Christianity. This was to be accomplished by reinforcing the restrictions on them. The Converso Geronimo de Santa Fe appealed for the Pope's consent to resolve the Jewish question definitively. The plan envisioned the collapse of rabbinic authority and legitimacy. The Pope agreed to Sante Fe's plan. In November 1412, the *aljamas* of Aragon were summoned

---

[72] Ibid., 51.
[73] Fernando Suárez Bilbao, *Cristianos Contra Judíos y Conversos* (Madrid : Universidad «Rey Juan Carlos», 2004), 462.
[74] Salo Wittmayer Baron, *A Social and the Religious History of the Jews: Volume X* (Philadelphia: Jewish Publication Society, 1965), 163.

to provide their representatives to Tortosa on January 15th, 1413, where they would be presented with irrefutable proof that Jesus was, indeed, the true Messiah. If the rabbis were shown the error of their ways and if they would submit to baptism, then surely the rest of the Jewish community would follow.

The rabbis who attended had little choice in the matter. The Tortosa affair lasted almost two years. Pope Benedict XIII clearly stipulated that this was not a debate, but rather an opportunity to reveal the Biblical and Talmudic evidence that confirmed the messianic claims of Christianity. Fernando Suarez Bilbao describes it as a dialogue of the deaf where the rabbis did not understand Christian syllogisms and the Christians did not comprehend the rabbis.[75]

The representatives of the Jewish community who attended the disputation included a large number of prominent individuals.[76] The pope presided at the first meeting, which occurred before an audience of more than a thousand people. The disputation was led by Geronimo de Santa Fé and another Converso Garci Alvarez de Alarcon and the theologian Andreas Beltran of Valencia. The Jewish opposition was led by Vidal Benveniste. During the sixty-fifth session, Joseph Albo and Astruc ha-Levi presented a resolute defense of the Talmud, on November 10th, 1414. Astruc ha-Levi, with the support of most of the Jewish representatives, declared that the aggadic passages were not regarded as authoritative by them.

In the summer of 1413 and the first six months of 1414, approximately 200 Jews from Saragossa, Calatayud, and Alcaniz acceded to baptism. Additional communities such as Guadalajara, Daroca, Fraga, Tamarite, Barbasto, Alcolea Caspe, and Maella also

---

[75] Fernando Suárez Bilbao, *Cristianos Contra Judíos y Conversos* (Madrid: Universidad «Rey Juan Carlos», 2004), 463.
[76] These included Rabbi Mattityahu Hayitzhari, Rabbi Ferrer Saladin, and Rabbi Moses aben Abez. The philosopher Joseph Albo of Monreal, Astruc ha-Levi of Alcañiz, Bonjudah Yehasel Hakaslari, and Profet Duran were also present among others. Yitzhak Baer, *A History of the Jews in Christian Spain Volume 2* (Philadelphia: Jewish Publication Society, 1961), 173.

submitted to baptism. The historian Zurita relates that more than 3,000 Jews were baptized in 1414. Hoping to build on the growing number of conversions that had occurred, Pope Benedict issued a bull on May 11th, 1415. This edict corresponded with the *Pragmatica* decree issued by Catalonia and which had been adopted in Aragon by King Ferdinand. The order prohibited Jews and Conversos from studying the Talmud, reading anti-Christian writings, manufacturing communion cups or other church vessels or accepting either as pledges, building new synagogues or restoring old ones.[77]

Each community was allowed to have only one synagogue. Jews were also denied previously held rights of self-jurisdiction, and they were also not authorized to seek retribution against accusers. Jews were also barred from holding public offices. As they had experienced previously, they were prohibited from serving as brokers, matrimonial agents, physicians, or apothecaries.

On a more religiously focused side, Jews were forbidden to bake or sell unleavened bread for Passover. Should their children become Christians, Jews were also prohibited from disinheriting them. They were to wear the distinctive badge at all times, and three times a year all those over the age of twelve were forced to listen to Christian sermons on the Messiah.[78]

---

[77] Amia Raphael. Jewish Virtual Library, "Goldsmiths and Silversmiths." Last modified 2008 – accessed July 31, 2015 https://goo.gl/uVeUGq See also Yitzhak Baer, *A History of the Jews in Christian Spain Volume 2* (Philadelphia: Jewish Publication Society, 1961), 229.

[78] "That in all cities, towns, and villages, where there may be the number of Jews the diocesan may deem sufficient, three public sermons are to be preached annually; one on the second Sunday in Advent; one on the festival of the Resurrection; and the other on the Sunday when the Gospel, 'And Jesus approached Jerusalem,' is chanted. All Jews above twelve years of age shall be compelled to attend to hear these sermons. The subjects are to be – the first, to show them that the true Messiah has already come, quoting the passages of the Holy Scripture and the Talmud that were argued in the disputation of Jerome of Santa Fe; the second, to make them see that the heresies, vanities and errors of the Talmud, prevent their knowing the truth; and the third, explaining to them the de-

Rabbis like Joseph Albo, a Jewish philosopher and author of *Sefer ha-Ikkarim* and others remained spiritually and intellectually committed to the survival of Judaism. King Ferdinand I of Aragon died in April 1416 and his successor King Alfonso V declared that he would not put the Papal Bull of 1415 into effect. The final solution to the Jewish dilemma was postponed for another time. In 1418, Martin V arrived as a representative of papal authority. He severely prohibited conversions by force, a measure that may indicate that they were still being applied, either directly or indirectly.

The Jewish community felt sufficiently secure to request a formal rescinding of the 1415 Papal Bull via Jewish representatives sent to Rome. This request was granted in 1419. Despite relief from this edict, the day to day conditions of Jews remained tenuous. They were driven towards social and economic marginalization. This economic marginalization lessened their importance to the Crown, which in turn, translated into less pressure on the local authorities to ensure their protection.

A partial turn of fortunes in Castile was brought about in large part by the efforts of Abraham Benveniste. Benveniste served as courtier to King Juan II beginning in 1420. His financial acumen proved invaluable to Alvaro de Luna, who succeeded Juan II. In the war of 1429 against Aragon, Abraham Benveniste had supported Alvaro with the financial resources at his disposal. As compensation for his support, Alvaro reestablished the position of Chief Rabbi of all Jewish communities and named him to the post. With it, the Jews of Castile regained a measure of their former glory. He restored the practice whereby representatives of the Jewish communities journeyed to the city in which the Cortes had convened with the acknowledgment of the King. Benveniste exploited his relationship with the King to accomplish a new chapter in the history of Iberian Jewry. From the 25th of April through to the 5th of May 1432 Jewish representatives from the various communities

---

struction of the Temple and the city of Jerusalem, and the perpetuity of their captivity, as our Lord Jesus Christ and the other prophets prophesied." Ibid.

of Castile gathered along with several Jewish courtiers in the city of Valladolid.

Under the direction of Benveniste, several *takkanot* (religious edicts) for the Jewish communities in Castile were issued. The key, however, was the fact that they were presented to the King for review and authorization. What may have seemed to be a mere ceremonial act effectively legitimatized the Jewish community, its laws, and its ability to self-govern. It restored a measure of Jewish autonomy, which mirrored that offered to other citizens and marked the first time a European monarch had ratified a Jewish law derived and deliberated exclusively by Jews. Benveniste offered a radical alternative to those who sought a resolution to the Jewish question by conversion or expulsion. Instead, the legitimacy and loyalty of the Jewish community could be recognized as a component of Castilian life and identity. This model, which saw Jews as members of a distinct religion, was not only based on the Torah, which Christians recognized but on the very Talmud that had previously proved the source of so much condemnation. Among the ordinances passed, were directives stipulating the educational responsibilities that rested on *aljamas* according to their size. The nature of the education which included Talmudic instruction was undoubtedly well known to the Crown. Benveniste's actions secured the Jewish communities of Castile a degree of autonomy. Even though it did not match that achieved during the 13$^{th}$ century, it certainly provided the stability necessary to begin the process of recovery in the aftermath of the physical violence and theological attacks of the previous forty years.[79]

The continued Jewish practices of many Conversos, their ongoing family, and Jewish cultural ties, coupled with the fact that the Old Christians were well aware that their conversions had occurred under coercion created an environment of suspicion. The success of many Conversos only added to the resentment. Many Conversos had entered into the army. Some had taken administra-

---

[79] Fernando Suárez Bilbao, *Cristianos Contra Judíos y Conversos* (Madrid: Universidad «Rey Juan Carlos», 2004), 466-467.

tive positions in local government; a number studied law while others entered the universities. Some even joined the Church. Conversos were eventually found at the highest positions at court.[80]

The financial success of many Conversos has been viewed as the primary motivator of anti-Converso sentiment. However, the religious undertones were always present. Christian anti-Judaism had an established history whose influence was not decoupled from Conversos simply by the fact that they had formally adopted Christianity. What had once been a Jewish problem was now being transformed into a Converso one with many clamoring for the separation of these New Christians just as they had done towards Jews. The motivation behind this was the seeming restoration of Iberian Judaism, which was drawing Conversos back to the fold. The recovery of the religious, intellectual, and moral life of the Jewish community was sufficiently strong to attract converts to return to their former religion, thus creating a dangerous infiltration into Christian society.[81]

In 1449, 1467, 1470, and 1473, violence broke out against Conversos. While financial considerations were part of the concern, Judaizing was also an essential element. The need to establish royal authority was evident to both Jews and Conversos alike.[82] The crisis of who would succeed King Juan II of Castile, led to a division among the nobility. Princess Juana's claim to the throne of Castile gained the support of Juan Fernández Pacheco, the Marquez of Villena—a powerful political operative. The violence and chaos provided him with the opportunity to get control of the city of Segovia. Two individuals, the Converso Andres Cabrera and Abraham Seneor, the chief tax-farmer, colluded to take control of the city and present it to Princess Isabella along with access to the

---

[80] Cecil Roth, *A History of the Marranos* (Philadelphia: Jewish Publication Society, 1947), 14.

[81] Fernando Suárez Bilbao, *Cristianos Contra Judíos y Conversos* (Madrid: Universidad «Rey Juan Carlos», 2004), 471.

[82] Ibid., 473.

Alcazar and the royal treasure. In return for their loyalty, Andres Cabrera was named Marquez of Moya and Abraham Seneor as Chief Rabbi. He also served as the royal tax farmer and the *Alguacil Mayor* of the *aljama* of Segovia.

The need to reestablish royal authority and quench the violence erupting against Jews and Conversos was entirely logical since it was for the benefit of the kingdom.[83] Both men believed that Isabella was best able to guarantee stability. The subsequent marriage of Ferdinand of Aragon and Isabella of Castile initiated a period of ten years, which were mostly marked by the well-being of the Jewish community and a return to order. This stability was soon to end, though. Converso critics pointed to the fact that not only untrustworthy Conversos were present at court, but that unconverted Jews had now re-entered the scene. In addition to Abraham Seneor, they could point to Vidal Astori, Meir Melamed, Samuel Abulafia, the grandsons of Abraham Benveniste, Abraham and Vidal, as well as the newly arrived Isaac Abravanel who would eventually rise as the leader of the Castilian Jewish community.

While the rise of these influential Jewish courtiers hearkened back to earlier days of seeming Jewish integration, the real life conditions of Jews was quite different. Royal protection granted to Jewish communities was often ineffectual. The towns and villages home to Jews were increasingly resistant to recommendations initiated by the royal counsel. The stability of Jewish communities of Castile and Aragon was increasingly fragile. The complexity of the Jewish situation was reflected by the fact that many Jews had reentered the royal court where their position and influence on royal dispositions towards the Jewish community were of paramount significance. Their service to the court increased the stability of the kingdom and strengthened the monarch's hand. Nevertheless, the socio-economic status of the majority of Jews ultimately diminished the importance of Jewish communities for the Crown. By the 1480s, many Jews were often small merchants selling dried

---

[83] Ibid., 474.

fish, shoemakers, and vendors of used clothing, pawnbrokers, jewelers, and the like. Jewish farmers, typically rare due to restrictions on land ownership and usages, were also present. The fanciful image of the powerful Jew critical to the financial well-being of the state, an image always exaggerated, had eroded.

## The Interwoven Destiny of Jews and Conversos

The continued Jewish presence was seen by individuals such as Fray Alonso de Espina and others as destructive and as a virus that was spreading among Conversos and could even infect Old Christians. Relentlessly, they sought to persuade Pope Sixtus IV that the reality of secret Jewish practices was both widespread and dangerous. The solution to the problem was the invigoration and intensification of the Inquisitorial process, which technically had been authorized under the reign of King Enrique IV, but had either not been implemented or was ineffectual. In October 1477, Nicolas Franco, the papal legate initiated significant discussions with King Ferdinand of Aragon and Queen Isabella of Castile in the city of Seville. Ferdinand and Isabella convinced the Pope that the control of the Inquisitorial process should be conceded to the Crown under the direction of the Dominicans and the secular authorities who would administer punishment. Whatever regret the Pope would later express towards the effective transfer of Papal power to the Crown, the new Inquisition was then unleashed in a manner that was far different from the earlier Papal Inquisitions.[84]

---

[84] The *Cronica de los Reyes Catolicos* authored by Hernando Pulgar relates that, "Some clerics and religious people and many other lay people informed King and the Queen, that in their kingdoms and lordships there were many Christians of the lineage of the Jews, who were Judaizing, and practicing Jewish rites secretly at home, and had not believed the Christian faith or works that Catholic Christians were supposed to observe. This known by the King and Queen, they expressed great regret, to see people who were not loyal to the Catholic Faith and were heretics and apostates ... Fray Tomas de Torquemada... placed inquisitors in all the cities and villages ... the Kingdoms of Castile and they placed them in his letters of edicts, founded by law, so that those who had Judaized or were not loyal to the faith were allowed to confess their sins within a certain time, and be reconciled to the Holy mother Church ... From these were burned at different times and in some cities and villas, two thousand men and women ... These were especially from Seville and Cordoba, and the cities and villages of Andalusia where four thousand homes

## The Establishment of the Inquisition

The new Inquisition in contrast to the earlier Papal Inquisitions was focused on the stated purpose of rooting out Judaizing among Conversos. Only later would both Inquisitions redirect their attention to *Moriscos* – Muslim converts to Christianity – who continued to practice Islam clandestinely, early Protestantism, witchcraft, bigamy, etc. Both institutions would arrest and try Conversos for Judaizing in the Iberian Peninsula, as well as throughout Spanish and Portuguese colonies across the world well into the 18th century.

Among the first moves of the Inquisition in the city of Seville was the forced relocation of Jewish communities to ensure that Jews and Christians were separated. Fray Miguel de Morillo ordered the relocation of the Jewish quarter to the Corral de Jerez, a smaller and squalid area. The move was sanctioned by Queen Isabella cloaked with guarantees of safety and security. The onset of this new empowered Inquisition appears to have kindled others ready to act on the unresolved place of Jews in Spain. In 1480, the Cortes assembled in Toledo where anti-Jewish regulations, dating back to 1412, were reissued. Two years were allotted for all Jewish quarters to be relocated far away from the center of the city. Each was to be furnished with walls and gates under watch. Both monarchs consented to the petition. Jewish business activity was curtailed. The forced move of Jews from one section of the city to another also caused financial difficulties for those who had to sell their houses at relatively low prices.

The inquisitors, if nothing else, were diligent in their work as they proceeded to collect information on Judaizers. They argued to the monarchs that the number of Judaizers was in the thousands. While they could punish Conversos, who relapsed into Judaism, the heart of the problem lay in the continued Jewish presence in

---

were to be found and many of this lineage lived there and they left the land with their wives and children." Rica Amran Cohen, "Judíos y conversos en las crónicas de los Reyes de Castilla (desde finales del siglo XIV hasta la expulsión)," Espacio, Tiempo y Forma. Serie III. Historia medieval 9 (1996): 267

the infected areas. The Inquisitor General, Miguel de Morillo, requested that the Jews be expelled from the principal cities of Andalusia including Seville, Cadiz, and Córdoba. The royal council ratified the move and Jews were given six months to vacate the area. The expulsion of Jews from the region of Andalusia was the first expulsion edict issued in the Peninsula.[85]

That expulsion impacted the neighboring kingdom of Portugal, where a burst of violence erupted in 1482 when a mob attacked several Jews. Jewish-owned stores and homes were destroyed in Lisbon. In the ensuing rampage, Don Isaac Abravanel lost his entire belongings including his precious library. The infamous epidemic of the Black Death also broke out concurrently with the arrival of the Jewish refugees from Castile. The city council ordered that all *émigrés* were to vacate the city immediately. Only two notables, Samuel Nayas, the Procurator of Castilian Jewry and the Castilian physician Samuel Judah, were allowed to remain and only through the intervention of King John II.

Many Jews believed the measures were temporary, and would continue only as long as the Inquisitional tribunals lasted. Before the courts initiated their proceedings, some Conversos had already abandoned the cities and escaped to the Castilian region of Extremadura, the Kingdom of Portugal, or the Kingdom of Granada.[86] Others sought refuge under the protection of the archbishops. The tribunals were in full swing with thousands of suspected Judaizers arrested and tortured and hundreds, if not thousands, sentenced to burn at the stake as unrepentant apostates.[87] As the courts expand-

---

[85] "... all... wanted to rid the land of this sin of heresy, because [they] understood that this was God's and his service." Yolanda Quesada Morillas "La expulsión de los judíos andaluces a finales del siglo xv y suprohibición de pase a Indias," Actas del I Congreso Internacional sobre Migraciones en Andalucía (2011): 2100.

[86] Ibid.

[87] The Cronica de los Reyes Catolicos written by Hernando del Pulgar states the following. "... [they] were and were still secret Jews, and were neither Jews nor Christians but they were baptized and were heretics.... they refused to eat pork unless they were forced, they ate beef ...and secretly kept the Passover and Saturdays as best they could, they sent to synagogues oil lamps, Jews preached to them at home in secret, especially to the women; they were very secret rabid Jews whose cattle and poultry were slaughtered at

ed their reach to other cities, the argument for segregation and expulsion intensified.

While thousands were burned, the Inquisitors continued to argue for their final solution to the root of the heresy. In 1490, their efforts were given a significant boost. The event was known as the incident of the *Santo Nino de la Guardia*. Jews and Conversos were accused of orchestrating the ritual murder of a Christian boy, profaning Christian symbols, and performing black magic in the process. It was no matter that the name of the boy, who was purportedly murdered, was not identified. The purported Jewish influence on Conversos was highlighted as another example of the danger the former's presence constituted.[88]

The drive against Jews was overshadowed by the final push against the last Muslim kingdom in Spain. The war against the Kingdom of Granada required support from all facets of Castilian and Aragonese society, including the valuable contributions of Jews. The need to maintain Jewish support was evidenced by King Ferdinand's refusal to implement an order in Aragon similar to that executed in Andalusia. Both monarchs had also guaranteed the property rights of those Jews forced to move from Andalusia. Jewish courtiers probably had sufficient reason for believing that their situation was not as unstable as it may have seemed. The success of the war in 1492 and the ongoing dilemma of Conversos and Judaizing appears to have resolved the matter. On March 20$^{th}$, the new Chief Inquisitor, Tomas de Torquemada, presented the monarchy with the plan for the complete expulsion of Jews and on the 31$^{st}$ of March, the edict was published in Granada. The need

---

their businesses; they ate unleavened bread at the appropriate time, ... they made all the Jewish ceremonies in secret, so the men and the women always excused themselves from receiving the sacraments of the Holy Church ... except by force in accordance with the ordinances of the Church." Rica Amran Cohen, "Judíos y conversos en las crónicas de los Reyes de Castilla (desde finales del siglo XIV hasta la expulsión)," Espacio, Tiempo y Forma. Serie III. Historia medieval 9 (1996): 269- 270.

[88] Fernando Suárez Bilbao, *Cristianos Contra Judíos y Conversos* (Madrid: Universidad «Rey Juan Carlos», 2004), 479.

for the Expulsion was rationalized as due to the failure of the Inquisition.[89]

The decree had an immediate effect. The Chief Rabbi, Abraham Seneor, converted. The defection of Seneor was devastating. Isaac Abravanel attempted to change the minds of both Ferdinand and Isabella and apparently, came close to achieving it. In the end, any hope for Spanish Jews to remain in the kingdoms of Castile and Aragon was crushed. Those Jews who fled to Portugal or Navarre soon faced a similar situation, only a few years later. The Inquisition remained focused on suspected Judaizers for years to come, reinforced by converted Jews in Portugal, as well as those Conversos who managed to escape to the various domains of the Spanish and Portuguese empires. The Chronicler Andres Bernaldez relates that the Spanish monarchs decided to expel Jews from Spain to put an end to the Mosaic heresy.[90] Some of the Jews who managed to flee Spain journeyed to Sicily and Naples, territories under or eventually under the control of King Ferdinand. Having escaped the Peninsula, many were overwhelmed by the possibility of another dangerous exit and opted for conversion.[91]

---

[89] Yolanda Quesada Morillas "La expulsión de los judíos andaluces a finales del siglo xv y suprohibición de pase a Indias," Actas del I Congreso Internacional sobre Migraciones en Andalucía (2011): 2101-2102.

[90] Eleazar Gutwirth, "The Jews in 15th Century Castilian Chronicles," The Jewish Quarterly Review, LXXIV. No.4 (1984): 395.

[91] In 1468, King Ferdinand of Aragon was crowned King of Sicily and in 1503, he assumed control of the Kingdom of Naples. As Nadia Zeldes relates: "Most scholars now agree that between 15,000 and 20,000 exiles reached the kingdom of Naples in the aftermath of the expulsions from the Iberian Peninsula and Sicily. King Ferrante I welcomed all the new immigrants, but shortly after this death (January 1494), hostility towards the Jews broke out through the kingdom…At Lecce, the crowds cried: [Death, death to the Jews unless they become Christians]' forcing the Jews to choose between death and conversion. In light of these circumstances, many exiles opted for conversion and journeyed back to Sicily." In 1503, King Ferdinand incorporated the Kingdom of Naples into his dominions when French claims to South Italy were ended when Spanish armies, under the command of Gonsalvo Hernandez de Aguilar, won a military victory. Nadia Zeldes, "Legal Status of Jewish Converts to Christianity to Southern Italy and Provence," California Italian Studies Journal, Vol.1:1 (2010): 5, 9. See also Abraham D. Lavender, "The Secret Jews (Neofiti) of Sicily: Religious and Social Status Before and

In the other fateful event of 1492, Spanish exploration under Christopher Columbus discovered the New World. The "Indies" provided opportunities for those Jews and Conversos caught in the current state of affairs, but a series of prohibitions regarding Jewish and Converso settlement in the newly discovered territories was implemented. Immigrating to the New World required royal permission.

In 1493, Ferdinand and Isabella decreed that royal licenses were needed for anyone wishing to travel to the New World. Hence, any person planning a trip to the New World had to meet with the Admiralty with the purpose registering each traveler. In 1501, Fray Nicolas de Obando issued further instructions for obtaining the royal license. Those wanting to travel to the new World had to provide information regarding their lives and practices to the "Tribunal de la Casa de Contratacion," which started issuing licenses as of 1503. The request for a permit was made to the court. While the majority of individuals were selected for a particular role based on their experience, permission was not granted to Moors, Jews, heretics, Gypsies, individuals reconciled by the Inquisition, or those recently converted to the Catholic faith.[92] Concerning those Jews who chose to leave, some of them faced severe challenges along the way and therefore decided to return to the Peninsula and submit to possible scrutiny of the Inquisition, as well as the increasing *Limpieza de Sangre* prohibitions being adopted.

## The Forced Conversions in Portugal

Following the expulsion orders of Castile and Aragon, the king of Portugal allowed Jewish refugees to reside in his kingdom for eight months in return for payment. He agreed to provide them with sufficient ships to carry them to their final destinations. The

---

After the Inquisition," Journal of Spanish, Portuguese, and Italian Crypto Jews. Volume 3 (2011): 119-131.

[92] For additional information see Yolanda Quesada Morillas "La expulsión de los judíos andaluces a finales del siglo xv y suprohibición de pase a Indias," Actas del I Congreso Internacional sobre Migraciones en Andalucía (2011): 2099, 2102-2104.

exact numbers of émigrés are difficult to confirm, but possibly up to 100,000 Jews entered Portugal from Castile. King John II did not keep his pledge, however. Some ships were provided, but the circumstances under which they arrived were terrible. Anyone who remained in the kingdom after the approved period was enslaved. King John also ordered that children be taken from parents who refused to convert. Some were sent to the recently discovered island of St. Thomas. Most of these died in route or from the severe conditions on the island.[93]

After King John's death, his cousin and brother-in-law Manuel was crowned king of Portugal. He ruled from 1495-1521. King Manuel granted freedom to those who had been enslaved. His marriage to the daughter of King Ferdinand and Queen Isabella radically changed the situation, however. King Ferdinand and Queen Isabella conceded to the wedding on the condition that King Manuel expel all the Jews from his territory.[94]

On December 4th, 1496, King Manuel issued the edict of expulsion. All Jews were ordered to leave the kingdom of Portugal by the end of October 1497. Failure to do so was punishable by death and confiscation of their property. The king allowed Jews to depart with all their property. Desperate to keep Jews from leaving the country, he ordered that all Jewish children between the ages of four to fourteen be taken from their parents and brought up as Christians. They were to be permanently separated from their parents if the latter rejected conversion. The forced baptisms were scheduled to start on the first day of the Passover, Sunday, March 19th. Some parents killed their children to prevent them from being baptized. The Portuguese king, much more concerned with the long-term economic impact their exit would pose, opted for a very different strategy than his Spanish counterparts. The king ordered that all remaining Jews were to go to Lisbon to board their waiting ships. They were informed that the time allocated for their depar-

---

[93] Jane S. Gerber, *The Jews of Spain* (New York: The Free Press, 1992), 141.
[94] Ibid., 141-142.

ture had lapsed. As a consequence, they were now the king's slaves. They were induced to convert to Christianity, but this failed. The king then ordered his agents to use force. Many were dragged into churches and baptized.[95]

On May 30, 1497, the king introduced a law protecting baptized Jews. The law stated that baptized Jews were to be left unmolested for twenty years. The authorities could not accuse them of Judaizing during this period. When this time expired, any complaint related to Jewish observance would only result in a civil suit being brought against them. If the person in question was convicted, their property was to pass to their Christian inheritors and not into the fiscal treasury. The possession of Hebrew books was prohibited excepting Jewish physicians and surgeons who were permitted to consult Hebrew medical works.

Some Conversos managed to sell their property and emigrate. The numbers were apparently significant enough to merit royal concern. In April 1499, King Manuel prohibited business transactions by Conversos which involved bills of exchange or selling their real estate. They were forbidden to leave Portugal without royal authorization. Those who assisted them in fleeing was subject to punishment.[96]

As in Castile, the animosity directed towards Jews was quickly transferred to these Conversos. King Emanuel attempted to assuage these new converts with the hope that they would sincerely adopt the Christian faith. The ability of the king to shelter them against provocative speeches of zealous priests was limited, however.

On May 25th 1504, several Conversos met in the Rua Nova, the former *Juderia*. As they conversed, they were encircled by a pack of

---

[95] Ibid., 142.
[96] Salo Wittmayer Baron, *A Social and the Religious History of the Jews: Volume XIII* (Philadelphia: Jewish Publication Society, 1969), 46.

angry youths who affronted them. One of the Conversos drew his sword and wounded some of them. An uproar followed but was ultimately checked by the governor of the city with an armed guard. Forty of the rioters were detained and convicted. They were flogged and were sentenced to banishment on the island of St. Thomas. The queen eventually interceded, and they were absolved.

This unrest was followed by the appalling massacre of Conversos in Lisbon two years later. A group of Conversos was attacked, and some Conversos were arrested, on the night of April 17, 1506. They were released after two days. The public was furious at their release and gossiped about bribery having secured their release. On April 19 another incident occurred when Old Christians and Conversos attended a Church service. Services were held to pray for the end of a devastating pestilence that had broken out. In a side chapel, a crucifix was reported to radiate an exceptional brilliance. This attracted the attention of Christians, who proclaimed it a miracle. A Converso voiced his lack of faith in the purported miracle sparking a riot. The Converso was grabbed by the hair, dragged out of the building, and immediately killed by a mob. Two Dominican monks, Joaõ Mocho from the city of Evora, and Bernardo from the Kingdom of Aragonese paraded through the streets carrying a crucifix and shouting "heresy." They urged the people to eradicate all heretics. The fury of the crowds was added to by German, Dutch, and French sailors in port at the time. The result was a widespread slaughter. On the first day of the violence, over five hundred Conversos were murdered. At the end of the violence between 2,000 and 4,000 Conversos were killed the course of forty-eight hours.

The king responded by arresting and executing the ringleaders and others involved in the violence. The two Dominican monks participating in the unrest were expelled from their order and strangled. Any resident who was found guilty of either theft or homicide was punished corporally and lay open to loss of their property. Friars who had taken part in the uprising were expelled from the monastery. Following the calamity some Conversos left the kingdom. Some apparently returned to Lisbon and for a time were sheltered by the King.

King Manuel also arranged new privileges to Conversos and issued an edict on March 1, 1507, allowing them to leave the country with their property. Those that stayed were also reassured by the renewal the law of May 30, 1497, protecting Conversos from inquisitorial prosecution. On April 21, 1512, it was prolonged for an additional period of twenty years. In 1521, emigration was again prohibited. Attempts to violate this ordinance resulted in the of confiscation of property and loss of freedom.[97]

Despite this, during the remainder of King Manuel's reign Conversos did not face further unrest. When King Manuel died, his son John III ascended the throne. He ruled from 1521-1557. On December 17, 1531, Pope Clement VII sanctioned the introduction of the Inquisition into the kingdom of Portugal. Some Conversos left the country. This occurred particularly during the reign of King Sebastian who ruled from 1557-1578. King Sebastian allowed New Christians to legally emigrate as long as they paid the enormous sum of 250,000 ducats.

In 1580, the Spanish Crown seized the Kingdom of Portugal. This initially had a positive impact on Portuguese Conversos as various economic opportunities were open to them particularly in centers such as Seville and Madrid. The new political reality also provided some relief to Portuguese Conversos fleeing from the

---

[97] In 1524, King John accepted a reported presented by Jorge Themudo. The report presented information gathered from parish priests on the activities of Conversos in their area. The report summarized by the Portuguese historian Alexandre Herculano related that "...the New Christians ceased to attend divine service on Sundays and religious holidays; that they did not bury their dead in the parish churchyards;...that when close to the death they neither received nor asked for extreme unction.; that in their wills they never provided for masses to be said for their souls;...that they were suspected of observing Saturdays and the ancient Passover;...that they practiced acts of charity among themselves, but not toward the Old Christians;...[yet] they got married at church doors, and baptized their children, observing precisely all the customary rites and solemnities." Salo Wittmayer Baron, *A Social and the Religious History of the Jews: Volume XIII* (Philadelphia: Jewish Publication Society, 1969), 48.

Portuguese Inquisition since they could not be tried in Spanish territory for purported crimes done in the Kingdom of Portugal. The Spanish Inquisition could try them for Judaizing on Castilian soil, however. Despite this, increased numbers of Portuguese Conversos journeyed to Castile where many of them became successful merchants and some even serving as conspicuous royal financiers. Portuguese Conversos became a focus of inquisitional queries, and the word Portuguese would increasingly become synonymous with the term Judaizer.[98]

## Conclusion

The Inquisition continued its campaign of targeting Conversos it believed were Judaizing. During the first forty years of the Holy Office's term, thousands of Conversos were burned at the stake with thousands more subject to protracted prison sentences and the confiscation of their property. After 1520, the focus of the Inquisition shifted towards other emerging threats with those accused of Judaizing representing only a small fraction of the total trials. This trend was interrupted by spells of activity particularly with the influx of Portuguese Conversos entering Spain in the late 16th and 17th centuries. The decline in prosecutions, however, has led many to believe that Conversos had integrated to the dominant Christian faith and culture.[99]

More likely, as Kevin Ingram suggests, is the rerouting of Conversos energies. The major reform movements of the early modern period in Spain were led by Conversos or strongly supported by them. One of the best examples is the *Alumbrado* or the Illuminist movement. The practitioners of this mystical form of Christianity rejected Catholic dogma by refraining from external worship common to conventional Catholicism. They also regarded the sacraments as useless. This movement was filled with Conversos, who

---

[98] Miriam Bodian, *Hebrews of the Portuguese Nation* (Bloomington: Indiana University Press, 1997), 13.

[99] Kevin Ingram, ed., *The Conversos and Moriscos in Late Medieval Spain and Beyond: Volume Two* (Leiden: Brill, 2012), 1.

also gravitated towards political movements like the Comunero Revolt of 1521. Converso craftsman and traders were disproportionately represented in this attack on the Crown, which had accumulated administrative power at the expense of the nobility and the aristocratic classes. Conversos, at the royal court and the universities, were also active in Spain's Erasmian movement. The reform movement entered the Iberian Peninsula in 1517 with the court of Charles I. The Erasmian humanistic movement provided Conversos with the opportunity to attack Catholic practices with cover. The trend continued until the 1530s when Charles V assumed the imperial throne. The political dangers associated with religious reform were too dangerous, given the spread of Luther's movement. The Inquisition now focused its attention on these reform movements, and Converso intellectuals opted for other means of conveying their dissent.[100]

As time passed, the majority of the 16th century Conversos in Spain may not have been active Judaizers, but as Kevin Ingram notes, to assume that they assimilated is also ill-advised. Conversos saw themselves as distinct if not superior to their Old Christian neighbors. While their knowledge of Judaism may have declined, their sense of higher status and distinction because of their Jewish background remained. The Conversos were the heirs of God's chosen people and not the descendants of "idol worshippers" like their Old Christian neighbors.[101] Many Conversos escaped to openly practicing Jewish communities from the 15th to the 17th centuries or created their own communities. Their struggles and successes drew other Conversos to join them in their recapturing of Jewish identity.

---

[100] Ibid., 5.
[101] Ibid., 8.

CHAPTER 2

# Christian Attitudes Towards Conversos

Christian attitudes towards Conversos were directly connected to the Church's understanding of forced conversions as well as its outlooks towards Jews. The compilation of Roman law known as the Theodosian code stated that "It is graver than death and crueler than massacre when someone abjures the Christian faith and becomes polluted with the Jewish incredulity."[1]

For the Church, abandoning Christianity presented a real danger to the spiritual welfare of those who remained Christians. The effect of baptism was irreversible, and the abandonment of the Christian faith was blasphemous.[2] In the 5$^{th}$ century CE, the Church permitted some Jewish converts who were lax in their Christian observance to return to Judaism if their conversions were deemed insincere. This was ultimately rejected by the Visigoth King Alaric II in his *Breviarium,* a collection of Roman law

---

[1] Codex Theodosianus 16.8.19 cited and translated by Ammon Linder, *The Jews in Roman Imperial Legislation* (Detroit: Wayne State University Press, 1987), 258.

[2] Edward Fram, "Perception and Reception of Repentant Apostates in Medieval Ashkenaz and Premodern Poland," AJS Review 21/2 (1996): 300.

disseminated in 506 CE, and by the Fourth Council of Toledo in 633 CE.³

The Second Council of Nicaea in 787 CE designated baptized Jews who continued to observe Jewish practices or hold Jewish beliefs as non-Christians. This measure was also rejected by Pope Adrian I.⁴ Pope Calixtus II affirmed that no Jew was to be converted by force. But those who had were not allowed to leave the Christian fold. In 1140, the Christian theologian John Gratian wrote that those who had been compelled were obligated to retain the Christian faith to prevent it from being blasphemed.⁵ In 1144, King Louis VII of France declared that baptized Jews who returned to Judaism had done so at the prompting of the devil. They were punished accordingly.

In 1201, Pope Innocent III stated that even if a person had been dragged violently by torture and accepted baptism to avoid loss, he had received the "impressed character of Christianity."⁶ He was compelled to observe Christianity "…as one-conditionally willing."⁷ Besides openly choosing death when threatened with forced conversion, there was very little any Jew could do to persuade the Church that they had not done so willingly.⁸ *Las Siete Partidas*, a Castilian law code compiled around 1265 under the di-

---

³ Ammon Linder, *The Jews in Roman Imperial Legislation* (Detroit: Wayne State University Press, 1987), 199-200.

⁴ Edward Synan, *The Popes and the Jews in the Middle Ages* (New York: Macmillan, 1965), 55, 58.

⁵ Edward Fram, "Perception and Reception of Repentant Apostates in Medieval Ashkenaz and Premodern Poland," AJS Review 21/2 (1996): 304-305.

⁶ Ibid., 305.

⁷ Nadia Zeldes, "Legal Status of Jewish Converts to Christianity to Southern Italy and Provence," California Italian Studies Journal, Vol.1:1 (2010): 7. According to Pope Innocent III... "[For] the grace of Baptism had been received, and they had been anointed with the sacred oil, and had participated in the body of the Lord, they might properly be forced to hold to the faith which they had accepted perforce, lest the name of the Lord be blasphemed, and lest they hold in contempt and consider vile the faith they had joined." Solomon Grayzel, *The Church and the Jews in the Thirteenth Century*, rev. ed., (New York: Hermon, 1966), 103.

⁸ Edward Fram, "Perception and Reception of Repentant Apostates in Medieval Ashkenaz and Premodern Poland," AJS Review 21/2 (1996): 305.

rection of King Alfonso X the Wise of Castile (1252-1284), also rejected coerced conversion.[9]

Concomitant with this, the Franciscan monk, Ramon Llull (1233-1316) argued that Jews who had embraced Christianity were in danger of returning to Judaism due to the influences of unbaptized Jews. The only solution was the physical separation of Jews and converts. Llull argued that since Christianity was the only true faith, Jews who refused to adopt it should be expelled from Christian territory. Tolerating Judaism guaranteed that it would flourish and present a strong temptation for converts to return to their Jewish ways.[10]

## The Theological Changes in Medieval Christianity

The violent attacks on the Jewish communities of Castile and Aragon at the end of the 14$^{th}$ century were ultimately underpinned by the religious attitudes that Christianity had adopted in earlier times towards Judaism. The medieval Church accepted the views of Saint Augustine, who saw the preservation and subjugation of those who had crucified Jesus as a testament to the Christian faith.[11] In 1199, Pope Innocent III expounded on Augustine's doc-

---

[9] "No force or compulsion shall be employed in any way against a Jew to induce him to become a Christian; but Christians should convert him to the faith of Our Lord Jesus Christ by means of the texts of the Holy Scriptures, and by kind words, for no one can love or appreciate a service which is done him by compulsion… and we also order that, after any Jews become Christians, all persons in our dominions shall honor them; and that no one shall dare to reproach them or their descendants, by way of insult, with having been Jews; and that they shall possess all their property, sharing the same with their brothers and inheriting it from their fathers and mothers and other relatives just as if they were Jews; and that they can hold all offices and dignities which other Christians can do." Jacob Marcus, *The Jew in the Medieval World: A Sourcebook, 315-1791* (New York: JPS, 1938), 34-42.

[10] Salo Witmayer Baron, *Social and Religious History of the Jews, Volume IX* (New York: Columbia University Press, 1965), 12.

[11] David Nirenberg, *Anti-Judaism: The Western Tradition* (W.W. Norton & Company, New York, 2013), 130. In the 10$^{th}$ century the choice between expulsion and conversion was also addressed by Pope Leo VII who declared that, "You should never cease preaching to them, with all the sagacity, prudent counsel and reverence toward God, the belief in the Sacred Trinity, and the mystery of the Lord's incarnation. If they wholeheartedly wish to believe and become baptized, we shall offer thanks and high praise to the om-

trine in the former's work titled *Constitutio Pro Iudaeis*. The Pope argued that the continued existence of Jews but the lack of self-determination was proof of their sins. The Church contended that Jews would ultimately embrace the Christian faith.

In 1215, the Council of Trent declared that Jews and Christians should be physically separated lest the former contaminate the latter. In 1236, a Jewish convert to Christianity named Nicolas Donin argued before Pope Gregory IX that contrary to popular belief, Jews were not faithful to the Bible. Instead, they adhered to false doctrines contained in the Talmud. He pointed to multiple Talmudic references which derided Jesus and the Virgin Mary. According to Donin, the rabbis conspired to prevent Jews from realizing the fulfillment of the messianic promises in Jesus.

## The Church's Missionary Drive

Disputations were held to convince Jews that Christianity was true. The Paris Disputation of 1240 was the first national dispute. In this case, Jewish representatives were questioned by Medieval Inquisitional authorities. Talmuds were seized and turned over to Dominican friars for "protection." In 1248, in the great Greve plaza of Paris, wagon-loads of Talmuds were burned. The message was clear. Judaism in its present form was a pernicious heresy; Jews were the bearers of this sacrilege.

In Aragon, King James I and subsequent kings allowed Mendicant orders to preach in the synagogues. James I ordered that Jews listen patiently during these lectures. The King did allow Jews to forgo answering Christian accusations that their religious works

---

nipotent God. Should they, however, refuse to believe, you shall expel them from your states with our permission. For we ought not to associate with the Lord's enemies, as the Apostle says: 'Be ye not unequally yoked together with unbelievers: for what fellowship hath righteousness with unrighteousness...or what part hath he that believeth with an infidel?' [II Cor. 6:14-15]. But you must not baptize with force, and without their wish and request. For it is written: 'Give not that which is holy unto the dogs, neither cast ye your pearls before swine, lest they trample them under their feet.'" Salo Witmayer Baron, *A Social and the Religious History of the Jews: Volume IV* (Philadelphia: Jewish Publication Society, 1957), 6.

contained attacks on Christianity, except those attacks against Jesus, the Virgin Mary, and the Saints.[12] The mounting pressure against Judaism was reflected in the great debate of 1263. Presided by King James I of Aragon, it pitted the famous Rabbi Moses ben Nachman against the Jewish apostate Pablo Christiani who argued that the messianic claims of Jesus were evident in rabbinic sources.

Charges of ritual murder and Host desecration were also promulgated by the clerics of some towns regardless of whether such charges were rejected or even condemned by their clerical elders.[13] The situation was particularly problematic for royal officials who were caught in a no-win situation. If they obeyed royal orders and protected the Jewish community, they faced the enmity of angry mobs. If they failed to protect Jews, they risked being punished by the king.

## The Miracle of Conversion

In 1391, the widespread violence against Jews in Castile and Aragon brought about the conversion of thousands. The incredible number convinced many Christian rioters that nothing short of the miraculous had occurred. In the city of Valencia, where many Jews converted, the clergy feared it would run out of holy chrism. In a tale oddly reminiscent of the Chanukah story, the priests returned to find the nearly empty vessels now brimming. The city council was amazed at this "miracle" and quickly forgot the violence that precipitated the conversions.

For all the excitement surrounding the conversions, Christian attitudes towards Conversos developed along three lines. The first was that Old Christians regarded Conversos as Jews. The second was a general apathy for educating Conversos in the Christian faith. The last was a belief that Conversos were not merely observing Jewish practices but actively poisoning the Christian faith.

---

[12] Ram Ben-Shalom, "Between Official and Private Dispute: The Case of Christian Spain and Provence in the Late Middle Ages," AJS Review, Vol. 27, No. 1 (2003): 37-38.

[13] Natalie Oeltjen, "Crisis and Regeneration: The Conversos of Majorca, 1391 - 1416." (PhD diss., University of Toronto, 2012), 9.

## Conversos Viewed as Still Jews

With thousands of neophytes, the previous focus on the Jewish problem slowly shifted to a Converso problem.[14] In earlier periods, Jews had been regarded as adherents to the Law of Moses to distinguish them from Christians who believed in Christ or Muslims who followed the teachings of Mohammed.[15] Jewish converts were theoretically viewed as Christians after their spiritual transformation without reference to their Jewish past.[16] A notable exception is the case of Pope Anacletus II (1130-1138) whose great-grandfather was Jewish. Anacletus served as a cardinal for years without any disapproval. When he was elected by a majority of the College of Cardinals to serve as Pope, Bernard of Clairvaux, a prominent preacher opposed him because of his Jewish background.[17]

Old Christians now regarded Jews as a religious and ethnic group. Even Jews who had converted were believed to retain the wicked characteristics attributed to Jews. Baptism did not remove the taint they bore. Converts remained Jews, and their descendants were suspect as far as Old Christians were concerned. Conversos who continued to observe Jewish practices reinforced these fears.

Conversos and their descendants were often insulated from Old Christians. In a bid towards social acceptance, some Conversos

---

[14] María del Pilar Rábade Obradó, "La instrucción cristiana de los conversos en la Castilla del siglo XV," En la España Medieval, 22 (1999): 370.

[15] Jacob Marcus, *The Jew in the Medieval World: A Sourcebook, 315-1791* (New York: JPS, 1938), 34-42.

[16] Fernando Suárez Bilbao, Cristianos Contra Judíos y Conversos (Madrid : Universidad «Rey Juan Carlos», 2004), 446. An exception can be found in the requirement that Jewish converts to Christianity from the Barcelona Jewish community provide Jewish witnesses in lawsuits that involved Christians and Jews. As Alexandra Guerson notes, "Baptism had not as Christian teaching says, made of the convert truly a 'new man,' even in the king's own perception, not to mention that of his legal advisors." Alexandra Guerson "Seeking Remission: Jewish Conversion in the Crown of Aragon, c. 1378-1391" Jewish History (2010): 38. Also Natalie Oeltjen, "Crisis and Regeneration: The Conversos of Majorca, 1391 - 1416." (PhD diss., University of Toronto, 2012), 41.

[17] Salo Wittmayer Baron, *A Social and the Religious History of the Jews: Volume IV* (Philadelphia: Jewish Publication Society, 1957), 10-11.

rejected the outward characteristics that were qualified as Jewish. Among these were physical cleanliness, industrial drive, thriftiness, and intellectual activity. For Old Christians, Conversos had converted to control or subvert Christian society.[18]

## The Lack of Christian Education among Conversos

There was a failure to instruct Conversos in the core tenets of Christianity. This left them ignorant of anything more than elementary Christian observances. The *jurados* of Valencia indicate that more than twenty years after the riots, Conversos had still not received instruction in the Christian faith.[19] They laid blame on the fact that Conversos and Jews continued to live together.[20]

In truth, this paucity of education was partially reflective of a general tendency among the clergy. Many priests were just incapable or insufficiently trained to convey the Christian faith to even true Christians. The efforts of inept priests were buttressed by brief compendiums on Christian doctrine, but the deficits were clear.[21] Prior to the reforms of the 15th century, the art of preaching was in decline as reflected by the fact that even bishops proved absent when the time for delivering sermons arrived. They foisted their responsibility onto friars who were apparently more capable.

For Conversos, the lack of instruction strengthened their ties to the faith of their ancestors.[22] The lack of meaningful education left

---

[18] Kevin Ingram, "Secret lives, public lies: the conversos and socio-religious nonconformism in the Spanish Golden Age." (PhD diss., UC San Diego, 2006), 2.

[19] "As experience, which is a good instructor, has shown that the new Christians who were converted nearly 23 years ago in the city of Valencia and were baptized without much information about or instruction in the holy Catholic faith, speak, live and reside together, they have received very little improvement in the Christian faith and are not well informed in what is necessary in order to believe, nor less in the devotions or acts of the holy law..." Jose Hinojosa Montalvo, *The Jews of the Kingdom of Valencia- Hispania Judaica Volume 9* (Jerusalem: The Magnes Press, 1993), 18.

[20] Ibid., 18.

[21] María del Pilar Rábade Obradó, "La instrucción cristiana de los conversos en la Castilla del siglo XV," En la España Medieval, 22 (1999): 378-379.

[22] Joaquim Carvalho ed., *Religion and Power in Europe: Conflict and Convergence* (Pisa: Edizioni Plus - Pisa University Press, 2007), 85.

them orphaned in the Christian religion, and only more likely to continue in or return to Jewish prayers and rites. The situation was not much better for those who were Conversos of the second and third generation. Their familial, ethnic, and cultural ties remained Jewish. The religious instruction they did receive was framed by the religious tradition of the Franciscans and Dominicans who had dedicated themselves to studying Hebrew and in certain cases Jewish theology. It was characterized by missionizing, polemicizing, and Inquisitorial tendencies.[23]

Near the end of the 15th century, the focus on educating Conversos in the Christian faith, as well as continuing the proselytization of Jews was augmented by a new strategy. Pope Sixtus IV authorized the Inquisition. María del Pilar Rábade Obrado maintains that the initiative towards doctrinal instruction was aimed at diminishing the scope of the Inquisitional tribunals. The enterprise was driven by Fray Hernando de Talavera, a one-time confessor to both monarchs and a descendant of Conversos.

The Church, particularly in Andalusia and in the kingdom of Aragon, launched various efforts to strengthen the faith of Conversos and end their Jewish practices. Talavera preached the superiority of Christianity over Judaism. Talavera was aided by Pedro Fernandez de Solis, the Bishop of Cadiz. Another component of Talavera's strategy was a catechism specifically intended to rectify the Conversos' lack of knowledge. The third part of Talavera's

---

[23] The religious instruction of the Dominicans was exemplified by individuals like Raimundo Marti of Aragon who had authored the work titled, *Pugio Fidei Adversus Mauros et Iudaeos,* in the 13th century. His work reflected an extensive knowledge of Jewish theology. De Marti's efforts were succeeded by his disciple Arnaldo de Vilanova whose work focused on the explanation of the Trinity. This genre of Christian literature was continued by other notables such as Fray Bernardo de Oliver from Aragon. Those hoping to catechize the Conversos looked to these works as resources. These texts were inherently polemical in nature and focused on convincing Jews that conversion to Christianity was the only hope for salvation. With its focus on the theological destruction of Judaism, they were ineffective in communicating the dogmas and doctrines of Christianity. Those who entered the Church struggled to acquire instruction in their new faith. María del Pilar Rábade Obradó, "La instrucción cristiana de los conversos en la Castilla del siglo XV," En la España Medieval, 22 (1999): 383, 389.

program was determining the extent of Crypto-Jewish practices. Cardinal Pedro Gonzalez de Mendoza, who had initially supported the creation of a new Inquisition, attempted to convince Conversos of the errors of their ways via his *Catecismo de la Doctrina Cristiana*. De Mendoza believed that instruction rather than prosecution was the way to bring Conversos in line with the Church.[24]

Talavera's efforts ended in failure. Heretics did not return to the faith as he had envisioned, and they continued to practice Jewish rites.[25] Hernando de Pulgar, a royal historiographer and a descendant of Conversos, noted that the lack of Christian knowledge further separated Conversos from a faith they already saw as foreign. The evangelistic endeavors of Talavera and others ended as the Inquisition began its operations in earnest. Pulgar criticized the Inquisition arguing that religious instruction and not persecution would have been much more successful in creating faithful Conversos.

The Edict of Expulsion in 1492 initiated another wave of evangelization intended to keep Jews in Castile and Aragon. The primary goal was conversion though it also included some minimal instruction in the Christian faith. King Ferdinand and Queen Isabella sponsored various initiatives designed to achieve this. Prelates were ordered to assign knowledgeable individuals to instruct these recent converts.[26] The mission to educate Conversos also included their relocation to neighborhoods inhabited by Old Christians. The purpose was to forestall the self-segregation which characterized Conversos of earlier decades. This rule was strictly applied to those Conversos who had been rabbis before their conversion. They were segregated from other converts with the purpose of diminishing the influence they could have on them. These Conversos were expected to derive a deeper understanding of Christianity with dai-

---

[24] Salo Wittmayer Baron, *A Social and the Religious History of the Jews: Volume XIII* (Philadelphia: Jewish Publication Society, 1969), 27.

[25] María del Pilar Rábade Obradó, "La instrucción cristiana de los conversos en la Castilla del siglo XV," En la España Medieval, 22 (1999): 385.

[26] Ibid., 388-389.

ly contact with Old Christians. If young Conversos became apprentices, they did so with Old Christian families that fostered their identity as Christians. The separation of reconciled Conversos from other Conversos was also implemented. Contact between Conversos and those reconciled only occurred in public in the presence of Old Christians.

The concern over Crypto-Judaism was so intense that the removal of children was also contemplated. The plan was not adopted but envisioned the removal of children from the age of five to sixteen from their Converso parents. They were to be placed with Old Christian families who would supervise their religious education. These foster parents were to oversee the contact they had with their natural families. The only Conversos who were to be exempted were those who had continued in the Christian faith for 20 years and had no issues with the Inquisition. The monarchs rightly believed Conversos would continue the observance of Jewish practices if left to themselves. The monarchs also sought to temper the Inquisition's queries concerning these new converts. This policy of moderation towards new converts was conveyed in a letter written by King Ferdinand to Fray Tomas de Torquemada.

The inquisitors of Granada, Martin Ponce, the bishop of Mesina, and Alfonso de Fuentelsaz, sought a practical guide for the considerable number of Conversos who dwelt in their designated area. They drafted a series of practices and norms that Conversos were expected to observe. Priests in parishes that included Conversos were urged to focus on their education. Particular attention was given to those who were fourteen years and younger. The underlying motivation was the fact that their parents had not stressed their Christian education. The Church sought to ensure that the younger generation of Conversos would be faithful to Christianity.[27]

## Second Thoughts on the Miracle of Conversion

---

[27] Ibid., 390-391.

The mass conversions of 1391 significantly altered age-old Christian notions of identity. Christians had devoted considerable energy in portraying themselves as the antithesis of Jews and Judaism. Christians were spiritual, whereas Jews were focused on the material. Christians were granted understanding to perceive the Gospel while Jews were blinded. Other dichotomies highlighting the differences between the two faiths were godly and satanic, good and evil, allegorical and literal. All of the positive elements were attributed to Christians while the negative ones were ascribed to Jews.[28] The mass conversions of 1391 now threatened notions of Christian identity. The possible elimination of Jews destabilized what had for so long been the foundations of Christian identity. David Nirenberg remarks that,

> "These were exciting times for a Christian society trained to see the advent of the Messiah in the conversion of the Jews. But they were also unsettling, destabilizing Christian identity in two important ways. First, the seeming messianic conversion of Jews promised to eliminate the living representatives of a negative pole vital to the coherence of Christian self-understanding. Second, the emergence of the converts as an intermediate class produced a rapid narrowing of the social space that had previously separated Christian from Jew and a consequent perception of the erosion of Christian privilege."[29]

As time passed, Jewish converts to Christianity as well as their descendants were seen as hybrid beasts who were neither Jew nor Christian. Some were suspected of converting in order to poison Christians while others were accused of having done so to have intercourse with Christian women.[30] Conversos were labeled as subversives in the infamous work of the middle decades of the 15th

---

[28] David Nirenberg, "Conversion, Sex, and Segregation: Jews and Christians in Medieval Spain," The American Historical Review, Vol. 107, no 4. (2002): 1086.

[29] Ibid., 1089.

[30] As Nirenberg notes: "Baptism could not alter the fact that the Jews' blood was corrupted by millennia of mixture and debasement, indelibly saturated with a hatred of everything Christian." Ibid., 1078.

century titled *El Alborayque*. Conversos who relapsed into Judaism were labeled rabid dogs.[31]

Intermarriage with Conversos was largely discouraged. This isolation reinforced the Jewish identity of Conversos. Surprisingly, in the first few decades following the mass conversions, Old Christians were not overly concerned with the religious practices of Conversos, nor even in instituting differences between them. David Nirenberg states that,

> "Christian authorities did worry that converts lingered in their old sensibilities, but voiced those worries rarely. This is in striking contrast with the litany of complaints about Judaizing that would arise in the 1440s, especially when we consider the fact that in the 1390s the thousands of converts who had entered Christianity by force and

---

[31] "Assi estos alboraycos son perros lebreles. Grandes perros son: y esto es verdad, que assi como el perro no ha verguenca de su senor de fazer sus faziendas delante d'el ni delante de las otras gentes, assi estos hombres-perros no han verguenca de D-os niaun del rey ni del las gentes de fazer sus faziendas ni cerimonias judaycas, ni de dezir sus heregias y mentiras. Y ostrosi, assi com el perro torna al vomio y a comer lo que bosso, ansi estos canes tornan al sabad e adafina e cacuelas e circumcision e cerminonias que usaron ya quando se baptizaron. E desto prophetizo Salomon, 'Tal es el loco que torna a fazer la segunda locura como el perro que torna a comer lo que bosso.' Assi eran locos los judios en guarder aquellas cosas judiegas, e agora tornan despues de baptizados a fazer otra vez su locura. Ytem, 'el can con ravia de su dueno trava'; ansi estos perros mordieron a sus senor con la ravia de la embidia diabolica. Circundederunt me canes multi, etc. cercaronme canes, conviene a saber, mucha companas de malvados me ceraron e foradaron mis pies e mis manos y echaron suertes sobre mis vestiduras. He aqui la quarta condiciom, de canes." "These Alboraycos are rabid dogs. Large dogs are they. And this is true that just as a dog has no shame...so too do these people have no shame before God or the King in performing their Jewish ceremonies or saying their heresy and lies. And just as a dog returns to its vomit and eats it, these dogs also turn to the Sabbath and to circumcision, and other ceremonies which they still observed when they were baptized. Of this Solomon prophesied...so too were the Jews crazy in observing their traditions and now they return their lunacy after having been baptized...and so too these dogs will bite their master with rage and with a diabolical jealousy… [Partial English translation]" Senal 394 cited in Jeremy Lawrance, "Alegoria Y Apocalipsis En El Alboraique," Revista de Poetica Medieval, 11 (2009): 21.

without catechism almost certainly had little sense of how to practice their new religion."[32]

The emphasis was focused primarily on establishing the indelible differences between Jews and Christians. King Joan I of Aragon, is an example. In 1393, he wrote to several cities to caution them on an increasing threat. It was becoming impossible for "natural Christians" or Old Christians to identify who was a Jew and who was a convert to Christianity. Converts were forbidden to live, eat, and socialize with Jews.[33] Also, Jews were ordered to dress distinctively which included the wearing of badges and hats which identified them.[34] The policy was not new, but its importance was intensified in the eyes of the King.[35] However, the continued Jewish practices of Conversos were disturbing to King Joan as Mark Meyerson explains.

> "For Joan, the Jewish practices of New Christians were not the only cause for concern. Being of 'an extraordinarily unstable and superstitious' nature, he could never quite allay his suspicions that Jews were allies of Satan, and perhaps of foreign Muslim enemies as well. These suspicions occasionally clouded the king's judgment and gave him additional reasons for investigating and penalizing Jews. Still, even in these instances, the Crown's near bankruptcy checked the worst excesses, moving Joan to fine rather than burn the accused."[36]

In 1398, King Marti of Aragon articulated his concern over the ongoing association of Conversos with Jews. He noted that they

---

[32] David Nirenberg, "Conversion, Sex, and Segregation: Jews and Christians in Medieval Spain," The American Historical Review, Vol. 107, no 4. (2002): 1085-1086.

[33] Yitzhak Baer, *A History of the Jews in Christian Spain, Volume 2* (Philadelphia: Jewish Publication Society, 1961), 125.

[34] David Nirenberg, "Conversion, Sex, and Segregation: Jews and Christians in Medieval Spain," The American Historical Review, Vol. 107, no 4. (2002): 1079.

[35] Nadia Zeldes, "Legal Status of Jewish Converts to Christianity to Southern Italy and Provence," California Italian Studies Journal, Vol.1:1 (2010): 2.

[36] Mark D. Meyerson, *A Jewish Renaissance in Fifteenth-Century Spain* (Princeton: Princeton University Press, 2004), 35.

met to keep the Sabbath and observed that many frequently Judaized. To combat this, he ordered all officials in his domain to assist papal inquisitors in their quest to extirpate this sacrilege. Judaizing continued as is revealed by King Marti's order in 1400 that any Converso observance of Jewish holidays would carry a fine of 100 sous.[37] Separation was still the preferred recourse. Vicente Ferrer who spearheaded the efforts for conversion during 1412-1415 stated that "he will never be a good Christian, who is a neighbor to a Jew."[38] Vicente Ferrer argued for harsh measures to be adopted to eliminate such interaction:

> "And above all, there should be no communication with them in the home, for Christian and infidel should not dwell together in the same house, for it is an evil which is contagious, that is luxury, for many are thought to be the children of Jews but are really Christian, and vice versa. And therefore just as Jews and Muslims are different from Christians in law, they should be different from them in habitation."[39]

## Growing Resentment against Conversos by Old Christians

The monarchy reinforced the ongoing association of Conversos with Jews. Despite their conversion, Conversos were forced to assume a proportional share of the debts and tax liabilities of their former Jewish communities. The tax burdens often matured over decades. Conversos were classified under a fiscal grouping distinct

---

[37] David Nirenberg, "Conversion, Sex, and Segregation: Jews and Christians in Medieval Spain," The American Historical Review, Vol. 107, no 4. (2002): 1086.

[38] As David Nirenberg explains: "Proximity destabilized an essential aspect of Christian identity, dishonored God, and put Christian society at risk of famine, plague, and other manifestations of divine displeasure." David Nirenberg, Mass Conversion and Genealogical Mentalities: Jews and Christians in Fifteenth-Century Spain," Past and Present 174(1) (2002): 11.

[39] Ibid., 12. The degree of integration of Jews and Muslims was purportedly of such a significant level that for Vincent Ferrer, Jews and Muslims lived among Christians, dressed like them, and at times even assumed Christian names. Thus he could state: "…by their appearance they are taken and reputed by many to be Christians." David Nirenberg, "Conversion, Sex, and Segregation: Jews and Christians in Medieval Spain," The American Historical Review, Vol. 107, no 4. (2002): 1083.

from Old Christians. As an example, Nadia Zeldes relates that the Jewish converts of Sicily, which were subject to the Crown of Aragon, were supposed to be equal in status to Old Christians. The reality was quite different.

> "Official policies tended to create a distinct status for the New Christians, at least in the first and second generations after the Expulsion, rather than to integrate them into Sicilian society."[40]

The business and social fraternities that Conversos formed only reinforced their distinct identity.[41] In 1402, the town of Valencia rejected the charge of a Converso against an Old Christian. The argument was that as a former professing Jew, he still "retained the accustomed calumnies of their ancient infidelity, which they have not yet purged from their character."[42] Given these social attitudes, most Conversos married other Conversos. This buttressed their existing social, ethnic, and religious ties.[43]

In the late 15th century, the Spanish historian Andres Bernaldez noted the similarities between Jews and Conversos. Bernaldez argued that Conversos remained part and parcel part of the Jewish community:[44]

---

[40] Nadia Zeldes, *The Former Jews of This Kingdom: Sicilian Converts After the Expulsion, 1492-1516* (Leiden: Brill, 2003), 70.

[41] David Nirenberg, Mass Conversion and Genealogical Mentalities: Jews and Christians in Fifteenth-Century Spain, Past and Present 174(1) (2002): 14.

[42] David Nirenberg, "Conversion, Sex, and Segregation: Jews and Christians in Medieval Spain," The American Historical Review, Vol. 107, no 4. (2002): 1092.

[43] "The Judeoconversos, even those who were not Judaising, were used to endogamy, and even those who retained their new religion seemed to form a caste, imbued with communal consciousness and a collective life instinct." Hilda Nissimi, "Religious Conversion, Covert Defiance and Social Identity," Numen, Vol. 51, No. 4 (2004): 385.

[44] El Alborayque also denotes the ways that Conversos could be identified. "And they can be known by the celebrations/feasts they observe and also by their observance of the Sabbath and in their eating and their blending/association with Jews and in their fasts and Passover that they observe and in the fact they never confess." Senal 1. 393 cited in Jeremy Lawrance, "Alegoria Y Apocalipsis En El Alboraique," Revista de Poetica Medieval, 11 (2009), 16.

"[They] stink...as they eat [as they did before] having never abandoned their Jewish customs of eating...corn and food made from onions and garlic fried with oil. And the meat they fried with oil and they used this instead of bacon or fat, to keep from eating bacon. And beef with oil and other things they fried...and these made a terrible smell. And their houses and doors stink of foul odors because of the food they eat. And they [i.e. the Conversos] have the same smell as the Jews, because of the food they eat and because they are not baptized." [45]

## The 1449 Riots of Toledo

While Conversos were still ethnically, culturally, if not religiously Jewish, their legal designation as Christians no longer subjected them to the limitations that had disadvantaged Jewish merchants and professionals in the past. Frequently skilled in trade and business, many Conversos retained essential contacts in Jewish financial and commercial circles that allowed them to compete successfully with Old Christians. In a letter written by a Converso named Francesc de Sant Jordi to an unconverted Jew named Shaltiel Bonafos, the former wrote that:

"Those who have emerged from the waters of baptism, from the fountains of salvation, are firmly established upon golden pedestals. They are all personages. In their courts and in their palaces there are ivories and monkeys and peacocks and dwarves; they divested themselves of their soiled attire...and donned the garments of salvation."[46]

The overwhelming majority of Conversos were poor, however. There was, though sufficient success among Conversos to draw the ire of many Old Christians. Many Old Christians viewed the

---

[45] Tratados de la Peste 97. See Andres Bernaldez, Memorias del Reinado de los Reyes Catolicos. Ed. M. Gomez Moreno and J. de Mata Carriazo, (Madrid: Real Academia de la Historia, 1962).
[46] David Nirenberg, "Conversion, Sex, and Segregation: Jews and Christians in Medieval Spain," The American Historical Review, Vol. 107, no 4. (2002): 1089.

financial success of many Conversos as having come about at their expense. While the envy was real, the relapse of Jewish converts to Judaism was the fundamental reason for the hatred against them. The religious factor was always present as J. Valdeon notes, "On their own, the social-economic issues would not have generated the conflict. The problem lay in the previously mentioned topic, the war of religion."[47]

Some Conversos amassed enormous fortunes and advanced their societal positions by acquiring administrative offices in the church and local governments. Other Conversos opted to create marriage alliances with Castile's nobility. With many Conversos prominent in commercial and social positions in the urban centers of Castile, social and even violent clashes with the Old Christian society arose. One of the most intense confrontations transpired in Toledo in 1449.[48]

With his treasury drained due to a civil war and the ongoing struggle against the Kingdom of Granada, King Juan II requested financial aid from the cities of Castile. In Toledo in 1449, Alvaro de Luna, King Juan's constable and master of the Order of Santiago, delegated the task of raising the required sum to the Converso merchant Alonso Cota.[49]

Suspicion fell on Conversos as the ringleaders of the special tax. Old Christians argued that Conversos had orchestrated it as a means to debase them. Pedro Sarmiento, the *alcalde mayor* and his assessor Marcos Garcia de Manzarambros, resisted the tax and pursued the intervention of the *Infante*, Don Enrique, with his father, the King. A riot began with a mob at the church of Santa

---

[47] María del Pilar Rábade Obradó, "La instrucción cristiana de los conversos en la Castilla del siglo XV," En la España Medieval, 22 (1999): 375.

[48] Kevin Ingram, "Secret lives, public lies: the conversos and socio-religious non-conformism in the Spanish Golden Age." (PhD diss., UC San Diego, 2006), 44.

[49] In 1443, Alvaro de Luna sponsored the Pragmatica of Arevalo which sought to restore Jews to more favorable conditions they had enjoyed before 1391. Under the Pragmatica, Jews would be allowed to assume certain positions which had been prohibited to them in addition to a restoration of the civil and religious privileges they had once experienced.

Maria. The house of the Converso Alonso Cota was burned. The homes of other Conversos were also attacked.[50] Alonso Cota managed to survive, but the result was open war climaxing in a cordon of the city by Alvaro de Luna.

In the midst of the violence, Juan de Ciudad, a Converso serving as tax collector, was killed and his body dragged to the Plaza de Zocodover. The *Cronica de D. Alvaro de Luna* relates that some of Juan de Ciudad's descendants eventually journeyed to other lands and returned openly to Judaism.[51] King Juan II arrived in Toledo in May of 1449. Sarmiento and his allies defended their actions and presented the King with a list of their demands. Sarmiento and his followers rejected the charge of treason levied against them but nevertheless refused to receive the King in Toledo. They maintained that Alvaro de Luna had given offices to "infidels and heretics, enemies of our sacred law." Sarmiento accused Alvaro of "publicly defending and receiving Conversos of Jewish lineage who for the most part are found to be infidels and heretics who have 'Judaized' and continued to do so and observe most of the Jewish rites and ceremonies."[52] Sarmiento gathered numerous officials in the city in June and distributed the *Sentencia-Estatuto,* which prohibited Conversos and their descendants from holding any public office or serving as witnesses against Old Christians.[53]

Sarmiento held that Conversos were known to belittle the Catholic faith with their Judaizing. He held that a significant portion of the city's Conversos subscribed to errors against the articles of the Catholic faith. They observed Jewish rites and ceremonies and asserted that Jesus was a Jewish man who was killed and whom the Christians worshiped as God. Some Conversos even

---

[50] Norman Roth, "Anti-Converso Riots of the Fifteenth Century, Pulgar and the Inquisition," En la España medieval 15 (1992): 369.

[51] Rica Amran Cohen, "Judíos y conversos en las crónicas de los Reyes de Castilla (desde finales del siglo XIV hasta la expulsión)," Espacio, Tiempo y Forma. Serie III. Historia Medieval 9 (1996): 262.

[52] Norman Roth, "Anti-Converso Riots of the Fifteenth Century, Pulgar and the Inquisition," En la España medieval 15 (1992): 370.

[53] Ibid.

interpreted Christianity as having a god and a goddess. On Holy Thursday while the holy oil and chrism were being consecrated in the Church of Toledo, Conversos slaughtered lambs and ate them in observance of Passover.

According to Sarmiento and his allies, Conversos were enemies of Old Christians. Their actions were consistent with those of their Jewish ancestors during the Moorish invasion centuries before. Sarmiento contended that Jews who lived in Toledo at the time of the invasion had betrayed the city into the hands of the invading Moors. Since Conversos were descended from Jews, they had robbed the king and had destroyed and ruined many noble ladies, knights, and *hidalgos*. Conversos intended on taking control of Toledo and throwing Old Christians out of the city and handing it over to their enemies.[54]

Sarmiento's *Sentencia-Estatuto* designated Conversos as Jews in "all their perversity." They could not be integrated into Old Christian society. The laws enacted in Toledo set the stage for a series of purity of blood laws that were gradually adopted across the Iberian Peninsula.

## The Violence in Ciudad Real

The animosity towards Conversos was often linked to a conflict between segments of the nobility and the monarchy. Various groups were vying for governmental control over cities. The hatred of Conversos was a weapon wielded by either side. But the political and economic issues that contributed to anti-Converso sentiment were never divorced from the Conversos' perceived lack of religious fidelity to Catholicism.

In June of 1449, Conversos in Ciudad Real responded to growing anti-Converso feelings. They organized themselves into a militia. The town's mayor, the bachiller Rodrigo, and a certain Juan

---

[54] Sentencia-Estatuto de Toledo, 1449 -Original text: Eloy Benito Ruano, Toledo en el siglo XV (Madrid, 1961). Baxter Wolf, Kenneth. Medieval Texts in Translation, "Sentencia-Estatuto de Toledo, 1449." Accessed March 17, 2014. htttps://goo.gl/stt6mi

Gonzalez encouraged hundreds of Conversos to protect themselves. Hoping to avert the violence in Toledo the armed band of Conversos in Ciudad Real issued a challenge. They promised to burn the town were anyone to try to lay a hand on them. Rodrigo was summoned to explain himself to the city council, but only a few days after this, the Converso militia returned to the town square and reiterated its warning. Somehow, in the shuffle, an Old Christian was killed.

The military Order of Calatrava was stationed nearby in Almagro. Soldiers from the Order were sent, and a battle ensued between the Converso militia and the Order. The commander of the Order was killed, and a full-fledged battle soon broke out. Rodrigo was killed as was his brother, Fernando. Two additional Conversos, Arias Diaz and Gonzalo Alonso de Siles, were accused of the death of the commander and were arrested and executed in the town square. The mob attacked the houses of many Conversos and set fire to a considerable portion of the city. The violence lasted for two days, and the bodies of several Converso officials who had been assassinated were dragged into the public square. In the end, a total of twenty-two people died in the riots, and property of several prominent Converso notaries was torched.[55]

King Juan II interceded forcefully and sought to punish those who instigated the violence. The king's attention spurred promises by the citizens of Ciudad Real to restore what had been robbed and to reinstate those Conversos who had been forcibly removed from their offices. In the end, the king relented and issued an unconditional pardon that exempted all inhabitants of the city from punishment.[56] Despite Converso attempts, prohibitions against their holding public office in Ciudad Real were enacted through an

---

[55] Haim Beinart, *Conversos on Trial: The Inquisition in Ciudad Real* (Jerusalem: The Magnes Press, 1981), 56.
[56] Norman Roth, "Anti-Converso Riots of the Fifteenth Century, Pulgar and the Inquisition," En la España medieval 15 (1992): 382.

official decree issued in 1468 under the reign of King Enrique IV.[57]

## An Ecclesiastical Defense of the Conversos

The growing anti-Converso sentiment added clout to those who had argued for the organization of a strengthened Inquisition. Juan de Torquemada, the future Inquisitor General, as well as other religious leaders convinced the Pope to issue a bull of excommunication against Pedro Sarmiento for his actions. At this stage, they hoped that Conversos could still be successfully integrated into Christian society. As far as they were concerned, Sarmiento's actions created a rift which prevented Conversos from becoming real Christians. King Juan II suspended the bull in October 1450. The king confirmed the prohibitions of Conversos holding office in Toledo in August of 1451. The pope pardoned Sarmiento. Sarmiento was absolved and reinstated to royal favor.

Lope de Barrientos, the Dominican bishop of Segovia, Avila, and Cuenca and the former confessor to King Juan II rejected Sarmiento's claims about Conversos. In his work *Contra Zizandoras de la Nacion de Los Convertidos del Pueblo de Israel*, Barrientos argued that Sarmiento's persecution disheartened other Jews from converting and lead to sacrilege among those already converted. Conversos were saying that it would have been better not to become Christians. Conversos were being persecuted more intensely than Jews. The crux of Barrientos' defense of the Conversos lay in his appeal to the Jewish lineage of biblical personages. The prophets and apostles were Jews. Per Sarmiento's position, the apostles would have suffered persecution as Conversos. Barrientos also appealed to the fact that even saints like St. Julian, the bishop of Toledo, were converts as were other church officials. Barrientos argued that dishonor would be brought to the Christian message if Jewish converts were subjected to insult, abuse, and discrimination

---

[57] Haim Beinart, *Conversos on Trial: The Inquisition in Ciudad Real* (Jerusalem: The Magnes Press, 1981), 57-58.

in secular and church offices. Barrientos appealed to the *Siete Partidas* and the views of the Cortes that Jewish converts were to be favored.

Barrientos pointed to that fact that hundreds of Christians had converted to Islam recently. One example was the case of Fray Alonso de Mella, a Franciscan monk and the brother of Juan de Mella, the bishop of Zamora and later a cardinal. Fray Alonso led the Durango heresy that saw many of its members imprisoned and burned at the order of the king. Fray Alonso managed to escape to the Kingdom of Granada. Barrientos noted that there were also many heretics among the Basques and Bohemians. Barrientos argued that no one persecuted the Basques as a whole because some of them were heretics or attacked Andalusians because many of them were journeying to Granada and converting to Islam. Barrientos also argued that since most of the Jews in the Visigoth kingdom had converted to Christianity, Old Christians in Spain could not be sure they were free of Jewish ancestry. Barrientos added that many noble families in Spain were of Converso origin. The royal families were not immune either. The royal families of Castile, Aragon, Navarre, and Portugal had also absorbed Converso blood.[58] Barrientos confirmed that Conversos in significant numbers were continuing to practice Judaism.[59] Barrientos depicted most Conversos as "good Christians" but admitted that some Conversos were leaving Toledo daily for the lands under Islamic control or other kingdoms and openly returning to Judaism. They left claiming that the Christian faith was worthless and failed to protect them against persecution.[60]

The Converso Fernan Diaz de Toledo (formerly Mose Hamomo) was a relator and secretary to King Juan II and King

---

[58] Norman Roth, "Anti-Converso Riots of the Fifteenth Century, Pulgar and the Inquisition," En la España medieval 15 (1992): 377.

[59] Ibid., 374-375.

[60] Haim Beinart, *Conversos on Trial: The Inquisition in Ciudad Real* (Jerusalem: The Magnes Press, 1981), 9.

Enrique IV.[61] He argued that bishops should act favorably towards Conversos whom he described as members of this "poor persecuted nation of the lineage of our Lord Jesus Christ according to the flesh, which above all things is blessed of God." He argued as others had, that the persecution of Conversos prevented other Jews from converting.

Diaz argued against any prohibition against Conversos holding office. This was contrary to civil and canon law. Any appeal to the Visigoth prohibition was mistaken since it only applied to apostates who had relapsed and returned to Judaism. According to Diaz, it was never intended to apply to those who remained Christians. Barrientos also pointed to the *Siete Partidas* as well as other laws issued by King Enrique III, which prohibited discrimination of Jewish converts from Toledo following the violence of 1391.[62]

A defense of the Conversos was also taken up by Alonso de Cartagena. Alonso was the son of Pablo de Santa Maria. Alonso succeeded his father as bishop of Burgos. Alonso argued for the harmony of Old and New Christians. He pointed to the Church Father Augustine as well as the council of Basil, the *Siete Partidas*, and the edicts enacted by King Enrique III. Alonso also pointed to a purportedly complete copy of the Toledo Councils convened during years of Visigoth reign.

Contrary to Alonso Gonzalez de Toledo's view regarding the Fourth Toledo Council, Alonso de Cartagena admitted that they

---

[61] Ibid., 7.

[62] Norman Roth, "Anti-Converso Riots of the Fifteenth Century, Pulgar and the Inquisition," En la España medieval 15 (1992): 374-376. The *bachiller* Alonso Gonzales de Toledo also wrote on the matter of the descendants of Jewish converts being excluded from holding public office. In an address to Barrientos, he stated that the Fourth Toledo council convened during the reign of the Visigoth Kingdom only stipulated that Jews should be prohibited from serving in public office. The descendants of Jews were not barred according to the glosses he had seen. In an interesting note, he related the prohibition as applying to "...aquellos que son de la fe de los Judios mas non delos que son de la gente de los judios." The proscription applied to those were of the "faith of the Jews," but not to those were of the Jewish people. Ibid., 378.

did prohibit Conversos from holding public office. He argued that the council's edicts were not sweeping, but rather particular in their scope and applicability. Consequently, the council's decisions were non-binding. References to Jews in the Fourth Toledo Council referred to unconverted Jews and those of "Jewish origin" referred to Judaizers. Alonso concluded by reproving the actions of those who had initiated the violence against Conversos and argued that they were the actual heretics.[63]

For Alonso de Cartagena, Christianity was a rerouting and an extension of the Jewish faith. The Torah or the Old Law had just evolved into a more idyllic form. Jews who converted to Christianity were accepting an enthusiastic spirit that had been existent in their own faith. Jews who converted to Christianity were likened to sons who after an extended absenteeism returned home.[64]

Alonso de Cartagena highlighted the religious, ethical, and political superiority of the ancient Israelite nation. Cartagena noted that this was not to deduce that all Jews were noblemen or noblewomen, but rather to say that they had the capability of constituting a

---

[63] Norman Roth, "Anti-Converso Riots of the Fifteenth Century, Pulgar and the Inquisition," En la España medieval 15 (1992): 379. Another text which contained the history of the rebellion was authored by Alonso Diaz de Montalvo who held posts under King Juan II and King Enrique IV. In his account, Alonso Diaz de Montalvo noted how certain Conversos were holding ecclesiastical and public offices. Those who were false converts were forever damned. He also made mentioned of the Visigoth laws that prohibited Jews and their descendants from holding office. Though he recognized the claims that the Visigoth codes barred Jewish converts from holding office, he argued that for the sake of peace and spiritual harmony, no differentiation should be made between Israelites and Gentiles as long as the former were true converts. If there were Conversos who Judaized, God would be capable of separating them from truly faithful Christians. Converts were not to be discriminated against, mechanically. Alonso Diaz de Montalvo appears to have been motivated in minimizing the potential existence of Judaizing among Conversos for political or social reasons. De Montalvo condemned the policy of King Enrique III, the father of King Juan II. The king's policy enacted at the advice of Pedro Tenorio, the archbishop of Toledo, restricted converts from both ecclesiastical and public offices. De Montalvo concluded his historical review of the Toledo uprising by condemning the persecution of Conversos as not being truly reflective of genuine zeal for God, but rather a zeal borne out of malice. This type of zeal was nothing more than hatred which should have been 'directed' at sin and not at men. Ibid., 380-381.

[64] Kevin Ingram, "Secret lives, public lies: the conversos and socio-religious nonconformism in the Spanish Golden Age." (PhD diss., UC San Diego, 2006), 45.

noble class. Kevin Ingram observes that this line of reasoning may have helped Cartagena, whose own ancestors had been members of the Sephardic elite. It was not as effective for the majority of Conversos, who had attained their positions through their own initiative or that of a contemporary member of the family.

## The Counter-Response

In 1449, Marcos Garcia de Mora refuted those who defended Conversos. He made no distinction between Jews and Conversos. He claimed that the entire kingdom was overwhelmed and dominated by Jews. While much of his response focused on a defense of his and Sarmiento's activities in Toledo, he included significant claims regarding Conversos in Toledo. He noted that Conversos kept Jewish holidays and the Sabbath. He charged that they worked on Sundays, maintained lamps in the synagogue, and went there to pray daily. For De Mora, these Conversos should be burned as heretics by canon law. Mora argued that any tolerance towards Conversos corrupted Christian society. He claimed that "whoever shows patience towards the criminals [Conversos] by tolerating them or omitting to punish them, is guilty of mortal sin because he leads into sin not only the good but also the evil."[65]

Old Christian attitudes towards Conversos were partially founded on the continued involvement of some Conversos in tax-collecting and usury. As Maria Dolores Cabanas relates,

> "...Conversos were tarred with the same brush as the Jews and regarded as the economic oppressors of the Christian population; the only difference was that, from the time of their integration, they now competed on an equal footing."

---

[65] Marcos Garcia Mora in his *El Memorial contra los conversos* wrote, "They were found to Judaize and to observe all the Jewish ceremonies, fasting on all the fast days prescribed by Mosaic law, respecting the Sabbath and working on Sundays and holy days, eating meat when they ought not during Lent and on other days set aside by the Church...saying and doing many foul, heretical things, to the great detriment of our Catholic faith." Joaquim Carvalho ed., *Religion and Power in Europe: Conflict and Convergence* (Pisa: Edizioni Plus - Pisa University Press, 2007), 88.

In his *Cronica de Enrique IV*, the historiographer Alonso de Palencia stated that Conversos achieved their wealth by strange arts. They were very proud and had the arrogance to aspire to public office once they attained the order of gentlemen. All of this was due to their money, which they acquired unlawfully even though they were of lowly extraction and familiar with hard work.[66] The chronicler Andres Bernaldez comments that Conversos were merchants, salesmen, moneylenders, pawnbrokers, silversmiths, weavers, or craftsman. They were for Bernaldez everything but laborers or builders. They sought to make significant amounts of money for little work.[67]

## The *Cortes* of 1462

In what seemed to be a reaction to the stabilization of the Jewish community and the rise of prominent Conversos, various cities petitioned the *Cortes* of 1462 to restrict Jewish contact with Christians. Many Jews left cities and instead settled in areas that lay under the authority of the counts. The extent of Converso success in tax-farming was confirmed at the *Cortes* of Fraga in 1460 when a large number of Conversos, much to the shock of many *hidalgos*, attended. The situation continued to deteriorate for the Jewish community when in 1465 King Enrique IV of Castile revived all the previously enacted anti-Jewish regulations.

In 1465, rebellious nobles officially overthrew King Enrique IV and appointed his brother Alfonso in his place. A rumor spread that King Alfonso intended to prosecute Conversos suspected of religious transgressions. This is mentioned by the chronicler and diplomat Alfonso de Palencia. Alfonso de Palencia had severely criticized King Enrique IV for the conditions under his rule and had advocated political and ecclesiastical reforms. Many Conversos opted to back King Enrique IV.

---

[66] Ibid., 90.
[67] Ibid.

King Alfonso arrived in Toledo in May 1467. After King Alfonso left Toledo in July, violence between Conversos and Old Christians erupted. An indictment was issued against the City of Toledo and a Converso named Alvar Gomez, who had served as *alcalde mayor* and former secretary to King Enrique IV. The letter of indictment referred to the payment of some ecclesiastical taxes and charges against Jews who had been granted rights to serve as tax farmers. In the midst of discussions regarding the issue, a group of armed Conversos broke into the cathedral with the resolve of killing their opponents. Street battles resulted once again.

Stores and homes owned by Conversos were burned. The fire spread through the surrounding neighborhood. Fernando de la Torre, brother of Alvaro de la Torre, one of the civic councilors, led a band of Conversos in the fighting. Fernando managed to gather weapons and even cannon in his house. Conversos endeavored to rally the support of the nobles who had supported King Alfonso. They argued that Old Christians had always demeaned them and were intimidating them with threats. They argued this was due to envy over their business success.

For a total of three days, Conversos and Old Christians fought in the streets of Toledo. Four streets where Conversos primarily lived were destroyed by fire. The leader of the Conversos, Fernando de la Torre tried to escape from the city but was captured and imprisoned in the tower of the Church of San Leocadia. He was hanged the next morning and his body, along with the body of his brother Alvaro, was dragged to the plaza of Zocodover. Conversos were alleged to have Hebrew books banned by the Church. Local Jews were called to inspect these books. When King Enrique IV was beaten at the battle near Olmedo, the city of Toledo asked King Alfonso to support its rules and activities against Conversos. King Alfonso confirmed the anti-Converso policies enacted by the city council.[68] King Alfonso died in 1468, leaving Enrique IV to assume the throne for the interim.

In a repeat of what his father had done previously, King Enrique IV in 1468 pardoned all those who had engaged in the anti-Converso riots. No Conversos were allowed to hold public office though he eventually reversed this order in 1471. In an attempt to lessen the acrimony, King Enrique IV tried to pacify the confraternities of Toledo, which had been divided between Old and New Christians. He united them and became a member. In 1480, the Synod of Alcala prohibited confraternities based on the "purity of blood". Despite this, King Enrique IV decreed that no Converso was to serve in public office in Toledo or Ciudad Real. The order was reissued in 1473. The law remained in place until 1501, when King Ferdinand amended the decree to exclude sons and grandsons of those reconciled by the Inquisition.[69]

### The Riots of Córdoba

Attacks on Conversos continued. Riots in Ciudad Real broke out and were followed by those in Córdoba in 1473. Rioting spread to other regions including Jaen.[70] On March 14, 1473, in Córdoba some Converso houses were invaded, plundered, and burned. A religious procession made its way through the streets when a young Converso girl emptied out some water from her

---

[68] Yitzhak Baer, *A History of the Jews in Christian Spain: Volume 2* (Philadelphia: Jewish Publication Society, 1961), 302-304.

[69] Salo Wittmayer Baron, *A Social and the Religious History of the Jews: Volume XIII* (Philadelphia: Jewish Publication Society, 1969), 23.

[70] There, the mayor, Miguel Lucas de Iranzo, was murdered in the church and his family intimidated and obliged to take refuge in the castle after he protected Conversos. The historian Alonso de Palencia, himself a Converso, blamed the riots on Juan Pacheco. According to the account of Miguel Lucas de Iranzo, the day before his death, the antagonism towards Conversos was unfounded since the Conversos were loyal to the king and to the city. Yet, De Iranzo noted that it would have been more impartial and truthful for those Conversos who acted inappropriately to be punished by the law rather than subject all of them to punishment.

home into the street. A blacksmith claimed she had thrown urine on the parade.

A Christian knight who tried to intervene and restore order was injured by the rioters. His relatives hurried to his assistance, and the conflict spread throughout the city. The blacksmith who had initiated the violence escaped to the Church of San Francisco. The blacksmith was coaxed into coming out to discuss the situation by a certain Alfonso de Aguilar. Alfonso's request was a ruse, and he threw a spear at the blacksmith. The blacksmith was mortally wounded. The Conversos collected weapons and fortified their residences. The blacksmith's death only served to spread further discord in the city.

Laborers and farmers entered the city from the villages with the intent of rioting and plundering. Some Conversos took refuge in the local fortress at the recommendation of Alfonso de Aguilar. The violence continued for sixteen successive days. The Conversos, who were able to flee from the city, wandered in the fields unable to find lodging. Peasants attacked and stole from Conversos everywhere they gathered.

The city council of Córdoba adopted an ordinance barring Conversos from public offices. Other towns in Andalusia also experienced the same chaos. In Seville, however, the nobles succeeded in suppressing the rioting. Unrest in Andalusia continued with many Conversos fleeing from Córdoba to Seville under the direction of Pedro de Cordova. They asked the Duke of Medina Sidonia for consent to settle in the stronghold of Gibraltar. The Duke of Medina Sidonia was inclined to approve the appeal in consideration of their help in defending the city against the Muslims. His counselors argued that the Conversos were inexperienced in warfare. They also argued that the Conversos were insincere Christians and observed Jewish practices. This fact they asserted was the real source of all their calamities. Were they to move to Gibraltar, it was improbable that they would alter their habits especially after settling in an area where they would not be overseen by the Church. They also argued that Gibraltar had been chosen to give them easy access to the sea to emigrate eastward. If they remained in Gibraltar, they could continue unabated in observing Jewish practices and even circumcise their sons without interference. The arguments made to the Duke were sufficiently plausible for him to believe. In 1476, the Duke rescinded the license he had given regarding settlement in Gibraltar.[71]

The chronicler Hernando del Pulgar acknowledged that punishment was appropriate for those Conversos who had relapsed, but should not be applicable to those who had not. Pulgar added that those Conversos who were Judaizing had done so because of the poor example of Old Christians.[72] Pulgar relates that because of the failure of proper leadership, once could not visibly recognize those who were Christians versus those who were Jews or Muslims.[73] Pulgar explains that "according to the laws of the realm, Jews and Muslims should wear (distinguishing) clothing and signs by which to be recognized." The law, however, was not enforced. The statement could also be interpreted to mean that the theological distinctions between Christians and Jews (i.e. Conversos) were muddled by the presence of Conversos, who were Judaizing and the mixing of Jewish and Christian practices.[74] In an account of the Toledo Inquisition, Pulgar noted the following:

> "In this year (1485) the Inquisition continued, which had begun against the Christians of Jewish lineage who began to 'Judaize.' In the city of Toledo some men and women were found who secretly observed Jewish rites, who in

---

[71] Yitzhak Baer, *A History of the Jews in Christian Spain*, Volume 2 (Philadelphia: Jewish Publication Society, 1961), 307-310.

[72] Norman Roth, "Anti-Converso Riots of the Fifteenth Century, Pulgar and the Inquisition," En la España medieval 15 (1992): 387.

[73] In the satirical poem titled *Coplas de Mingo Revulgo*, the religious condition during the reign of King Enrique IV is described. The *Coplas* states that the religious conditions had worsened so significantly that one could not distinguish the "flock of Christ," "nor that of the other stammerer [Moses] nor the keen Moor of Meca."

[74] Norman Roth, "Anti-Converso Riots of the Fifteenth Century, Pulgar and the Inquisition," En la España medieval 15 (1992): 387.

great ignorance and danger of their souls kept neither the one nor the other law because they were not circumcised like Jews...and although they observed the Sabbath and some Jewish fasts, they did not observe all the Sabbaths nor all the fasts and if they observed one rite they did not observe another, so that they were false to both laws (Christians and Jewish). It happened in some cases that the husband kept certain Jewish ceremonies and the wife was a good Christian and that one son and daughter would be good Christians and another hold the Jewish opinion. Thus, in one house there was a diversity of belief, and one would hide from the others."[75]

## The Purity of Blood Statutes

Those who defended Conversos against the proliferation of purity of blood laws were not entirely altruistic. In his *Instrucción del Relator*, the previously mentioned Diáz de Toledo, a 15th century jurist, humanist, and nephew of the first bishop of Málaga, argued that the foremost challenge created by *Limpieza de Sangre* statutes was their potential to marginalize Spain's highest nobility. All or many of them included Jews in their lineage. To combat the possible pitfall in this, Diáz educated his readers that Jews historically were the first and the finest Christians. That being said, Jews and not the Gentiles, were the offspring of God's chosen people.

The adoption of purity of blood statutes was countered by attempts to situate the arrival of Iberian Jewry in Spain before the birth of Christ. This it was hoped would excuse Jews and Conversos of any culpability in the crime of deicide. The first account mentioning the purported antiquity of Jewish settlement on the Peninsula was the *Refundición de la Cronica de 1344* written at the time of the 1449 *Sentencia Estatuto*. The author of the *Refundición* was purportedly a Converso from Toledo. The Chronicle refers to the biblical Tubal, the son of Japheth, the son of Noah. The Chronicle states that Tubal inhabited the Peninsula and a surge of

---

[75] Ibid., 393.

Jewish settlement by the heirs of King David eventually took place. Contemporaneous with this work, Juan de Valera claimed that the Goths who conquered the Peninsula from the Roman Empire were the descendants of an Israelite tribe.

Pope Nicholas V condemned purity of blood laws in two bulls issued in 1449 and 1451. A Castilian Church Synod chaired by Archbishop Alphonso Carrillo of Toledo also adopted the following resolution:

> "We reprimand and excommunicate all fraternities, colleges, chapters and assemblies which may in the future introduce such divisions between nations and groups [of Christians], whether publicly or clandestinely, under whatever guise. We order that those who would enact a statute or constitution imposing the observance of such divisions [be placed under a ban] so long as they persevere in this schismatic behavior. We prohibit all ecclesiastical persons, under the sanction of a major excommunication, from permitting the said persons to congregate in their churches or parishes; nor shall they celebrate masses or divine services for them as long as the transgressors shall obstinately adhere to the said schism."[76]

Jaime de Salazar Acha argues that the statutes were primarily ideological in nature and not racial. The goal of the laws was to maintain doctrinal purity. The elimination of someone with Jewish ancestry was assumed to reduce the possibility that the individual maintained Jewish practices or heretical beliefs. The statutes required individuals to demonstrate pure blood for filling certain institutional, religious, or governmental roles. Acha argues that the underlying motivation of the laws was due to social, class, and economic envy, even though the basis for the discrimination was, in fact, religious. The ultimate definitive source for determining the impure status of an individual was the Inquisitorial tribunal.

---

[76] Salo Wittmayer Baron, *A Social and the Religious History of the Jews: Volume XIII* (Philadelphia: Jewish Publication Society, 1969), 66.

The purity of blood statutes first adopted in Toledo and then in other cities were primarily related to municipal government positions. The expansion of these laws into others areas of Castilian society occurred gradually. Several members of the religious order of San Geronimo, for example, were accused of having observed the Law of Moses. This discovery led to the adoption of purity of blood requirements in 1489 though they do not appear to have been entirely implemented until 1540.[77] Pope Alexander VI's authorization for the religious order of San Geronimo to adopt this requirement enabled other institutions to implement similar requirements. In 1496, the Pope granted permission for the Dominican monastery of Santo Tomás de Aquino to adopt these standards. In Avila, in 1531, converts to the whole Dominican Order were excluded. The order of Augustine adopted the policy in 1520. In 1525, the purity of blood requirements were established for the Franciscan order. The Church of Seville approved the purity of blood requirement in 1515. Diego de Deza, a descendant of Conversos and the former grand inquisitor and then the archbishop of Seville, prohibited second generation descendants of heretics from all clerical offices and benefices in his cathedral.[78] The statute was sanctioned by Pope Leo X in 1516 and once again by Pope Clement VII in 1532. In the case of the latter, he extended the prohibition to the grandchildren of heretics. In 1546, Pope Paul III included great-grandchildren in the ban.[79]

Church orders in Córdoba adopted them in 1530. In 1547, the Church of Toledo excluded the descendants of Moors and Jews from their religious orders. Only the Jesuits appear to have resisted this, a fact that may be explained by the fact that several of the key

---

[77] Jaime de Salazar Acha, "La Limpieza de Sangre," Revista de la Inquisición, Vol 1 (1991): 293.

[78] Salo Wittmayer Baron, *A Social and the Religious History of the Jews: Volume XIII* (Philadelphia: Jewish Publication Society, 1969), 88.

[79] Ibid.

founders of the movement had Converso backgrounds. The purity of blood laws were finally adopted by the order in 1593.[80]

King Ferdinand and Queen Isabella initially opposed the adoption of the purity of blood statutes by the order of San Geronimo. In 1501, however, they consented to the exclusion of anyone who had been reconciled for the crime of heresy. They also agreed to exclude the descendants of those burned at the stake up to the second generation to the positions of royal counselor, judge, administrator, mayor, sheriff, bailiff, treasurer, and other posts, without special consent from the Crown.

The purity of blood statutes were gradually adopted by universities as well as the various military orders of the day. In January 1497, the *Colegio de San Antonio de Siguenza* passed this requirement. The provisions were adopted by the *Colegio de San Ildefonso* in 1519. In 1522, the charter for the universities of Salamanca, Valladolid, and Toledo were modified accordingly. There were attempts to forestall this trend. Rodrigo de Santaella (Maese Rodrigo), a wealthy canon established the college of Santa Maria de Jesus, with professorships in theology, canon law, civil law, medicine, and the liberal arts. Santaella firmly prohibited his institution from discriminating against professors or students on the basis of lineage. The College was to admit all Christians, whether their ancestors were 'Canarians, Indians, gentiles [Old Christians], pagans, Jews, Saracens, nobles, non-nobles, rich, poor, good, bad, urbanites, rustics, free men or slaves.' Santaella died before the college was opened. In 1516, its first rector Martín Navarro eliminated the nondiscriminatory policy and adopted a Limpieza de Sangre requirement.[81] Over time, the statutes spread to the rest of Spanish society. A person's purity had to be established in order for them

---

[80] Jaime de Salazar Acha, "La Limpieza de Sangre," Revista de la Inquisición, Vol 1 (1991): 294.

[81] Kevin Ingram, "Secret lives, public lies: the conversos and socio-religious nonconformism in the Spanish Golden Age." (PhD diss., UC San Diego, 2006), 53.

to enter various fraternities, obtain licenses to practice law, become a teacher, and become a notary.[82]

## The Plan to Resolve the Converso Problem

A seeming resurgence of Judaism in the 1460s initiated a new phase in the Christian polemic against both Jews and Conversos. The charges against Conversos were apparent. Many of them circumcised their sons, observed Jewish rituals, and remained theologically Jewish. To combat this pernicious heresy, the Franciscan preacher, writer, and later bishop, Fray Alonso de Espina, authored the work *Fortalitium Fidei* (The Fortress of Faith). His treatise which sought to combat various heresies, included Judaism. For de Espina, the solution was clear. To properly fight heresy among Conversos, Judaism had to be uprooted.

In 1459, in Segovia, he learned that the local Conversos had gone to the synagogue on the holiday of Succot. In 1459, in Fromista a Converso barber declared that he did not believe in Jesus, but rather in the God alone. The barber's declaration was reported to the bishop of the diocese of Palencia who, in turn, related it to Alfonso de Espina. The barber was originally sentenced to lifetime imprisonment, but his conviction was ultimately commuted to ten years' banishment from the town. De Espina charged inquisitors and the secular authorities to levy harsh penalties on Conversos who practiced circumcision.

On another occasion, De Espina spoke in the town of Medina del Campo against the heretics who pointed to errors in the New

---

[82] The purity of blood statues were definitively suppressed by law on the 16th of May 1865. Jaime de Salazar Acha, "La Limpieza de Sangre," Revista de la Inquisición, Vol 1 (1991): 294. There were individuals in Spain who became known as *los linajudos*. Contrary to the implication of the name, the individuals were not of Jewish blood but were instead purported genealogical researchers who investigated the backgrounds of families to point out the impurities that they possessed. This of course could be silenced at a price. Acha states that in the 17th century, there were no engagements between families which did not include a visit from the aforementioned *linajudos* ready to point out the maculate genealogies they had for the families involved. Jaime de Salazar Acha, "La Limpieza de Sangre," Revista de la Inquisición, Vol 1 (1991): 306.

Testament. The heretics claimed it contained quotations from the prophets that were not found in the same usage as in the Hebrew Bible. De Espina argued that several Converso traders had heard a Converso monk make these statements while they visited Flanders. This had prompted them to undergo circumcision secretly when they returned to Medina del Campo. They were now about to set sail for North Africa while their associates were waiting for them in Seville.[83] According to De Espina, there were those who practiced circumcision on the ground that Jesus had also been circumcised. De Espina claimed he had seen Conversos circumcise themselves and their sons. De Espina preached in Medina del Campo in 1459 against Conversos practicing Jewish customs. Concurrent with his visit, thirty Conversos had just been circumcised and were secretly resting in the home of a friend during their recovery. De Espina claimed that one of them, a physician named Magister Franciscus, had even traveled to Jerusalem. This fact is confirmed by official records.[84]

On August 10th, 1461 he approached Alonso de Oropesa, the head of the Order of Saint Jerome, with this manuscript.[85] Alonso de Oropesa defended Conversos on the basis that it was not just to suspect them simply because of their Jewish ancestry. He did, however, refer to Jews who were enticing Conversos and even old Christians to embrace Judaism in unforgiving terms.[86] Alonso de Oropesa argued that the medieval Inquisition, which had operated in the Kingdom of Aragon, should be similarly introduced into Castile. The King acceded to Oropesa's request, but Alonso de Espina was not satisfied. The medieval Inquisition had been limited in scope if not inefficient. In 1461, King Enrique IV peti-

---

[83] Yitzhak Baer, *A History of the Jews in Christian Spain: Volume 2* (Philadelphia: Jewish Publication Society, 1961), 285-286.

[84] Yitzhak Baer notes that the official confirmation of Espina's claim regarding Magister Franciscus adds veracity to other stories related by him. He also adds that some other *Conversos* also intended to travel to Jerusalem. Ibid., 284-285.

[85] Cecil Roth, *the Spanish Inquisition* (New York: W.W. Norton and Company, 1964), 40.

[86] Yitzhak Baer, *A History of the Jews in Christian Spain: Volume 2* (Philadelphia: Jewish Publication Society, 1961), 291.

tioned Pope Pius II to establish an Inquisition in Castile. No response was apparently given, and the pope died shortly after.[87]

De Spina spread rumors of ritual slaughter of Christian children by Jews. The stories were accepted and in the cities of Tavara, Toro, and Avila plays depicting this were acted out. In the city of Sepulveda, the accusations reached such a level that Rabbi Solomon Pichon was accused of the murder of a Christian boy. In Medina del Campo, Jews were killed and burned due to the same acaccusations.

The pressure for action against Conversos and Jews was increasing. The fall of Constantinople to the Ottoman Turks ten years earlier in 1453 and the concern over purported Turkish overtures to Jews to settle in their domains added to the view that Jews were subversive. Alonso de Espina drafted a complete plan for the formation of an organization dedicated to investigating heresy among Conversos. For him, all Conversos were religiously suspect.

His treatise provides twenty-five transgressions that Conversos committed. They bear a striking resemblance to the accusations that would be recorded in tribunal records in subsequent decades.[88] Haim Beinart classifies the transgressions into three divisions. The first involved the observance of Jewish practices and beliefs. Among these is circumcision, the observance of the Sabbath, Jewish burial customs, the education of Converso children in synagogues, contributions of oil for synagogue lamps, taking Jewish oaths, and the expressions of belief in the Jewish faith.[89] The second category included a broad range of actions committed against Christianity. Among the accusations were evading the Sacraments, working on Sundays, avoiding mention of Jesus or Mary, slandering Mary and Christianity, eating lamb on Easter, attending Mass only for the purpose of throwing off

---

[87] Norman Roth, "Anti-Converso Riots of the Fifteenth Century, Pulgar and the Inquisition," En la España medieval 15 (1992): 383.

[88] Haim Beinart, *Conversos on Trial: The Inquisition in Ciudad Real* (Jerusalem: The Magnes Press, 1981), 13.

[89] Ibid., 13.

suspicion to avoid excommunication, abstaining from making the sign of the cross, pretending that the lives of their babies were at danger at birth in order to prevent a formal church baptism, lending money at interest to Christians (as a means of atonement for their conversion to Christianity), false confessions, and theft or desecration of the Host.[90] Many of the elements are attested to by the earlier papal inquisitions operating in the kingdom of Aragon half a century earlier.

The final category included marriages among the various prohibited degrees of consanguinity. Alonso de Espina also accused Conversos of having abandoned belief in an afterlife. Strangely enough, he remarked that Conversos also worshiped strange images, an accusation that remains obscure.[91]

## The Solution to the Converso Problem

Alonso de Espina maintained that faithful Christians should keep as far away from Conversos as possible. He rejected the proposition that integration and assimilation would ultimately resolve the continued Jewish practices of Conversos. Segregation was the key to ensuring that faithful Christians were not dragged into heresy as well. The policy of separation was adopted by the Cortes of Toledo in 1480. Nevertheless, as the very Edict of Expulsion relates, the policy was ultimately a failure.[92]

De Spina argued that the Converso heresy should be dealt with by active investigation. The method for investigation was straightforward. Informers on individuals suspected of heresy were sought out. In short, as Beinart notes, de Espina called on every faithful Christian to seek out heretics. The actual examination of witnesses was to be done under the supervision of two members of the clergy, and ideally a public notary would record their statements. As would be the case under the Inquisition, a mere rumor of here-

---

[90] Ibid.
[91] Ibid.
[92] Ibid., 14.

sy was sufficient to initiate an investigation by archbishops, bishops, or archdeacons. Suspects would be subject to examination at least once a year. If the accused confessed of their accord, then a light punishment sufficed to absolve the guilty party. If the accused did not confess within a year, he would be punished. The secular authorities handled carrying out punishment directed by the religious authorities. Their failure to do so would result in their dismissal. The inquisitors were also given the ability to act directly and arrest suspects themselves if warranted. Alonso de Espina laid the groundwork for the eventual rise of the national Inquisition.[93]

He stipulated that heretics would be excommunicated and divested of all ranks and honors. Excommunication was levied whether the individual was a member of the clergy or a public official. Confiscation of property would be applied to all heretics. The death penalty would be implemented as appropriate. Those heretics who abjured but later relapsed were to serve lifelong imprisonment. Descendants of heretics were barred from public office until the second generation. Anyone providing refuge to a heretic was to be excommunicated from the Church and ineligible for public office. They were also ineligible to serve as witnesses in court. Any Christian supporting Converso heretics and providing them with Christian burials would be excommunicated. They would not receive pardon unless they exhumed the corpse in question with their hands and discarded the bodies into a field.[94]

---

[93] Ibid., 15.

[94] Ibid., 16. The danger of ignoring the Converso problem is in the work *El Alboraique*, which relates words ascribed to St. Isidore of Seville."Esta gente, si freno no les puiessen, sin rienda fuera a caer en mayors danos; pero darles-han una sofrenada e seguirse-ha la muerte de espada cruel en ellos, e cumplirse-a lo que dixo Moysen, Deuteronomio cap. Xxxii [...] 'oyd, cielos, el mi cuchillo cortara la carne', que quiere dezir: 'dara venganza a mis apasionadores e a mis malquerientes dare mal galardon. 'E Sant Ysidoro dize, levantarse-ha una heregia en Espana de las gentes que crucifaron a Christo, e durara setenta anos, y al cabo del ano de senteta sera destruydos por fuego y espada.'" "These people, if they are not stopped, without reigns they will fall into terrible danger...and St. Isidore said a great heresy in Spain has emerged from those who crucified Christ and it will last for seventy years. At the end of the seventy years it will end in fire and sword." Prologo 403 cited in Jeremy Lawrance, "Alegoria Y Apocalipsis En El Alboraique," Revista de Poetica Medieval, 11 (2009): 34.

Alonso de Espina also sought to address the possibility of any favorable disposition towards Conversos. To ensure that priests extended no support or clemency to heretics, any priest who urged a heretic to conceal his heresy was to be punished. Any bishop failing to impose adequately severe punishments would be removed from office for three years. Lower rank clergy were to be excommunicated and were to be granted pardon by the Pope alone or on their death bed.[95]

Alonso de Espina regarded the forced baptism of children as acceptable even if their parents protested. Expulsion proved to be the only real remedy for obstinate Jews as far as De Espina was concerned.[96] His proposal enjoyed some success with the establishment of inquisitional tribunals in the episcopal courts of Toledo and Castilian localities. By the following decade, however, his views were adopted by those spearheading the charge against Converso integration in Spanish society.[97]

## The Final Effort: The Spanish Inquisition

In 1474, Ciudad Real was the site of further anti-Converso attacks. With mounting civil disorder, a group of aristocrats complained to King Enrique IV regarding the inability of the Crown to deal with the Converso crisis. Ladero Quesada explains the relationship between the need to address civil unrest and the eventual rise of the Inquisition:

> "In the long-term, this use of the Converso issue as a political tool helped transform it into a matter of public order, whereby everyone had to respect the sovereign capacity of the crown to perform justice with the aid of the instruments of the law and there was to be no tolerance of any disturbances which might damage the image of regal

---

[95] Haim Beinart, *Conversos on Trial: The Inquisition in Ciudad Real* (Jerusalem: The Magnes Press, 1981), 18.
[96] Ibid., 20.
[97] Ibid.

authority. The influence of this idea on the birth of the Inquisition should not be overlooked."[98]

Whatever hopes Conversos had for stability were shattered in 1475. The Archbishop of Toledo, Alonso de Carrillo inspected the diocese of Ciudad Real and came to the conclusion that Conversos were by and large covert Judaizers.[99] Carrillo's motivation may have been politically motivated because Conversos had opposed Isabella's ascension to the Crown of Castile. While this may have been an issue, the likelihood is that sufficient, crypto-Jewish activity provided the rationale for any action taken. During their journey through their new holdings, King Ferdinand and Queen Isabella were informed of the full measure of secret Jewish practices among Conversos. The monarchs were apprised to what extent crypto-Jewish practices were the source of significant disruptions in the civic order. The establishment of the Inquisition was viewed as the best way to root out heresy and the public outbreaks that resulted from it. The chronicler Andres Bernaldez records the purported conversation related to a Converso, who went to confess.

> "They would never make true confession, and it happened that one of these people went to confession, and the confessor cut a bit of his clothing, saying, 'As you have never sinned, I wish to retain something of your clothing as a reliquary to cure the sick.'"[100]

The Inquisition's reign was secured by parties who were actively opposed to Conversos as well as those who supported them. The anti-Conversos groups characterized Conversos and Jews as constituting the same community. Those who were favorable to Conversos and argued against their indiscriminate marginalization

---

[98] Joaquim Carvalho ed., *Religion and Power in Europe: Conflict and Convergence* (Pisa: Edizioni Plus - Pisa University Press, 2007), 91.

[99] Ibid.

[100] Eleazar Gutwirth, "The Jews in 15th Century Castilian Chronicles," The Jewish Quarterly Review, LXXIV. No.4 (1984): 393.

based on their ancestry agreed that Judaizing was present among some. The only solution was rooting out this heresy.[101]

In the Kingdom of Aragon, the tension that rocked the Crown of Castile was largely absent though a change began near the end of King Juan II's reign. The *jurats* of Valencia attempted to prohibit Conversos from serving in public office. In 1478, the King refused to agree to the ban despite his acknowledgment that "it is very true that the conversos practice Jewish [practices] so much…among the Christians that in their way of life they are Jewish and not Christian."

> "Reports of converso Judaizing may not have greatly bothered Juan, but they deeply disturbed Fernando and Isabel, who viewed the cells of Judaizers, wherever they lived, as so many threats to their project to reform the Catholic church."[102]

King Ferdinand and Queen Isabella set a path of religious reform which included the religious orders of Aragon and set Castilian clergy to oversee this program. Mark Meyerson relates that,

> "Since they had no qualms in sending, for instance, Castilian observant Dominicans to reform Dominican houses in Aragon and Catalonia, small surprise that they extended the new Castilian inquisition to Aragon, Catalonia, and Valencia to eradicate the Judaizing New Christians who lived in these territories just as they did in Castile."[103]

The segregation of Jews from Conversos was an essential element in the early reign of King Ferdinand and Isabella. Segregation was intended to promote the assimilation of Conversos. The goal

---

[101] Joaquim Carvalho ed., *Religion and Power in Europe: Conflict and Convergence* (Pisa : Edizioni Plus - Pisa University Press, 2007), 92.

[102] Mark D. Meyerson, *A Jewish Renaissance in Fifteenth-Century Spain* (Princeton: Princeton University Press, 2004), 228.

[103] Ibid.

was to forcibly separate Jews from Conversos so that the former would lose their influence on Conversos. In December 1477, King Ferdinand ordered the segregation of Jews in Soria. This was followed by the separation of Jews in Caceres in 1478. By 1480, the *Cortes* of Toledo ordered the segregation of Jews in all communities in Castile.[104] The forced relocation of Jews often placed them in areas of the cities where no one wanted to live. The relocation to the least desirable sections of the towns which were often dirty and run down only enhanced the image of Jews as undesirables.

On November 1, 1478, Pope Sixtus IV issued the Papal *bull*, *Exigit Sinceras Devotionis Affectus*, which gave the Spanish monarchs exclusive authority to designate inquisitors in their respective kingdoms. The establishment of the Inquisition in Seville happened two years after Pope Sixtus IV authorized its creation. The papal *bull* gave King Ferdinand and Queen Isabella unprecedented control over the Inquisition in contrast to the more limited influence that the monarchs of Aragon had experienced with the earlier Papal Inquisitions. In the end, despite tens of thousands of trials, the Inquisition failed. Despite its intensity, a different approach towards definitively resolving the Converso problem was taken.

The only solution was the complete expulsion of the Jewish community.

---

[104] S. Haliczer, "Conversos y Judios en tiempos de la expulsion: Un analisis critico de investigacion y analisis," Espacio, Tiempo y Forma, Serie III, H. Medieval, t. 6, (1993): 290.

CHAPTER 3

# Jewish Attitudes Towards Apostates

The conversion of thousands of Spanish Jews in the 14th and 15th centuries was a catastrophe for the Jewish community. The status of Conversos and how they were perceived by the Jewish community was dictated in part by Jewish attitudes towards apostasy. In Judaism, an apostate is defined as a Jew in rebellion against God, the Torah, and the faith of Israel.

[1] The rabbis of the Babylonian Talmud believed that apostasy could be limited to the intentional rejection of even a single commandment. There was a distinction, however, between individuals who apostatized with respect to circumcision, dietary laws or Shabbat observance, and those who participated in *Avodah Zarah* (e.g. offering libations to or worshiping of idols). Only the

---

[1] The Greek term ἀποστασία means defection or revolt. Apostate and apostasy are found in I Maccabees 11: 14, 8:16; Josephus, "Contra Apion." i. 19, § 4 and are used to signify rebellion against God and the Torah. The terms are used in the Septuagint in Numbers 14:9; Joshua 22: 19, 22; II Chronicles 28: 19, 33:19; Isaiah. 30:1; and in I Kings 21:13; Judges 19:22; I Samuel. 25:17. I Maccabees 2:15 states that "the officers of the king compelled the people to apostatize." Jason, the high priest siding with the Seleucids, was "pursued by all and hated as a deserter of the law"; II Maccabees 5: 8. Singer, Isidore; Adler, Cyrus; (eds.) Jewish Encyclopedia, "Apostasy and Apostates from Judaism." Accessed December 21, 2012. https://goo.gl/msqt5j

latter, as well as those who had abandoned the entire Torah, were regarded as complete apostates.

In rabbinic literature, various terms were applied to apostates.[2] One such term was *mumar*[3] while the term *meshumad*[4] typically referred to voluntary converts to another religion. [5] Whether a Jew was an apostate out of convenience or conviction, the Talmud condemned either type equally and without leniency.[6] Apostates were counted as the enemies of Israel per the *Mekhilta*, a halakhic Midrash on the Book of Exodus. They were also to be hated as instructed in the *Avot de Rabi Natan,* an aggadic work likely compiled in the Geonic era.[7] There were various restrictions placed on the apostate. The Talmudic Tractate Hullin (5a) deemed that any ritual slaughtering carried out by the apostate was invalid and equivalent to the slaughter done by a non-Jew. This was true even if the slaughtering was executed in an accurate fashion.[8]

---

[2] Ibid. Regarding apostates and heretics, the Talmud states, "But as to the heretics (minim), the apostates (meshummadim), the informers, the apoqorsim, who have denied the Torah, those who have separated from the ways of the community, those who have denied the resurrection of the dead, and everyone who has transgressed and caused the public to transgress…Gehenna is shut in their faces, and they are punished in Gehenna for ever and ever." Tractate Sanhedrin 13:5.

[3] i.e. the one that is changed.

[4] i.e. meaning to destroy or annihilate.

[5] The Mishnah does not use either *mumar* or *meshumad*, but the Tosefta does. Tosefta Horayot 1, 5; See also Horayot 11a cited in Sacha Stern, *Jewish Identity in Early Rabbinic Writings* (New York: Brill, 1994), 106. "He who eats carrion and non-kosher meat, abominations and 'creepies' and pork, who drinks forbidden wine, or who desecrates the Shabbat and who is decircumcised. R. Yose b. Yehuda says even he who wears a garment of wool and linen; R. Shimon b. El'azar adds, even he who commits a transgression for which there is no natural desire."

[6] There were distinctions among those who were deemed full apostates. The *mumar le-te'avon* (i.e. the apostate out of appetite or convenience) was distinguished from the *mumar le-hakh'is* (i.e. the apostate out of conviction or spite). Sacha Stern also associates the apostate out of conviction with the *mumar be-gilluy panim*- the overt or open apostate mentioned in Talmud Yerushalmi Eruvin 6, 2 and the Bavli Eruvin 69a-b. Sacha Stern, *Jewish Identity in Early Rabbinic Writings* (New York: Brill, 1994), 106-107.

[7] Mekhilta Kaspa 2 and Avot de Rabi Natan 16.

[8] Hullin 4b-5a.

Despite this and other exclusions, the apostate was still desig-designated as *Israel mumar*. The term Israel remained the substantive identity while *mumar* was the descriptive element. The Talmud in Sanhedrin 44a refers to the story of the fall of Jericho.[9] The Torah states that Israel had sinned and violated the covenant. The story recounts that the only sinner was Achan, who kept proscribed spoils from Jericho. Despite his sin, Achan was still called "Israel."[10]

The marriage of an apostate to a Jewish woman was deemed lawful per the Talmudic Tractate Yevamot (47b). Consequently, a woman was required to obtain a divorce document from her apostate husband if she wished to marry someone else lawfully. The continuing obligation of the apostate to observe the com-commandments is not found explicitly in rabbinic texts, but the *Midrash Tanhuma* relates that the children of Israel cannot dissoci-dissociate themselves from their pledge of loyalty to God. The Talmud correspondingly notes that every Jew is obligated by oath to observe all the commandments.[11] The apostate was expected to repent.[12]

## Apostates in the Medieval Period

The instance of a Jew converting to another religion arose more prominently with the emergence of Christianity and Islam.

---

[9] Joshua 7:1–26.

[10] The first biblical reference to a heretic is that of the dissenter who appeals to others to go and worship the gods of others. The biblical punishment for worshiping foreign gods was death. The Bible records that idolatry was prevalent among many Israelites, but this was not viewed as sufficient cause for negating their status as the Children of Israel. The confrontation between the prophet Elijah and the prophets of the Canaanite deity Baal in the book of Kings (chapter 17) provides one illustration. This account relates that many Israelites were worshipping Baal. While Elijah challenged the priests of Baal and the people's idolatry, they remained identified as Jews/Israelites. Sacha Stern, *Jewish Identity in Early Rabbinic Writings* (New York: Brill, 1994), 11.

[11] Shevuot 21b; 22b; 23b. Yoma 73b.

[12] Sacha Stern, *Jewish Identity in Early Rabbinic Writings* (New York: Brill, 1994), 107. See also Jacob Katz, *Exclusiveness and Tolerance: Studies in Jewish-Gentile Relations in Medieval & Modern Times* (West Orange: Behrman House, 1961), 68-69.

Whether either religion qualified as *Avodah Zarah* (i.e. idolatry) was an issue of debate and had practical implications regarding the manner in which Jews interacted with the practitioners of these religions. If they did indeed qualify as *Avodah Zarah*, the prohibi-prohibition against socializing with idolaters was applied, as laid out by the Talmudic tractate *Avodah Zarah*. If, however, they did not, greater latitude was possible in social and business spheres.

With the majority of Jews living in Islamic lands in the early medieval period, Islam was first deliberated on by the Geonim, the heads of the two great Babylonian Talmudic academies of Sura and Pumbedita. Some rules forbidding Gentile wine were relaxed during this era on the basis that Muslims were not idolaters. Since Muslims were monotheists and claimed to worship the God of Abraham, concerns over their wine being used for idolatrous purposes was lessened. Jews were allowed to benefit from the sale of wine but were not authorized to drink it. It was forbidden to drink pagan wine or to derive any benefit from its sale during the Talmudic period.

Whether a Jew who converted to Islam was still a Jew was an issue considered by the Geonim.[13] Some contended that conversion to Islam detached the individual from their connections to Judaism. They argued that the willing convert was not to be considered as a brother. Consequently, levirate marriage or its alternative, *haliza* (i.e. the procedure for the *yavam/levir* to forgo marriage and release the widow to remarry whomever she wished), did not apply.[14] The physical death of the *levir*, which ended the obligation of levirate marriage, was now coupled with the view that death to the faith also severed the requirement. Other Geonim continued to treat the apostate in the same manner as the *meshumad* of the Talmud. Just as the *meshumad* had not lost their Jewish status, neither did these converts. The wife of an apostate

---

[13] Louis Jacobs. "Attitudes towards Christianity in the Halakhah." Accessed January 30, 2014. https://goo.gl/r9AaAa

[14] See Deuteronomy 25: 5-10.

still required a *get* (i.e. divorce document) before she could marry another.

The question of whether a Jew must lay down his or her life ra-rather than adopt Islam also arose. Talmudic law mandated that a Jew undergo martyrdom rather than worship idols. In the 12$^{th}$ century, Maimonides ruled that Islam was not a pagan religion.[15] Maimonides declared that if a Jew was threatened with death if he refused to accept Islam, martyrdom was not required. A Jew could adopt Islam to save his or her life. [16] Regarding conversions under duress, the outrage was the disloyalty to their religion and people when confronted with persecution. Theological, as well as social and ethnic considerations, were introduced into what was once solely a matter of Jewish law.

Christianity presented more complex issues since it embraced the doctrines of the Trinity and the Incarnation. These beliefs were augmented by observances such as bowing to crosses and saints. It was considered to be idolatry by rabbis living in Christian lands. Some of the more restrictive rules between Jews and non-Jews were relaxed solely on the grounds of economic necessity, but the differences with Islam were clear.[17]

The Talmud had ruled that a Jew was forbidden to enter into a business relationship with a non-Jew.[18] The reason being the possibility that, if a dispute arose, an oath might be required by either party. The Gentile, it was assumed, would take the oath by his gods. This was forbidden for a Jew to bring about, even circuitous-

---

[15] Louis Jacobs. "Attitudes towards Christianity in the Halakhah." Accessed January 30, 2014. https://goo.gl/r9AaAa

[16] Other authorities were not willing to adopt such a position on martyrdom. The responsa of Rabbi David ben Solomon ibn Avi Zimra cited Rabbi Yom Tov Ishbili's assertion that converting to Islam involved a denial and renunciation of the Torah.ibid.

[17] Louis Jacobs. "Attitudes towards Christianity in the Halakhah." Accessed January 30, 2014. https://goo.gl/r9AaAa

[18] See Sanhedrin 63b and Bekhorot 2b.

ly. Venerating idols violated the Noahide laws that all Gentiles were obligated to observe.[19]

Ultimately, Christianity was viewed as idolatry for Jews, but not for Gentiles. The rationale for this view was based on a passage in the Tosafot that was understood to imply that a Christian did not violate the Noahide laws by his belief. The Christian was not to be regarded as an idolater since *shituf* (divine association with God) was not forbidden to a Noahide.[20] None of the halakhists, however, were prepared to assert that Christianity was pure monotheism, as was the case with Islam.[21]

The Tosafists defended their position by arguing that when Christians took an oath, they did so in God's name. The position was controversial, given the Tosafists' admission that Christians associated God's name with that of Jesus. Christians as Noahides were not forbidden to associate the name of God with another. They argued that the principle of *shituf* was only applicable where there was a belief in One Supreme Being along with lesser deities and not the Trinitarian view that the Godhead was composed of three co-equal persons. This view allowed Jews to enter into business relationships with Christians.[22] This view stood in con-

---

[19] Sanhedrin 56b.

[20] Louis Jacobs. "Attitudes towards Christianity in the Halakhah." Accessed January 30, 2014. https://goo.gl/r9AaAa Also Jacob Katz, *Exclusiveness and Tolerance: Studies in Jewish-Gentile Relations in Medieval & Modern Times* (West Orange: Berhman House, 1961), 163.

[21] In the 16th century, Rabbi Moses Isserles stated: "Some authorities are lenient in the matter of a Jew becoming a business partner with a Gentile, nowadays, for their intention (when they take an oath) is to the Creator of heaven and earth." Rabbi Moses Isserles commenting on 'Orah Hayim' 215: 2 argued that it was permitted to answer 'Amen' to the benediction of a Christian. Rabbi Isserles' position was regularly cited by later halakhists who saw it as a decision that a Noahide was allowed *shituf* in the theological context of the term. In consequence, a Christian did not transgress the Noahide laws by accepting as true, the doctrines of Trinity and in the Incarnation. The 16th-century Italian Rabbi Solomon Modena argued that Christianity was in fact pure monotheism. Modena rejected the view that the doctrine of the Incarnation compromised true monotheism. Louis Jacobs. "Attitudes towards Christianity in the Halakhah." Accessed January 30, 2014. https://goo.gl/r9AaAa

[22] Rabbi Isserles permitted a Gentile Christian to give contributions to a synagogue. It was forbidden however, to receive donations from a Jewish convert to Christianity. Yoreh De'ah 254: 2; cf. Orah Hayim 154: 11. This latter prohibition was also disregarded

trast to that of Maimonides, who stated that Christians were, in fact, idolaters.[23]

In the 13th century, Rabbi Menachem Meiri of Perpignan concontended that Christians were not idolaters. Rabbi Meiri argued that the prohibitions laid out in the Talmud could not be applied to those nations that were governed by a moral religion. Christians were not to be considered pagans. They had a religion that imimposed substantial moral expectations on its followers, not unlike the manner in which Judaism did so for Jews. In a striking attempt to reinterpret the prohibition of doing business with Christians (*Notzerim*), Rabbi Meiri argued that *Notzerim* did not refer to Chris-Christians but rather to the Babylonians. The reference to "the first day" was not a reference to the Christian Sabbath, but instead to sun-worship, which purportedly took place on the first day of each new week. While Rabbi Meiri retained the prohibition on drinking wine handled by Christians, it could be bought and sold.

## The Status of Jewish Converts to Christianity

Rabbi Solomon ben Isaac (*Rashi*) in the 11th century argued that whatever sins a Jew committed, including apostasy, the individual remained a Jew. His stance countered the Church's position that baptism was indelible.[24] Had the rabbis acknowledged that a Jewish convert to Christianity was a non-Jew, they would have admitted that baptism had magical powers capable of transforming an individual. Giving such power to Christian baptism was unacceptable. Despite their behavior, even a baptized Jew had never truly apostatized according to Jewish law.[25]

---

repeatedly in Spain where Conversos often contributed to the welfare of the synagogue as a means of affirming their continuing connection to the Jewish people.

[23] Despite this, he permitted the Torah to be taught to Christians while forbidding it to be taught to Muslims. The reason for this lay in the fact that Muslims accused Jews of having forged parts of the Torah. Louis Jacobs. "Attitudes towards Christianity in the Halakhah." Accessed January 30, 2014. https://goo.gl/r9AaAa

[24] Solomon Katz, *The Jews in the Visigothic and Frankish Kingdoms of Spain and Gaul* (New York: Kraus, 1970), 13, 15.

[25] Jacob Katz, *Halakhah ve-Qabbalah* (Jerusalem: Magnes, 1984), 264.

Rabbi Solomon ben Isaac and his successors rejected severing an apostate's Jewish connections entirely. The apostate's wife required a *get* and, in the event of the death of the apostate's brother, his sister-in-law needed *haliza* if she were childless. When asked about the requirement of *haliza* in this situation, Rabbi Solomon ben Isaac wrote that the woman needed a bill of divorce before she could marry another man. The marriage of a Jew, who had voluntarily apostatized was legal, according to Jewish law.[26] Baptism was not sufficient cause for severing the halakhic status of a Jew.

In contrast, Maimonides believed that those who converted willingly were no longer considered members of the Jewish People.[27] His position was founded on the biblical verse dealing with adultery that states that "None that go to her repent, nor will they regain the paths of life."[28] Maimonides sought to prevent such converts from returning to Judaism even if they repented. In his Mishneh Torah, Maimonides states:

> "A Jew who serves false gods is considered like a Gentile in all regards and is not comparable to a Jew who violated another transgression punishable by being stoned to death. An apostate who worships false gods is considered to be an apostate with regard to the entire Torah. Similarly, Jewish *minnim* are not considered to be Jews with regard to

---

[26] Paul Halsall, Fordham University, "Medieval Sourcebook: Rashi (1040-1105): Communal Affairs in Troyes, c.1100." Last modified October 1997. Accessed March 17, 2014. http://www.fordham.edu/halsall/source/1105rashi.asp.

[27] Mishneh Torah, Hilkhot Mamrim 3:2. "Since it has become known that such a person denies the Oral Law, he may be pushed into a pit and may not be helped out. He is like all the rest of the heretics who say that the Torah is not Divine in origin, those who inform on their fellow Jews, and the apostates. All of these are not considered as members of the Jewish people. There is no need for witnesses, a warning, or judges for them to be executed. Instead, whoever kills them performs a great mitzvah and removes an obstacle from people at large." See Touger, Eliyahu. "Hilchot Mamrim - Chapter 3 - Texts & Writings." Hilchot Mamrim - Chapter 3 - Texts & Writings. https://goo.gl/UnFu56 accessed May 16, 2014.

[28] Proverbs 2:19.

any matter. Their repentance should never be accepted, as [implied by Proverbs 2:19]: 'None that go to her repent, nor will they regain the paths of life.' It is forbidden to talk to them or to reply to them at all, as [Proverbs 5:8] states: 'Do not come close to her door.' [It can be assumed that] a *min's* thoughts are concerned with false gods."[29]

## The Case of the Returning Apostate

The possibility that an apostate might return to Judaism was a reality that was hoped for, but the implications of his return were debated. Rabbi Moshe Gaon in the early part of the 9th century CE was asked whether a Jew, who had apostatized but later returned to Judaism, was to be trusted with regards to the permissibility of wine under his care. Gaon responded that if he observed the Sabbath in public and kept all the commandments, he was to be counted as a kosher Jew without restriction. One could drink a glass of wine with him, forgoing the mistrust that it may have been handled by a Gentile.

Rav Amram Gaon in the 9th century required lashes as well as a public confession for the returning convert. He argued that lashes were obligatory because the apostate had violated various positive and negative commandments, including those punishable by spiritual excision and the death penalty, during his apostasy. He nevertheless argued that immersion was unnecessary since the returnee was not a convert. Once this was completed, the former apostate was received into the community without restriction.[30]

---

[29] Mishnah Torah, Hilkhot Avodah Kochavim 2:5. Touger, Eliyahu. "Avodah Kochavim - Chapter Two - Texts & Writings." https://goo.gl/R1EDuZ accessed May 16, 2014.

[30] David Golinkin "How Can Apostates Such as the Falash Mura Return to Judaism?" Responsa in a Moment 1, no. 5 (2007). Accessed June 9, 2015. http://www.schechter.edu/responsa.aspx?ID=30.

Rabbi Solomon ben Isaac argued that forced converts who were sincerely returning to Judaism should be embraced.[31] He referred to the fact that Rabbi Gershom ben Judah Me'or ha-Golah in the 11th century Germany, had issued excommunication decrees for any individual who reminded a repentant apostate of their past. With regards to the common concern over wine handled by forced converts, as long as they returned to Judaism, their wine was considered acceptable without further validation. Following Rabbi Gershom's lead, Rabbi Solomon ben Isaac stated:

> "Let us beware of alienating those who have returned to us by repulsing them. They became Christians only through fear of death; and as soon as the danger disappeared, they hastened to return to their faith."

Rabbi Solomon ben Isaac's acceptance of forced converts without formal procedures was not accepted by all rabbis. The French rabbi, Yitzhak ben Shmuel, also known as the *Ri* of Dampierre (1110-1189) required immersion for forced converts wishing to return to Judaism.[32] With regards to marriage, the relapsed convert, like the apostate Jew, remained eligible to marry marriage in accordance with Jewish law.[33]

---

[31] Taitz 90. Rabbi Solomon ben Isaac commented: "Repentance reaches as high as the Throne of Glory, and even the most righteous individuals do not reach the level of those who repent, as it is written: 'peace, peace to the far and to the near (Isaiah 50: 7, 19).' " Perlmann, Moshe. "Apostasy." Jewish Virtual Library, Accessed January 9, 2013. http://www.jewishvirtuallibrary.org/jsource/judaica/ejud_0002_0002_0_01188.html.

[32] In the specific case that Shmuel addressed, the individual in question was already openly living again as a religious Jew. The requirement for ritual immersion was apparently aimed at addressing the community's concern over the acceptability of wine handled by the individual in question. Louis Jacobs. "Attitudes towards Christianity in the Halakhah." Accessed January 30, 2014. https://goo.gl/r9AaAa

[33] The Shulchan Aruch, the Code of Jewish law authored in the century following the Spanish and Portuguese Expulsions, ruled that a marriage between a Jewish man and a Jewish woman who converted to another religion remained valid. The children were Jewish and could also marry other Jews. Shulchan Aruch, Even Ha-ezer 44:9. According to Nelson Zalman, this is very important. "Marriage, however, is the real test of Jewishness. Even if a non-Jew would marry a Jew with a chupah and a rabbi presiding with all the procedures 'by the book,' the marriage does not have the validity of a marriage sanctified in accordance with Jewish law." Nelson, Zalman. *Is a Jew Who Converts Still Jewish?* Retrieved 21 December 2012 from Chabad.org: https://goo.gl/ZQeHXQ Rabbi Aharon

*Sefer Hasidim* authored by Rabbi Yehudah heHasid relates the matter of an apostate who returned to Judaism. If he submitted himself to repent as the sages instructed him, it was permitted to drink his wine and pray with him from the instant he accepted the stipulated requirements.[34] There were others such as Rabbi Eleazar of Worms who included long penances for returning apostates.[35] He believed self-mortification for a former apostate was appropri-appropriate. He wrote that an apostate was to grieve and fast every day for several years, repent three times daily, and undergo enormous anguish to atone for his sin.

In the 11th century, Rav Hai Gaon was asked about a slave who had been circumcised by his master but who later abandoned Juda-Judaism. Rav Hai Gaon was asked whether it was necessary to perform *hatafat dam brit* (i.e. extracting a drop of blood from the male member). He was also asked if ritual immersion in a *mikveh* was sufficient to accept the slave as a Jew once more. Rav Hai Gaon responded that neither was necessary since the slave was equivalent to an apostate Jew, who had repented.

In the 11th century, Rabbeinu Gershom ruled that a formerly apostate *Cohen*, who repented, was allowed to recite the Priestly Blessing.[36] The French Tosafist of the late 12th and early 13th centuries, Rabbi Yitzhak ben Avraham also argued that repentance for the returning convert was sufficient. Neither immersion nor ap-

---

Lichtenstein argues that a Jew who has adopted another religion remains a Jew without Jewishness. The individual according to Lichtenstein is bereft of a sacred Jewish identity. With regards to a Jewish apostate to Christianity, such an individual probably alienates himself more than Jews who adopted idolatry during Talmudic times. This is due to the fact that Christians make up a separate social group in a way in which other religious societies did not. Aharon Lichtenstein, *Brother Daniel and Jewish Fraternity, Leaves of Faith: The World of Jewish Living* (Jersey City: Ktav, 2004), 67-68.

[34] Siman 203. Reuven Margaliot, ed. *Rabbi Yehudah he-Hasid, Sefer Hasidim* (Jerusalem: Mosad ha-Rav Kook, 1956), 192.

[35] Edward Fram, "Perception and Reception of Repentant Apostates in Medieval Ashkenaz and Premodern Poland," AJS Review 21/2 (1996): 304.

[36] Rabbi Elazar of Worms, Sefer ha-Rokeah, Laws of Repentance, siman 24.

pearance before a *Beit Din* was required.[37] The French Tosafist Rabbi Samson explained that an apostate was to be accepted if he repented publicly, without further encumbrances.[38]

Rabbi Solomon ben Aderet of Barcelona (1235-1310) asserted that the apostate who wished to return to the Jewish community must repent, and endure punishments and reprimands for the sins he had committed.[39] The returning apostate was not required to undergo immersion since he remained a Jew despite his prior conversion to Christianity. He "deserved stripes as he transgressed in several positive and negative precepts, and this deserved premature death by divine visitation (karet) as well as capital punishment by (regular) courts."[40] The returning apostate needed to repent but not convert. To require immersion for the returning apostate would have admitted the significance and efficacy of Christian baptism.[41] Rabbi Yom Tov ben Avraham Ishbili, living in the 13th and 14th centuries, wrote about the necessity of a returning apostate to accept the *mitzvot* before a *Beit Din*, to be allowed back into the community. Rabbi Ishbili commented that all authorities agreed that a Jew, who had sinned but then repented, was required to undergo immersion by rabbinic decree and not by Torah law.[42]

---

[37] David Golinkin "How Can Apostates Such as the Falash Mura Return to Judaism?" Responsa in a Moment 1, no. 5 (2007). Accessed June 9, 2015. http://www.schechter.edu/responsa.aspx?ID=30.

[38] David Golinkin notes that the unabridged version of the Mordekhai, as quoted in the Responsa of the Maharik (par. 85), added that "since he was permitted in the congregation and accepted the obligation to fast, even though he has not finished, when he recanted and repented he immediately returned to his acceptable status." Ibid.

[39] "Stripes, to be sure, he does deserve as he did commit several transgressions. Immersion, on the other hand, is not required as he was born a Jew. [The same way] as a proselyte who converted does not require immersion, being an Israelite for any purpose. He has, nonetheless, to undergo public admonition and repent for anything he committed. From that moment on, nobody fears deceit in the case." Joseph Shatzmiller, "Converts and Judaizers in the Early Fourteenth Century," HTR, Vol. 74, No 1. (1981): 65.

[40] Ibid., 65.

[41] Kristine T. Utterback, "Conversi-Revert: Voluntary and Forced Return to Judaism in the Early Fourteenth Century," Church History, Vol. 64. No. 1 (1995): 25

[42] Joseph Shatzmiller, "Converts and Judaizers in the Early Fourteenth Century," HTR, Vol. 74, No 1. (1981): 66.

In the 15th century, Rabbi Shlomo ben Shimon Duran, known as the *Rashbash* wrote about repentance, circumcision, and ritual immersion among forced converts who were uncircumcised. He determined that these converts remained Jewish even though they had sinned. Their marriages were valid, and money could not be loaned to them at interest. He differentiated between descendants of converts who returned to Judaism (i.e. hence the fact that they were uncircumcised) and converts to Judaism. Unlike the latter, the descendants of returning converts were not to be instructed in various minor and major commandments or the corresponding punishments for their transgression, as stipulated in the Talmud for a convert.[43] Rabbi Shlomo ben Shimon Duran was focused on ensuring the community's warm embrace of returning converts since they had already entered the covenant at Sinai by virtue of their lineage. Immersion was also not necessary since the returning converts were not proselytes.

In the 14th century, Rabbi Jacob ben Asher known as the *Baal Ha-Turim* questioned whether a former apostate Cohen could administer the priestly blessing.[44] While finding objection to the former, he ruled that the returning convert should be called up first when the Torah was read. In the 16th century, the *Maran*, Rabbi Joseph Caro permitted a Cohen, who had apostatized but consequently repented, to recite the priestly blessing. This was to be done if only to provide an opening for those who might repent. Conscious of Maimonides' ruling prohibiting such a Cohen from performing the priestly blessing even if he had repented, Rabbi Caro argued that the proscription did not apply to cases in which the apostasy was coerced.[45]

In the 16th century, the *Maharshal*, Rabbi Solomon Luria noted that it was his community's practice for a returning apostate to undergo immersion to purify himself from the transgressions and

---

[43] Yevamot 47a
[44] Tur, Orah Hayyim 128.
[45] Shulchan Aruch, Orach Ḥayyim 128, 37. Perlmann, Moshe. Jewish Virtual Library, "Apostasy." Accessed January 9, 2013. https://goo.gl/Auisfo

sins he had committed.[46] Rabbi Luria stated: "It is our custom that the convert (who reverted) require a *tebila* because of the sins (he committed) and the precepts he broke."[47] Rabbi Moses Isserles (the *Rema*), who lived during the sixteenth century in Poland, ar- argued that a Jewish apostate looking to return to Judaism was to be accepted if he repented before a *beit din*. The obligation for the returning convert to immerse in a *mikveh* was held out of rabbinic rigorousness.[48]

## The Mystical Aspect of Jewish Identity

The general acceptance of returning converts to Judaism was based on the view that the converts remained a part of Israel despite their voluntary conversion or their failure to choose martyrdom when persecuted. The legal aspect of Jewish identity was certainly a factor, but there were other possibilities for believing Jewish links were unbreakable. One such approach was put forward by Rabbi Judah Loew of Prague.

Rabbi Judah Loew of Prague argued for an innate essence in Jews that could not be changed. Rabbi Loew maintained that Israel's redemption from Egypt and the subsequent revelation at Sinai was not predicated on the outward merits of the people of Israel. Israel received the Torah at Sinai because of the innate superiority of its members' souls. This factor separated Israel from the rest of the nations.[49] Rabbi Loew maintained that, just as according to the Torah, a man who coerced a woman into marriage by raping her could never divorce her, so too had God forced Israel into the covenant. The Talmud states, "The Holy One, blessed be He, overturned the mountain [i.e. Sinai] upon them like an [inverted] cask and said to them-If you accept the Torah, it will be

---

[46] Ibid.
[47] Joseph Shatzmiller, "Converts and Judaizers in the Early Fourteenth Century," HTR, Vol. 74, No 1. (1981): 66.
[48] Shulhan Arukh, Yoreh De'ah 268:12.
[49] Byron L. Sherwin, *Mystical Theology and Social Dissent* (Oxford: Littman Library of Jewish Civilization, 2006), 84.

well; if not, here shall be your burial." As a consequence, God's relationship with Israel was unbreakable and eternal. It could never be replaced, nor could it be negated.[50]

For Rabbi Loew, every nation on earth possessed a particular characteristic that contributed to the world's makeup. Each nation was tasked with perfecting this unique feature. Israel's existence was vital to the survival of the world. The presence of other peoples was, in many ways, mere chance. Rabbi Loew stated:

> "The matter is as we have explained. Unlike the Gentiles, Israel was created in essence by God. Though the Gentiles were also created by God, their creation was not essential. For the essence of Creation was Israel. The creation of the [other] nations was accidental and only follows from the formation of the essence of creation."[51]

Rabbi Loew believed that certain peoples were complimentary opposites of Israel while others were contradictory opposites. The descendants of Ishmael according to Rabbi Loew were an example of complimentary opposites. The children of Israel could dwell among the descendants of Ishmael (i.e. Arabs). Another example was the case of Egypt. Other nations like the descendants of Edom and Amalek were contradictory opposites. Consequently, the children of Israel could not dwell or coexist with such nations. This description may have highlighted Loew's view of the Spanish and Portuguese expulsion.[52] It was evident to Rabbi Loew that Christians were the spiritual successors of Edom and were the contradictory opposites of Jews. Jews and Christians were different physically, communally, and metaphysically.[53] Rabbi Loew believed that it was impossible for an individual to change their fundamental essence. It was impossible for someone to abandon, willingly or unwillingly, his defining nature and become a member

---

[50] Ibid., 86.
[51] Ibid., 88-89.
[52] Ibid., 90, 92.
[53] Ibid., 98.

of another people. The impact on the question of Conversos and Jewish identity is astounding. As Byron Sherwin summarizes:

> "For Rabbi Loew, as for many sixteenth-century Jewish scholars, the problem of Jews who had converted to Catholicism at the end of the fifteenth century in Spain wanting to return to Judaism after having left Spain appears to have been a constant issue. Loew refuses to close the door back into Judaism for those wishing to re-enter. For Loew, the Jews can never cease being a Jew. The apostate need not be readmitted because he never left."[54]

This allowed those who converted, whether by compulsion or of their own volition, to rejoin the Jewish community.

## Conclusion

In the majority of the cases discussed, the idea of a returning apostate was focused on localized circumstances. In the aftermath of the widespread violence in the Iberian Peninsula in 1391, few Jewish families were left unaffected. Most had family members that had succumbed to the violence or acted to forestall it. The view that these Conversos were forever cut off from the Jewish people was, therefore, much harder to espouse.

The evidence points not only to Jewish compassion for Conversos but also to a willingness to help them maintain or return to the faith of their fathers. This usually occurred outside of the Peninsula, but Conversos were also supported in their Jewish endeavors in the Peninsula. The acceptance of returning Conversos without overly burdensome requirements became the general rule, as evidenced in particular by the attitudes adopted by communities comprised of former Conversos in the 17th century. This topic, as well as the attitudes of Jews towards Conversos, will be addressed more extensively in chapter six.

---

[54] Ibid., 102-103.

CHAPTER 4

# Types of Conversos

The Jews who converted in 1391 and throughout the 15th century had different reasons for doing so. However, the impetus for the majority was simply to survive the violence. In an environment of fear, few Conversos genuinely embraced the Catholic Church. Most still lived in Jewish, or Converso dominated neighborhoods where Jewish religion and culture exerted a continuing influence on them. Old Christians did little to cajole Conversos to embrace their new faith sincerely. The tendency of many Conversos to retain Jewish praxis and belief ultimately stirred the mistrust of Old Christians. These feelings grew throughout the 15th century as many Conversos now liberated from the social and economic limits applied to the Jewish community excelled in business and public office.[1]

Converso identity was complex. Religious affiliation, family bonds, economic opportunity, and political connections all played a part in defining them. Many fled to Jewish communities in North Africa or in the Ottoman Empire. Over a period of centuries, many Conversos journeyed to northern Europe, England, and the New World where some established openly Jewish communities. Some of those who found safety outside of the Peninsula found it difficult to fully embrace a faith they had been disconnected from

---

[1] Kevin Ingram, "Secret lives, public lies: the conversos and socio-religious non-conformism in the Spanish Golden Age." (PhD diss., UC San Diego, 2006), 43-44.

for centuries. Others were able to integrate successfully into the Jewish community. Many remained on the edges of these newly formed Jewish communities and had to be cajoled or even threat-threatened into joining. Still, others who did embrace Judaism opted to return to the Peninsula even if it meant reverting to Catholicism.

There were, however, Jews who had converted sincerely. The violence may have only spurred their previous doubts regarding Judaism or made them realize the declining fortunes of their people and faith. Many were content to not only embrace their new faith but were also driven to attack their former coreligionists. Some desired to maintain a measure of their former identity. They believed that their Jewish heritage made them exemplary Christians and that they represented a nobility from which Jesus and the early Church had emerged. Because of discrimination and persecution, even sincere converts often found it more expedient to leave the Iberian Peninsula.

## Opportunistic Conversos, Troubled Souls, and Erratic Individuals

The largest group of Conversos was those who were swept up by the violence into converting. They were often ordinary folk who were not scholars of the Jewish faith but were faithful to Judaism. Having seen rabbis and community leaders convert, including the famed Rabbi Isaac bar Sheshet Perfet of Valencia, who eventually escaped to North Africa and returned to Judaism, many followed suit.

Any suggestion that their ongoing Jewish observances were simply a matter of sociological customs as opposed to actual religious practice assumes that Conversos distinguished between those Jewish practices that were cultural and those that were religious in nature. Jewish identity was not compartmentalized with Christian notions of Jewish customs. Jewish faith was lived out practically in daily dietary, social, and familial experiences. Conversos continued to have family and friends who were openly

Jewish and their social, and economic bonds continued after bap-baptism.

The passage of time lessened the connections that linked subsequent generations of Conversos and Jews. The reason is not difficult to imagine since in certain areas entire Jewish communities had converted. The decline was also attributable to the fact that Conversos and Jews could not legally marry. With the majority of Conversos marrying among themselves, ties to their openly Jewish family members still existed, but at increasingly removed levels.[2]

After the initial violence of 1391, different attitudes towards Jewish observance began to emerge. The case of Aldonca and Angelina, both Conversas, serves as an example. Angelina and her husband observed the Sabbath, Passover, and other Jewish holidays to the best of their ability. Angelina also had a brother who had left the Peninsula, returned to Judaism, and journeyed to Jerusalem. Her brother was daring enough to go back for a visit and gave her a stone he claimed was from the ruins of the Temple. Angelina was active in donating to the poor Jews of Morvedre and even attended the synagogue there. Angelina was well known by fellow Conversos who commended her knowledge of Judaism.[3]

In contrast, Aldonca had married an Old Christian. On one Friday night, Angelina passed by and saw Aldonca spinning yarn. She confronted Aldonca and chastised her for violating the Sabbath. Aldonca retorted that her criticism was better apt for the Jewish women of Morvedre. Angelina related the story to her husband who cautioned her to avoid Aldonca. A separation between Conversos was emerging.

## Opportunistic Conversos: Pedro de la Cavalleria

---

[2] Mark D. Meyerson, *A Jewish Renaissance in Fifteenth-Century Spain* (Princeton: Princeton University Press, 2004), 199-200.

[3] Ibid., 201.

Some Conversos who Judaized were quite adept at living dou-double lives. Pedro de la Cavalleria was a member of a famous Saragossa family and a first-generation convert. He was baptized along with the rest of his family during the Tortosa Disputation. As a convert, he took full advantage of the economic opportunities that became open to him. He became an authority on jurisprudence in the 1430s. He was killed in 1461, during the initial phases of the rebellion in Catalonia against King John II of Aragon.

While baptism opened up opportunities, Pedro was cognizant that his Jewish past was a liability. In 1447, he falsified evidence which was signed by noted Christian personalities corroborating his pure Christian ancestry. In 1450, perhaps to buttress his claims, he even wrote a defense of Christianity titled *Zelus Christi contra Judaeos, Saracenos et infidels*. In it, he quoted passages from the works of the Kabbalist Rabbi Joseph Chicatilla confirming his familiarity with Jewish books.

Despite this, there was another side to Pedro. During an inquisitional trial in the 1480s, a Jewish weaver swore that at the time of the plague, Pedro de la Cavalleria had fled with his family from Saragossa to a village in Aragon. While there, the weaver claimed he had often visited him at his home. He enjoyed spending the Sabbath with him and partook of the wine and various Jewish delicacies.

Pedro participated when *Birkat Hamazon*, grace after meals, was recited. He had also spoken Hebrew to his host and even conversed about Jewish religious matters. The weaver asked him: "Sir, why, being so learned in the Torah, didst thou hasten to embrace Christianity?" To this Pedro responded:

> "Silence, fool! Could I, as a Jew, ever have risen higher than a rabbinical post? But now, see, I am one of the chief councilors (*jurado*) of the city. For the sake of the little man who was hanged (Jesus), I am accorded every honor, and I issue orders

and decrees to the whole city of Saragossa. Who hinders me—if I choose—from fasting on Yom Kippur and keeping your festivals and all the rest? When I was a Jew I dared not walk as far as this (i.e., beyond the prescribed limits of a Sabbath day's walk); but now I do as I please. "

The weaver continued the dialogue and Pedro replied: "So it was formerly. Now I am free to do as I please."[4] Some Conversos were capable of achieving a very high level of integration into the larger society while still retaining their connections and links to the Jewish community when they chose to do so.

## Confused Conversos: Juan del Hoyo

Many Conversos combined Christian and Jewish observances and beliefs. Since Christianity possessed elements which were derived from the Hebrew Scriptures, the dividing line between Jewish and Christian beliefs might not have been visible to many. The fact that Conversos received little Christian education only confused things more. The case of Juan del Hoyo provides one example.

Hoyo was an orphan at an early age and was raised by various members of the Converso community of his native town. Later in life, he was questioned by the Inquisition and found to be completely devoid of any significant knowledge of the Christian faith. When asked if he was a Christian, he surprisingly answered that he was not sure. Astounded by his reply, the Inquisitors questioned him regarding his beliefs. He stated he believed in Jesus and that he was born of the Virgin Mary, but then shockingly added that Christ had not suffered or died. This was to come.

Hoyo added that he did not believe in the resurrection of the dead. He doubted the miracle of the transubstantiation. The Inquisitors realized that he lacked even minimal instruction, yet

---

[4] Yitzhak Baer, *A History of the Jews in Christian Spain: Volume 2* (Philadelphia, Jewish Publication Society, 1961), 274-275.

they still sentenced him to imprisonment. While confined, he was ordered to receive religious instruction.[5]

## Troubled Souls: Juan Poeta and Anton Montoro

While conversion opened up economic and social opportunities for many, some Conversos were anguished by the inability to find real acceptance in Christian circles. A poem written by the Count of Paredes attributes a complex identity to the aspiring Converso poet, Juan Poeta of Valladolid.

> "Each one of the following is his name- Juan, Simuel (Shemuel) and Reduan [Arabic name]. A Moor, so he won't be dead, A Christian, so he will have more worth, But a Jew he is for certain, As far as I can know."

For the Count of Paredes, each identity was part of Juan's complex character. Juan Poeta rejected accusations against these multiple personalities. His goal, to be at court, required the status of a full-fledged Christian. Conscious of the challenges that Conversos faced, a fellow Converso poet named Anton Montoro attacked Juan Poeta for his seeming naivety.

> "Juan, *señor* and great friend: with my very whole heart I wish to chastise you; take it as I say, as coming from a father or a brother because we (are) of a common tribe being Jews you and I, and my pains are also yours."[6]

According to Yirmiyahu Yovel, Montoro's poem was an expose of Juan Poeta's unsuccessful attempts to hide his Jewish past.[7] Montoro recognized that no matter what Poeta did, he could not

---

[5] María del Pilar Rábade Obradó, "La instrucción cristiana de los conversos en la Castilla del siglo XV," En la España Medieval, 22 (1999): 393.

[6] Montoro 139a.

[7] Yirmiyahu Yovel, "Converso Dualities in the First Generation: The Cancioneros," Jewish Social Studies 4, no. 3 (1998): 2.

escape his heritage. He would never be free of his Jewish back-background.[8]

Montoro was born around the year 1404 near the town of Cór-Córdoba. Montoro conceivably converted before the age of thirteen possibly as a result of the Tortosa Disputation and anti-Jewish decrees enacted in 1414. His mother remained a Jew.[9] Montoro was eventually known as *El Ropero* in literary circles, which means a clothes peddler due to his clothing business. Montoro wrote a poem to Queen Isabella describing the disappointments he had experienced as a result of his Jewish background.

> "To the Queen Isabel- O sad, bitter clothes-peddler who does not feel your sorrow! Here you are, seventy years of age, and have always said [to the Virgin]: 'you remained immaculate.' And have never sworn [directly] to the Creator. I recite the *credo*, I worship pots full of greasy pork, I eat bacon half-cooked, listen to Mass, cross myself while touching holy waters- and never could I kill these traces of the confeso...I pray rosary in hand, reciting the beads of the Passion, adoring the God-and-man as my highest Lord, but because of the remnants of my guilt I cannot lose the name of an old Jewish son of a whore." [10]

Montoro's claim that he worshiped pork and accepted Catholic doctrine reveals a measure of satire and lack of true belief. As Kevin Ingram notes:

> "In sixteenth-century Spain pork eating had become something of a shibboleth: the test of one's Limpieza de Sangre [purity of blood]. Although many conversos were physically nauseated by the taste of pork, they often ate

---

[8] See also Yitzhak Baer, *A History of the Jews in Christian Spain: Volume 2* (Philadelphia, Jewish Publication Society, 1961), 310-311.

[9] Yom Tov Assis and Yosef Kaplan, eds. *Jews and Conversos at the Time of the Expulsion* (Jerusalem: The Zalman Shazar Center for Jewish History, 1999), 117.

[10] Yirmiyahu Yovel, "Converso Dualities in the First Generation: The Cancioneros," Jewish Social Studies 4, no. 3 (1998): 5-6.

pork products in public to reinforce their claim to Old-Christian blood. Other conversos—Arias Montano is an example—disguised their distaste for pork by presenting themselves as vegetarians. Golden Age literature contains many furtive references to the converso's distaste for pork..."[11]

With the approach of the Inquisition, the city of Toledo or-ordered all butcher shops only to sell pork. This was an overt effort to thwart any Judaizing tendencies among Conversos. In response, Montoro composed a poem to the Corregidor of Córdoba. *"To the Corregidor of Córdoba Because the Butcher Shop Has Nothing but Pork*- One of the true servants of our mighty Lord the King, has given the meat dealers a reason to make me a perjurer. Not finding, to my grief, with what to kill my hunger, they made me break the vow I had made to my forefathers."[12]

The fact that Montoro had sworn to his grandparents that he would abstain from pork is interesting. It may reveal that some Jews understood the reasons that other Jews adopted Christianity. Nevertheless, they requested they do their best to retain some fundamental aspect of Jewish identity. For Montoro it was abstaining from pork, and while he may have only done it for the sake of honoring his forefathers, the very act itself reveals an individual who was not convinced as to the efficacy of Christianity.

## Erratic Individuals: The Case of Guillem Ramon Splugues

---

[11] Kevin Ingram, "Secret lives, public lies: the conversos and socio-religious non-conformism in the Spanish Golden Age." (PhD diss., UC San Diego, 2006), 16. Yovel speculates that perhaps Montoro was appealing to the story in the Haggadah of Rabbi Elazar who states that he is 70 years of age and had never seen the story of Exodus told at nighttime and viewed his life as an inversion of the story. Yirmiyahu Yovel, "Converso Dualities in the First Generation: The Cancioneros," Jewish Social Studies 4, no. 3 (1998): 6.

[12] Yirmiyahu Yovel, "Converso Dualities in the First Generation: The Cancioneros," Jewish Social Studies 4, no. 3 (1998): 8.

Guillem Ramon Splugues was a respected member of the Jew-Jewish community and a lay scholar. He served as the administrator for the synagogue of Morvedre and even gave sermons there. The problem with Splugues was his romantic exploits. Splugues had various affairs with Christian women and fathered a child with at least one of them. He objected to the child being baptized and argued that he would instead be raised as a Jew. Splugues fell out with his parents and was not invited to his sister's wedding over the matter. Infuriated by this, he was baptized.[13]

Despite his conversion, Splugues did not conform to Christian life, even outwardly. He regretted his baptism immediately. In re-relating his baptism to his Christian paramour Cathalina, he explained, "...first I had a dispute with [Christian] masters in theology." Cathalina asked if he was persuaded that the Christian law was true and that the Torah was false. Splugues responded that he could have defeated them in a religious debate. He asserted that anger alone was the cause for his decision. Splugues openly practiced Judaism for twenty-seven years between his baptism and his final arrest by the Inquisition. He related to Cathalina several times, "I am what I used to be; I am a Jew."[14] Splugues even broke down in tears before her relating that he was stirred by the miracles of Queen Esther and the Torah.[15]

Splugues was uncharacteristically bold in maintaining his Jewish identity and even proselytized. Ursula Trilles was an Old Christian, who served as a maidservant in the Splugues home. Splugues along with this wife convinced Ursula to participate in their Jewish customs. They explained that Passover was similar to the Last Supper. They also argued that Jews had similar practices to Christians and that these observances were in the "service of God." Ursula remained unconvinced stating that she knew that these practices were not in concert with Christianity. Splugues was

---

[13] Mark D. Meyerson, *A Jewish Renaissance in Fifteenth-Century Spain* (Princeton: Princeton University Press, 2004), 216.
[14] Ibid., 216- 217.
[15] Ibid., 217.

nevertheless capable of convincing her to marry the Converso Joan Aguilaret. Aguilaret had been recently baptized and was even-eventually burned for Judaizing. Splugues unsuccessfully tried to bribe Ursula to keep quiet about Jewish practices she had seen the Converso named Jaume Viabrera and Splugues observe.[16]

After Splugues's wife Barbara died, Splugues married a Conver-Conversa named Gonstanca shortly after. She had initially served in Splugues' household along with her husband and continued to serve even after her husband's death. Splugues romantically pursued Gonstanca and by 1477, she was expecting. Splugues sent Gonstanca to the town of Almenara for the birth. There a Jewish physician named Vidal visited her and provided her with an amulet carved with Hebrew letters to give her a prompt and benign delivery. The amulet's purported healing powers gained notoriety and other Conversos, and even Old Christians borrowed it to assist their own wives in delivery. The willingness of Jews to interact with Splugues' wife reveals the complexity of the situation that many Conversos faced. As Meyerson notes:

> "The entrance of a Jew, master Vidal, into the comfortable world of Splugues some fourteen years after his baptism was not wholly fortuitous, an anomaly in the life of a converso who had abandoned the Jewish community. Splugues may well have asked his brother in Xativa, the Kabbalist Yosef Alcastiel, to send Vidal with the Hebrew amulet to Gostanca. Despite his painful and abrupt break with this family in Morvedre, Splugues had not severed all ties with the Jewish community."[17]

Splugues's family eventually mended fences with him. His father left him part of his library and Splugues read these Hebrew books until the Inquisition was established in Valencia in 1482. After this, he transferred them to one of his brothers.

---

[16] Ibid., 219.
[17] Ibid.

Splugues also maintained good relations with his Uncle Gento Tarfon in Morvedre. Splugues hired Tarfon as well as other Jews to produce significant amounts of kosher wine to distribute to Jewish communities in North Africa. Tarfon was apparently a ca-capable butcher, and Splugues requested that he ritually slaughter a cow on his behalf. He received an invitation from Jews to attend a wedding in the Jewish quarter of Morvedre.[18]

Splugues' renewed association with Jews, his extensive Jewish education, and his continued Jewish practices ultimately presented a problem that could not be ignored. By the time of his arrest, most Conversos were second and third generation converts and lacked his Jewish education. Splugues was in effect a Converso proselytizer. His first wife Barbara, an Old Christian, participated in his Jewish observances and lived as a Jewess while married to him. In the case of Gonstanca, a Conversa, her knowledge of Jewish practice was apparently slight. But Splugues and his wife Barbara convinced her that she would receive salvation by observing the Law. As Mark Meyerson notes:

> "Before and after Barbara's death, and before and after she and Splugues first abjured their Jewish errors before the Inquisition, Gostanca practiced Judaism with Splugues. Her love for her husband and devotion to the Law of Moses would earn her the same terrible end as him."[19]

Splugues reached out to Conversos and encouraged them to hear him read the stories of Queen Esther. Proficient in Hebrew, he used his Hebrew books as teaching resources and translated them impromptu from Hebrew into the Valencian dialect. Splugues even lead services for Conversos.

Splugues was bold enough to engage with Old Christians publicly on theological matters. While in the bookstore of the Converso Francesc Castellar, Splugues discussed the messiah's

---

[18] Ibid., 220-221.
[19] Ibid., 221.

coming and stated that since the return of the exiles to the land of Israel had not taken place, the Messiah could not have come. An educated Old Christian named Joan Cirera countered by stating that the prophecies that Splugues referred to were in fact in refer-reference to the exiles which returned from Babylonia. Splugues and Cirera continued their public debate by challenging each other with various biblical verses and counter-interpretations. Splugues' confidence and lack of trepidation in this era before the establishment of the Spanish Inquisition demonstrates how some Conversos continued to observe and circulate Jewish beliefs.[20]

## Sincere Converts: Solomon Ha-Levi-Pablo de Santa Maria

Some Conversos sincerely adopted Christianity. Some believed they exemplified the highest Christian model- a Jew, who had accepted the messianic claims of Jesus. As neophytes, they were very zealous for their new faith. Their enthusiasm led them to stoke further the fires of anti-Judaism already present among the Christian populace. These Conversos often proselytized aggressively among their former co-religionists.[21]

Pablo de Santa Maria, the former rabbi of Burgos, is without a doubt the most famous sincere convert. Shortly before or perhaps during the violence of 1391 he underwent baptism. Pablo de Santa Maria was born Solomon Ha-Levi. He was a part of a prominent Jewish family in Burgos. Several members of the family had served as tax farmers and financiers for the kingdom of Castile. Ha-Levi continued this trend and eventually served as part of a Castilian diplomatic mission to Aquitaine under English rule at the time. Ha-Levi interacted with a number of prominent rabbis and individuals including his relative Don Meir Alguades, as well as Don Joseph Orabuena and Don Benveniste de la Cavallería. During the early 1380s, he communicated with Rabbi Isaac ben Sheshet on halakhic issues. He studied Jewish and Arabic philoso-

---

[20] Ibid., 221- 222.
[21] Alexandra Guerson, "Seeking Remission: Jewish Conversion in the Crown of Aragon, c. 1378-1391," Jewish History Volume 24 Issue 1 (2010): 43.

phy and was familiar with Christian theological works.[22] The works of Thomas Aquinas are viewed as a critical influence in his conversion.[23]

Ha-Levi wrote that scrutinizing the foundations of a person's faith was paramount. Responding to Joshua Lorqui over why he had converted, he noted that "...this scrutiny is the door of hope through which I entered the New Covenant- I and my friends- and this is the gate of the LORD through which the righteous enter."[24] The writings of the older apostate Abner of Burgos were influential in his decision. While Ha-Levi converted to Christianity in 1391, his mother and wife remained Jewish.[25] Ha-Levi's four sons, his daughter, and his three brothers were baptized along with him.

After his conversion, he wrote to Rabbi Joseph Orabuena explaining what prompted his conversion. He explained that he had concluded that the messianic prophecies relating to Jesus were real. He then journeyed to Paris where he studied theology and

---

[22] Yitzhak Baer, *A History of the Jews in Christian Spain: Volume 2* (Philadelphia, Jewish Publication Society, 1961), 139-140.

[23] Ibid., 143.

[24] Ibid., 149.

[25] While his wife initially refused, she accepted baptism later as evidenced by her burial in a Christian church. Yitzhak Baer, *A History of the Jews in Christian Spain: Volume 2* (Philadelphia: Jewish Publication Society, 1961), 141. The idea of predestination and theodicy was an issue of critical concern in the second half of the 14th century. This was reflected in the works of Abner of Burgos and Isaac Polgar and was also reflected in *Maamar Habehira* written by Moses Narboni. Ram Ben Shalom argues that the idea of predestination may have played a key part in the conversion of Solomon HaLevi. He had argued that his belief in predestination caused him to adopt the name of the apostle Paul, a proponent of predestination in the New Testament. Abner of Burgos and Solomon Halevi were both interested in Kabbalah and M. Glatzer has argued that Kabbalah brought HaLevi close to Christianity. The possibility of this idea having influenced many Jews, who were confronted with the option of conversion of death, was significant enough for Hasdai Crescas to address this issue. In his work, *Or Elohim*, Crescas effectively argued that even if God had issued an edict which caused many Jews to convert; they still bore responsibility for their actions. Ram Ben-Shalom, "Between Official and Private Dispute: The Case of Christian Spain and Provence in the Late Middle Ages," AJS Review, Vol. 27, No. 1 (2003): 32.

was ordained a priest in 1394. He settled in Avignon and became friends with Cardinal Pedro de Luna, who eventually became Pope Benedict XIII. During his service to Pope Benedict XIII, Pablo began his anti-Jewish activity. He attempted to convince King John I of Aragon to enact anti-Jewish laws. In 1396, he was made archdeacon of Treviño. In 1403, he was designated the bish-bishop of Cartagena. In 1415, he was appointed bishop of Burgos, which he served as until his death. He also held the position of chief counselor to the king of Castile from 1407.

Pablo wrote a number of theological works. The first was titled *Scrutinium Scripturarum* and was completed in 1432. In it, a fictional dialogue between a Jew named Saul and a Christian named Paul is detailed. The Jew disputed the doctrines of Christi-Christianity while the Christian rebutted all his protests. The work also includes a dialogue in which a convert asked his tutor to clarify various points of Christian doctrine which were not clear to him. His wide-ranging familiarity of the Talmud, the classical Jewish commentators (i.e. Rashi, Ibn Ezra, Nachmanides), and Maimonides are ostensible.[26]

The converted members of his family held important posts. His son Alonso de Cartagena succeeded his father as bishop of Burgos and composed *Defensorium unitatis christianae* in defense of the Conversos. Another son, named Gonzalo Garcia dei Santa Maria, also served as a bishop. Another son, Pedro de Cartagena, became a military commander while Alvar Sanchez de Cartagena was a diplomat in royal service. The brothers of Pablo de Santa Maria served as governors and notaries, military leaders, and royal diplomats.

## Joshua Lorqui- Geronimo de Santa Fe

---

[26] Yitzhak Baer, *A History of the Jews in Christian Spain: Volume 2* (Philadelphia: Jewish Publication Society, 1961),142.

The physician Joshua Lorqui is another example of a genuine convert to Christianity. During his youth, he studied under Solo-Solomon Ha-Levi in Alcañiz. Joshua Lorqui's path to Christianity was not a simple one but appears to reflect an inner struggle to face the reality of a decimated Jewish community and the theological arguments used to prove the messianic fulfillment of Jesus. Lorqui wrote Ha-Levi a letter that contained four conceivable explanations for the latter's conversion to Christianity.

Firstly, Lorqui asked Ha-Levi if riches and honor were the motivations for his conversion. Secondly, Lorqui questioned if the study of philosophy had led him to conclude that true faith was a delusion and that it was better to side with the dominant faith. Thirdly, he inquired if the recent devastation the Jewish community had suffered had convinced him to abandon the Jewish religion. Lastly, he enquired whether Ha-Levi had received an actual revelation which led him to conclude that Judaism was wrong.[27]

Lorqui rejected the first three possibilities as the reasons for Ha-Levi's conversion. Lorqui stated: "I can find in your case only the last reason, namely, examination and testing of different religions and prophecies. Furthermore, I knew you delved into the hidden treasure of Christian books, commentaries, and principles, having a mastery of their language, and there found many things not discerned by any of the Jewish scholars of our times."[28]

Lorqui was apparently already drawn to Christianity as a viable religious option. While he included traditional Jewish objections to Jesus as the Messiah in his letter, Lorqui returned to his interest in Christian theology. He stated: "And also concerning the Trinity, which the theologians make plausible by their marvelously delicate analysis of the Divinity, it should be said that this is an ancient belief which was held by some men even in the age of the proph-

---

[27] Ibid., 143-144.
[28] Ibid., 145.

ets."²⁹ He also noted that it was everyone's duty to search for true faith.³⁰

Lorqui possibly converted under the influence of the Domini-Dominican preacher Vicente Ferrer. After his baptism, Lorqui adopted the name Gerónimo de Santa Fé and served as the personal physician to Pope Benedict XIII. Lorqui proposed holding a disputation with the leading Jews of Alcañiz. He submitted his proposal to the Pope. Pope Benedict suggested that the debate should be held at Tortosa. Lorqui treated Jews with disrespect and threatened them with punishment by Papal Inquisitors. He was referred to as *megaddef* by Jews, meaning the blasphemer. After the Tortosa Disputation, Lorqui traveled extensively on missionary activities.

Lorqui composed two polemical works against Judaism. The first was *Contra perfidiam Judaeorum*, in which he cites aggadic passages allegedly attesting to the coming of Jesus. The second work titled *De Judaeis erroribus ex Talmuth* reviewed the Talmud as the principal source of Jewish errors. Both works were written about the time of the Tortosa Disputation and were used during the debates.

Interestingly, a descendant of Lorqui, Francisco de Fé served in various important public offices. In 1485, Francisco was implicated in the murder of Pedro de Arbues, the inquisitor of Saragossa and detained. He committed suicide in an Inquisitional prison. His body was burned, and his ashes thrown into the Ebro River.

## Juan Luis Vives

---

[29] Ibid., 146.

[30] Yitzhak Baer relates that "The truth of the matter is that Joshua Halorki wrote as one whose faith had long before been undermined." Ibid., 148. Ram Ben-Shalom, "Between Official and Private Dispute: The Case of Christian Spain and Provence in the Late Middle Ages," AJS Review, Vol. 27, No. 1 (2003): 56.

Juan Luis Vives was a significant figure of the Renaissance, a student, and friend of the humanist Erasmus and was mainly known for his learning and innovation. Juan Luis Vives was born to a Converso family in Valencia in 1493.[31] Vives' immediate family circle were victims of the Inquisition.

In 1524, his father, Luis Vives Valeriola, was burned at the stake for Judaizing. His father had been initially arrested in 1500 when a secret synagogue was discovered in Valencia. His mother, Blanquina March y Almenara, was detained by the Inquisition twice, but subsequently released. She first encountered the Inquisition in 1487 when she repudiated Judaism.[32] She appeared before the Inquisition again in 1491 when she rejected the influence of her mother and confessed to observing a fast on Yom Kippur and to reading Hebrew books. She was subsequently accused of Judaizing several more times.[33] His mother was initially cleared but died of the plague. In 1520, Luis Salvador reported that he had found the entire Vives family observing the Yom Kippur fast. In 1529, Blanquina was disinterred, and her bones burned by the Inquisition.[34]

Given the extent of his family's Judaizing, Vives was certainly exposed to Jewish practices and faith.[35] Despite this, his enthusiastic embrace of Christianity and his identity as a Christian appears to have remained complete and unblemished by regret. He saw himself as fully included in the mystical body of Christ to the exclusion of any other identity.

---

[31] Jose Antonio Escudero, "Luis Vives y La Inquisicion," Revista de la Inquisicion Volumen 13 (2009): 11. According to Angel Amillo, both of Vives' parents were 4th generation Conversos. His father's family was descendant of Abraham Abenfacam who converted in 1391. Angel Gomez-Hortiguela Amillo, "La vida sine querella de Juan Luis Vives," eHumanista 26 (2014): 346.

[32] Jose Antonio Escudero, "Luis Vives y La Inquisicion," Revista de la Inquisicion Volumen 13 (2009): 13.

[33] Ibid., 21.

[34] Ibid., 12.

[35] Angel Gomez-Hortiguela Amillo, "La vida sine querella de Juan Luis Vives," eHumanista 26 (2014): 347.

In 1509, after his mother's death, he traveled to Paris to pursue his studies. He was most likely forced into exile to escape persecution by the Inquisition. Vives also married the Conversa Margarita Valdaura.[36] In 1514, he moved to Flanders. Two years later he met the famed Erasmus at the court of Brussels.

Vives began his literary career in earnest with a stream of writ-writings during this period. These included an extensive commentary on St. Augustine's *City of God*. He also wrote treatises on the relief of the poor and on nonviolence. He addressed these via letters to monarchs and clerics and even to Emperor Charles V. With controversy surrounding King Henry VIII's desire for a divorce from Catherine of Aragon, Vives fell from royal favor and returned to Bruges where he produced a twenty volume set titled *De disciplinis* which provided a wide-ranging review and critique of academic disciplines in his day.

Perhaps most ominously, Vives produced a work on human emotions. In it, he investigated the actions and purposes of the soul. His investigation earned him the designation as the father of modern psychology. His most significant work was his polemic against Judaism and Islam authored in 1543. The work was titled *De veritate fidei christianae*. The third book of *De veritate* was directed specifically towards Judaism and was titled *Contra los judios: Jesucristo es el Mesias*. The book followed the structure of other polemical works against Judaism dating back to the Middle Ages in that it featured a dialogue between a Jew and a Christian debating Scripture.[37]

His goal was to prove the superiority of the Law of Christ over the Law of Moses. Like other Christian apologists, Vives portrayed man as bound to the limitations of the body and a slave to his passions. Only as an immortal being could man experience true

---

[36] Jose Antonio Escudero, "Luis Vives y La Inquisicion," Revista de la Inquisicion Volumen 13 (2009): 19.
[37] Vincent Parello, "La apologetica antijudia de Juan Luis Vives (1543)," Melanges de la Casa de Velazquez 38-2 (2008): 2, 4.

freedom, peace, and joy. Vives degrades man's corporeal existence while exalting the soul's eternality. Once man was freed from the slavery of his corrupted body, he was capable of achieving his true state. In this manner, the spirit gained victory over the flesh and a glorified body over one wrought with misery.[38]

Vives viewed Judaism as embracing the flesh. This was evi-evidenced by the Talmudic and rabbinic use of anthropomorphisms. Vives rejected descriptions which portrayed God as sitting on a throne in Jerusalem, being prone to good or ill disposition, and having physical appendages. Vives attacked Judaism on the basis of what he considered irrational and illogical. How could all the resurrected fit within Jerusalem? Why are some resurrected but others are not? How could a real messianic era be reduced to a life of physical pleasures in the land of Israel? How could death be part of the messianic age? For Vives, Jewish rituals were senseless. He pointed to the prohibition of pork as an example. The purpose of the commandments was their fulfillment in Christ. The Jew was bound to his literal interpretation of the Scripture and was incapable of understanding its true spiritual meaning. Jewish preoccupation with the literal text prevented the Jew from recognizing the Messiah.

For Vives, the Christian is bound to study the Scripture in a manner which applies reason and judgment. The Scripture must be scrutinized. To fail to do so results in nothing more than childish games to which the student was bound by empty rhetoric. The Jew according to Vives accepts his tradition without any examination. He accepts the commandments as he perceives they were given, without any contemplation of their real meaning. Human reason can provide the spiritual rationale for the commandments to those who are willing to search for it.[39]

Like others before him, Vives contended that Christianity was the true spiritual Judaism. The Law that God entrusted to the

---

[38] Ibid., 5-6.
[39] Ibid., 7-8.

Jewish people is abrogated only in its literal meaning. The real spirspiritual meaning is understood by Christians, and hence Christians observed the Law as it was intended. For Vives, with the exception of individuals like Moses, David or the prophets, Jews are like children to whom God must promise material blessings for them to realize spiritual ones.[40]

In 1523, he wrote a letter in which he related the tragedy of his family situation. Vives was disconcerted by the news of the death of his brother, his father's arrest, the endangerment of the family fortune as well as the status of his three unwed sisters. He was unsure whether to return to Spain or to stay.[41] He did not, despite his wide-ranging contacts including the Inquisitor General, appeal for intervention on his father's behalf. Whether he failed to do so for fear that he would be entangled and subsequently accused of Judaizing is unclear. In 1529, following his father's death and in the midst of the posthumous trial of his mother, Vives dedicated his work titled *Sobre la pacificacion* to none other than the Inquisitor General Alonso Manrique the bishop of Seville.[42]

Unlike Alonso de Cartagena, Vives did not see his Jewish background as a badge of merit or honor. His Jewish ancestry did not link him to the first Jewish followers of Jesus. He saw no benefit in the being part of the people of Israel. For Vives, Christianity entailed the loss of personal identity. His identity was inextricably linked to his faith in Christ.

> "Entering into the mystical body of the Christ, which is the Church, wherein no one lives for himself. Just as with the

---

[40] Ibid., 9.

[41] Vives stated, "…me dice que mi padre esta tambien enfermo de mucha gravedad y que se muere con mu pocas esperanzas; que had entablado un pleito muy serio y con gran sana contra nuestros bienes; que sobreviven tres hermanas mias, pobres ye menores de edad…con estas noticias aumento mi anguista y la inquietude de mi espiritu… No se si en estas circunstancias es conveniente que vaya alli o que me quede…"Angel Gomez-Hortiguela Amillo, "La vida sine querella de Juan Luis Vives," eHumanista 26 (2014): 351.

[42] Angel Gomez-Hortiguela Amillo, "La vida sine querella de Juan Luis Vives," eHumanista 26 (2014): 352.

bread, the grain of wheat is no longer present, but it is ground and made into flour, forming now a mass of dough; [and just as] with many clusters of grapes, once crushed they become wine, the same takes place with the fusion and unification [of individuals] within the Church through charity, in such a fashion that no one lives any longer his own life, but in him lives Christ. The incorpora- incorporation of our being in Christ takes place at the moment that we take him within ourselves. Since it gives peace to each one, one knows that Christ not only inhabits spiritually within, but also bodily, and [he] is the death and life of each one, because in [his] breast he received life."[43]

## Wavering Conversos

Once they escaped from the Iberian Peninsula, practicing Judaism openly was often a challenge for many Conversos. This was particularly true for Conversos of subsequent generations. Some Conversos did not join the Jewish community immediately but hesitated to do so until late in life. Part of this may have been the halakhic obligations and most significantly an unwillingness to be circumcised. Manuel Carvalho for example, claimed to have lived in Amsterdam since the 1560s. He did not embrace Jewish life until 1616. The grandfather of Baruch Spinoza, Henriques Garces arrived in Amsterdam somewhere around 1598. He was not actively religious by 1614. When he died in 1619, he was circumcised after his death to allow his burial in the Jewish cemetery.[44]

A prominent Converso, Duarte da Silva arrived in England in the 1660s with the retinue of Catherine of Braganza, who married King Charles II of England. Duarte did not join the London Jewish community until the end of his life. The same was the case

---

[43] Jose Faur, *In the Shadow of History: Jews and Conversos at the Dawn of Modernity* (New York: SUNY, 1992), 44.
[44] Miriam Bodian, *Hebrews of the Portuguese Nation* (Bloomington: Indiana University Press, 1997), 33.

for other prominent Conversos such as Fernando Mendes da Cos-Costa who had contemplated the return of Conversos to the Portugal if social discrimination and the threat of Inquisitorial persecution ended even if this required a reversion to Catholicism.[45] He and his son Alvaro da Costa were listed as uncircumcised members of the London congregation in the 1680s. Another individual, Solomon Franco, along with his brother came into conflict with Rabbi Jacob Sasportas in 1664-1665 over their unwillingness to follow Halakhah entirely and undergo circumcision.[46]

To individuals who wavered in rejoining the Jewish community, the former Converso Daniel Levi de Barrios of the Amsterdam community wrote the following lines in his poem titled, *Epistola a un mal Encaminado* (i.e. Letter to one who walks a crooked path):

> "You are not liked by one people because you abandoned it; The other people do regard you as faithful because it saw you pretending…You shall depart from (this world) victorious if, before your death you row to the holy shores…Abandon the glorious illusions and then you will surely attain the light of truth in the heavenly spheres of Judaism…Return to the House of God with a loving heart."[47]

The governing board of the Amsterdam community adopted a strict approach to the matter of circumcision. In 1622 for example, it ordered a certain Francisco Lopes Capadosse and his sons to be circumcised. It also ordered that they join the community or be placed under *herem* (i.e. a ban). The *Mahamad* recognized the inherent Jewish status of Conversos arriving in Amsterdam by threatening to punish them. The threat of excommunication

---

[45] Yosef Kaplan, "The Jewish Profile of the Spanish-Portuguese Community of London during the Seventeenth Century," Judaism 41 (1992): 239.

[46] Ibid., 233.

[47] Yosef Kaplan, "The Portuguese Jews in Amsterdam: From Forced Conversion to a Return to Judaism," Studia Rosenthaliana XV, No. 1 (1981): 41.

failed.[48] The goal of the *Mahamad* was to demarcate between those who were circumcised (i.e. demonstrating their commitment to Jewish life) and those who refused to do so.

Cristobal Mendez who was eventually arrested by the Inquisi-Inquisition in Madrid in 1661, related the events that characterized his formal return to Judaism. In 1643, Cristobal had left the Peninsula for Venice where his uncle Abraham Suarez lived. Cristobal was persuaded to undergo circumcision by his uncle and a rabbi named Moses of Toledo. The latter was also former Converso. The rabbi provided Cristobal with a Bible in Spanish and discussed Psalm 19:18 which states "The Law of the LORD is perfect." Cristobal was circumcised a month later. After his circumcision, his uncle provided him with a *tallit* and a set of *tefillin*. He was also given a prayer book which he reviewed during his recovery. Once he recovered he attended the *Scuola Spagnola*, the Spanish Synagogue in Venice where he was called to open the ark and recite *Birkat haGomel* (blessing of deliverance).[49]

Some of those who accepted Jewish life unreservedly nevertheless retained connections to the Christian milieu they had

---

[48] Yosef Kaplan explains that "Francisco Lopez Capadosse was a 'member of the Hebrew Nation' in the ethnic and national sense of the term, who also 'openly acknowledged the unity of the Divinity.' Had he lived in France, Flanders, or England, he would have been considered a respected member of the Nacao. Moreover, had he remained in Spain or Portugal, he would have been regarded as 'one of the conversos of the seed of Israel,' 'a child imprisoned among the gentiles,' in whom the best efforts must be invested to remove him from the valley of the shadow of death and bring him to the open practice of Judaism…Yet upon his arrival in Amsterdam, Francisco was expected to become a fully practicing Jew, a Jew by religion, since equivocating there blurred the boundaries of the renewed Jewish identity, that of the 'New Jews' who had fully detached themselves from their past as Catholic New Christians." Yosef Kaplan, "Wayward New Christians and Stubborn New Jews: The Shaping of a Jewish Identity," Jewish History Volume 8, No. 102 (1994): 30.

[49] Yosef Yerushalmi notes that some rabbis saw fit to impose floggings on Conversos as a sign of contrition. He notes that "in most cases Marranos sought and undertook them voluntarily." He also notes that the matter of an ordained rabbinical court authorized to order biblical stripes on Conversos was a major aspect of the controversy over the revival of ordination between Rabbi Jacob Berab and Rabbi Levin Ibn Habib in 1538. Yosef Hayyim Yerushalmi, *The Re-Education of the Marranos in the Seventeenth Century*. lecture., Hebrew Union College, 1980.

been part of before their public embrace of Judaism. Still other Conversos preferred to live along the edges of the emerging Jewish community.[50] An ordinance adopted by the London Jewish community on January 2, 1678, relates the following:

> "…If a Jewish woman…married someone who is not circumcised- no Jew, *whether or not he is a member of this congregation*, shall attend such a wedding or a party taking place following it. Moreover, it is forbidden for anyone to serve as a witness to such a wedding, or to write out the marriage contract, or to sign it, or to pronounce the seven marriage benedictions, or to be present when they are recited to make up the prayer quorum. Anyone violating any of these prohibitions will be excommunicated, and with him will be banned anyone knowing of such activity who does not inform the lords of the Mahamad that it is taking place."[51]

Many of those on the fringes of the community still married Jewish women and did so according to Jewish law. They maintained their Jewish identity primarily as an inward reality and kept Christian appearances. Their primary connection to other Jews was their ethnic commonality.

Until the end of the seventeenth century, some former Conversos who were now openly Jewish continued to donate to St. Catherine's church in London which was situated close to the synagogue. Church bells were tolled at the passing of several

---

[50] Conversos on the fringes of the community who refused to identify themselves as Jews and to behave in accordance with Jewish were viewed as a threat. The lines defining Jewish identity were blurred. The phenomenon of Jewish identity apart from Judaism was emerging. Yosef Kaplan explains: "…the social and national relation to conversos, even to New Christians whose Jewish identity was faint, differed from the official *Halakhic* view. In the consciousness of the entire community, Conversos were viewed as an integral part of the socio-national group known as the 'Nation.'" Yosef Kaplan, "Wayward New Christians and Stubborn New Jews: The Shaping of a Jewish Identity," Jewish History Volume 8, No. 102 (1994): 27, 30.

[51] Yosef Kaplan, "The Jewish Profile of the Spanish-Portuguese Community of London during the Seventeenth Century," Judaism 41 (1992): 235-236.

members including Mrs. De Brito, Sara Athias, and Antonio Fer-Fernandes Carvajal. This was done despite their burial in accordance with Jewish law. The funeral records of the London community indicate that between 1656 and 1684 only 54% of the dead were buried in the community cemetery. The number of uncircumcised males was quite low indicating that many of even the most involved members of the Spanish-Portuguese nation opted to be buried in plots they had acquired prior to 1656 or next to spouses who had expired before Jews received official recognition to live in London. Being buried in a Jewish cemetery may have brought concern that their Jewish affiliation would negatively impact their economic connections with family members still residing in the Iberian Peninsula.[52]

## Conversos who Rejected Judaism

There were also cases of those who chose not to reintegrate into Jewish life. Antonio Ferreira, who served as Queen Catherine's physician, and his brother Francisco, returned to Portugal and never attempted to join the emerging community in London. Esteban de Ares Fonseca, originally from Lisbon arrived in Amsterdam via Bayonne. The date of his arrival is unclear but likely occurred in the 1620s. His relatives, now openly living as Jews, tried to persuade him to undergo circumcision and live as a Jew. He made it clear that he was not interested in doing so. Their efforts frustrated, they turned to Rabbi Morteira for help in convincing Esteban to embrace Judaism. Esteban lived with Rabbi Morteira for six months but in the end refused to live as a Jew.

Rabbi Morteira issued a ban against him in the synagogue.[53] So strongly did Rabbi Morteira believe in the Jewish status of Esteban, that he was willing to excommunicate him for failing to return to Judaism, a faith neither he nor his ancestors had fully

---

[52] Ibid., 34- 235.
[53] Marc Saperstein, "Christianity, Christians, and 'New Christians' in the Sermons of Saul Levi Morteira," Hebrew Union College Annual, Vol. 70/71, One Hundred Twenty-Fifth Anniversary (1999-2000): 374.

known for generations. After having been excommunicated for approximately two weeks, Esteban acceded and underwent circumcision. The story did not end there, however, and in 1635 he voluntarily presented himself before the Inquisition in Madrid testifying that it had never been his intention to embrace Judaism nor undergo circumcision.[54]

There were others who, after having adopted Judaism officially, opted to return to Christianity. Prominent individuals such as Augstin Coronel Chacon, Solomon Franco, Eliahu de Lima, Isaac de Azevedo, Aaron Gabay, David Gabay, and Jonah Gabay reverted to Christianity after having embraced Judaism. Even Thomas de Rojas, the son of Duarte Enriques Alvares one of the founders of the community in London journeyed to the Canary Islands. There he voluntarily presented evidence before the Inquisition regarding his father and stepmother's adherence to Judaism.[55]

There were others who for whatever reason rejected Judaism and preferred to return to Spain. Gabriel da Costa, Francisco Tomas de Miranda, and Bartolome Mendez Trancoso were among those who desired to go back to the Peninsula. Trancoso requested "safe-conduct so that he, his wife, children and family should not be punished by the Holy Inquisition" if they returned to Spain. To secure this, Trancoso was willing to provide economic information that would prove beneficial to the Spanish Crown. He also named several New Christians in Spain whom he accused of receiving false coinage and were involved in other illegal activity. Francisco Tomas de Miranda offered the Crown information that would purportedly benefit the Spanish treasury. He described himself as "residing in Holland where I live as a Catholic as is well-known and can be checked." Miranda's self-description was not so accurate, however. Yosef Kaplan explains,

---

[54] Yosef Kaplan, "Wayward New Christians and Stubborn New Jews: The Shaping of a Jewish Identity," Jewish History Volume 8, No. 102 (1994): 28.
[55] Yosef Kaplan, "The Jewish Profile of the Spanish-Portuguese Community of London during the Seventeenth Century, " Judaism 41 (1992): 235.

"Still, being compelled by Dutch circumstances to pose outwardly as a Jew, he had no illusions about his status in the eyes of the Inquisition and requested a safe-conduct so that he would be able to go to Madrid. He elicited at least some interest in Madrid though not enough evidently to procure his immunity from the Inquisition."[56]

Rabbi Immanuel Aboab wrote in 1626 or 1627, that "From letters that have arrived from this land [France], it can be seen how many persons of our nation return to Spain."[57] Family members often tried to coax family members still living in the Iberian Peninsula to leave. Some attempted to induce them to do so by excluding them from inheritance should they fail to leave. Others tried to make theological arguments for their family to flee the lands of idolatry.[58]

## Sincere Returnees to Judaism: Abraham Israel Pereyra

Of all the Conversos who escaped the Peninsula and returned to Judaism, few are as intriguing as Abraham Israel Pereyra. Pereyra's path reflects the challenges of many Conversos who struggled to embrace Judaism. While he eventually became a pious Jew in the Amsterdam community, he spent years dismissing the calls to embrace Judaism.

Thomas Rodriguez-Pereyra served at the Spanish court where he managed the royal finances. He arrived in Amsterdam in 1647 preceded by his brother, Isaac. He grew wealthy through the sugar trade and became the most prominent and richest Jewish merchant in the city. He focused on his business affairs. He dismissed the authority of the rabbis and saw himself as more learned that they were. He disdained the rabbis and treated them without respect

---

[56] Ibid., 11-12.
[57] Miriam Bodian, *Hebrews of the Portuguese Nation* (Bloomington: Indiana University Press, 1997), 77.
[58] Ibid., 139.

and focused his life on worldly pleasures. As Pereyra later admit-admitted, "The flesh with its false appetite defeated me..."[59]

Pereyra underwent an unexplained spiritual transformation somewhere between 1647 and 1656. Now known as Abraham Is-Israel Pereyra, he established a *Yeshiva* named *Torah Or* in conjunc-conjunction with Abraham Bueno in 1656. Rabbi Menasseh ben Israel served as its head. In 1659, he also founded another Yeshiva. This one named, *Hessed le Abraham*, was set up in the city of Hebron. He financially supported the printing and publishing endeavors of Rabbi Menasseh ben Israel. While Pereyra changed his ways and became a devout Jew, his Catholic past and education remained a part of him. Even as he attempted to do penance for his dissimulation in the Iberian Peninsula and for his delayed returned to Judaism in Amsterdam, the ongoing influences of Christianity remain clear in his writing. Pereyra was in effect terrified by his past actions and distressed about his future in the World to Come. Pereyra wrote of the grief he felt.[60]

> "Shall I escape from the falsehoods into which I sank? But woe to me! They are so deeply submerged within me that only with difficulty shall I be able to free myself from the false views that dominated me....Use your sense and strength of will and if you have already succeeded in fleeing from the danger of the Inquisition and come to worship the LORD, throw off your (mental) weakness for it shall sentence you to prison...for hundreds of years in

---

[59] Charles Myers and Norman Simms, eds. *Troubled Souls: Conversos, Crypto-Jews, and other Confused Jewish Intellectuals from the Fourteenth through the Eighteenth Century* (Hamilton: Outriggers Publishers: 2001), 57-58.

[60] Yosef Kaplan, "The Portuguese Jews in Amsterdam: From Forced Conversion to a Return to Judaism," *Studia Rosenthaliana* XV, No. 1 (1981): 39. Daniel Levi de Barrios wrote the following sonnet, "Not with tears (LORD) shall I wipe out the stain that de-prives my soul of Thy divine light. For my sin, my terrible foolishness shall I feel more if I do not put a stop to my weeping? Behold, I –of humble spirit- obey thee and praise Thee and seek the path to salvation. In my blindness I delivered myself to the cruel fate of the falsehood that enslaved me...Have mercy (Oh LORD) for I shall flee from myself and in Your loving kindness I shall try not to belong to myself in order to attain the glory of belonging to Thee."

which you shall undergo punishment and torture of which the most difficult will be God's hiding His face from you."[61]

The fact that he had squandered several years in Amsterdam be-before committing himself to live an observant Jewish life motivated him to relate the errors of his ways to other Conversos wavering in their commitment. He also targeted the Conversos, who remained on the Iberian Peninsula. Pereyra appealed to Conversos in his work titled *La Certeza del Camino* (*The Certitude of the Way*). Pereyra contended that Conversos were bound to remove the stain of sin they had acquired by dissimulating in the land of idolatry. In Spain, the purity of blood laws had designated Conversos as tainted by their Jewish ancestry. In 1671, Pereyra also condemned those who failed to leave out of financial consideration and concern for affluence. Pereyra wrote:

> "Let us not be so cruel and because of matters of assets which are not durable, or due to a fear of their loss, endanger the essential thing. A person must devote all he possesses for (the salvation of) his soul. As the King of Sodom said, even though he was an idolater: 'Give me the persons and take the goods to thyself.' (Genesis XIV, 21). We are acting in the opposite way and say to our enemies: Take the persons and give us the goods. The reason that those who remained in those places did so was not, we know, lack of true and good will but a lack of capability to grasp (the severity of) the duty imposed on them."[62]

For Pereyra, Conversos because of their Jewish background and status as Jews were condemned if they did not revert openly to Judaism. Their retention of a limited number of Jewish observances or beliefs while living in the lands of idolatry was

---

[61] Yosef Kaplan, "The Portuguese Jews in Amsterdam: From Forced Conversion to a Return to Judaism," *Studia Rosenthaliana* XV, No. 1 (1981): 43.
[62] Ibid.

insufficient. God would not forgive them for participating in Christian worship. The oddity of Pereyra's heartfelt appeal to Conversos is his predominant use of Christian modes of thought and texts to make his case. Henry Méchoulan contends this is partly the result of Pereyra's ignorance of Hebrew. But it reflected the reality that Conversos, particularly educated ones, were more fluent in Christian and non-Jewish texts that in Jewish ones. The abundance of Christian sources in Pereyra's works led Van Praag to characterize elements of Pereyra's treatises as portions of the Gospel written under rabbinic supervision.[63] The continuing influence of Christian thought coupled with the paucity of Jewish sources in *La Certeza* reveal the seminal challenge that Conversos faced even after having returned to organized Jewish communities.[64]

In one example of his reliance on Christian modes of thought, Pereyra related the responsibility to reproach a neighbor committing a sin per Leviticus 19:17 via the words of Thomas Aquinas who stated that, "The human and divine law is to correct one's neighbor fraternally." Once Conversos fled the lands of idolatry and returned openly to Judaism, Pereyra called them to a life of sanctity and piety that mimicked Christian views on sin. Pereyra considered the soul as trapped in the prison of the body. This state led to sin, and the Jew was tasked with an ever-present struggle to fight his base desires. In the tradition of Plato and Augustine, Pereyra believed that only then could the soul free itself and return to its original home. Pereyra saw the path to God via the hatred of the self. In a manner reflective of Christian asceticism, the flesh was to be mortified, and the Jew was to deny himself at everyone turn.

---

[63] Charles Myers and Norman Simms, eds. *Troubled Souls: Conversos, Crypto-Jews, and other Confused Jewish Intellectuals from the Fourteenth through the Eighteenth Century* (Hamilton: Outriggers Publishers: 2001), 58-61.

[64] Pereyra's later work titled *Espejo de la vanidad del mundo* (The Mirror of the World's Vanity) included many more reference to rabbinic texts though Christian influences were still present. Ibid., 62.

The Converso was to live in a state of continual prayer, fasting, and contrition. He was to suffer in order to atone for his past failures in the hope that he would avoid the fires of hell. The Inquisitional pyres, as horrific as they may have been, were sublime when compared to the prospect of eternal damnation.[65] The physical body was to be maintained at its most minimal level since its only purpose was to provide the individual with the strength necessary to beg God for forgiveness evidenced by self-mortification. Pereyra held that one should fast most of the week excepting Shabbat. Self-flagellation was also encouraged. Pereyra supported regular Jewish observances such as Torah study, *tevilah*, and the recitation of one hundred *Berachot* daily. But even while embracing normative Jewish commandments, he also included foreign elements such as solitude and avoidance of the world. His desire to do so was based on his frustration with many fellow Jews in Amsterdam whom he saw as uncommitted or insufficiently focused on the supremacy of a Torah observant life.

It is no surprise that given his fixation with his pasts sins, that Pereyra like so many other former Conversos was also drawn to the messianic movement of Sabbatai Zevi. The possibility that the messiah might be revealed elated him. The supporters of Sabbatai Zevi in Amsterdam met in the home of the community's cantor. The fact that they were not sanctioned by the *Mahamad* was likely due to Pereyra's presence among them. Zevi's conversion to Islam was naturally a severe blow and according to Méchoulan only convinced Pereyra that the necessity of self-mortification, constant repentance, and prayer was critical.[66]

Abraham Israel Pereyra admitted that when he first arrived in Amsterdam, his own attitude was less than congenial to learning a new way of life.

> "Only with difficulty can I free myself from the false opinions that dominated me for it is difficult to alter

---

[65] Ibid., 59.
[66] Ibid., 60.

oneself...since I was acquainted with secular works (what ignorance!) I considered myself wiser than the sages of the Torah...and when I spoke about them I did so with little respect; since my will then tended towards things of delight I thought up reasons (which I believed) to confound vir-virtue."[67]

Abraham Israel Pereyra recommended that a returning Converso pursue the following plan of study.

"You must when leaving the synagogue and arriving home, take a Bible and read it...and when studying it concentrate all your attention and do not read without it...stop at each difficulty and enquire about it, and fix yourself an exact time in one of the Yeshivot for this is the true remedy and you shall learn by means of it, by presenting your doubts...and listening to the answers of the experts and you shall thus heal your soul at that time...and in this way, you shall enjoy the persistency and attention that you devote to learning the Bible and studying other books, and it was in this way that I studied at Yeshiva 'Torah Or' under our faithful shepherd, the noble Haham Ishac Aboab. I enjoyed his teaching and the sweet company of the other gentlemen and friends."[68]

---

[67] Yosef Kaplan, "The Portuguese Jews in Amsterdam: From Forced Conversion to a Return to Judaism," *Studia Rosenthaliana* XV, No. 1 (1981): 48.

[68] Ibid., 47. Regarding Abraham Israel Pereyra's own return to Judaism and study, Rabbi Raphael d'Aguilar noted that "This magnificent person arrived from Spain with only a simple and vague knowledge of the truth of our holy Torah which those countries allow one to obtain; he came here to a place in which one can observe it and study it in ample freedom; but (he arrived) at a late age when study of the holy language was difficult and tiring for him. But since righteousness was part and parcel of his nature and character, he first of all began to attend Yeshivot regularly, to listen attentively to the words of learning that were uttered in them and to study books of faith; in this way he accumulated a precious store of holy wisdom...but this pious man was not content with knowledge for himself but tried to get others to participate in his religious doctrines for 'it is not good for man to be alone' ...and with this aim in mind he abandoned worldly

## Isaac Orobio de Castro

Balthazar Orobio de Castro was born in Bragança, Portugal in 1617. He died in 1687. He studied philosophy at Alcalá de Henares and taught philosophy at the University of Salamanca. He eventu-eventually studied medicine and practiced in Seville. He served as the physician to the duke of Medina-Celi. De Castro was arrested by the Inquisition after a servant had testified he was a Judaizer. He spent three years in prison. He eventually confessed under torture and was finally released.

He moved to Toulouse where he taught medicine at the univer-university. He was granted the title of councilor by Louis XIV. De Castro eventually moved to Amsterdam in the middle of the 1660s and openly returned to Judaism where he changed his name to Isaac. De Castro practiced medicine in Amsterdam and served as a member of the *Mahamad*.

De Castro was a prolific author. One work critiqued Spinoza's ethics. Despite opposition to his views, de Castro maintained an affable correspondence with Spinoza. He also authored works against idolatry and a commentary on Isaiah 53. He wrote the work titled *Epistola Invectiva Contra un Judio Philosopho Médico, que Negava la Ley de Mosse, y Siendo Atheista Affectava la Ley de Naturaleza*. This manuscript was directed against Juan de Prado, a physician and former colleague who now lived in Amsterdam and had influenced Spinoza.

De Castro's successful integration into Judaism was extraordinary as evidenced by his literary accomplishments. He described two types of Conversos who reached Jewish communities and their reactions to this new life. In the prologue to his work, titled *Epistola Invectiva*, he related that,

---

affairs, refrained from idle talk and devoted himself to the inner contemplative life…"
Ibid.

"Those who make [their] away from idolatry [i.e. Christian-Christianity] to the provinces where there is freedom for Judaism are of two kinds; here are some who upon arriving at a [place] of harbor, apply their entire will to love the divine Law, and procure (as much as the power of their understanding allows them) to learn what is required of them in order to observe religiously the sacred commandments, laws, and ceremonies that they and their elders had forgotten during the Captivity [in the Iberian Peninsula]. Humbly, they listen to those who, since were brought up in Judaism and studied the Law, can explain it. They endeavor (as much as their understanding permits them) to adopt the style and worthy traditions and customs observed by Israel throughout the whole world, everyone in accordance with his state and possibility, [in order] to arrange his life in the service of God and avoid the errors that previously his ignorance gave occasion to. Those who had arrived sick with ignorance, were easily healed, enjoying the holy and healthy medicine that the piety of their brethren offered them; since, upon arrival – from the greatest Haham[rabbinic scholar] to the lowliest lay person- all try to teach them in order that they would not err in the observance of the divine Law."[69]

Other Conversos were not as enthusiastic. Isaac Orobio de Castro also described another type of Converso, who was less inclined to conform to this new life. The university education that many had received in Spain or Portugal was an impediment to embracing the Torah and its commandments.

"Others who come to Judaism have learned certain profane sciences [while] in Idolatry [Christianity], such as logic, physics, metaphysics, and medicine. These are no less ignorant of God's Law than the first ones. However,

---

[69] Jose Faur, *In the Shadow of History: Jews and Conversos at the Dawn of Modernity* ( New York: State University of New York Press, 1992), 111.

because they are full of vanity, arrogance and pride, [they] are] convinced to be extremely wise in every subject, [and that] they know everything; and although they ignore the most essential [elements of Judaism], they believe that they know everything. When they enter under the happy yoke of Judaism, [and] proceed to hear from those who know that which they ignore, their vanity and arrogance does not permit them to receive [the] doctrine [of Judaism and] escape their ignorance. They believe that if they would be taught by those who are truly [the sages] of the holy Law, they would no longer be credited as learned. They pretend [to have] a great science by contradicting that which they do not understand, although it is all true, all holy, all divine. They think that by making sophisticated arguments without any foundation, they are accrediting themselves as ingenious and scientific."[70]

In Spain or Portugal Conversos had actually served as their own "halakhic authorities." Since they had rejected the authority of the Church, the tendency to question authority was present making the path towards integration in the synagogue that much harder.[71] The Judaizing practices and beliefs they observed in the Peninsula often stood in contrast to standard Jewish practices. The latter were likely seen as unfamiliar at best, and alien at worst. As Miriam Bodian notes, the Law of Moses was often more of a symbol than a practical reality to most Conversos.[72] But the goal of collectively returning openly to Judaism required that rabbinic norms be adopted and upheld.[73]

---

[70] Ibid., 112.

[71] Yosef Hayyim Yerushalmi, *The Re-Education of the Marranos in the Seventeenth Century.* lecture., Hebrew Union College, 1980.

[72] Miriam Bodian, *Hebrews of the Portuguese Nation* (Bloomington: Indiana University Press, 1997), 30.

[73] ibid. 19.

De Castro revealed his questions regarding the commandments. Unlike others, though, he did not transform such issues into a rejection of rabbinic authority or of the Torah. De Castro wrote:

> "Of what importance is it that this or that limitation ap-appears to be inappropriate to our understanding? Of what significance is it that the prohibition to eat dairy products and poultry together is incomprehensible to us...? Shall we, due to (our lack of understanding) desecrate the Sabbath? Or shall we eat well on the Day of Atonement? Or shall we drink blood...Whoever loves (the Torah), believes in it and fears God, does not seek reasons to forsake it...it is not sensible to upset the tranquility of others with these doubts and lead them to meditation."[74]

De Castro regularly turned towards the rabbis when doubts or questions arose regarding the observance of the commandments or Judaism in general. There were cases, however when the arguments put forward by them were insufficient to convince De Castro that the arguments being made were correct. Yosef Kaplan argues that De Castro's previous theological and philosophical training may have contributed to his struggle in accepting certain arguments given for justifying certain observances. In the end, honest as he was regarding those elements of Jewish law that troubled him, De Castro wrote that "...it is necessary at all times that the Law be taught to the people by those sages who delve into its significance as did the priests, the judges and the prophets in the past, for no one is an expert in the Law from birth."[75] Like the case of David Farrar, and in contrast to that of Uriel da Costa, De Castro was content to express his doubts without undermining rabbinic authority or ritual observance.[76]

---

[74] Yosef Kaplan, "The Portuguese Jews in Amsterdam: From Forced Conversion to a Return to Judaism," *Studia Rosenthaliana* XV, No. 1 (1981): 49.
[75] Ibid., 49.
[76] Ibid., 50.

De Castro admitted he had found it difficult to leave Spain for financial reasons. In his response to Juan de Prado, Baruch Spino-Spinoza's mentor, De Castro wrote that,

> "In Spain, I pretended to be a Christian because life is pleasant, but I was never a good pretender, and I was found to be a Jew. And if there – were ones' freedom, honour, and property and even life were in danger- I was, in fact, a Jew and only outwardly a Christian, it may be assumed that where divine providence grants me a life of liberty, I shall be a real Jew."

Once confronted with reality, De Castro unreservedly embraced Jewish life.[77] The challenge of leaving the Peninsula or other lands where Judaism was prohibited often entailed the separation of families. Parents, siblings and even spouses were left behind at times. For some, the ability to join the Jewish community compensated for this enormous loss.

## Samuel Yahya

An intriguing figure in the Converso community in Hamburg was Alvaro Dinis, who was also known by the alias Samuel Yahya. Samuel was born in Antwerp in 1576 and settled in Hamburg in 1605. Samuel was critical in the formation of the Hamburg Converso community. His Jewish education was extensive as revealed in his sermons. He was conversant in Hebrew and was able to reference various sources including Rashi, Maimonides, Abravanel, and the Shulchan Aruch. He was also familiar with the Zohar.[78]

Two of his sermons focused on the validity of the Oral Torah showing that even in a community that was still dissimulating, the proper observance of the Law was a concern. Yahya was aware of

---

[77] Ibid., 39.
[78] Julia R. Lieberman, "Sermons and the Construct of a Jewish Identity: The Hamburg Sephardic Community in the 1620s," Jewish Studies Quarterly, Vol. 10, No. 1 (2003): 50, 52.

the sensitivity this issue presented among his community of Con-Conversos. Uriel de Costa lived in Hamburg between 1614 and 1618 and may have been the target of some of Yahya's sermons. When his sermons were published, he purposely omitted one of these sermons out of deference to the dissenters in his group. Yahya was particularly concerned with ensuring that the incumbency of Torah observance was clear to all members.

One of his sermons focused on doubts (*dudas*), an indication of the place many Conversos found themselves. Yahya referred to God's love which demands loyalty while simultaneously allowing free will. Based on Psalm 44:21, Yahya offered the following interpretation: "If we forgot the name of our God/and spread forth our hands to a foreign god, God would surely search it out/for He knows the secrets of the heart."[79] Whatever had transpired in or outside the Peninsula, a genuine love for God would guarantee that God would not abandon His people. This was proven by the verse from Deuteronomy 4:31 stating, "For the LORD your God…will not fail you, nor He will let you perish." Having participated in idolatrous practices was a personal matter between each individual and God.[80] The challenge was the fact those in that the Hamburg community were still forced to hide their Jewish identity from their neighbors until 1652, seven years after Yahya's passing.[81]

Yahya related that God's love for Israel was natural and could never be detached. Conversos had little choice on the question of Jewish identity. They were born Jewish and would remain so despite their having lived as Christians for generations. Yahya appealed to the idea that all souls had been created at the beginning of the world and that the souls of all Jews were present

---

[79] Ibid., 62.
[80] Ibid., 53, 60.
[81] Ibid., 51.

at Sinai. Consequently, Jews could not reject or release themselves from the covenant.[82]

In another sermon, Yahya focused on the incumbency of the Oral Torah. In the vein of works like Rabbi Immanuel Aboab's *Nomologia* and Rabbi Leon Modena's *Magen ve-Tsinnah,* Yahya deliv-delivered the sermon "in order to show the responsibility of all of the seed of Israel to believe the declaration of the Oral Law, received in Sinai [and was] preached on the occasion and in the presence of some of our own who did not understand the truth."[83] The commandment of circumcision was critical. Yahya referenced the Zohar in stating that through circumcision God saves Israel from the fires of Gehinnom. He cautioned that ongoing sin would nevertheless make salvation a painful process.[84]

Yahya argued the Oral Torah was necessary to understand the Written Torah. He also explained the rationale for the Oral Torah not having been originally written down. The rabbis were entrusted with the responsibility for determining how the commandments were observed. Yahya provided various examples highlighting the vagueness of certain biblical texts and the illumination given by the Oral Torah.

In an attempt to convince his listeners not to reject the Oral Torah in favor of their own interpretation of the Written Torah, Yahya pointed his listeners to the passage in the *Pirke Avot* which instructed the children of Israel to warm themselves by the fire of the sages. *Pirke Avot* warns readers to be careful lest they are burned by the glowing coals of the fire. All Jews were responsible for observing the Oral Torah, and Yahya issued an explicit threat of excommunication for those failing to keep it.[85] The fact that Yahya was able to threaten such punishment to members of a

---

[82] Ibid., 61, 63.
[83] Ibid., 63, 64.
[84] Ibid., 59.
[85] Ibid., 64, 70.

secret community reveals the complex identity of Conversos, who endeavored to maintain Jewish practices.

## Abraham Miguel Cardozo

In 1665, Sabbatai Zevi traveled to Gaza and was declared the Messiah by Nathan Ashkenazi, a Kabbalist, and purported prophet.[86] Sabbatai Zevi and his messianic movement thrust much of the Jewish world into an eschatological frenzy.[87] The movement was widely supported by former Conversos.[88]

Cities like Istanbul, Salonika, Livorno, Amsterdam, and Venice were centers of Sabbateanism and were hubs of Converso settlement. [89] Former Conversos were among Zevi's closest

---

[86] David J. Halperin, trans., *Abraham Miguel Cardozo: Selected Writings* (New York: Paulist Press, 2001), 46.

[87] In 1666, the governing board of the *Beit Israel* community of Hamburg composed of former Conversos debated whether a delegation should be sent out to the Levant to pay respect to king Sabbatai Zevi who was anointed by the God of Jacob. The *Mahamad* adopted a resolution to sell all communally owned buildings since "with the grace of God, we hope to set out soon" to the Land of Israel. Ezer Kahanoff, "On Marranos and Sabbateans: a reexamination of charismatic religiosity - its roots, its place and its significance in the life of the Western Sephardi diaspora," Ma'of u-Ma'aseh 8 (2002): 112-113.

[88] In 1666, many of the members of the community in Amsterdam succumbed to the predominant enthusiasm, as had their sister community in Hamburg. Prayers were offered in the synagogue denoting Zevi as King Messiah. Some prayer books were printed which included reference to year one of the Messiah, and even incorporated etchings portraying Sabbatai Zevi. Some members of the community traveled to Adrianople to meet the professed messiah. Moshe Idel *,Messianic Mystics* (New Haven: Yale University Press, 1998), 152. See also Gershom Scholem, *The Messianic Idea in Judaism*, (New York: Shocken, 1972), 41. Samuel Primo, Sabbatai Zevi's personal secretary voiced his belief in who Zevi truly was. According to Primo, Zevi was "King of the World…your king and savor, who brings your dead back to life, who saves you from the oppression of the Gentiles and the punishments of Hell." For Primo, Zevi was the Almighty and the Sabbath incarnate. Primo eventually served as rabbi in Adrianople. David J. Halperin, trans., *Abraham Miguel Cardozo: Selected Writings* (New York: Paulist Press, 2001), 52.

[89] Matt Goldish, *The Sabbatean Prophets*, (Cambridge: Harvard University Press, 2004), 45. According to Moshe Idel, "The presence of significant numbers of former conversos in many centers of Jewish population paved the way for a positive response to Sabbatean nihilistic and antinomian doctrines. These doctrines struck a deep chord within those religiously tormented people, sometimes unsatisfied or in many cases also more strongly uneasy with the painful process of acceptance of rabbinic Judaism." Moshe Idel, *Messianic Mystics* (New Haven: Yale University Press, 1998), 184.

associates in his youth, and several were among the first to support his messianic claims. [90] These included Rabbi Moses HaCohen Isaac Silveyra, the physician Abraham Baruch, and Rabbi Moses Pinheiro.[91]

## Abraham Miguel Cardozo and Sabbatai Zevi

Abraham Miguel Cardozo was born in 1626 to a Converso family in Rio Seco, Spain and played a key role in the evolving Sabbatean movement. Cardozo studied medicine and possibly theology at the University of Salamanca. Cardozo later recalled that,

> "When I was six years old, my parents made known to me that I was a Jew. When I was twelve...I took to reading the [Old Testament] Scriptures in Latin, despite the tremendous danger that this entails everywhere in Spain."[92]

Michael and his older brother left Spain in 1648 and journeyed to Italy where they returned to Judaism. Abraham lived in Italy for a time and continued his medical studies. He found success as a physician. He also studied rabbinic texts extensively but eventually grew dissatisfied with traditional Jewish theology and the rabbinic

---

[90] The Sabbatean pamphlet titled *Fin de los dia* was an assortment of sermons on the looming redemption authored by Gideon Abudiente, a former Converso. Gershom Scholem: *Sabbatai Sevi: The Mystical Messiah: 1626-1676* (London: Routledge Kegan Paul: 1973), 529.

[91] Jacob Barnai identified Rabbi Moses Pinheiro as a former Portuguese Converso. Ezer Kahanoff, "On Marranos and Sabbateans: a reexamination of charismatic religiosity - its roots, its place and its significance in the life of the Western Sephardi diaspora," Ma'of u-Ma'aseh 8 (2002): 133. Yosef Kaplan views the unique backgrounds of Conversos as a critical reason for Zevi's initial success among them. "...as crypto-Jews, they had been precluded from sharing a mode of life founded by Jewish Law, many of them came to feel that an interior, emotionally-felt identity with the Jewish heritage was more important than the actual implementation of the commandments." Yosef Kaplan, *From Christianity to Judaism* (Oxford: Oxford University Press, 1989), 380.

[92] David J. Halperin, trans., *Abraham Miguel Cardozo: Selected Writings* (New York: Paulist Press, 2001), 7.

establishment.⁹³ He claimed that a monk who was trained in rabbinic texts challenged the Jewish community to explain the true nature of God given the complexity of Kabbalistic phrases and ideas. Unsettled by this, he left Livorno and Venice and headed for Egypt where he studied Kabbalah.⁹⁴ He eventually settled in Tripoli.⁹⁵ Cardozo had high expectations and believed he was instrumental in the eventual revelation of the Davidic Messiah. In a story reminiscent of the tale of St. Christopher, Cardozo stated,

> "In the year 5409 [1648-1649] I was studying the Torah in Venice...I had a dream that the Messiah had appeared and that the people of Venice did not believe in him. But God gave me strength, and I seated him on my shoulders and proclaimed through the market-places, 'This is the true Messiah!'"⁹⁶

Cardozo claimed to have received spiritual revelations beginning in Livorno in 1659 and continuing thereafter. Cardozo claimed to have received one such revelation in Tripoli in 1665. The revelations were generally given through the women of his household, but Cardozo was the only one capable of interpreting them. The heavens related to him that King Messiah would soon be revealed. He was told that one of his wives would become pregnant with a male child.⁹⁷ The child would "give the light of

---

⁹³ Cardozo states, "I learned Scriptures, Mishnah, and Gemara. My teachers were the flawless scholars Rabbi Abraham Vallensi, Samuel Aboab, and Moses Zacuto...[I studied] the Bible commentators, the Geonim, and the midrashim." David J. Halperin, trans., *Abraham Miguel Cardozo: Selected Writings* (New York: Paulist Press, 2001), 13.

⁹⁴ Cardozo states, "My head swirled. I found myself once gain caught in a web of doubts. To escape them, to find for myself some kind of spiritual equilibrium, I set out for Egypt...I wanted medicine to heal this wound of mine." David J. Halperin, trans., *Abraham Miguel Cardozo: Selected Writings* (New York: Paulist Press, 2001), 21.

⁹⁵ Matt Goldish, *The Sabbatean Prophets*, (Cambridge: Harvard University Press, 2004), 97.

⁹⁶ David J. Halperin, trans., *Abraham Miguel Cardozo: Selected Writings* (New York: Paulist Press, 2001), 37.

⁹⁷ Cardozo had a large household that by 1674 included four wives. David J. Halperin, trans., *Abraham Miguel Cardozo: Selected Writings* (New York: Paulist Press, 2001), 44.

the king messiah, but then fall ill in within ten days and die." The baby was born, and according to Cardozo, news arrived that day in Tripoli that the King Messiah (i.e. Sabbatai Zevi) had been revealed. The baby died shortly afterward as predicted.[98] Other revelations occurred, and some were accompanied by miracles. Cardozo claimed he was partially healed of cataracts and his sister in law had her crippled hand and foot healed as signs these visions were true.[99]

In the spring of 1666, Cardozo was told that a heavenly sign would appear. The sign would be "a great star as big as the full moon, in order to strengthen my faith concerning the messiah…" In May of 1666, Cardozo claimed that on the 15$^{th}$ day of the counting of the Omer, which fell on a Sabbath, a star "was revealed in the east, big as the sun and distant from it be ten cubits to the right."[100] Cardozo claimed other people also witnessed the event. Cardozo questioned what these portents meant. He asked God for direction and was told that Sabbatai Zevi was destined to rule.[101] His support of Sabbatai Zevi eventually led to a severing of the relationship with his brother who rejected Zevi's messianic claims.[102] His brother Isaac Cardozo won fame on his own accord when he wrote the book titled *Las Excelencias y Calumnias de los Hebreos*. In it, he defended the virtues of traditional Judaism.[103]

---

[98] Goldish notes that Cardozo may have seen himself as a harbinger of the messiah but modeled on the Christian interpretation of the prophet Isaiah. This is particularly reflected in case of his son, which bears similarity to Isaiah 9:5. This pass is a passage traditionally interpreted as messianic by Christian interpretation. Interestingly, Sabbatai Zevi made a similar pronouncement regarding the birth of his own son whom he said would not survive. Matt Goldish, *The Sabbatean Prophets* (Cambridge: Harvard University Press, 2004), 100.

[99] Matt Goldish, *The Sabbatean Prophet* (Cambridge: Harvard University Press, 2004), 98.

[100] Goldish is quick to point out the similarity between the gospel of Matthew's story (2:2, 9-10) about the birth of Jesus and the appearance of the star in the east. Ibid., 101.

[101] Ibid., 99.

[102] Bruce Rosenstock, "Abraham Miguel Cardozo's Messianism: A Reappraisal," AJS Review, Vol. 23, No. 1 (1998): 63.

[103] David J. Halperin, trans., *Abraham Miguel Cardozo: Selected Writings* (New York: Paulist Press, 2001), 12. Cardozo also claimed that the coming of the Messiah had been revealed to him previously. He states, "After the year 5423 [1662-1663] had begun… I

On September 15, 1666, the Zevi appeared before the Sultan of the Ottoman Empire.[104] Sabbatai Zevi emerged from his session with the Sultan a convert to Islam. He was now proclaimed as the hidden Messiah of Israel by many of his followers. Some Sabbateans followed Zevi's example and converted to Islam.

Interestingly, Cardozo unlike Nathan of Gaza or Samuel Primo was never part of Zevi's inner circle. Cardozo never even met Sabbatai Zevi, at least while he was alive. Cardozo claimed that Sabbatai appeared to him after the latter's death. For all his passion and support, Cardozo was viewed as following his own path.[105] Cardozo emphasized that the Torah as it then existed would soon no longer be needed. To achieve this, there was a need to cast off the yoke of Exile and all it involved. Gershom Scholem explains this required "...negating its religious and institutional forms as well as returning to the original fountainheads of the Jewish faith."[106] Cardozo believed the humiliation of Messiah ben David was alluded to in Isaiah 53. This meant that,

> "The Messiah will perform actions that are beyond the Torah's limits, and that break the commandments. He will say things that must be seen violent and deceitful to all who see him or hear about him. They will repudiate him. They will declare him loathsome and contemptible, scoundrel and criminal; they will refuse to him all credence."[107]

---

saw in a dream the following words written out: 'The Redeemer will come in that year 5425 [1664-1665]...And so it happened." Ibid., 43.

[104] Ibid. 66.

[105] David J. Halperin, trans., *Abraham Miguel Cardozo: Selected Writings* (New York: Paulist Press, 2001), 54.

[106] Ezer Kahanoff, "On Marranos and Sabbateans: a reexamination of charismatic religiosity - its roots, its place and its significance in the life of the Western Sephardi diaspora," Ma'of u-Ma'aseh 8 (2002): 128.

[107] David J. Halperin, trans., *Abraham Miguel Cardozo: Selected Writings* (New York: Paulist Press, 2001), 137-138.

Consequently, Zevi's conversion to Islam was not a treacherous act. It was a necessary action to begin the redemptive process. Na-Nathan of Gaza, Zevi's principal supporter had already asserted that Sabbatai was "…good on the inside but his garment is evil." With his strange acts and debasement, Sabbatai was actually demonstrating a mastery over the demonic realm. He had become subservient and debased himself in order to set free the fallen sparks.[108] Cardozo noted that,

> "… The King Messiah wanted nothing other than to sanctify God's name and the Turkish king wanted nothing other than according to his counsel to dress him in garments of shame. Thus, he was violated (*anus*) in every way and from every quarter. And the reason for our iniquities and the prime secret to which we are obligated by the Torah is that all of us must be *anusim* before we leave the Galut, as it is written in the Torah that 'you shall serve other gods of wood and stone' …and of their abandoning Torah, defamation was destined for the Messiah the son of David so that he will be forced against his will in such a way that he will not be able to obey the Torah."[109]

Cardozo argued, however, that the extraordinary act of apostasy committed by Zevi was a singular act, which was not to be followed by Sabbatean supporters.[110]

---

[108] Ibid., xiii.

[109] Rabbi Jacob Sasportas had noted that "…the sages say that in the future Israel will sing, but will not do so until the Messiah be abused, and it is written: "wherewith they have taunted the footsteps of Thine anointed…" For Sabbateans this may have been replaced by the idea that the Messiah was to undergo humiliation. Here the words of Nathan the Prophet prior to his Zevi's conversion stated the messiah would be: "…oppressed among the kelippot, to cleanse all our sins, to repair all that we have injured." Even Don Isaac Abravanel spoke of a Messiah who is to be born in one of the Christian countries, and tortured and humiliated like his Jewish brethren, the Converso Molcho (formerly Diogo Pires) spoke of a Messiah actually born into Christianity. Ezer Kahanoff, "On Marranos and Sabbateans: a reexamination of charismatic religiosity - its roots, its place and its significance in the life of the Western Sephardi diaspora," Ma'of u-Ma'aseh 8 (2002): 125-126.

[110] ibid. 66.

Cardozo's views on a debased Messiah were partly influenced by the Kabbalistic text known as *The Faithful Shepherd* (*Ra'ya Mehmna*) which was incorporated into the Zohar. In the text, the faithful shepherd is none other than Moses. Elijah, Rabbi Shimon bar Yohai, and even Moses himself portray Moses as a suffering servant. The imagery of Isaiah 53 was evident to Cardozo. He believed that the sufferings and profanations that Moses endured on behalf of Israel were a foreshadowing of what Sabbatai Zevi endured.[111] Cardozo strove to show that his belief in Sabbatai Zevi did not stem from any personal sense of suffering or exile. From a purely physical perspective, he enjoyed material success and had the opportunity to study Torah with little interruption. His goal was the redemption of Israel.[112]

Despite his commitment, Cardozo struggled to define Sabbatean faith amidst the reality of a degraded Messiah. Zevi's apostasy and self-humiliation were eerily close to that of Jesus in Christianity. Notwithstanding the challenge, Cardozo was determined to use biblical passages most often associated by Christians asserting the messianic claims of Jesus. Bruce Rosenstock comments that,

> "Although he was not afraid to use the Suffering Servant passage in Isaiah 53 as a proof text for the messianic status of the debased Sabbatai Zevi, he sought to distinguish Sabbatai Zevi's debasement from that of Jesus by claiming that Sabbatai Zevi would not die in a condition of debasement as Jesus had: 'And we say that between the abasement and the glory of the Messiah son of David,

---

[111] Citing the *Faithful Shepherd*, Cardozo writes "The Holy Lamp [Rabbi Simeon ben Yohai] stood up and said: Master of the world! Here is the Faithful Shepherd...the equal of six hundred thousand Israelites...Of him it is said, with reference to he generation of the Last Exile: 'The Lord inflicted upon him the sin of us all' [Isa 53:6]...Yet the rabbinic scholars have now awareness of the Faithful Shepherd." David J. Halperin, trans., *Abraham Miguel Cardozo: Selected Writings* (New York: Paulist Press, 2001), 123, 127-128.

[112] Ibid.,161.

there must be no death, for the Messiah son of David does not have to die.'"[113]

When Zevi died in 1676, Cardozo retooled his theory yet again to incorporate the traditional idea of Messiah ben Joseph and Messiah ben David. Cardozo remained intensely engaged in the surviving movement debating against other Sabbateans who adopted the view that the Messiah was divine. Cardozo rejected these views arguing that they had in short adopted Christian beliefs.

Cardozo argued that Sabbatai Zevi was the Davidic Messiah and in an interesting twist claimed that he, David Cardozo was the Messiah ben Joseph. The influences of his Converso past reveal themselves. In viewing himself as Messiah ben Ephraim, Cardozo related that he was,

> "destined to be born among the uncircumcised. Unwillingly, therefore, will he worship their idols. He will learn their sciences, including the science of Divinity that they call *teologia*. As a result, there will not be a single one, of all the distorted doctrines to which the uncircumcised give credence, with which I am not conversant."[114]

In his treatise titled *Qodesh Yisrael*, Cardozo laid out the case for his own claims to fill this role. Cardozo worked with the various acronyms resulting from the first and last letters of various biblical phrases. He also did this with the phrases "Messiah son of David" and "Messiah, son of Ephraim." Cardozo derived that his name "Michael son of Abraham" equated the sequence of "Messiah, son of Ephraim."[115] In a complex argument, Cardozo saw himself

---

[113] Bruce Rosenstock, "Abraham Miguel Cardozo's Messianism: A Reappraisal," AJS Review, Vol. 23, No. 1 (1998): 66-67.

[114] David J. Halperin, trans., *Abraham Miguel Cardozo: Selected Writings* (New York: Paulist Press, 2001), 10.

[115] Ibid., 10. Cardozo also wrote that "I am the man they call, at times, *mem-bet-aleph*, which are the [Hebrew] initials of *Michael ben Abraham*, At other times I am called *aleph-mem-koph: Abraham Michael Cardozo*. I am of the Marranos of Spain." As Halperin points out, the Hebrew letters *mem-bet-aleph* could also render *Messiah ben Ephraim*. Ibid., 5, 42.

fulfilling a critical role in Israel's redemption. Cardozo argued that he as the Messiah ben Ephraim would provide a more lucid and intelligible understanding of the Messiah's message regarding true faith. Cardozo viewed himself as a speculum that shined in contrast to that Sabbatai Zevi, who did not. Cardozo believed his role was essential to Sabbatai's mission. Cardozo wrote that "Messiah ben David and Messiah ben Ephraim are called Messiah when the two of them are together. Each of them is a half Messiah."[116] Bruce Rosenstock argues that the reference here is tied to the Kabbalistic terminology reflective of male energy within *sefirotic* arrangements. Cardozo argued that he possessed a greater clarity of the divine than even Sabbatai Zevi had obtained.[117] Despite his aversion to emulating anything Christian, Cardozo appears to have done just that by arguing for an inherent unity between both messianic figures.[118]

Bruce Rosenstock asserts that the death of Sabbatai forced Cardozo to revise his earlier views regarding the splendor and mission of his co-Messiah.[119] In a text written before Sabbatai's death, Cardozo had described Zevi in the following terms:

> "Now we must make clear that no creature is able to grasp with knowledge the affairs of the King Messiah because his knowledge is greater and higher than of all who have ever passed through the world or whoever will, whether in purity or its opposite [i.e. whether members of Israel or

---

[116] David J. Halperin, trans., *Abraham Miguel Cardozo: Selected Writings* (New York: Paulist Press, 2001), 245.

[117] Bruce Rosenstock, "Abraham Miguel Cardozo's Messianism: A Reappraisal," AJS Review, Vol. 23, No. 1 (1998): 70- 71.

[118] Bruce Rosenstock argues that while Cardozo's claiming to be the Messiah ben Joseph may seem odd at first glance, it was not as awkward as might first appear. He points to the fact that Rabbi Isaac Luria's disciples considered him the Messiah ben Joseph. Rosenstock also points to the case of Rabbi Samson b. Pesah of Ostropol. Pesah died during the 1648 disasters. A contemporary of Sabbatai Zevi, Rabbi Nehemiah Cohen even argued with Zevi because he believed that he and not Zevi was the Messiah ben Joseph. ibid. 67-68.

[119] Ibid., 71.

not]. And this is what the sages hinted at in saying [TB San83b] that the Hole One, blessed be He, would lay upon the Messiah commandments as a heavy burden which enjoins upon him strange things which will be done by the King messiah to the point that they will appear strange in the eyes of all the world. Indeed, because they are established as a remedy for their own heavy burdens, the deeds which are strange in the eyes of all people are heavy [for the King Messiah]. There is no one who is able to comprehend them in any way or manner because they are profoundly hidden acts of reparation [tiqqunim]... (Maggen 'Abraham, p.137)."[120]

Following the death of Zevi, Cardozo constructed an interpretation of Zevi's conversion to Islam as a test of faith for the Jewish people. Rosenstock describes Cardozo's description as

"...a stage in Israel's path to knowledge from out the blindness of its faith. I see this reconceptualization of the strange deeds of the Messiah as springing from Cardozo's desire to present an image of a Messiah without the taint of debasement, even it if means presenting another Messiah, the Messiah son of Ephraim, as the one who fulfills what Sabbatai Zevi began."[121]

Cardozo nevertheless asserted that faith in Zevi, as the Messiah son of David was necessary, as Zevi had done what no Jewish messianic figure would have done- apostatize. Zevi was a debased figure rather than a great king. To offset the obvious problem, Cardozo laid the responsibility on the Jewish people for the ultimate success or failure of his mission. Without the faith of the Jewish people, Zevi's mission and hence Israel's redemption could not be realized. Cardozo stated: "Faith is a speculum which does not shine, and knowledge is a speculum which does shine, and

---

[120] Ibid.,71.
[121] Ibid., 72.

someone who wishes to ascent to knowledge must enter through the door of faith because this is the gate of the LORD."[122]

Cardozo's beliefs embraced anti-elitism and anti-rabbinic sentiment. In his role as an anti-elitist Messiah, Cardozo believed he would share the secrets of Israel's redemption bearing knowledge to the masses of Israel. Cardozo believed the experience of Conversos was critical to understanding the messianic redemption. He stated, "the King Messiah was destined to wear the clothes of a converso [*anus*] because of which the Jews would not recognize him...he was destined to be a converso like me."[123] The purpose of this was to atone for Israel's sin of idolatry. His past as a Converso and his inability to escape this identity is revealed in his treatise, *Qodesh Yisra'el*:

> "Abraham Cardozo...was destined to be born among the uncircumcised in order to bring forth the sparks which fell from holiness and also the sparks which fell from Yesod in accordance with the secret of the emission. And the gazelle [Zevi] always turns its face towards the place from which it came, and this relates to the Messiah son of David, who had to depart from the entirety of Israel, from the Torah, and from holiness into impurity and even from his body, which must return to him, in order to hasten the ingathering, and because of all this his name is Zevi. But the Messiah son of Ephraim shall go from impurity into holiness, and it is not fitting for him to turn his face back toward the place from he came. Because the uncircumcised are now declaring Jesus to be like God, it is fitting for the Messiah son of Ephraim to say 'Who is like God?'...and

---

[122] Ibid., 74.

[123] Ibid., 90. Matt Goldish, *The Sabbatean Prophets*, (Cambridge: Harvard University Press, 2004), 99. According to Halperin, this statement reveals the heart of Cardozo's messianic faith. "Cardozo believed in Sabbatai Zevi, because he saw in Sabbatai Zevi *a mirror of the most painful and shameful, yet most essential, aspects of his own experience.*" David J. Halperin, trans., *Abraham Miguel Cardozo: Selected Writings* (New York: Paulist Press, 2001), 55.

that is why from all time his name was Michael and not Zevi."[124]

His birth in the land of idolatry was now transformed into part God's plan to bring about Israel's redemption.

## The Uncircumcised Messiah

Despite his return to Judaism in Italy, two women accused Cardozo of having a blemish on the site of his circumcision. According to Cardozo, the women who made the accusation argued that the blemish was preventing the coming of the Messiah. This apparent jab was likely intended to put an end to Cardozo's claims. The women stated that his salvation was dependent on his repairing his circumcision, a possible allusion that he like other Conversos needed to submit to rabbinic authority. Bruce Rosenstock summarizes Cardozo's remarkable claims:

> "The circumcision was faulty, he tells us, because he had been born without a foreskin, and after he left Spain, a *mohel* had removed skin unnecessarily…what this must have mean to Cardozo was that while may have been born in a land of impurity, and considered by its people to be of 'impure blood' as a New Christian, his true identity was that of purity, indeed a natal purity that put him on a plane beyond other Jews."[125]

Rosenstock argues that in this may lie another reason for Cardozo's belief in the unification of the two Messiahs and the unification of all Israel- i.e. the house of Judah and the dispersed tribes of Israel, which had been previously lost.[126] Cardozo saw the unification of the two Messiahs as rectifying the breach that had

---

[124] Bruce Rosenstock, "Abraham Miguel Cardozo's Messianism: A Reappraisal," AJS Review, Vol. 23, No. 1 (1998): 91.
[125] Ibid., 96.
[126] Ibid., 97.

divided the two houses of Israel. "You have already noted the affair of Jeroboam son of Nebat, and this extends all the way down to the Messiah son David and the Messiah son of Ephraim, between whom there will be conflict and jealousy until the end of time, and then 'Ephraim shall not be jealous of Judah, and Judah shall not harass Ephraim." Because of Jeroboam's action, Cardozo states that he was predestined to live in a land of idolatry and force to be an "idol worshipper." Just the apostasy of Zevi had atoned for Israel's adoption of foreign conceptions about God which were tantamount to idolatry, so too was Cardozo's own Converso past atonement for the sin of Jeroboam who had introduced idol worship among the Northern Kingdom of Israel and resulted in the assimilation of these tribes among the Gentiles. [127]

Cardozo gradually deemphasized Zevi as a model. Cardozo attempted to circumvent the issue of apostasy. Sabbatai was in fact, Cardozo argued, the precursor to another messianic figure. This messianic figure would, in turn, bring about the full manifestation of Sabbatai's teaching and hence redemption. In 1680, Cardozo relates that he and his students began to await the looming end of the exile. Cardozo and his students hoped that the redemption would not tarry beyond the celebration of Passover in 1682. In the end, the mass apostasy of Sabbateans in Salonika in the year 1683 dashed Cardozo's hopes that the redemption might be revealed.[128] Cardozo wandered to various places and was often expelled from the local Jewish community. Cardozo was unable to find rest and his hope for redemption ended unfulfilled. Near the end of his life, Cardozo abandoned his belief about his own messiahship. Cardozo wrote,

> "I am no Messiah. But I am the man of whom the Faithful Shepherd [Moses] spoke when he addressed Rabi Simeon ben Yochai and his companions: 'Worthy is he who struggles, in the final generations, to know the Shechinah,

---

[127] Ibid., 98.
[128] Ibid., 68.

to honor Her through the Torah's commandments, and to endure much distress for Her sake."[129]

His life ended tragically and violently at the hands of a begrudged nephew in 1706. Despite his amazing mastery of Jewish texts, he was unable to extricate himself from the Christian past he so reviled.

## Conclusions

The accounts that have been reviewed reveal the unique circumstances of each individual. Their experiences and motivations for conversion were distinctive. Each of them represents a point of Jewish identity along a broad spectrum. Even in the cases where individuals genuinely accepted Christianity, they appear to have placed themselves in opposition to their former Jewish identity in a manner that at times can only be called obsessive. They seemed in many ways incapable of truly escaping their past status. Juan Luis Vives, for example, married a Conversa, and his father and mother suffered Inquisitional prosecution.

For others, the inevitable decline of Judaic knowledge and the growing influence of Christian faith saw a unique fusing of Jewish and Christian beliefs. Conversos like Juan del Hoyo, were unclear where the boundaries and distinctions between each faith lay. Other Conversos like Anton Montoro understood that their Jewish identity could never be truly erased, even as they tried to excel in a Christian society. The emptiness of Christian faith for many of these individuals is apparent.

While the Jewish identity of Conversos lay along a broad spectrum, the individual Converso often changed their place along that continuum. This was especially true for Conversos of later generations. Perhaps, the best example is that of Abraham Israel

---

[129] David J. Halperin, trans., *Abraham Miguel Cardozo: Selected Writings* (New York: Paulist Press, 2001), 305.

Pereyra, who changed his disinterest in Judaism to that of a zeal-zealous adherent. Amazingly, in his new fervor, he remained linked to the Christian motifs he was familiar with before his spiritual transformation. The same is the case for Abraham Miguel Cardozo. Cardozo was able to master rabbinic texts in a manner that Pereyra was not. Despite this, he too was unable to separate his past from his Jewish identity. In most of the cases discussed, the complexity of struggling with multiple identities is evident. All of these individuals exhibited a complex identity regardless of where along the spectrum of Jewish identity they lay.

CHAPTER 5

# Skeptical Conversos

Some Conversos remained steadfast in their commitment to Judaism. Others sincerely adopted Christianity. Still other Conversos abandoned belief in any religious system. Their philosophical inclinations were largely anti-religious or at least free from the typical structures of traditional religions.[1]

Having witnessed the near destruction of Jewish life in the Peninsula by the very faith that they were now legally a part of, some Conversos became skeptical about any religious tradition. Becoming a Christian for them was not an act of faith, but an act of surrender. The chances of survival were at least theoretically improved.[2] Many Conversos resigned themselves to their status as

---

[1] Jose Faur, "Four Classes of Conversos: A Typological Study," Revue des Etudes Juives, CXLIX (1-3), (1990): 113-124.

[2] Don Isaac Abravanel saw those Conversos who had turned skeptical towards all religious practice as *minim* for their total abandonment of Jewish belief and theology. He also believed that these "Averroistic" Conversos served a subversive role which would undermine the foundations of Christian theology and in fact promote Jewish monotheism. In his *Yeshuot Meshiho*, Abravanel stated: "When a man subscribes to no faith, when he is void of religion, he will more easily accept the true religion than will someone else who follows a rival faith. Thus, it was God's wisdom that before the arrival of the messiah and the revelation of God's faith, the entire Kingdom will be afflicted with heresy." quoted in Ram Ben-Shalom, "The Typology of the Converso in Isaac Abravanel's Biblical Exegesis," Jewish History 23:9 (2009): 281-292.

"New Christians," and abandoned Jewish praxis for practical rea-reasons. Don Isaac Abravanel states:

> "They don't observe God's laws, rituals, and commandments for fear of the Gentiles. Lest they [the Christians] should say that since now they form part of them and their society, if they observe the laws of Israel they would be killed as sectarians and heretics."[3]

Their new faith was spiritually empty. Don Isaac Abravanel adds: "And they don't observe the religion of the Gentiles, because they don't believe in their religion." [4] Conversos raised questions about Christian doctrines such as image worship, the cult of saints, and classical Christian approaches to interpreting Scripture. These issues heralded the very same problems that arose during the Protestant Reformation.[5] Regarding these skeptical Conversos, Abravanel also wrote:

> "…you have also failed to observe the laws which are in accordance with the dictates of reason [i.e. morality]. This is so because you have abandoned [the Jewish] religion, but on the other hand, the [rational] laws of the nations around you, you have not observed. This means that although the

---

[3] Jose Faur, *In the Shadow of History: Jews and Conversos at the Dawn of Modernity* (New York: SUNY, 1992), 50. Rabbi Isaac Arama remarked that Jewish and Converso intellectuals effectively agreed with Christian views regarding the lapse of Israel's election. "The length and depth of our Exile' had led the freethinkers to disbelieve in the Election of their people, and this disbelief was in itself a cause of the Exile's prolongation. And these men [the Jewish intellectuals] followed them [the Christians] in thinking—as did the others who departed [i.e., the *anussim*]—that the Torah had lost its taste and fragrance and ceased to yield its strength. They interpreted the Torah not at all in the way of tradition. God forgive me for thinking that they would willingly deny the entire tradition, except that they may consider that, if there was no truth in the religion of Israel, there was even less in the Christian religion; also that the Christians would never allow such complete religious infidelity and that the land would tolerate neither their views nor their sayings." Yitzhak Baer, *A History of the Jews in Christian Spain: Volume 1* (Philadelphia: Jewish Publication Society, 1961), 258-259.

[4] Jose Faur, *In the Shadow of History: Jews and Conversos at the Dawn of Modernity* (New York: SUNY, 1992), 50.

[5] Ibid., 40.

[Conversos] have made themselves as if they were just like the rest of the people of the world, they have failed to ob-observe the [moral] laws of these people. Accordingly, they are like heretics and sectarians, because they don't believe in either of the two religions: in the law of God or in the [moral] laws of the nations." [6]

These Conversos often joined existing Converso communities where family and business ties bridged the religious gaps between them. They often remained hesitant to adopt the religious views of openly Jewish communities. Many of them also espoused skeptical attitudes towards the intellectual foundations of medieval scholas-scholasticism. They embraced empiricism as the basis of human knowledge. This approach was also adopted towards the study of the scriptural and rabbinic texts. The application of scientific methodology towards sacred texts opened the doors of critique towards religion.

While these tendencies existed in the 15th century, Conversos who particularly associated with these positions arose in the 16th and 17th centuries. Among these were Francisco Sanchez, Isaac La Peyrère, Michel de Montaigne, Uriel da Costa, and Benedict Spinoza.[7]

## The Case of Francisco Sanchez

Francisco Sanchez was born in Tuy in northwestern Spain in 1551 to Converso parents. He died in 1623. His family was originally from Aragon where his Converso ancestors served in the court of King Ferdinand. Some of his ancestors appear to have been involved in a conspiracy in Zaragoza resulting in the deaths of a friar and a priest responsible for establishing the Inquisition in

---

[6] Abravanel's Commentary on Ezekiel 5:7 cited Jose Faur, In the Shadow of History: Jews and Conversos at the Dawn of Modernity (New York: SUNY, 1992), 50-51. Ram Ben-Shalom, "The Typology of the Converso in Isaac Abravanel's Biblical Exegesis," Jewish History 23:9 (2009): 283.

[7] David B. Ruderman, *Jewish Thought and Scientific Discovery in Early Modern Europe* (Detroit: Wayne State University, 2001), 276.

Aragon.[8] The family relocated to Galicia. According to Manuel Vázquez, this area offered greater tolerance for Conversos as well as an easy path to exit should it have proven necessary.[9]

He studied medicine at the College of Guyenne in Bordeaux, the home of many Conversos who had abandoned Spain and Portugal.[10] The College of Guyenne had been established by the Converso *André de Gouveia in 1533*. In 1550, King Henry II extended permission to all Portuguese Conversos allowing them to dwell in any French city and enjoy all the privileges of French citizens. After completing his doctoral studies at the University of Montpellier in 1574, he eventually taught philosophy and medicine at the University of Toulouse.[11] There he joined the ranks of other well-known Conversos on the faculty including Manuel Alvares, Pedro Vaz Castelo, and the previously mentioned Baltazar Orobio de Castro. The latter eventually journeyed to Amsterdam and embraced Judaism openly where he was known as Isaac Orobio de Castro.[12]

Sanchez authored his signature work titled *Quod nihil scitur* (That Nothing is Known) in 1576 and published it in 1581. Sanchez began his work by declaring that he was not sure if he even knew anything. He then proceeded to examine the Aristotelian concept of knowledge to demonstrate why this was the case.[13] As a consequence, Francisco Sanchez was widely known as Sanchez, the skeptic. He argued for practical education centered on empiricism

---

[8] Elaine Limbrick and Douglas F.S. Thomson, eds. *Francisco Sanches, That Nothing is Known* (Cambridge: Cambridge University Press, 1988), 6.

[9] Manuel Bermúdez Vázquez, "La influencia del pensamiento judeo-cristiano en Michel de Montaigne, Giordano Bruno y Francisco Sanchez," Ambitos, Num. 23 (2010): 24.

[10] Elaine Limbrick and Douglas F.S. Thomson, eds. *Francisco Sanches, That Nothing is Known* (Cambridge: Cambridge University Press, 1988), 5.

[11] Ibid., 1.

[12] Jose Faur, *In the Shadow of History: Jews and Conversos at the Dawn of Modernity* (New York: SUNY, 1992), 109.

[13] Richard H. Popkin, *The History of Skepticism from Erasmus to Spinoza* (Berkeley: University of California Press, 1979), 37.

and investigation.[14] He remained a Catholic in the city of Toulouse and never revealed his opinions openly about Judaism. However, there is sufficient evidence showing Jewish influence in his thought and a seemingly favorable disposition towards the faith of his fathers.[15] This is especially so in his early writings.[16]

His writings do not characterize him as a Judaizing Converso, but a Jewish influence is arguably apparent.[17] He was influenced by Conversos like Juan Luis Vives and the Converso doctor Amatus Lusitanus.[18] In his *Quod nihil scitur*, he extended a heartfelt dedication to the Converso doctor Jacob de Castro using his Hebrew name after the latter had openly returned to Judaism. This is an action that could have been precarious given Inquisitional scrutiny.[19] Sanchez appears to have been aware of this since he mentions his reticence for publishing anything philosophically oriented.[20] For Jose Faur, the fact that Sanchez dedicated his most significant philosophical work to Jacob Castro reveals the former's intention

---

[14] In the 17th century, his promotion of skepticism was opposed by Martin Schoock, a Utrecht theologian and philosopher opposed to Descartes, and the German theologian Gabriel Wedderkopff. They placed him on their list of the greatest enemies of Christianity. Wedderkopff labeled Sanchez as the "most ruinous of the Skeptics." Elaine Limbrick and Douglas F.S. Thomson, eds. *Francisco Sanches, That Nothing is Known* (Cambridge: Cambridge University Press, 1988), 1.

[15] David B. Ruderman, *Jewish Thought and Scientific Discovery in Early Modern Europe* (Detroit: Wayne State University, 2001), 277.

[16] Manuel Bermúdez Vázquez, "Intuiciones De Criptojudaismo En El Quod Nihil Scitur De Francisco Sanchez." LusoSofia - Biblioteca On-line De Filosofia E Cultura. January 1, 2008. Accessed December 26, 2014.

[17] Ibid.

[18] David B. Ruderman, *Jewish Thought and Scientific Discovery in Early Modern Europe* (Detroit: Wayne State University, 2001), 278.

[19] *Quod nihil scitur* is dedicated to "the most integral and eloquent man, Jacob de Castro." Jose Faur, *In the Shadow of History: Jews and Conversos at the Dawn of Modernity* (New York: SUNY, 1992), 93.

[20] In his introduction to *De diviantione per somnum, ad Aristotelem*, Sanchez wrote "For a long time I have decided to keep silent and not to publish anything on philosophy, since this would be better than to express my insanity in public discussions, lectures, and works, and what can still be worse, to bring others into a similar situation…" Jose Faur, *In the Shadow of History: Jews and Conversos at the Dawn of Modernity* (New York: SUNY, 1992), 102.

to not sever his ties with the Jewish people.[21] Sanchez also quoted frequently from the Hebrew Scriptures, in particular, the book of Ecclesiastes. Sanchez referenced 12 Biblical passages. Ten of these were from the Hebrew Bible while the two passages from the New Testament are arguably out of place and artificially included.[22] He referred to Moses as a "divine legislator…inspired by the Holy Spirit" and as God's "faithful servant."[23] In relating Moses' encounter with God, Sanchez wrote:

> "But God, who can know Him perfectly? ' Man cannot see me and live.' Therefore, only Moses was allowed to see Him through His works. From there another says: 'The in-invisible God is understood through His creation.'"[24]

Sanchez's knowledge of Maimonides' *Guide to the Perplexed* is evident but is couched with a verse from Paul's epistle to the Romans to mask his reference to the former.[25] Jose Faur and Manuel Vázquez both contend that the ending line from Paul's epistle to the Romans is superfluous.[26] The inclusion of the New Testament references even seems forced. According to Elaine Limbrick, Sanchez went to great steps to convince his readers of his traditional Catholic views. He customarily ended his philosophical and medical essays with praise for the Virgin Mary. His orthodoxy was

---

[21] Jose Faur, *In the Shadow of History: Jews and Conversos at the Dawn of Modernity* (New York: SUNY, 1992), 93.

[22] Manuel Bermúdez Vázquez, "La influencia del pensamiento judeo-cristiano en Michel de Montaigne, Giordano Bruno y Francisco Sanchez," Ambitos, Num. 23 (2010): 25. The Biblical passages referenced are Exodus 7:7-11, 33:20, 3:2, 14:24, 14:24; Genesis 2:19-20; Ecclesiastes 1:48; Psalm 101 and 102; Romans 1:20; and Acts 2:3.

[23] Jose Faur, *In the Shadow of History: Jews and Conversos at the Dawn of Modernity* (New York: SUNY, 1992), 94.

[24] Translated from Q.N.S. P. 117 Cited in Manuel Bermúdez Vázquez, "Intuiciones De Criptojudaismo En El Quod Nihil Scitur De Francisco Sanchez." LusoSofia - Biblioteca On-line De Filosofia E Cultura. January 1, 2008. Accessed December 26, 2014.

[25] Jose Faur, *In the Shadow of History: Jews and Conversos at the Dawn of Modernity*, (New York: SUNY, 1992), 95.

[26] Cited in Manuel Bermúdez Vázquez, "Intuiciones De Criptojudaismo En El Quod Nihil Scitur De Francisco Sanchez." LusoSofia - Biblioteca On-line De Filosofia E Cultura. January 1, 2008. Accessed December 26, 2014. Jose Faur, *In the Shadow of History: Jews and Conversos at the Dawn of Modernity* (New York: SUNY, 1992), 95.

unquestioned by his contemporaries, and two of his sons became priests.[27] Given this, his omission in *Quod nihil scitur* and *Carmen de Cometa,* of the customary praise for the Virgin is noteworthy. He also quoted from the *Ethics of the Fathers*.[28] In one of his later works titled *Opera Medica* published in 1636, Sanchez included the pig and various other animals prohibited by the Torah in his list of unhealthy animals to be shunned.[29]

In *Quod nihil scitur,* Sanchez refers to the unique integration of the soul and the body in contrast to Christian views that character-characterized them as two distinct entities with little in common. Christianity embraced the Platonic view that the soul was trapped in the body. Sanchez noted that it was incorrect to characterize the soul as understanding or hearing on its own.[30] A man uses both the soul and the body and cannot accomplish anything without the two elements working together. For the scholar Manuel Vázquez, this is a reflection of Jewish views that highlight the integration and connection that body and soul form in the holistic human being.

For Jose Faur, Sanchez's Converso background is crucial to understanding his philosophical skepticism. Jose Faur argues that the

---

[27] Elaine Limbrick and Douglas F.S. Thomson, eds. *Francisco Sanches, That Nothing is Known* (Cambridge: Cambridge University Press, 1988), 7.

[28] David B. Ruderman, *Jewish Thought and Scientific Discovery in Early Modern Europe* (Detroit: Wayne State University, 2001), 278. Sanchez states that "Life is short, and the work is long, infinite." See Pirke Avot 2:15 for similiarities. Sanchez also writes, "You miserable work, who can hardly know who you are, where you come from and where you are going." See Pirke Avot 3:1 for comparison. Jose Faur, *In the Shadow of History: Jews and Conversos at the Dawn of Modernity* (New York: SUNY, 1992), 248.

[29] Jose Faur, *In the Shadow of History: Jews and Conversos at the Dawn of Modernity* (New York: SUNY, 1992), 94.

[30] Sanchez states: "What may be gathered from all this? That the human soul, which is the most perfect of God's creations, should need for the most perfect of all actions, which is perfect knowledge, a most perfect body. How come!- you'd say: knowledge does not depend in any way on the body, but exclusively on the perfect soul. This is false as I'll prove to you elsewhere. It is vain to say that the soul understands that the soul hears. It is man as a unit that acts, as a unit of body and soul, and neither one by itself can function without the other." Jose Faur, *In the Shadow of History: Jews and Conversos at the Dawn of Modernity* (New York: SUNY, 1992), 97.

doubt embraced by individuals like Sanchez was ultimately rooted in the spiritual crisis borne by Conversos in the Iberian Peninsula. Conversos faced a sense of alienation from Old Christian society.[31] Sanchez is an anti-dogmatist precisely because of his past. Sanchez rejected the possibility of outright certainty and the right to foist "absolute truth" onto others. The idea that an individual could possess "perfect truth" was the source of the backwardness, disagreement, and religious wars afflicting the various kingdoms of Europe. Violence and conflict were the consequences of the false view that perfect knowledge was attainable. Sanchez believed that human knowledge was ever changing. He held, like Maimonides, that the entire universe was like a clock. The workings of a clock could not be understood by only reviewing a few of its components. Instead, all of the elements making up the clock had to be taken apart, and their individual functions understood. Each part was not independent. The movement of one part affected the others. Consequently, since perfect knowledge was dependent on a complete understanding of everything, no absolute knowledge could be known with certainty.[32]

Sanchez was particularly critical of the Aristotelian focus on definitions rather than on a direct analysis of natural occurrences. When purported science or philosophy began with definitions that were arbitrarily imposed on things in a whimsical fashion, this approach did not reflect the real nature of an object. For Sanchez, the use of words and definitions in describing the nature of things was inherently problematic. They often resulted in superfluous descriptions or wholly inadequate ones.[33] The Western philosophical tradition's focus on words and their definitions had created the web that imprisoned the mind.

---

[31] David B. Ruderman, *Jewish Thought and Scientific Discovery in Early Modern Europe* (Detroit: Wayne State University, 2001), 278.

[32] Jose Faur, *In the Shadow of History: Jews and Conversos at the Dawn of Modernity* (New York: SUNY, 1992), 98.

[33] Richard H. Popkin, *The History of Skepticism from Erasmus to Spinoza* (Berkeley: University of California Press, 1979), 37.

Sanchez viewed Aristotle's *Metaphysics* and other works as focused on the classification of names. Sanchez asserted that "words do not possess the faculty to reflect the nature of things," a view Jose Faur contends resonates with the Sephardic philosophical tradition. Aristotelian definitions were nothing more than abstractions. Out of these constructs, Sanchez accused philosophers of creating a fictitious world that no sane mind could accept.[34] According to Sanchez, purported scientists were describing nothing more than falsehoods and theoretical concepts. Sanchez also attacked the use of syllogisms arguing that they only produced circular reasoning.[35]

The resolution was the adoption of a scientific methodology that combined critical judgment with experimentation. Sanchez believed that despite this approach, the real essence of things could never be known. True science was dependent on perfect knowledge of a thing. But a human understanding of the natural world remained marginal and imprecise not only due to the nature of objects but also due to the nature of man.[36] This led Sanchez to conclude that "There is only [information] on what is probable, nothing is known with certainty."[37] For Sanchez, all that man could achieve was a partial and imperfect knowledge of some things derived from observation and judgment.[38]

Theology, philosophy, and science in the medieval period rested on the premise that there existed a higher and perfect truth. This truth was timeless and absolute. Human beings could consider it with their limited intellect, but could contribute to its creation. According to this view, a fact that resulted from human involvement

---

[34] Jose Faur, *In the Shadow of History: Jews and Conversos at the Dawn of Modernity* (New York: SUNY, 1992), 99.
[35] Richard H. Popkin, *The History of Skepticism from Erasmus to Spinoza* (Berkeley: University of California Press, 1979), 38.
[36] Ibid., 38-39.
[37] Jose Faur, *In the Shadow of History: Jews and Conversos at the Dawn of Modernity* (New York: SUNY, 1992), 99.
[38] Richard H. Popkin, *The History of Skepticism from Erasmus to Spinoza* (Berkeley: University of California Press, 1979), 39.

was artificial and consequently false. There were two options in this worldview. The first was truth without science. This manifested itself via revelation and mysticism. The other option was a science derived from the Aristotelian and the scholastic tra- tradition of the medieval period but yielded no truth. Sanchez rejected both the notion of a perfect knowledge and the ineffectiveness of Aristotelian metaphysics. He proposed "truth" derived from scientific methodology. Here, the individual through his experimentation was the author.[39]

## The Case of Isaac La Peyrère

The Jewish background of Isaac La Peyrère is hard to confirm, but Richard Popkin maintains he had Converso ancestry. This assertion is partly based on what Popkin refers to as La Peyrère's Marrano theology that fused Jewish and Christian elements into a unique messianism.[40] For Popkin, the struggle between faith and science in modernity materialized as a result of the use of "scientific" methods applied to all biblical research. This in due course undermined the miraculous and mysterious fundamentals of Judaism and Christianity.[41] Among the drivers of this, was Isaac La Peyrère. La Peyrère is often regarded as the father of Bible criticism. His approach to Biblical texts influenced Juan de Prado, Baruch Spinoza, and Richard Simon.[42] For Richard Popkin, La Peyrère prepared the way for anthropological studies and biblical

---

[39] For Jose Faur, this confirms rabbinic thought that views human creativity as superior to the natural creativity. For Faur, this is Sanchez's contribution to Western intellectual history. Truth is not a given, but rather the result of human involvement. Jose Faur, *In the Shadow of History: Jews and Conversos at the Dawn of Modernity* (New York: SUNY, 1992), 105.

[40] Regarding Popkin's contention, Ruderman notes that, "Popkin admits that the circumstantial evidence for La Peyrère's converso background is not overwhelming and that all one can conclude is that he was most likely of Jewish origin." David B. Ruderman, *Jewish Thought and Scientific Discovery in Early Modern Europe* (Detroit: Wayne State University, 2001), 280-281.

[41] Ibid., 280.

[42] Richard H. Popkin, *The History of Skepticism from Erasmus to Spinoza* (Berkeley: University of California Press, 1979), 227. Juan de Prado agreed with La Peyrère that the world was eternal and that human history was older than Jewish history.

criticism in successive centuries by his secularization of human history.[43] La Peyrère was accused of atheism, but while he sharply deviated from traditional Jewish or Christian views, he maintained a passionate belief in a messianic theology.[44]

He was born in Bordeaux in 1596 and raised as a Calvinist. He was accused of atheism and irreverence by a local Calvinist Synod but was defended and acquitted by a group of sixty pastors.[45] In 1640, he served as secretary to the Prince of Condé.

He is best known for his two controversial works, titled *Praead-Praeadamitae* (Men Before Adam) and *Du Rappel des Juifs* (Reminder of the Jews), which focused on his theory of Biblical criticism and messianism. The first work was banned but was disseminated clandestinely in France, Holland, and Denmark. After seeing the manuscript of *Praeadamitae* in Brussels, Queen Christina of Sweden subsidized its publication. It was printed in Amsterdam and Basle. The book was banned and burned for its heterodox claims that Adam was not the first man. The Bible, La Peyrère contended was not the history of mankind, but the history of the Jewish people. He endeavored to distinguish between human and Jewish history as reflected in the Bible given the physical, social, and geographical dissimilarities among various human groups. La Peyrère maintained that the Biblical Flood was a local event. Most significantly, he argued that Moses did not write the Torah and that no precise manuscript of the Bible existed. When it was published, it was condemned by the President and the Council of Holland and Zeeland as scandalous, false, contrary to God's Word, and a danger to the state. The bishop of Namur had him condemned as a "Calvinist and as a Jew." [46]

---

[43] David B. Ruderman, *Jewish Thought and Scientific Discovery in Early Modern Europe* (Detroit: Wayne State University, 2001), 281.

[44] Richard H. Popkin, *The History of Skepticism from Erasmus to Spinoza* (Berkeley: University of California Press, 1979), 215.

[45] Ibid.

[46] Richard H. Popkin, *The History of Skepticism from Erasmus to Spinoza* (Berkeley: University of California Press, 1979), 220.

His *Rappel des Juifs* was published anonymously in 1643. In it, he anticipated the pending revelation of the Jewish Messiah. La Peyrère held that the only significant history was that of the Jewish people. History was divided into three periods. The first was the history of the Jewish people and their election from the time of Adam to the time of Jesus. Divine History began when God fash-fashioned the first Jew. The Jewish people alone were actors, but non-Jews also participated. He explained that a Messiah, Jesus in the spirit, had already come in the first century for non-Jews. At that point, Jews had been cast away from divine history, and this continued until the 17$^{th}$ century. During this period, non-Jews had been grafted onto the Jewish stock. The last period of history was the redemption of the Jewish people. They would now be restored, and the Jewish Messiah in the flesh would be revealed soon.[47]

La Peyrère argued that Jews should be allowed into France. They should be treated well and placed in a "Jewish Christian" church consisting of only Jews. No doctrines or observances that were offensive to Jews should be allowed. There they would prepare for the coming of what their brothers in the first century had expected, the Messiah in the flesh. The Messiah would lead Jews to the land of Israel and Jerusalem would be rebuilt. Jews would constitute the Messianic court and the King of France, who had gathered Jews together and enabled their return to the Holy Land, would rule the world alongside the Messiah.[48] La Peyrère also maintained that everyone would be saved regardless of what they believed.[49]

Former Conversos including Rabbi Menasseh ben Israel and Isaac Orobio de Castro were familiar with his works. While they rejected his views on the Torah, his messianic beliefs were posi-

---

[47] Ibid., 216-217.
[48] Richard Popkin, "Jewish-Christian Relations in the Sixteenth and Seventeenth Centuries: The Conception of the Messiah," Jewish History Vol. 6., No. 1-2 (1992): 165.
[49] Richard H. Popkin, *The History of Skepticism from Erasmus to Spinoza* (Berkeley: University of California Press, 1979), 216.

tively received.⁵⁰ La Peyrère was ultimately arrested. He was offered a pardon if he embraced Catholicism and recanted. In a Converso like manner, he did so and claimed that his heterodoxies were derived from his Calvinist education. La Peyrère recanted while arguing that he could not find any Scriptural or rational evi-evidence against his ideas. He repudiated them because the Church said they were erroneous. Pope Alexander VII offered La Peyrère a post, but he returned to Paris. He served as the Prince of Con-Condé's librarian where he gathered more evidence for his pre-Adamite theory. Upon his death in 1676, a friend characterized La Peyrère as a good Israelite, a Huguenot, a Catholic and finally a Pre-Adamite who ultimately rejected all established religious traditions.⁵¹

## The Case of Michel de Montaigne

Michel de Montaigne was born in 1533 and died in 1592. The French writer and philosopher Michel de Montaigne is regarded by Richard Popkin as the most prominent figure in the 16th-century resurgence of early skepticism. Montaigne was interested in the ideas put forward by Academic and Pyrrhonian skeptics. Most importantly, he was influenced by Pyrrhonian skepticism that argued for complete doubt and related it to the ongoing religious conflict engendered by the Reformation. Montaigne recognized the relativity of man's intellectual, social, and spiritual experiences.⁵²

---

⁵⁰ David B. Ruderman, *Jewish Thought and Scientific Discovery in Early Modern Europe* (Detroit: Wayne State University, 2001), p. 282. In his work titled, *Vindiciae Judaeorum*, Menasseh ben Israel wrote "…for as much as a most learned Christian of our time hath written, in a French book, which he calleth the *Rappel of the Jews* (in which he makes the King of France to be their leader, when they shall return to their country), the Jews, saith he, shall be saved, for yet we expect a second coming of the same Messiah, and the Jews believe that that coming is the first and not the second, and by that faith they shall be saved, for the difference consists only in the circumstance of time." Richard Popkin, "Jewish-Christian Relations in the Sixteenth and Seventeenth Centuries: The Conception of the Messiah," Jewish History Vol. 6., No. 1-2 (1992): 166.

⁵¹ Richard H. Popkin, *The History of Skepticism from Erasmus to Spinoza* (Berkeley: University of California Press, 1979), 223.

⁵² Ibid., 42.

Montaigne and Francisco Sanchez were distantly related. Montaigne's mother, Antoinette de Loupes de Villanueva, was of Converso ancestry and had become a Protestant. One of her ancestors, Mayer Pacagon of Calatayud, had converted to Catholicism under duress. He adopted the name Lopez de Villanueva.[53] Some of his offsprings observed Jewish customs and several of them were arrested by the Inquisition. One of them, Juan de Villanueva fled to Toulouse, France. Montaigne's mother was a descendant of Juan de Villanueva. Whether Antoinette was aware of her Jewish ancestry is unclear, but given the social segregation often experienced by Conversos and their descendants, even those who were from mixed families were reminded of their backgrounds. Antoinette married Eyquem de Montaigne. Eyquem's Old Christian background has been assumed, but new research points to his Converso ancestry. Montaigne's great-great-great grandfather Ramon Sante was from Portugal and converted to Christianity.[54]

Montaigne's family had significant relationships with some Conversos. These included Simon Milanges, who taught at the College of Guyenne and published portions of Montaigne's *Essais*. Other Conversos that the Montaigne family was intimate with were the Govea brothers whose family had fled to Paris from Portugal after they were accused of Judaizing.[55]

Michel de Montaigne studied at the College de Guyenne which included a large number of prominent Portuguese Conversos and where Francisco Sanchez also studied. He also studied at Toulouse University, another center of Converso activity. Montaigne served in the Bordeaux Parliament and at the Court of France from 1557 to 1570. He inaugurated his literary vocation in the late 1560s.

---

[53] Charles Myers and Norman Simms, eds. *Troubled Souls: Conversos, Crypto-Jews, and other Confused Jewish Intellectuals from the Fourteenth through the Eighteenth Century* (Hamilton: Outriggers Publishers, 2001), 129.

[54] Ibid., 131.

[55] Elizabeth Mendes da' Costa suggests that given the extent of the relationships Montaigne's family had with Conversos it is conceivable that they belonged to the crypto-Jewish community in the area. Ibid., 133.

In 1571, after retiring from public life, Montaigne penned his famed *Essais*.[56] With this work, Montaigne created the essay as a literary form. His book on skepticism is titled *Apologie de Raimon Sebond*. He returned to public office and was voted mayor of Bor-Bordeaux. Despite his official responsibilities, Montaigne continued work on the *Essais*. Montaigne was critical of the authority attributed to Aristotelian thought. Montaigne wrote:

> "Before the principles that Aristotle introduced were in credit, other principles satisfied human reason, as his satisfy us at this moment. What letter-patent have these, what special privilege, that the course of our invention stops at them, and that to them belongs possession of our belief for all time to come? They are no more exempt from being thrown out than were their predecessors."[57]

Montaigne battled against academic pretenses behind the idea of total certainty. Montaigne held that "The impression of certainty is a certain token of folly and extreme uncertainty."[58] Montaigne like Sanchez rejected the notions of absolute certainty. He denied that dogmatism was rational or logically inevitable. Humans rendered judgment on appearances and were influenced by various elements.[59] Only a genuinely impartial judge could

---

[56] Sophie Jama points out an interesting fact regarding the publication of the *Essais*. The first edition of Montaigne's work was printed by Simon de Millange. Millange's father was a Converso. The date of the publication was March 1, 1580. The date corresponds in the Hebrew calendar as 14 Adar 5340. This corresponds to the first day of Purim. Charles Myers and Norman Simms, eds. *Troubled Souls: Conversos, Crypto-Jews, and other Confused Jewish Intellectuals from the Fourteenth through the Eighteenth Century* (Hamilton: Outriggers Publishers, 2001), 147.

[57] Jose Faur, *In the Shadow of History: Jews and Conversos at the Dawn of Modernity* (New York: SUNY, 1992), 106.

[58] Ibid.

[59] Jose Faur contends that this also extends to the matter of forced conversions, though Montaigne only ever laments the persecution of Jews in the Peninsula. Ibid.

determine what and who is right. In the realm of religion, Montaigne recognized that this was not possible.[60]

The fundamental characteristic of skepticism in relation to religion is the belief that human reason and experience are largely incapable of understanding the Divine. God and His creation are well beyond the faculties of the human being.[61] For skeptics, the person is severely limited by his inability to understand the world around him fully.[62] Montaigne was unusually tolerant with regards to religious beliefs. Montaigne stated that "An untoward disease that a man should be so riveted to his own belief as to fancy that others cannot believe otherwise than as he does…"[63] For Montaigne, religion was based solely on faith given to an individual by God's grace.[64] Montaigne's attitude towards Jews was sympathetic and was reflective of his view that religion was a product of circumstances, history, and emotion.[65] Perhaps aware of his family history, Montaigne related that authority and not reason was the source of "our religions." The human intellect is

---

[60] "As we say in dispute about religion that we need to judge not attached to either party, free from preference and passion which is impossible among Christians, so it is in this." Apology for Raymond Sebond. Ibid.

[61] Montaigne saw nothing wrong with using reason to buttress faith, "but always with this reservation, not to think that it is on us that faith depends, or that our efforts and arguments can attain a knowledge so supernatural and divine." Richard H. Popkin, *The History of Skepticism from Erasmus to Spinoza* (Berkeley: University of California Press, 1979), 44.

[62] Manuel Bermúdez Vázquez, "La influencia del pensamiento judeo-cristiano en Michel de Montaigne, Giordano Bruno y Francisco Sanchez," Ambitos, Num. 23 (2010): 20.

[63] Harry Friedenwald, "Montaigne's Relation to Judaism and the Jews," The Jewish Quarterly Review, New Series, Vol. 31, No. 2 (1940): 141.

[64] Richard H. Popkin, *The History of Skepticism from Erasmus to Spinoza* (Berkeley: University of California Press, 1979), 44. Montaigne wrote that, "The participation that we have in the knowledge of truth, whatever it may be, has not been acquired by our own powers…Our faith is not of our own acquiring, it is a pure present of another's liberality. It is not by reasoning or by our understanding that we have received our religion; it is by external authority and command." Ibid., 46.

[65] Harry Friedenwald, "Montaigne's Relation to Judaism and the Jews," The Jewish Quarterly Review, New Series, Vol. 31, No. 2 (1940): 144.

restricted in its ability to understand divine knowledge.[66] Consequently, Montaigne noted that,

> "All this is a most evident sign that we only receive our religion after our own fashion by our own hand, and not otherwise than other religions are received. Either we are in the country where it is in practice, or we have a reverence to its antiquity, or to the authority of the men who have maintained it, or we fear the menaces it fulminates against unbelievers, or we are allured by its promises...We are Christians by the same title that we are Perigordins or Germans."[67]

According to Jose Faur, Montaigne's reference to "our religions" was a call for religious tolerance. Since the faith a person practiced was the product of authority and external circumstances, it did not automatically eliminate the private beliefs of the individual.[68] For Montaigne, pure faith was the foundation of religion.[69] Montaigne maintained that "...there cannot be first principles for men unless the Divinity has revealed them; all the rest - beginning, middle, and end- is nothing but dreams and smoke."[70] Oddly enough, Montaigne's adoption of Pyrrhonist doubt provided a defense against the Reformation. The complete skeptic did not hold positive views and did not run counter to the laws and customs of his community. Hence, the real skeptic accepted Catholicism if that were the religion dominant in his area.[71] Montaigne noted that,

---

[66] Richard H. Popkin, *The History of Skepticism from Erasmus to Spinoza* (Berkeley: University of California Press, 1979), 44.

[67] Harry Friedenwald, "Montaigne's Relation to Judaism and the Jews, " The Jewish Quarterly Review, New Series, Vol. 31, No. 2 (1940): 142.

[68] Jose Faur, *In the Shadow of History: Jews and Conversos at the Dawn of Modernity* (New York: SUNY, 1992), 107.

[69] Richard H. Popkin, *The History of Skepticism from Erasmus to Spinoza* (Berkeley: University of California Press, 1979), 44.

[70] Ibid., 48.

[71] Ibid., 47.

"...since I am not capable of choosing, I accept other people's choice and stay in the position where God put me. Otherwise, I could not keep myself from rolling around incessantly. Thus I have, by the grace of God, kept myself intact, without agitation or disturbance of conscience, in the ancient beliefs of our religion, in the midst of so many sects and divisions that our century has produced."[72]

Montaigne's statement is perhaps a resignation to his status of a Christian. Religion should not be imposed on anyone, as it had on the Jews of Spain and Portugal. Montaigne notes that "the things that come to us from heaven have alone the right and authority for persuasion, alone the stamp of truth…"[73] The challenges and the "agitation" that Montaigne may have seen confronting other Conversos struggling to return to Judaism may have added to the resignation of his own state. Unforced conformity to the religion of an area was ideal, but did not reflect an embrace of the absolute truth as only revelation could provide that.[74] Montaigne was willing to surrender his actions, efforts, wealth, and life to the state, but not his thoughts. This attitude implied conformity, at least outwardly, with the dominant religion.[75]

Montaigne was present at the death and reversion to Judaism of his closest friend, the poet Etienne de la Boétie. Boétie was from a Converso background and authored the work, On Voluntary Servitude. Montaigne witnessed Boétie receive last rites but at the

---

[72] Ibid., 49.

[73] Ibid.

[74] In relating his opinion on Montaigne's personal religiosity, Popkin notes, "My own view is that, at best, Montaigne was probably mildly religious. His attitude appears to be more that of indifference or involvement. He was opposed to fanaticism, primarily as displayed by the French Reformers, but at the same time he certainly seems to have lacked the spiritual qualities that characterized such great French Counter-Reformers as St. Francois de Sales, Cardinal Berulle, or St. Vincent de Paul." Ibid., 55.

[75] Charles Myers and Norman Simms, eds. *Troubled Souls: Conversos, Crypto-Jews, and other Confused Jewish Intellectuals from the Fourteenth through the Eighteenth Century* (Hamilton: Outriggers Publishers, 2001), 136.

end related that he wished to die in the faith of Moses. Montaigne wrote his father an extensive essay on the event. Harry Freidenwald notes that the minute details and the lack of comment reveal a profound interest in this significant event.[76]

Montaigne repeatedly described himself as a faithful Catholic subservient to ecclesiastical authority.[77] Indeed, in his essay on prayer, perhaps fearful of Inquisitional oversight, he submitted his views to those who were responsible for regulating his writings, actions, and his very thoughts.[78] But Montaigne's references to Christianity appear detached. Montaigne refers to religion, but never to Christ. He does not reference the sayings of Jesus and his knowledge of the Gospels does not seem to have been extensive. His reverence for Catholicism was likely out of prudence rather than devotion.[79] Montaigne may have reached a compromise given the religious wars tearing France apart and his family history. Montaigne may have resigned himself to relinquish Judaism and embrace Catholicism not out of faith, but for safety sake.[80]

In his essay, titled *Apology for Sebonde,* Montaigne highlights his skepticism regarding the veracity of truth since thoughts are uncontrollable. He references the unreliability of confessions obtained under torture. In this essay, Montaigne notes his famous

---

[76] Harry Freidenwald, "Montaigne's Relation to Judaism and the Jews," The Jewish Quarterly Review, New Series, Vol. 31, No. 2 (1940): 145.

[77] Manuel Bermúdez Vázquez, "La influencia del pensamiento judeo-cristiano en Michel de Montaigne, Giordano Bruno y Francisco Sanchez," Ambitos, Num. 23 (2010): 20.

[78] Inquisitorial prosecution was always a possibility. While the Inquisition was not as active as in the Peninsula, the danger was real. In 1619, a Portuguese woman was burned alive for not having swallowed the Host at Church. The priest of the Church who was a Converso fled fearing that he would liable to the same punishment. All of the "Portuguese" were ordered to leave the town the following day. Charles Myers and Norman Simms, eds. *Troubled Souls: Conversos, Crypto-Jews, and other Confused Jewish Intellectuals from the Fourteenth through the Eighteenth Century* (Hamilton: Outriggers Publishers, 2001), 134.

[79] Harry Freidenwald, "Montaigne's Relation to Judaism and the Jews," The Jewish Quarterly Review, New Series, Vol. 31, No. 2 (1940): 143.

[80] Charles Myers and Norman Simms, eds. *Troubled Souls: Conversos, Crypto-Jews, and other Confused Jewish Intellectuals from the Fourteenth through the Eighteenth Century* (Hamilton: Outriggers Publishers, 2001), 134.

motto "What do I know?" What is most significant about the *Apology* is that while it was written as a defense of Christianity, it never mentions the Trinity. Instead, he includes a quotation from Plutarch which states "So that it was a sinful saying to say of God, who is *He* only *is*, that *He was* or that *He shall be*...and there is nothing that truly is, but *He* alone, with one being able to say *He has been*, or *shall be*, without beginning and without end."[81] Here, Harry Freidenwald contends that the allusion to the Exodus 3:14 "I am that I am" is evident. Out of apprehension, Montaigne uses the religious quotation of a pagan to express an explicitly Jewish idea. Somewhat less discreet, Montaigne noted that of all the nations, the Jewish people alone had the true God at its head.[82]

In the *Essais*, he references the maltreatment of Conversos in Portugal. In his *Travel Diary* (Journal de Voyage), he references Jewish customs he witnessed during his Italian excursion in the cities of Verona and Rome. He visited synagogues on the Sabbath, attended Jewish observances including a circumcision, and, as his secretary notes, spoke with Jews intensely about their customs.[83] He commented on the congregational involvement in prayer and study. He also mentioned the extensive familiarity of Hebrew among all ages. On February 6, 1581, he observed half-naked Jews forced to participate in a pre-Lent event. He also attended a conversion homily given by converted Jew. His observations appear free from the conventional biases against Jews.

Montaigne's skepticism is arguably derived from his Jewish background. Montaigne may have been intrigued by his Jewish past, but avoided any reference to it out of fear of the consequences it might stir. His father shaped his education and to some extent this determined his philosophical path. Montaigne's

---

[81] Harry Friedenwald, "Montaigne's Relation to Judaism and the Jews, " The Jewish Quarterly Review, New Series, Vol. 31, No. 2 (1940): 145-146.

[82] Ibid., 146.

[83] Charles Myers and Norman Simms, eds. *Troubled Souls: Conversos, Crypto-Jews, and other Confused Jewish Intellectuals from the Fourteenth through the Eighteenth Century* (Hamilton: Outriggers Publishers, 2001), 135.

curiosity about Jewish life is fascinating given his failure to make any mention of his mother in the *Essais*. A possible reason for not mentioning his mother is her conversion to Protestantism. Protestant family members would not have been a benefit to a public figure in the middle of ongoing religious wars. Nevertheless, his mother lived with him all his life and even survived him by several years.[84] The fact that his mother, as well as two siblings converted to Protestantism, may have also played a factor in Montaigne's tolerance of variant religious beliefs. But his awareness of the situation in Portugal and the other experiences of his life make it clear that Jewishness played a role in his life.

## The Case of Uriel da Costa

Many Conversos who fled the Peninsula experienced issues with acceptance of rabbinic authority upon their entry into the Jewish community. Noteworthy individuals were Juan de Prado and Daniel Ribera. Juan de Prado held deistic beliefs and rejected the divine origin of the Law and the immortality of the soul. He also believed God existed only philosophically. Daniel Ribera was reputed to be an atheist. [85] The most notable cases of rejection of rabbinic authority are those of Uriel da Costa, and of Baruch Spinoza.

The more tragic of these individuals is Uriel da Costa. Da Costa was born in Porto in Portugal in 1583 or 1584 as Gabriel da Costa. His parents were Conversos. According to Da Costa, while he was a student of canon law at the University of Coimbra, his reading of the Bible led him to question Christianity and consider a return to Judaism. The Inquisitional trials of his sister Maria da Costa, however, indicate that Jewish practices were already being

---

[84] Harry Friedenwald, "Montaigne's Relation to Judaism and the Jews," The Jewish Quarterly Review, New Series, Vol. 31, No. 2 (1940): 143.

[85] Miriam Bodian, *Hebrews of the Portuguese Nation* (Bloomington: Indiana University Press, 1997), 123. Prado would write, "The truth is that many customs, response and decisions that do not concern the actual Law of God are not consistent with my understanding and it rejects them." Yosef Kaplan, "The Portuguese Jews in Amsterdam: From Forced Conversion to a Return to Judaism," *Studia Rosenthaliana* XV, No. 1 (1981): 48.

observed by the family before his purported crisis of faith. At personal risk, Da Costa was even involved in coaxing at least three Conversos to embrace Judaism.[86]

Increasing inquisitional activities were the likely reasons for Da Costa's departure from Oporto. From 1618 to 1625, approximately 143 Conversos were arrested in Oporto for Judaizing.[87] Sometime between 1612 and 1615, Da Costa along with his mother and two brothers fled Portugal for Amsterdam where his family openly returned to Judaism.[88]

Shortly after his arrival in Amsterdam, Da Costa moved to Hamburg. He became quickly disillusioned with traditional Judaism. In his work titled *Exemplar*, he wrote,

> "After a few days I realized that the mores and ordinances of the Jews hardly agreed with those which were ordered by Moses. If the law were to have been truly observed in its purity, those whom the Jews incorrectly call wise [i.e. the rabbis] had invented everything that the law abhors. Therefore, I could not contain myself, and thought it would be pleasing to God if I would freely defend the law."[89]

Jose Faur believes that Da Costa's representation is false given the extent of his family's familiarity with Judaism.[90] In 1616, while, in Hamburg, he penned a tract that promoted unorthodox views on rabbinic tradition and authority. Da Costa was not content to keep his ideas local. He sent his tract to the community of Venice. Rabbi Leon de Modena contacted the community in Hamburg

---

[86] Jose Faur, *In the Shadow of History: Jews and Conversos at the Dawn of Modernity* (New York: SUNY, 1992), 126.

[87] Ibid., 119, 121.

[88] Miriam Bodian, *Hebrews of the Portuguese Nation* (Bloomington: Indiana University Press, 1997), 49.

[89] Jose Faur, *In the Shadow of History: Jews and Conversos at the Dawn of Modernity* (New York: SUNY, 1992), 122.

[90] Ibid., 123.

where da Costa resided. He demanded that he and his followers be excommunicated.[91] In August 1618, the Venetian community excommunicated Da Costa and Rabbi Leon de Modena contacted the Hamburg community and informing them of Da Costa's ex-excommunication.[92]

According to the refutation of Da Costa authored by Rabbi Le-Leon de Modena, the former argued that the Oral Torah was not a fundamental component of the Torah. It was instead, a "new To-Torah" which controverted the old. Da Costa argued against the hedges or fences around the Torah on the basis that they were "not all good because people may easily be misled into thinking that this is the principal offense." He believed that the fences around the Torah had complicated observance so extensively that they made the Torah "almost impossible to observe."[93] The concern was that returning Conversos unschooled in rabbinic thought and practice would find Da Costa's argument's convincing.

Da Costa's move to Amsterdam in 1623 eventually placed him on a collision course with the *Mahamad*, the governing board of the unified Amsterdam Jewish community. While the *Mahamad* did not immediately officially excommunicate him, the *Mahamad* honored the excommunications from Hamburg and Venice.[94] The Amsterdam community expelled him in May 1623 given his intent on publishing his work. Unrepentant, Da Costa continued and printed his book titled *An Examination of the Traditions of the Pharisees*.

The book questioned fundamental aspects of Judaism including the immortality of the soul. Da Costa argued this was not deeply rooted in biblical texts. It was instead expressed principally by rab-

---

[91] Miriam Bodian, *Hebrews of the Portuguese Nation* (Bloomington: Indiana University Press, 1997), 49.
[92] Ibid., 119.
[93] Yosef Kaplan, "The Portuguese Jews in Amsterdam: From Forced Conversion to a Return to Judaism," *Studia Rosenthaliana* XV, No. 1 (1981): 47.
[94] Daniel Frank and Matt Goldish, eds. *Rabbinic Culture and Its Critics: Jewish Authority, Dissent, and Heresy in the Medieval and Early Modern Times* (Detroit: Wayne State University Press: 2007), 314-315.

binic tradition. This fact further highlighted the discrepancies between biblical texts and rabbinic thought. He regarded rabbinic Judaism as the ongoing accretion of ceremonies and practices. For Da Costa, the rabbis were the "real renegades and heretics who are accursed."[95] Judaism was bereft of transcendent and philosophical ideas. He mocked the notion of martyrdom and argued that God did not require or want such a sacrifice. In doing so, he struck a raw nerve among Conversos as he scorned the martyrdom of Conversos in the Peninsula. More serious was the potential danger he was placing the community in since his attack on the idea of an afterlife extended to Christianity as well. The rabbinate could not tolerate open doubts about any of these views or the veracity of the Oral tradition, however, as Miriam Bodian notes,

> "Da Costa's insinuations on this matter notwithstanding, the Amsterdam communal authorities were never interested in applying inquisitorial methods to impose conformity of private belief."[96]

Da Costa ultimately recanted in 1628 only to undergo another ban in 1632 or 1633. He continued to express his skeptical views, expressing doubts as to whether biblical law was divinely sanctioned or whether Moses authored it. He concluded that all religions were a human invention and rejected formalized religions. Da Costa believed that religion should be based solely on natural law. Consequently, ceremonies were empty and meaningless.

He eventually recanted again around 1640, but the process of repentance was apparently harsh, and he committed suicide. He

---

[95] Miriam Bodian, *Hebrews of the Portuguese Nation* (Bloomington: Indiana University Press, 1997), 119.

[96] Miriam Bodian, "Hebrews of the Portuguese Nation: The Ambiguous Boundaries of Self-Definition," Jewish Social Studies, New Series, Vol. 15, No. 1, Sephardi Identities (2008): 76.

ended his life a deist having rejected the Written and Oral Law and the involvement of God in creation.[97]

## The Case of Baruch Spinoza

Baruch Spinoza was born to a family of former Conversos, who had moved to Amsterdam. He received a thorough Jewish educa-education. This is evidenced by the notes and references in his theological-political treatise that make mention of Maimonides, Moses ibn Ezra, and David Kimchi (Qamhi) among others.[98] His philosophical perspectives and critique of fundamental Jewish concepts of God ultimately led to his excommunication.[99]

Spinoza was the product of two distinct traditions both rooted in the Jewish experience. The first as previously mentioned was connected to classical Jewish education. The other was the skepticism of Conversos like Francisco Sanchez and Uriel da Costa. Spinoza's direct mentor was Juan (Daniel) de Prado who tutored the former in deistic theology.[100]

For Spinoza, the methods for interpreting Scripture were not significantly different from those used to understand nature. Nature was understood by examining the history of nature and by inferring meanings of natural occurrences on definite axioms. The same was the case for Scripture. The Bible was to be scrutinized, and inferences of the original authors' intention derived. Also, like the study of nature, an understanding of the Bible could only

---

[97] Miriam Bodian, *Hebrews of the Portuguese Nation* (Bloomington: Indiana University Press, 1997), 121.

[98] R.H.M. Elwes, trans., Benedict de Spinoza, A Theologico-Political Treatise (New York: Dover Publications, 1951), Reference to Maimonides are found on 17, 114, 115, 127, to Rabbi David Kimchi on 273, and Ibn Ezra Chapter 1 notes.

[99] Perhaps Spinoza's most contentious perspective is the equating of Nature with God. Spinoza states: "Everything takes place by the power of God. Nature herself is the power of God under another name, and our ignorance of the power of God is co-extensive with our ignorance of Nature. It is absolute folly, therefore, to ascribe an event to the power of God when we know not its natural cause, which is the power of God. R.H.M. Elwes, trans., Benedict de Spinoza, A Theologico-Political Treatise (New York: Dover Publications, 1951), 25.

[100] ibid. 143.

emerge directly from the text. Subsequently, rabbinic interpretation and elucidation of the Bible was inconsequential to its meaning.

For Spinoza, Scriptural definitions were reached at by consider- considering the different stories about a particular topic. Most significantly, like nature, alternate meanings from the text could not be mined to suit the prescriptions of reason. Spinoza disavowed the miracles detailed in the Bible and attributes their description as the product of unscientific minds. The study of the Bible was to be inductive and unbiased by prior suppositions. The objective was attaining dispassionate information.[101]

Spinoza extended the scientific approach to the Bible which Azariah de Rossi had applied to rabbinic *aggadah*. De Rossi had used scientific and historical criteria in evaluating the veracity of non-legal statements made by the rabbis. De Rossi cited Moses Maimonides' position that when the rabbis commented on natural phenomena (e.g. heavens), they did so on the basis of their knowledge and not as representatives of the tradition from Sinai. In these cases, the rabbis were liable to make errors. De Rossi enlarged the applicability of Maimonides' view to all of rabbinic *aggadah*. Spinoza continued along this path by approaching the Bible with the same historical and scientific tools. While he rejected Maimonides' use of allegorical interpretations to resolve problematic passages, Spinoza continued the former's approach.[102]

Despite a thorough knowledge of and, in fact, a great affinity for the New Testament which he displayed throughout his Treatise, Spinoza never formally adopted Christianity.[103] Indeed, while

---

[101] David B. Ruderman, *Jewish Thought and Scientific Discovery in Early Modern Europe* (Detroit: Wayne State University, 2001), 282-283.

[102] Ibid., 283.

[103] Spinoza's constant references to Christianity are found throughout his work and are especially poignant in the area of the continuing relevance of the Torah. Spinoza states: "If a people wished to transfer their rights to God, it would be necessary to make an express covenant with Him, and for this would be needed not only the consent of those transferring their rights, but also the consent of God. God, however, has revealed through his Apostles that the covenant of God is no longer written in ink, or on tables of stone, but with the Spirit of God in the fleshy tables of the heart." Ibid., 237.

honoring "true religion" (i.e. religious beliefs) that built up or directed humanity toward greater good; he rejected the conventional emphasis and ideas of both Jewish and Christian circles.[104]

## Baruch Spinoza's Approach to Torah

Spinoza's notions of Jewish identity and Jewish thought were ultimately founded on his critical approach to the Bible. His treatment of the Torah and the Jewish people appears focused primarily on the issue of peoplehood- a people tied to a particular land and history, language, and culture. These factors were funda-fundamental to his understanding of who was a Jew. He rejected covenantal identity. The Torah, Spinoza argued, did not serve as a unique spiritual covenant but served rather as the governing document of the Jewish nation. The promise of obedience to the law for Spinoza was at most the basis for a free commonwealth and did not reflect a spiritual elevation of the Jewish people.[105]

Once an independent Jewish state was no longer in existence, the need for and in fact viability of Jewish law was for Spinoza pointless and meaningless. The continued observance of the Torah was in actuality problematic. For Spinoza, Jewish chosenness was at most geographical, and the importance of the Torah related only to the duration of the Israelite state:

> "I learned that the Law revealed by God to Moses was merely the law of the individual Hebrew state; therefore that it was binding on none but Hebrews, and not even on Hebrews after the downfall of their nation."[106]

---

[104] In response to an inquiry by his landlord as to whether she might be saved in her religious tradition, Spinoza reportedly remarked: "Your religion is a very good one; you need not look for another, nor doubt that you may be saved in it, provided, whilst you apply yourself to piety, you live at the same time a peaceable and quiet life." Ibid., xix.

[105] Ibid., 47.

[106] R.H.M. Elwes, trans., Benedict de Spinoza, A Theologico-Political Treatise, (New York: Dover Publications, 1951), 8. Spinoza further stressed the existence of pre-Mosaic priests and kings serving in Jerusalem with God ordained laws and rituals. Ibid., 48.

Such a view, of course, is in direct conflict with classical Jewish perspectives on the covenantal nature of Jewish identity. The peo-people of Israel according to Judaism are a people brought into being by the establishment of a covenant. In the biblical view, the parameters of the covenant establish the definition of who is a Jew.

Spinoza rejected this view. In its place, he argued that the ritual components of the Torah were unrelated to what he referred to as a "state of blessedness."[107] In fact, Spinoza asserted that the continuation of Jewish identity was the ultimate source of anti-Semitism. Spinoza did foresee the possibility of a resurgent Jewish state. Spinoza recognized that circumcision was a key marker of Jewish identity.[108] Spinoza explained the nature of Jewish identity as related to the distinguishing features of any nation with regards to another.

> "Nations, then, are distinguished from one another in respect to the social organization and the laws under which they live and are governed: the Hebrew nation was not chosen by God in respect to its wisdom nor its tranquility of mind, but in respect to its social organization and the good fortune with which it obtained supremacy and kept it so many years."[109]

---

[107] Ibid., 76. "…if anyone wishes to maintain that the Jews, from this or from any other cause, have been chosen by God forever, I will not gainsay him if he will admit that this choice, whether temporary or eternal, has no regard, in so far as it is peculiar to the Jews, to aught but dominion and physical advantages (for by such alone can one nation be distinguished from another), whereas in regard to intellect and true virtue, every nation is on a par with the rest, and God has not in these respects chosen one people rather than another." Ibid., 56.

[108] "The sign of circumcision is, as I think, so important that I could persuade myself that it alone would preserve the nation forever. Nay, I would go as far as to believe that if the foundations of their religion have not emasculated their minds they may even, if occasion offers, so changeable are human affairs, raise up their empire afresh, and that God may a second time elect them." Ibid., 56.

[109] Ibid., 46.

For Spinoza, Jewish distinctiveness was a problem to be corrected. The rabbis of Amsterdam could not allow Spinoza's views to spread.

## Conclusion

The violence of the late 14$^{th}$ century not only destroyed physical lives but the faith of many who survived. While many Conversos were committed to observing Judaism to the best of their ability, others abandoned Jewish belief entirely. Many did not, however sincerely embrace Christianity. Their lives as Christians were characterized by a desire to succeed in the here and now and not from a genuine belief. Such attitudes may have been espoused by the severity of the destruction they witnessed. It may also have come from a belief that in the end, all religious traditions were equally valid or equally worthless. Moral failings of individual rabbis, a lack of belief in eternal punishment due to the influence of philosophy, belief in the transmigration of souls, or a decline of rabbinic scholarship may have also contributed to the loss of faith of among certain Conversos and a resignation to their current circumstances.

In the cases of Sanchez, La Peyrère, and Montaigne, their Jewish background was remote. But the social and religious impact of their ancestors having undergone conversion were still strong enough to influence their identity and thought. The challenges faced by Conversos coupled with the Renaissance, Reformation and discovery of the New World forged a unique identity. The religious wars that ravaged Europe during their lifetimes likely convinced them that absolute views on religious beliefs were misguided and untenable. The spiritual world of their Jewish ancestors was undermined violently. Decades later, Sanchez, La Peyrère, and Montaigne exposed the weaknesses of the religious systems they were now part of. By doing so, they helped set the stage for the reevaluation of religious and scientific beliefs.

In contrast to them, Da Costa and Spinoza were exposed to traditional Jewish identity. Their embrace of skepticism and rejec-rejection of conventional religious life, however, came about through elements of doubt that had been forged by the Converso experience. Spinoza, in particular, was influenced by other Conversos who ultimately seemed to be inclined towards challenging established authority whatever religious label it bore.[110] Having been forced to live in a Christian environment they did not freely espouse, many Conversos, who did join openly Jewish communities, equally resented what they regarded as the imposition of Jewish beliefs and rites. The fact that many were university-educated often prevented them from embracing a faith that claimed divine authority even if it was a Jewish one. The skeptical beliefs towards Christianity that many Conversos held following their coerced conversions was knowingly or unknowingly transmitted to their descendants.

---

[110] Jose Faur, *In the Shadow of History: Jews and Conversos at the Dawn of Modernity* (New York: SUNY, 1992), 142. Despite Spinoza's rejection of classical Jewish ideas, his views have been seen as a harbinger of later "Jewish" thought. Dagobert D. Runes went as far as to note the following: "One can say that through every thought and word of the philosopher Spinoza there breathes the Ruach Hakodesh, the Spirit of Holiness of Judaism. Spinoza might rightly be called *Judaissimus*. The most Jewish of all thinkers…Ruach Hakodesh pervades the writings of Baruch Spinoza, the Holy Spirit that has breathed through the wisdom of literature of Israel from the days of the philosopher king, Solomon, and even earlier. Spinoza's *amor Dei intellectualis*, the spiritual love of God, is the closest to the Hebrew *simchah shel mitzvah*, the joy of faith, the joy of the law. In the ideology of Spinoza, living by the law of wisdom was identical with obedience to divine principle." Dagobert D. Runes, *The Ethics of Spinoza: The Road to Inner Freedom* (Secaucus: The Citadel Press, 1976), 1, 13.

CHAPTER 6

# Jewish Attitudes Towards Conversos

Few Jewish families were left untouched by the attacks of 1391 and the upheaval that followed. While some saw loved ones die as martyrs, many more saw family members succumb to the violence and undergo conversion. Jewish attitudes towards Conversos were expressed in three ways.

The first was practical and involved everyday relationships. The interaction between Jews and Conversos was not theoretical, but an everyday occurrence. The relationships between Jews and Conversos at the family level often remained positive since Jews understood that the conversions had occurred under duress. Since Conversos often remained in Jewish neighborhoods for decades, their family relationships were also reinforced.

The second area involved rabbinic considerations as to how Conversos were treated in relation to various areas of Jewish law. Rabbinic attitudes towards Conversos were driven in part by how or whether Conversos observed Jewish practices. Some responses were determined by circumstances beyond the control of Conversos. This was especially true in cases of marriage and divorce, but also included the permissibility of food and wine prepared by Conversos. There were also questions regarding Conversos who fled the Peninsula and openly returned to Judaism. These included the status of uncircumcised Conversos and how their return to Judaism was realized. Most rabbis did everything possible to ensure they were welcomed and helped in their journey back to Judaism. Rabbinic discussions on Conversos often reveal the Jewish practices and the beliefs they held.

The last area of concern was theological and revolved around the spiritual condition of Conversos. In the 17$^{th}$ century, with the creation of openly Jewish communities comprised of former Conversos in cities like Amsterdam, Hamburg, and London rabbis faced a new series of issues. The Conversos who escaped the lands of idolatry were well received. However, others who reached safety refused to join the community. Those who remained on the Peninsula or in other areas where Judaism could not be practiced openly were condemned for failing to join the Jewish community. The goal of this chastisement was to challenge them to journey to lands where they could openly practice Judaism. The rabbis' anger was predicated on the assumption that the Conversos were Jewish. In not leaving the lands of idolatry, they failed to live out proper Jewish lives, they prevented the redemption of Israel and endangered their eternal souls.

## The Connection of Conversos to the Jewish Community

The continuing family associations between Conversos and Jews served to reinforce the identification of the former with the Jewish community. As Mark Meyerson notes the enduring bond between Jews and Conversos was to be expected:

> "…because the baptism had been so obviously coerced, because the converts had only yesterday been Jews, and because the sense of community among Jews and conversos was thus spontaneous and natural, social relations – and machinations- among Jews and conversos

were, in several respects, continuous with those among just Jews before 1391."[1]

Jews were aware that some Jews had converted willingly, and others had converted under duress. The anti-Jewish polemical pamphlet of the late 15<sup>th</sup> century titled, *El Alboraique*, provides confirmation of how Jews responded differently towards voluntary and forced converts:

> "And they took among themselves the Hebrew term *anusim*, meaning forced converts and if one had converted to Christianity sincerely and adhered to Christian law/faith they called them a *Meshumad* which means he who mixes because they mixed with Christians. And if someone from this background arrives at a place where this evil generation [dwells], they [the Jews] ask, 'Are you an *anus* or a *meshumad*?' If they respond, 'I am an *Anus*,' they honor him and provide him with support. If he responds, 'I am a *meshumad*,' they do not speak to him again.'" [2]

Family bonds were a critical factor in the assistance Jews provided to Conversos. In 1393, for example, King Joan of Aragon punished two of the wealthiest members of the Jewish community in Morvedre. The two Jews in question were David el Rau and Jacob Facan. They sent their sons who had been baptized during the riots to North Africa. There they could live openly as Jews. In Facan's case, he along with his wife Ceti, their daughter Jamila, and their son in law Isaac Xamblell were accused of encouraging David to return to Judaism.[3] David Facan was persuaded by his family that the "Hebrew law is worth more than the Catholic faith" and he agreed to flee. A bribe secured David's

---

[1] Mark D. Meyerson, *A Jewish Renaissance in Fifteenth-Century Spain* (Princeton: Princeton University Press, 2004), 188.

[2] Prologo 391 quoted in Jeremy Lawrence, "Alegoria Y Apocalipsis En El Alboraique, Revista de Poetica Medieval," 11 (2009): 17. Mark D. Meyerson, *A Jewish Renaissance in Fifteenth-Century Spain* (Princeton: Princeton University Press, 2004), 39.

[3] Ibid., 37.

passage and other Conversos also boarded the ship bound for "the parts of Barbary and of the Saracen..."[4]

Jacob Facan was also active in helping other Conversos. He made *matzah* and delivered it to the town of Sogorb so that Con-Conversos could observe Passover correctly. The Converso Gaspar Sayes received *matzah* for Passover from Jewish friends in Morvedre. Abraham and Jacob Adzoni provided their converted relative Clara Fuster with *matzah*, kosher wine, and kosher meat. Salamo Caporta also gave kosher wine to Conversos. The Converso Pere Alfonso obtained kosher wine via the Jewish tavern in Morvedre.[5] Conversos from Valencia visited Morvedre and received kosher meat and food prepared by openly practicing Jews.

Jews and Conversos often shared Passover meals together and stayed in one another's home.[6] Since Conversos married other Conversos, the connections of husbands and wives to the Jewish family were strengthened.[7] The bonds were so strong that some Conversos were even involved in the politics of the *aljama* although they were technically no longer members of it.[8]

---

[4] Ibid., 39.

[5] Ibid., 206.

[6] One example of the continuing relationships between Conversos and Jews is the case of two Jewish families in Morvedre in the 1430s. The Maymo and Agi families received the backing of Converso families from Valencia in a feud that erupted between them. The blood feud centered on Pau de Sant Marti, a Converso who was murdered by Mosse Maymo. The sister of Mosse and Jahuda Maymo was Cinha. She learned of the attack on her brother while she was staying at the home of her Converso brother-in-law. In the court case, a witness testified to the closeness between Catala a Conversa and the Agi brothers who were Jews "He had heard them [Catala and the Agi brothers] call each other cousins all the time...and had seen the said Agis, Jewish brothers, entering and leaving, and in the time when the wounds were inflicted on the person Jahuda [Maymo]... and there they stayed eating and drinking." Ibid., 197.

[7] They married among themselves; it may at first be a matter of racial preference, but of course, for the most part was due to the disgust that Old Christians felt in marrying them. Besides this, they were strongly related to each other or their businesses, their friends were mutually supportive in everything that they learned." Jaime de Salazar Acha, "La Limpieza de Sangre," Revista de la Inquisición, Vol 1 (1991): 297-298.

[8] Mark D. Meyerson, *A Jewish Renaissance in Fifteenth-Century Spain* (Princeton: Princeton University Press, 2004), 188.

While some Jewish knowledge could be passed on from one generation of Conversos to the next, openly professing Jews still represented the ideal Jewish expression. Jews welcomed Conversos to eat with them in their homes. Salamo Caporta was ultimately arrested by the Inquisition and tried for having invited Conversos to Jewish festivals such as Sukkot and giving them kosher food.[9] Beatriu Guimera, a Conversa fasted on the Ninth of Av and then joined a Jew in breaking the fast. As Mark Meyerson explains:

> "…actually eating at a Jew's table in a Jewish home power-powerfully enhanced the conversos' sense of belonging to the Jewish community. Here conversos could witness a Jewish family eating, talking, and praying together- real flesh-and-blood people more tangible that the archetypal guardians of the Law of Moses of the converso's imagination."[10]

Conversos also invited Jews to their homes and provided ko-kosher food for their guests. An indication of this is found in the writings of Rabbi Isaac ben Sheshet Perfet (1326–1408).[11] He was asked about the kosher status of wine and meat prepared and handled by forced converts. Rabbi Perfet was asked if Jews were

---

[9] The celebratory nature of Sukkot provided a natural opportunity to join together. A Conversa named Aldonca later recalled: "I ate in the home of a certain Jew, and a table we ate chicken and other viands slaughtered and prepared by him. The Jew made a great festivity adorning the whole house [or booth] with green reeds and other things." Ibid., 208.

[10] Ibid.

[11] He was born in Barcelona and studied under a number of eminent Spanish rabbis. A. M. Hershman, *Rabbi Isaac bar Sheshet Perfet and his Times* (New York: The Jewish Theological Seminary, 1943), 3. The court records of Valencia reveal that he had been asked to convert as a means of ending the riots. He refused but converted once false charges that would have resulted in his death were levied against him. Rabbi Perfet was baptized on July 4, 1391. Within a year and a half's time, he escaped to North Africa and was able to return to an openly Jewish life. Isaac ben Sheshet Perfet, *Encyclopaedia Judaica*. Ed. Michael Berenbaum and Fred Skolnik. Vol. 10. 2nd ed. (Detroit: Macmillan Reference USA, 2007), 49.

allowed to rely on Converso testimony that their wine and food were kosher.[12]

Rabbi Sheshet responded that while a Jew should have chosen martyrdom when faced with conversion, a person who had proven weak in the face of persecution and accepted baptism should not automatically be considered as an invalid witness. These individuals were complete Jews since God forgave them for their weakness. A Jew, who sinned, was still a Jew and consequently, their wine and meat were kosher and available to other Jews.

The support given to Conversos was not limited to food. The connections that Clara Fuster's family maintained with her Jewish relatives were leveraged to secure a rabbi to officiate at the wedding of Clara's daughter Beatriu. Her daughter was less than ecstatic about this though the source of her discontent was likely due to the potential exposure this might bring. Her husband welcomed the rabbi's participation and in the end both man and wife observed the Sabbath and some Jewish holidays, albeit perhaps less unswervingly as her parents had.[13]

The support that Conversos received from the Jewish community was not a one-way street. Some Conversos who served as diplomats continued serving Jewish communities even after their conversion.[14] Many Conversos donated to synagogues and provided oil for synagogue lamps. Some gave money for dowries for poor Jewish girls. Others used their positions to promote the wel-

---

[12] Jews dietary laws specify that wine that a non-Jew handles is forbidden to be drunk by a Jew. A Jew is prohibited from even deriving benefit from it. See Mishneh Torah Sefer Kedushah *Ma'achalot Assurot*; Chapter 17, Halachah 9. See Touger, Eliyahu. "Ma'achalot Assurot - Chapter 17 - Texts & Writings." Ma'achalot Assurot - Chapter 17 - Texts & Writings. https://goo.gl/74NEE1 (accessed May 13, 2014).

[13] Mark D. Meyerson, *A Jewish Renaissance in Fifteenth-Century Spain* (Princeton: Princeton University Press, 2004), 203.

[14] Salo Wittmayer Baron, *A Social and the Religious History of the Jews: Volume X* (Philadelphia: Jewish Publication Society, 1965),180.

fare of the Jewish community. In Majorca, a Converso even authored a divorce document for a Jewish couple.[15]

## Marriage and Divorce among Conversos and Jews

Jewish parents often provided for their baptized children in their wills. Even the baptism of a spouse did not necessarily imply hostility or separation. Records indicate that a certain Samuel's wife, Bonafilla, resisted the urges to convert by her husband and even by those of the Crown with whom Samuel was associated. Despite this, they remained married.[16] Bonafilla even transferred ownership of some property she owned to Samuel. In 1419, she was still referred to as his wife when she granted him authority to lease property she owned.[17]

There were cases, however where continuing a marriage was untenable for the unconverted spouse or even those who had also converted. Some women left the Iberian Peninsula in the hope of practicing Judaism openly while their Converso husbands re-

---

[15] In *She'elot u-Teshuvot Tashbez* 3:43, Rabbi Simeon Ben Zemah Duran was asked about the legitimacy of a divorce document written by a Converso who violated Shabbat publicly. Unconverted Jews testified that he had converted under duress. He observed Judaism secretly to the best of his ability. Maimonides in his Mishneh Torah, Hilkhot Gerushin 3:15 wrote on the basis of Hullin 5a, that an apostate who practiced idolatry and publicly violated Shabbat was to be considered like a Gentile in every respect. Such an individual was not permitted to author valid divorce documents. Rabbi Duran noted that the witnesses testified that this Converso's conversion was false and his heart remained towards Heaven. Maimonides, Rabbi Duran contended, would have regarded the divorce document valid, because he had not converted voluntarily. The only disqualifier lay in whether the author's intention was to author the text as a divorce document. See Touger, Eliyahu . "Gerushin - Chapter Three - Texts & Writings." Gerushin - Chapter Three - Texts & Writings. https://goo.gl/HrTakr (accessed May 13, 2014).

[16] The possibility of divided households is brought up by Benjamin Gampel who describes the case of a Jewish family in Girona in 1391. The husband hand converted, while the wife refused to convert and cohabit with him as a married couple. Surprisingly, the presbyter of Girona was brought in to appeal to her to remain married to her now Christian husband albeit without blaspheming the Christian faith. In the end she refused, but reveals that the idea of a "mixed" marriage was possible. Benjamin R. Gampel, "The "Identity" of Sephardim of Medieval Christian Iberia," Jewish Social Studies Volume 8, Number 2/3, (2002): 136.

[17] Mark D. Meyerson, *A Jewish Renaissance in Fifteenth-Century Spain* (Princeton: Princeton University Press, 2004), 196.

mained. Rabbi Sheshet was asked about the case of a Conversa woman who had divorced her Converso husband. The woman escaped to Islamic territory. She had obtained a *get*, a Jewish writ of divorce but it was signed by other Conversos. This led some to question the legitimacy of the *get* and the ability of the woman to marry again. Rabbi Perfet contended that the forced converts who signed the *get* and had not fled the Peninsula had to be investigated carefully to ascertain whether they were legitimate witnesses.

He held that after having converted, some Conversos had purportedly let go of the yoke of the Torah and were willingly going the way of the Gentiles and violating all the commandments. Some were even informing to the government on other Conversos whose hearts were directed toward heaven and observed Jewish law to the best of their ability.[18] These Conversos would not have a share in the world to come. If the divorce document were witnessed by these types of persons, the divorce certificate was invalid.

Rabbi Perfet recognized that many Conversos stayed in the Peninsula for the sake of maintaining their family unity and did their best to observe the Torah. While this was admirable, service to God superseded everything. Even if this meant leaving children behind, this was to be done. While having stayed for seemingly right reasons, these Conversos were acting improperly. *Like Maimonides in his Iggeret Hashamad, Rabbi Perfet labeled a person who was capable of leaving a land of persecution but failed to do so* as an *almost* wanton sinner. Despite this, they were not automatically considered non-kosher witnesses since they did not believe they were committing a sin. If they were proper witnesses, the divorce document was legal. If not then the *divorcée* was an *agunah* (i.e. a bound woman) and

---

[18] Samuel Usque wrote: " I do not want to be remiss in tell you that in addition to the enemies, there were at the time some confesos who delivered their own brothers into this cruel monster's (i.e. the Inquisition's) power. Poverty was the spur and the reason for most of their evil acts. Many poor confesos went to the houses of their richer brothers to ask for a loan of fifty or a hundred crusados for their needs. If any refused them, they accused him of Judaizing with them." Martin A. Cohen. Trans. *Consolation for the Tribulations of Israel* (Philadelphia: Jewish Publication Society, 1977), 199.

could not remarry without obtaining an acceptable divorce document.[19]

## The Case of Levirate Marriage

A recurring topic related to Conversos was levirate marriage (a case in which the husband had died and his wife remained childless, and the brother in law was required to marry the widow in accordance with biblical law). The obligation of levirate marriage among Conversos was a subject discussed by numerous rabbinic authorities. Among the first was Rabbi Simeon ben Zemah Duran. He fled Majorca in 1391 in the wake of the violence. He settled in Algiers and served under Rabbi Perfet's rabbinic court until the latter's demise. He then succeeded him as chief rabbi of Algiers.

Rabbi Duran addressed the validity of Jewish marriages contracted by Conversos.[20] In one case, the party in question had married according to Jewish practice (i.e. with a *ketubah*, two witnesses, etc.). After her husband's death, the widow fled the Peninsula and openly returned to Judaism. Rabbi Duran ruled on whether a levirate marriage was applicable when the *yavam* (i.e. brother in law bound to perform levirate marriage) was a Converso and remained in the lands of idolatry.

Rabbi Duran cited the *Sefer Halakhot Gedolot* (a work on Jewish law dating from the Geonic period) which argued that even if the *yavam* were a voluntary convert, the obligation of levirate marriage continued. He also revealed the dissenting view of Rav Yehuda. Rav Yehuda stated that if at the time of the wedding, the *yavam* has already converted there was, in fact, no obligation of *haliza* (i.e. the procedure for the *yavam* to forgo marriage and release the widow to remarry whomever she wished).

Despite the fact that most authorities maintained that *haliza* was in force, in this case Rabbi Simeon ben Zemah Duran opted for

---

[19] Rabbi Nissan Antine, Lecture at Beth Sholom and Talmud Torah, 2010.
[20] *She'elot u-Teshuvot Tashbez* 3:47.

the minority view.[21] The decision allowed this Conversa to begin her life anew as a Jewess without restrictions. Doing otherwise would have left her ineligible for remarriage and could have easily caused her to return to the Peninsula as a Christian.

Another rabbi who agreed with this view was Rabbi David ibn Avi Zimra who was born in 1479 and left the Iberian Peninsula in the wake of the Expulsion decree. According to his view, if a Converso remained in Christian territory, this released his brother's widow from the obligation of levirate marriage to him.[22]

Rabbi Zimra appealed to any elements that cast doubt on the eligibility of a Converso to serve as a *yavam* or the obligation of levirate marriage.[23] For Rabbi Zimra, the Jewish ancestry of Conversos of later generations was always questionable. This was because they could not definitively tell that from the point of the first generation of converts until their own that none of their ancestors had married a Gentile.[24] If all Conversos were suspect, then levirate marriage was inapplicable. If the other brother remained a convert, the wife was free to marry whom she desired and no obligation of levirate marriage existed.[25]

Rabbi Zimra also argued that immersion for a Converso returning to Judaism was preferable in cases where uncertainty existed about the individual's matrilineal line.[26] Rabbi Zimra did not regard

---

[21] Maimonides, Rav Sherira Gaon, Rabbi Solomon ben Aderet, Rabbi Yakov ben Asher, and Rav Moshe ha-Kohen also held that an apostate was still a viable yavam.

[22] Dora Zsom, "Converts in the Responsa of R. David ibn Avi Zimra: An Analysis of the Texts," Hispania Judaica 6 (2008): 283. See Maimonides' Mishne Torah, Hilkhot Yibum ve-Halitsah 1:6: Touger, Eliyahu . "Yibbum vChalitzah - Chapter One - Texts & Writings." Yibbum vChalitzah - Chapter One - Texts & Writings. http://www.chabad.org/library/article_cdo/aid/960619/jewish/Yibbum-vChalitzah-Chapter-One.htm (accessed May 13, 2014).

[23] Dora Zsom, "Converts in the Responsa of R. David Ibn Avi Zimra: An Analysis of the Texts," Hispania Judaica 6 (2008): 284.

[24] Ibid.

[25] Ibid., 288.

[26] Responsa 3:415. Dora Zsom, "Uncircumcised Converts in Sephardi Responsa from the Fifteenth and Sixteenth Centuries," IberoAmerica Global Volume 1 No. 3. (2008): 169.

such a Converso as a Jew until he underwent circumcision and ritual immersion.[27] In contrast, Rabbi Simeon ben Shlomo Duran (*Rashbash*) (1400 – 1467) accepted the Jewish claims of Conversos without any concrete proof.[28] He considered forced converts fit for marriage, divorce, and levirate marriage. Their marriages were valid, and money could not be loaned to them at interest in accordance with biblical law.[29] The descendants of Conversos were considered Jews as long as the mother was a descendant of a Jewish woman. Intermarriage was uncommon because it resulted in estrangement from other Conversos who regarded children born from non-Converso women as idolaters.[30]

---

[27] This opinion is opposed to the widespread view that converts did not marry Gentiles, which was so well-established that a number of halakhic authorities even based their ruling on this legal presumption (Regarding the legal presumption see : Yakhin u-Boaz 2: 3, 31; Mahari ben Lev, Responsa, 1:15; R. Moshe of Trani, Responsa 2:83; R.Shemuel de Medina, Responsa, Even ha-'Ezer 112).

[28] One example is that of a Converso who arrived in Salonika. He was not aware of his original Jewish family name. Accordingly, he picked one at random after returning to Judaism. He subsequently received a message from an old woman in Safed, who claimed she knew he was descended from a priestly family. Based on this information, he adopted the name Cohen for himself. On this evidence alone he was given synagogue duties performed by *Kohanim*. The responsum relating this case stated, "And thus it is the custom with regard to all Marranos ('anusim) who declare themselves to be kohanim, and they are called thus upon their own word, and there is no suspicion whatever." Yosef Hayyim Yerushalmi, *The Re-Education of the Marranos in the Seventeenth Century*. lecture., Hebrew Union College, 1980. In Amsterdam, unless there was an obvious maternal ancestor who was an Old Christian, the community adopted what Miriam Bodian describes as a "don't ask, don't tell" policy. The returning Conversos had no ketubot or other documents that would provide indisputable proof regarding their background. The ancestral pedigree of Converso families was generally acknowledged as sufficient. Miriam Bodian writes that, "Communal leaders probably hesitated to act on such matters unless, as in the cases mentioned, the problematic female relative was a very recent ancestor and a person whose gentile status was well known. Given 'Portuguese' ideas about the purity of Jewish blood, members of the Mahamad would not have been eager to uncover gentile blood in respected families." Miriam Bodian, *Hebrews of the Portuguese Nation* (Bloomington: Indiana University Press, 1997), 113.

[29] Dora Zsom, "Converts in the Responsa of R. David Ibn Avi Zimra: An Analysis of the Texts" Hispania Judaica 6: (2008): 269.

[30] "This presumption [that the mother of the convert is Jewish] is proven by the common practice of the reputed authorities everywhere, that they oblige the returning converts only to circumcision and not to ritual immersion, since we do not suspect them to have Gentile mother. It is a common presumption that the converts do not marry Gentiles." Yachin u'Boaz 2:31 quoted in Dora Zsom, "Uncircumcised Converts in Se-

Another rabbi who held the continuing obligation of *haliza* for Conversos was Rabbi Yakov ibn Habib, who had left the Iberian Peninsula in the wake of the edict of expulsion.[31] His son, Levi ibn Habib, was forced to undergo conversion in Portugal. He eventually fled to Salonika where he returned openly to Judaism. Rabbi Habib's objective may have been to include as many Conversos in the category fit to serve as potential *yavamim*, perhaps to remind them of their Jewish background. This is seen in his reference to the Talmudic tractate Hullin (13b), which identified contemporary Gentiles as not real idolaters when compared to those mentioned in the Torah. Conversos had not adopted a pagan religion in the vein of the Canaanite religions mentioned in the Torah. As a consequence, Conversos had not truly left the Jewish fold.[32] The obligation of the levirate marriage was, therefore, binding on them.

## The Process of Return for Conversos

Conversos returning to Judaism were well received by local communities even though some acrimony did occasionally exist.[33]

---

phardi Responsa from the Fifteenth and Sixteenth Centuries," IberoAmerica Global Volume 1 No. 3. (2008): 169. Another member of the Duran dynasty was Rabbi Zemah ben Shlomo Duran who also addressed priestly lineage claimed by Conversos. Rabbi Duran was contacted by Rabbi Nathan Busti of Fez. Rabbi Busti had referred to Conversos fleeing to Fez as Gentile converts to Judaism. Some of these Conversos claimed that they were of priestly ancestry. Rabbi Duran rebuked Rabbi Busti for designating them as Gentile proselytes to Judaism and simultaneously asking if their priestly claims were to be believed. Rabbi Duran explained that non-Jews converting to Judaism could never claim priestly descent. The Conversos fleeing to North Africa were "not called by the term gerim [i.e., 'converts'] for they are [Isaiah 41:14] the worm of Jacob; they are considered [ibid] maggots of Israel, and are not called gerim for this purpose, but rather, penitents..." Rabbi Busti was "mistaken in referring to the penitents of the anusim as gerim..." Talya Fishman, Zemah ben Shlomo Duran, She'elot u-Teshuvot Yachin u-Vo'az,(Jerusalem, 1995) II.3, selections from pp. 23-25.. (Manuscript, University of Pennsylvania, 2004), http://www.wesleyan.edu/socsci/Develop/emw/workshops/summer04/fishman/duran_2/english.html.

[31] Eliyahu Mizrahi, no. 47. *She'elot u'Teshuvot Rabi Eliyahu Mizrahi*, Yerushalayim, 1984. Elliot N. Dorff and Arthur Rosett, *A Living Tree: The Roots and Growth of Jewish Law* (Albany: State University Press of New York, 1988), 329.

[32] Dora Zsom, "The Levirate Marriage of Converts in the Responsa of Some Sephardic Authorities," Kut 3 (2008): 106.

[33] An Algerian Jew who had undergone conversion and then returned to Judaism argued that returning Conversos would pose a financial hardship on the local community.

Rabbi Simeon ben Shlomo Duran worked to ensure that returning converts were warmly embraced since he held they had already entered the covenant at Sinai by virtue of their lineage. Rabbi Duran's views were supported by Rabbi Saadia ben Maimon ibn Danan (d. 1493). Rabbi Danan's overriding concern was that Conversos return to Judaism. Rabbi Danan rejected any approach which likened Conversos to non-Jews.

> "If the Anusim are to be considered as Gentiles and those who return to Judaism as proselytes, their desire to return to the fold will weaken, so that finally they will assimilate among the Gentiles, add crime to their sin and even their name will be forgotten from Israel." [34]

He argued that adherence to a foreign religion could not remove their status as Jews. He wrote:

> "The Gentiles insult and attack them every day, calling them Jews and hating them...By God, there is reward for many of them – I mean for those who expose themselves to great danger in observing some of the commandments- a reward much greater indeed than for Jews who have no fears nor face any danger but rather are praised by the Gentiles for observing the law of the LORD and His commandments, and even [though] they do not do it properly." [35]

---

This position was rejected outright by Rabbi Isaac ben Sheshet. Edward Fram, "Perception and Reception of Repentant Apostates in Medieval Ashkenaz and Premodern Poland," AJS Review 21/2 (1996): 338.

[34] Hemdah Genuzah 16b, ed. Edelmann, Koenigsberg, 1856 quoted in Benzion Netanyahu, *The Marranos of Spain: From the Late 14th to the Early 16th Century, According to Contemporary Hebrew Sources* (Ithaca: Cornell University Press, 1999), 64.

[35] The concern over the acceptance of Conversos was also echoed by Rabbi Joseph Caro, the author of the *Shulchan Aruch*. Both expected punishment for anyone reminding a returning forced convert of his former state. Caro also understood the complicated real life situation that Conversos faced and their inability to meticulously observe all commandments. Salo Baron, *Social and Religious History of the Jews: Volume XIII*, (New York: Columbia University Press, 1958), 95, 153.

Like Rabbi Danan, Rabbi Simeon ben Shlomo Duran also differentiated between descendants of converts to Christianity who returned to Judaism and contemporary proselytes to Judaism.[36] Unlike present-day Gentile converts, Conversos were not instructed in various commandments and the corresponding punishments for transgressing them as stipulated in the Talmud. They did not undergo immersion either.[37] This view was not universally accepted but was dominant among most Sephardic rabbis.[38]

Regarding Conversos returning to Judaism, Rabbi Zimra maintained that since their ancestors had already accepted the commandments at Sinai, this act also counted for all their offspring. Rabbi Zimra's position was based on the biblical account of Joshua's circumcision of the Israelites born in the wilderness after the Exodus.[39] Joshua did not require that they undergo immersion. Rabbi Zimra reasoned that the first generation of forced converts was similar to the generation of the wilderness in that both were compelled by circumstances to act in an unusual manner. Rabbi Benjamin Zev also explained that saving one's life took precedence over the commandment of circumcision. Jews who had been converted by physical force were regarded as uncircumcised Jews who did not need immersion and were to be deemed to be Jews in most

---

[36] The responsum in *Yachin u-Boaz 1:75* relates that: "Ritual immersion was not prescribed for the converts reverting to Judaism, and they are not called *gerim* but *baalei-tshuva*. These returning converts are similar to the Jew who does not perform the precept of circumcision [but performs the other precepts], or to one who was not circumcised by his father and mother, and has to be circumcised by the rabbinical court of law, or by himself: none of these persons need ritual immersion. Thus decided the French rabbis as well: the convert, even if he was idolater, does not need ritual immersion [if he wants to return to Judaism] and neither has to declare in the presence of three men that he has the intention of observe the precepts." Quoted in Dora Zsom, "Uncircumcised Converts in Sephardi Responsa from the Fifteenth and Sixteenth Centuries," IberoAmerica Global Volume 1 No. 3. (2008): 168-169.

[37] Yevamot 47a

[38] Dora Zsom, "Converts in the Responsa of R. David ibn Avi Zimra: An Analysis of the Texts," Hispania Judaica 6: (2008): 269.

[39] Rabbi David ben Solomon ibn Avi Zimra, Responsa, 3, 415. Ibid., 270.

areas. The failure to undergo immersion did not prevent Conversos from returning as full members of the community.[40]

Consequently, a first generation Converso was reintegrated without an official ceremony.[41] Mortification of the flesh was mentioned by Rabbi David Zimra (1479-1573) but mainly seen as unnecessary. Rabbi Benjamin Zev also rejected mortification as superfluous.[42]

## Circumcision

To the Inquisition, circumcision could not be explained away, and so most Conversos of the second and subsequent generations were uncircumcised. The lack of circumcision was generally recognized not to pose a disqualification in cases of marriage, divorce, and levirate marriage. Some Jews, however still questioned whether an uncircumcised Converso or one with an uncircumcised father was actually Jewish.[43]

If returning Conversos were not circumcised, this was remedied as quickly as possible.[44] The rabbis, however, confirmed that the lack of circumcision did not affect their halakhic standing or their marital status.[45] Rabbi Duran ruled that the Jewish status of an un-

---

[40] Ibid.

[41] Dora Zsom, "Uncircumcised Converts in Sephardi Responsa from the Fifteenth and Sixteenth Centuries," IberoAmerica Global Volume 1 No. 3. (2008): 163, 168.

[42] Benjamin Ze'ev no. 72 states: "I think that he does not need to chastise himself, since there is no greater mortification of the flesh than what he suffers each and every day anyway: namely, that he has to abstain from all those pleasures which are permitted to the Gentiles, and were permitted to him also formerly [before his reversion]." quoted in Dora Zsom, "Uncircumcised Converts in Sephardi Responsa from the Fifteenth and Sixteenth Centuries," IberoAmerica Global Volume 1 No. 3. (2008): 170.

[43] See David Silberg, Yeshivat Har Etzion, "Parashat Lekh Lekha." Accessed January 9, 2013. http://www.vbm-torah.org/archive/salt-bereishit/03-11lekh.htm.

[44] Yachin u-Boaz, 2, 3. Dora Zsom, "Uncircumcised Converts in Sephardi Responsa from the Fifteenth and Sixteenth Centuries," IberoAmerica Global Volume 1 No. 3. (2008): 163-164.

[45] Maimonides in Hilchos Nedarim 9:21, Chidushei Ha'Ran (Rabbi Nissim Ben Reuven), and Rabbi Menachem Meiri argued that even a Jew who intentionally refused to be circumcised was not to be deemed an *arel*. They derived this position from Mishnah that

circumcised male born to a Conversos family was unaffected.[46] If a child of a Jewish mother had an uncircumcised or non-Jewish father, their halakhic status remained intact.[47]

Rabbi Zimra contended that an uncircumcised Converso was eligible for counting in a minyan. A Jew even if he was uncircumcised was regarded as being circumcised.[48] Rabbi Zimra agreed that the failure to observe the commandment of circumcision was a transgression, but the individual remained a Jew. Rabbi Duran's position was echoed in *Yachin u-Boaz* 2:31. It stated that an uncircumcised Converso was also similar to a child that was not circumcised for life-saving health reasons, a view also supported by Rabbi Benjamin Mattathias Zev. For Rabbi Zev, remedying the lack of circumcision was in actuality no more important than the observance of any formerly unobserved commandment. There were some restrictions. If the uncircumcised Converso was a *Cohen*, he was ineligible to eat *terumah* or the Passover sacrifice as the Torah specifically restricted these actions to circumcised Jews.[49]

## The Importance of Circumcision for Later Conversos

---

says that an *arel* refers only to a *Nochri* (foreign or Gentile). For more a more extensive discussion see Kollel Iyun Hadaf of Yerushalayim Insights to the Daily Daf, "Nedarim 31." Accessed January 1, 2013. http://dafyomi.co.il/nedarim/insites/nd-dt-031.htm.

[46] "All the more in the case of these converts, if one of them marries a woman, his marriage is valid, and also the marriage of the child who was born after the conversion of the parents and is uncircumcised: for everybody, whose mother is a convert, even if the father is Gentile, is Jewish; so similarly, if the father is uncircumcised, the child is Jewish." Tashbez, 3, 47 quoted in Dora Zsom, "Uncircumcised Converts in Sephardi Responsa from the Fifteenth and Sixteenth Centuries," IberoAmerica Global Volume 1 No. 3. (2008): 166. The same arguments are also found in the decisions of Rabbi Solomon Ben Simon Duran no. 89 and in Yachin u-Boaz 2:19 and 2:31.

[47] Yebamoth 23a. "The son of your daughter who derives from a heathen is called 'thy son.'" Isidore Epstein, *The Babylonian Talmud* (London: Soncino Press, 1984).

[48] Rabbi Simeon ben Zemah Duran stated that "a Gentile is called uncircumcised even if he is circumcised, while a Jew is called circumcised even if he is uncircumcised." Yachin u-Boaz, 1,107 quoted in Dora Zsom, "Uncircumcised Converts in Sephardi Responsa from the Fifteenth and Sixteenth Centuries," IberoAmerica Global Volume 1 No. 3. (2008): 166. See Mishnah Nedarim 31 B.

[49] Exodus 12:48.

Declining knowledge of Jewish practices increased the importance of circumcision among Conversos. Conversos attributed the same special role to circumcision that Christians credited to baptism. The Conversos of the city of Bayonne in France highlight this. In 1663, Conversos there corresponded with Rabbi Moses Raphael D'Aguilar of Amsterdam.

Living an openly Jewish life was still prohibited in France. These Conversos were troubled by the arrival of Dr. Isaac de Avila from Amsterdam. He circulated a letter he claimed was authored by Rabbi Isaac Aboab, which condemned Conversos living in Southern France. The letter stated:

> "Those members of the Nation who keep the commandments of the Torah before being circumcised have no part in divine grace, and they are condemned to eternal damnation. Hence, every converso who arrives from the Iberian Peninsula must be circumcised within three months of his arrival. If not, he will be excommunicated."[50]

The Conversos of Bayonne were stunned by the severity of these words. One of the Conversos, David Manuel Isidro wrote to Rabbi Moses Raphael D'Aguilar hoping to understand the ramifications of the letter. Isidro asked whether the Conversos of France, who by law were not allowed to practice Judaism openly, would be forgiven for foregoing the commandment of circumcision. Isidro wondered whether uncircumcised males were prohibited from keeping any other commandments. He also inquired about the eternal state of someone who had been buried according to Christian burial rites. Isidro questioned if it were prohibited for uncircumcised males to enter a synagogue. Lastly, he asked about the fate of those who returned to the Peninsula because of financial necessity. Isidro understood the limitations of the "Judaism" that Conversos in France observed and was cognizant that they were

---

[50] Yosef Kaplan, "Wayward New Christians and Stubborn New Jews: The Shaping of a Jewish Identity," Jewish History, Vol. 8, No. ½ The Rober Cohen Memorial Volume (1994): 31-32.

failing to fulfill their responsibilities. Isidro pleaded with Rabbi D'Aguilar to allow them to continue praying to the God of Israel.[51]

Rabbi D'Aguilar dismissed the letter as a forgery and also addressed the near sacramental status that circumcision had attained among Conversos. Rabbi D'Aguilar explained that circumcision could not purify or redeem. It could not bring salvation or transform Conversos into pure Jews. Circumcision did not bring salvation, particularly to those who still pretended to be Christians. It could not atone for the sin of idolatry. Conversos were baptized as Christians, ate non-kosher foods, neglected the laws of *niddah*, violated the Sabbath, and even lent money at interest.

Despite their failings, uncircumcised Conversos were not exempt from the observance of the commandments.[52] Rabbi D'Aguilar did not view the Conversos of France as forced converts since he argued they could leave whenever they wanted. This fact compounded the gravity of their sins. D'Aguilar then provided

---

[51] Ibid., 33.

[52] A rabbi of Pisa in Italy was asked about a former Converso who had returned to Judaism. The former Converso was devout. He prayed three times a day, wore a tallit, and observed the mitzvoth, but was not circumcised. The reason was his need to return to the lands of idolatry to secure his fortune. A controversy erupted over whether a Converso was permitted to observe *mitzvot* and to hold a Torah scroll if he was not circumcised and had not immersed himself. The rabbi was inclined to allow him. He even leaned towards allowing him to wear *tefillin*. His position was rejected by the sages of Livorno. The sages did not argue against the merits of allowing this specific individual from doing so. They acknowledged that the law permitted this, but believed that making the former Converso equal to a full Jew without undergoing circumcision undermined the return of other Conversos. They believed they would put off circumcision indefinitely. The rabbis acknowledged that this former Converso was in effect still an *anus* in the literal sense, in that, even though he was outside the Peninsula, he was still subject to duress and could not be circumcised yet. They recognized that his whole heart was directed with Heaven, and he was scrupulous regarding all the other mitzvoth. Regarding this type of forced convert, they made no distinction apart from the matter of *tefillin*. Regarding those who postponed circumcision not out of duress, but because of lethargy were to refrain from wearing *tzitzit* and even attend synagogue services until they repented. Responsa Mayim Rabim, Rabbi Rafael Mildula (Amsterdam, 5497 [=1737], Pt. 10, §§51, 52; quoted in El Libro de los Acuerdos (Oxford, 1931). Translation provided by Rabbi Yehonatan Chipman. Also see David Graizbord, "Religion and Ethnicity among "Men of the Nation": Toward a Realistic Interpretation," Jewish Social Studies: History, Culture, Society. n.s. 15 (2008): 54-55.

conflicting advice. Even though those who lived in idolatrous lands had no hope of salvation in the World to Come, they were still obligated to keep the commandments. Observing the commandments could take them to the right path one day. D'Aguilar sought to encourage the Conversos of France to flee. He ended his letter with "...you are our brethren, and we do not wish to cut you off from the body of Israel!"[53]

## Circumcision as the Rite of Passage

Since Conversos regarded circumcision so powerfully, many believed that any sins committed before undergoing circumcision were not counted. The lack of circumcision effectively removed their obligation to the Torah, or at least protected them from the consequences of violating it. This idea was extremely troubling to rabbis such as Rabbi Samuel Aboab, who believed this view was keeping Conversos from fully returning to Judaism. Rabbi Aboab wrote:

> "The vain idea which has spread among almost all sons of our people who come from the servitude of the soul [i.e., the Peninsula]..., that so long as a man is not circumcised he is not part of Israel [and] his sins are not sins....And some claim that the day of their circumcision is the first day on which their sins begin to count." [54]

Rabbi Aboab insisted that circumcision was a commandment like all the other commandments of the Torah and that all male Israelites were bound to keep them regardless of whether they were circumcised or not. Former Conversos who had already undergone circumcision, along with other rabbis encouraged vacillating Conversos to observe the commandment. The rabbis

---

[53] Yosef Kaplan, "Wayward New Christians and Stubborn New Jews: The Shaping of a Jewish Identity," Jewish History, Vol. 8, No. ½ The Rober Cohen Memorial Volume (1994): 33.

[54] Miriam Bodian, *Hebrews of the Portuguese Nation* (Bloomington: Indiana University Press, 1997), 98.

understood circumcision as *the* ceremony of return, the presumptive Jewish status of former Conversos notwithstanding.[55] An adult male undergoing circumcision was nevertheless not an easy proposition. The Converso Isaac Cardoso fled Madrid at the age of forty-five. In Venice, he observed Judaism openly and was circumcised. He noted that:

> "...it is not like some light wound in the leg or an easy bruise on the arm, but rather something hard and difficult which no one would undertake unless he were moved by great awareness and zeal to embrace the Law of the LORD. This is also the reason why it is done at the tender age of eight days when the pain is not so great as later, and the imagination is still weak. But all this increases with maturity when a man becomes apprehensive and fears things before they happen..." [56]

Rabbi Saul Levi Morteira of Amsterdam who was typically very strict noted that God pardoned the sins of those who lived among Gentiles if they returned to Judaism. In commenting on the story of Moses' journey to the land of Egypt, Morteira wrote:

> "From this we learn how God pardons the sin of those who dwell among the Gentiles and were not able to be circumcised because their lives would be endangered. However, once they have the opportunity [and neglect it], God punishes them immediately."[57]

Postponing circumcision provided the individual with the option of returning to the lands of idolatry. Even if he were arrested, he could protest that he had not reverted to Judaism. Once

---

[55] Ibid., 98-99.

[56] Yosef Hayyim Yerushalmi, *The Re-Education of the Marranos in the Seventeenth Century.* lecture., Hebrew Union College, 1980.

[57] Marc Saperstein, "Christianity, Christians, and 'New Christians' in the Sermons of Saul Levi Morteira,' Hebrew Union College Annual, Vol. 70/71, One Hundred Twenty-Fifth Anniversary (1999-2000): 378-379.

circumcised, no argument could deny this reality. Circumcision was a definitive act that effectively ended the connection with the individual's former life. With that in mind, the rabbis of Amsterdam strove to have Conversos undergo circumcision as quickly as possible to prevent any wavering.[58] Rabbi Morteira commented the following:

> "One who is able to be circumcised and is not circumcised is guilty every passing moment of a new punishment of karet, making for infinite punishment, and he cannot be saved. However, one who is circumcised and circumcises his sons at this time when there is no longer a paschal sacrifice- the Bible speaks of him [in Ps. 50:51] as if he had offered the paschal sacrifice as well."[59]

The *Mahamad* of Amsterdam imposed a ban on travel to the lands of idolatry. Circumcising Conversos was apparently so important, however, that they were willing to look the other way if not directly support emissaries traveling to the Peninsula for that purpose. In the 1630s, *mohelim*, ritual circumcisers, from Amsterdam were reportedly active in Castile. According to evidence presented in 1635 by the Inquisitional Tribunal of Toledo, a certain David Farhi, a *mohel* from Amsterdam, had circumcised Conversos in Castile. A Converso testifying in this investigation noted he had undergone circumcision by David Farhi while he was in Amsterdam. He had moreover, seen David Farhi in Madrid only eight days before his testimony. In 1635, another Converso testified before the Inquisition in Brazil that he had personally heard Rabbi Menasseh ben Israel note that every year certain Jews left Holland and journeyed to the Peninsula, to circumcise Conversos.[60]

---

[58] Ibid., 377.
[59] Ibid., 378.
[60] Miriam Bodian, *Hebrews of the Portuguese Nation* (Bloomington: Indiana University Press, 1997), 146. Various figures in Amsterdam including Eliahu Montalto, Rabbi Immanuel Aboab, and Abraham Idana (Gaspar Mendez del Arroyo) were involved in a campaign to convince Conversos to flee the lands of idolatry. The arguments included

## The Eternality of Punishment

The integration of Conversos and their adherence to Judaism were of paramount importance to the community of Amsterdam and other communities composed primarily of former Conversos. Rabbi Saul Levi Morteira, the head rabbi of the community, held an unforgiving stance against Conversos, who failed to immigrate to lands where they could openly observe Judaism. For Morteira, Conversos were Jews who would be punished eternally if they failed to return to the Torah.[61]

Rabbi Isaac Aboab Fonseca, a student of the former Converso and Kabbalist Abraham Cohen de Herrera who in turn was a student of Israel Sarug believed that "All Israelites are a single body (*guf echad*) and their soul is hewn from the place of Unity."[62] Every Jew no matter where they resided or how deficient their connection to Torah may have been was still an essential component of the transcendent body of Israel.[63] Aboab was focused on ensuring the acknowledgment of Conversos as part of the people

---

the practical such as leaving the Peninsula to avoid potential arrest by the Inquisition but most were theologically focused. Idana for example argued against the view that the Law of Moses could be kept in one's heart as opposed to actual observance. He also argued against the notion that the lack of circumcision absolved Conversos from their failure or inability to observe certain commandments. According to an ecclesiastical and royal investigation into crypto-Jewish activity in Rouen in France, two Jews from Amsterdam Eliahu Montalto and Rafael Buendia visited Rouen in 1631. While there, they conducted a Passover *Seder* for Conversos in the area. In 1633, another report regarding Rouen related that Jao (Moses) Pinto Delgado had learned Hebrew from two rabbis who had visited the area. The report also claimed that Delgado had received aid from the Jewish communities in the Netherlands, Livorno, and Venice among others. In the end, the investigation was dropped thanks in large part to large financial inducement. In 1673, an inquisitorial report suggested that Conversos in Bayonne and Peyrehorade traveled to Spain on business or for the purpose of instructing other Conversos in Jewish observance. Ibid., 143, 145.

[61] Alexander Altmann, "Eternality of Punishment: A Theological Controversy within the Amsterdam Rabbinate in the Thirties of the Seventeenth Century," Proceedings of the American Academy for Jewish Research, Vol. 40 (1972): 1-2.

[62] Sarug in turn was a student of Hayyim Vital, the famed pupil of Isaac Luria. Ibid., 19.

[63] Noah H. Rosenbloom, "Menasseh Ben Israel and the Eternality of Punishment Issue," Proceedings of the American Academy for Jewish Research, Vol. 60 (1994): 251.

of Israel without any qualification. This was predicated on Aboab's Kabbalistic belief that Jewish souls were distinct.[64]

Rabbi Aboab was also a former Converso. Aboab believed that Conversos were Jews who had a share in the world to come. Aboab believed that when the Sages stated that "a Jew, even though he sinned, is a Jew" this meant the following:

> "Even though he sinned, he shall not be cut off forever from the tree because of this; he is indeed a Jew and even though he has exchanged God for new gods, he will still be called a Jew again through the transfiguration and punishment, all according to a trial of justice, as explained."[65]

Rabbi Morteira opposed Rabbi Aboab fiercely on this issue. Morteira was more skeptical regarding Kabbalistic tradition than Aboab was. Morteira refused to accept this belief that Conversos that failed to rejoin the community would share in the World to Come. The conflict pitted Morteira, an eminent Talmudic scholar against Aboab, a leading Kabbalist.[66] Morteira believed the existence of eternal punishment was key in ensuring his community remained faithful to Torah observance without deviation.[67] Morteira was so troubled by the potential consequences of Abo-

---

[64] Ibid., 17. Rabbi Isaac Aboab did not dismiss the idea of punishment. His belief in *gilgul* did not promise a pass for those who had transgressed the Torah. The souls of every Jew were to be purged of their transgressions through the process of transmigration. Transmigration was characterized by suffering. Aboab also dismissed the notion that belief in *gilgul* would sway Conversos towards remaining in their present condition. Alexander Altmann, "Eternality of Punishment: A Theological Controversy within the Amsterdam Rabbinate in the Thirties of the Seventeenth Century," Proceedings of the American Academy for Jewish Research, Vol. 40 (1972): 19.

[65] Yosef Kaplan, "The Portuguese Jews in Amsterdam: From Forced Conversion to a Return to Judaism," *Studia Rosenthaliana* XV, No. 1 (1981): 40-41.

[66] Noah H. Rosenbloom, "Menasseh Ben Israel and the Eternality of Punishment Issue," Proceedings of the American Academy for Jewish Research, Vol. 60 (1994): 246.

[67] Ibid., 258.

ab's views, that he designated this belief as heresy.[68] Rabbi Morteira believed that Rabbi Aboab's position effectively encouraged Conversos, who remained in the lands of idolatry to linger there.[69] Morteira was resolute in his interpretation of classical Jewish sources on this issue.[70] For Morteira, the Mishnah's statement that "all Israel (Israelites) have a share in the world to come" was not to be regarded as an unqualified judgment.[71]

Morteira was concerned that the Aboab's interpretations were gaining currency among many of the community's youth.[72] The

---

[68] "It is blasphemy to believe that these extremely wicked people have not been given an eternal punishment…those who believe in their salvation are relying on a falsehood when they say that they will not suffer the ultimate evil since they are Jews." Yosef Kaplan, "The Portuguese Jews in Amsterdam: From Forced Conversion to a Return to Judaism," *Studia Rosenthaliana* XV, No. 1 (1981): 41.

[69] Ibid.

[70] He stated: "But the minim, informers and apikorosim…descend to hell (le-dorey dorot), as it says, 'and they shall go forth, and look upon their carcasses of the men that have transgressed against me: for their worm shall not die, neither shall their fire be quenched, and they shall be an abhorring unto all flesh. (Isa. 66:24)'"Alexander Altmann, "Eternality of Punishment: A Theological Controversy within the Amsterdam Rabbinate in the Thirties of the Seventeenth Century," Proceedings of the American Academy for Jewish Research, Vol. 40 (1972): 24. Also see Noah H. Rosenbloom, "Menasseh Ben Israel and the Eternality of Punishment Issue," Proceedings of the American Academy for Jewish Research, Vol. 60 (1994): 257.

[71] In concert with Isaac Arama, Morteira agreed that the term "Israelite" was identical with the word "righteous." Isaac Arama stated: "If he (the Tanna) meant to state that every Israelite, regardless –whether wise, wicked or indifferent, has a share in the word-to-come, then this is an absolute injustice…It is justifiable that the children of His servant Israel, just or unjust, should all merit the world-to-come? Heaven forbid. However, if he (the Tanna) meant that anyone bearing the name Israelite is assuredly righteous and, therefore, entitled to a share in the world-to-come, it is impossible, since it is at variance with the facts, as evident by the many heretics in their midst…The true meaning and novelty in his dictum, however, is that one is not called a true Israelite unless he is righteous, because 'Israelite' and 'righteous' are interchangeable synonyms…Every Israelite is assured of the world-to-come and everyone who is assured of the world-to-come is an Israelite." Noah H. Rosenbloom, "Menasseh Ben Israel and the Eternality of Punishment Issue," Proceedings of the American Academy for Jewish Research, Vol. 60 (1994): 252.

[72] Rabbi Morteira wrote "…some of those young men who were deficient (*bilti shelemim*) in this belief, and their party lodged such vigorous complaint against me in that in my anguish I was compelled to admit as controversial a perfect doctrine of our faith which we received from our Fathers, the Prophets, the *Tanna'im* and the *Amora'im*, and which, permitting no doubt, was upheld by the more recent authorities." Alexander Altmann, "Eternality of Punishment: A Theological Controversy within the Amsterdam

opponents of Rabbi Morteira assumed that his position was reflective of Christian perspectives. Ever sensitive to their Christian backgrounds, these former Conversos were against anything that they identified as foreign.[73]

They approached the communal leaders and demanded that Rabbi Morteira be prevented from disseminating his views on the eternality of punishment. The debate quickly escalated to a matter of heresy with Morteira appealing to the rabbinic court in Venice.[74] The leaders of the community approached Rabbi Abraham Aboab first and not the *Bet Din* directly for his review of the matter.

Rabbi Abraham Aboab pleaded with Rabbi Isaac Aboab Fonseca to reject his views on the afterlife and abstain from disseminating these opinions. Chief among Rabbi Abraham Aboab's concern was the dangerous implications it could have for former Conversos. He wrote that it was especially necessary to relate this warning to "those of our people who came from those places…[who] would seek only one thing, namely the way how to serve God in sincerity (*bitemimut*) and how to fulfill the *miswot* according to Halakah in all their minutiae."[75]

Morteira's belief in eternal punishment did not sever the halakhic status of Conversos. It was Rabbi Morteira's recognition of Conversos as Jews that upset him so much. Conversos were bound to suffer as Jewish sinners if they failed to leave or escape the lands of idolatry when the opportunity presented itself.

---

Rabbinate in the Thirties of the Seventeenth Century," Proceedings of the American Academy for Jewish Research, Vol. 40 (1972): 12.

[73] Noah H. Rosenbloom, "Menasseh Ben Israel and the Eternality of Punishment Issue," Proceedings of the American Academy for Jewish Research, Vol. 60 (1994): 254, 256.

[74] Alexander Altmann, "Eternality of Punishment: A Theological Controversy within the Amsterdam Rabbinate in the Thirties of the Seventeenth Century," Proceedings of the American Academy for Jewish Research, Vol. 40 (1972): 12.

[75] Ibid., 15. For Rabbi Menasseh ben Israel's views on the afterlife see Noah H. Rosenbloom, "Menasseh Ben Israel and the Eternality of Punishment Issue," Proceedings of the American Academy for Jewish Research, Vol. 60 (1994): 253.

## Visiting the Land of Idolatry

The Amsterdam community was very concerned about former Conversos returning to Catholic lands on business. Even prominent members of the community visited Spanish-controlled areas of the Netherlands where living as a Jew was prohibited and subject to Inquisitional scrutiny. Rabbi Morteira, the head rabbi of the community was severely critical of those who chose to return on even a temporary basis.

> "Because of their money they abandon God, remaining in the lands of their enemies and worshipping another god in order to care for their wealth, their lands, and their houses. Worse than this: some of them go back there, like Lot's wife, who looked behind her and became a pillar of salt (cf Gen 19:26). She did not understand the great act of kindness God had performed for her in saving her from that conflagration but looked behind her, in defiance of God's command. Her concern was for her property rather than for God's act of kindness; therefore she became a pillar of salt. And this is the fate that will befall those who have escaped from the conflagration yet return here to take out their property; they will remain a useless pillar of salt burnt by brimstone. We see examples of this every day."[76]

---

[76] Marc Saperstein, "Christianity, Christians, and 'New Christians' in the Sermons of Saul Levi Morteira,' Hebrew Union College Annual, Vol. 70/71, One Hundred Twenty-Fifth Anniversary (1999-2000): 383. Morteira went on to compare the return of Conversos to the lands of idolatry to Egypt and Babylon. "God commanded that from that first evil and sin-producing land from which He brought the Israelites out the king must not get horses lest he bring the people back there (Deut 17:16). It was against God's will for the people to return to that evil land. From that example, we learn about others. When God brought the Jews out of Babylonia, some of them brought forbidden wives- Sidonian, Moabite, Hittite- as is written in the Book of Ezra. When they divorced them, following Ezra's counsel, it is obvious that these women returned to their father's homes in their own countries, lest they take up again with these women. Similarly, when God has brought out a number of the 'children of Israel' from the sin-producing Iberia, it is certainly an abomination in God's sight for someone to return there in order to increase his

In 1644, the community of Amsterdam instituted a rule that required any member who journeyed to the lands of idolatry, upon their return to ask for forgiveness, publicly. The primary concern was the concealment of their Jewish identity since they had to live as Christians in these lands.[77]

Despite this rule, approximately 82 members of the Amsterdam community are noted to have traveled to the Peninsula over a period of 80 years (from 1644-1724).[78] The transgressor was called up to the Ark in the synagogue and required to ask for clemency. Even after this, they were to suffer sanction by not being permitted to fulfill any public role for four years following their return to Amsterdam.[79]

## Indifference among Some Conversos

While some Conversos thrived in an open Jewish environment, some were hesitant to leave their familiar surroundings in "the lands of idolatry" out of a measure of indifference. While most Conversos did marry other Conversos, Rabbi Morteira recognized that some did not and used this relationship to justify remaining in the lands of idolatry.[80] In a comparison to the Hebrew slave mentioned in the book of Exodus, Rabbi Morteira writes that in

---

wealth. God has said to you, (Deut 17:16), for it is like Egypt, nay even worse in its sins. Those who have not paid heed have aroused God's wrath." Ibid., 383-384.

[77] Harm den Boer, "Exile in Sephardic Literature of Amsterdam Studia Rosenthaliana," Vol. 35, No. 2 (2001): 195.

[78] Moises Orfali, "The Portuguese Dowry Society in Livorno and the Marrano Diaspora," Studia Rosenthaliana, Vol. 35, No. 2 (2001): 153.

[79] Yosef Kaplan, "The Portuguese Jews in Amsterdam: From Forced Conversion to a Return to Judaism," Studia Rosenthaliana XV, No. 1 (1981): 43.

[80] Rabbi Morteira recognized that Conversos tended towards endogamy. In 1624, he wrote: "How much God warned us against intermarriage, for this causes a blurring of the identity of peoples. Even today we have seen God's gracious love in this matter. What has enabled the last remnant of the exile of Jerusalem which is in Sefarad (Obadiah 20) to preserve its identity is their refusal to intermarry with the Gentiles of that land. This has preserved their lineage and their identity, so that they are not lost to the community of the Eternal." Marc Saperstein, "Christianity, Christians, and 'New Christians' in the Sermons of Saul Levi Morteira,' Hebrew Union College Annual, Vol. 70/71, One Hundred Twenty-Fifth Anniversary (1999-2000): 361.

cases of intermarriage since "...the wife belongs to an alien faith, they are not truly his children...He will go forth alone, and be counted with his people." But not all Conversos in this arrangement were willing to abandon their families. Were they to state, 'I love the master and my wife and my children, I will not go forth to freedom" God would "bring him to judgment (Exod 21:6), removing him from the exile to pass sentence against him..." He would, "be laid to rest with the uncircumcised (Ezek 32:19), for there worm will never die and there fire will never be extinguished (Isa 66:24).[81]

The consequences for failing to leave the Peninsula were not only reserved for the future but experienced in the present day. The Inquisition, Morteira argued was an instrument of divine punishment.[82] Rabbi Morteira explained why such Conversos would be punished. "For this hypocrisy and this concealing of their true faith in God is detested by Him. It is truly a violation of their oath, which our ancestors explicitly accepted, making it a futile oath."[83] Rabbi Morteira believed that the souls of Jews were naturally inclined towards the Torah. Many ex-Conversos in Amsterdam had exhibited a sincere embrace of Torah study and devoted the energy necessary to achieve a mastery of it. The fact that some

---

[81] Ibid., 367-368.

[82] "...You will confess to them in humiliation and disgrace what you did not want to affirm with honor and joy in other places. And this is three ways. *With a strong hand*, namely, through the power of a strong Inquisition investigating all the laws of the realm. *And with an outstretched arm*: an arm extended and stretched for a long, long time, a period of imprisonment and punishment lasting many years. *And with overflowing fury* (Ezek 20:33), which they pour out to each other, by calling each other to pay their debts to this punishment. All of this is the result of the violation of their oath for God wants them to fulfill it against their will, and not to their good." Ibid., 369.

[83] Ibid., 370. Rabbi Morteira wrote: "But the Eternal will never forgive him [...] Every sanction...will come down upon him (Deut 29:19), meaning that he casts his oath to the ground, yet despite it all, he will not accomplish what he wants, for The Eternal will single him out from all the tribes of Israel for misfortune (Deut 2:20), single him out not for good but for evil, so that he too will admit being of the tribes of Israel, admitting against his will what he wanted to conceal." Ibid., 370-371.

Conversos remained in lands where they could not study the Torah pointed to the suppression of their natural affinity for it.[84]

In a manner reflective of Rabbi Judah Loew's view that something physical as well as metaphysical distinguished Jews from non-Jews, Rabbi Morteira held that Conversos were imbued with Jewish attributes that readily explained their return to Jewish life after many generations had passed. Rabbi Morteira also made it clear that Conversos were not proselytes but had returned to their true selves. Finally, it was likely that his congregants in Amsterdam needed to be reminded that there was a consequence for abandoning or refusing to embrace the covenant. As Marc Saperstein notes:

> "Even those whom the Inquisition had robbed of any future stake in Portugal must have felt something of a loss. Amsterdam, with all its attractions, was not a paradise, and not all were successfully integrated into the community. Many experienced severe economic hardship, others spiritual and intellectual dislocation. Lingering doubts as to whether they had made the right decision would have been normal."[85]

---

[84] Commenting on the weekly parashah of Shemot, Morteira wrote: "This is the meaning of God's Torah is perfect, restoring the soul (Ps 19:8), namely that the soul of the Israelite and the Torah dwell serenely and peacefully together, but not with any other religious teaching…Thus, we have seen that the conversos of Jewish descent immediately embrace the Torah when they hear something from it, for there is a close affinity between them. By contrast, it is extremely difficult for Gentile proselytes to understand it, with rare exception of those who devote enormous energy and intense prayer." Ibid., 373.

[85] Ibid., 375. Rabbi Morteira was cognizant that not all who had left the Peninsula and joined the community of Amsterdam had necessarily done so with the sole motive of embracing Judaism openly: "There are those who dwell at ease in the lands of God's enemies. Their children are with them, and their houses are filled with possessions. Feeling secure and serene, as if they lack nothing, they do not remember God or ever call Him to mind. Then, suddenly, when disaster strikes, they flee for their lives from the oppressor's wrath. They arrive in these lands and return to Judaism, thinking that God owes them much because they have done a great deed. This is not the repentance that God wants. It is rather repentance that occurs 'in the very context in which they sinned.' (cf b.Yoma 86b), while they are living in peace and quiet and contentment: to leave it all—

Rabbi Morteira was cognizant that even for those who had earnestly sought to recapture Jewish life, the daily challenges in Amsterdam were sufficient to cause some to deviate from their original spiritual goals.[86] Their struggles were real, but he contended that such suffering was not comparable to the past.[87]

## Doubts Regarding the Oral Law

There were other concerns. Skepticism towards the Oral Torah was prevalent among many former Conversos. This doubt was directed at the observance of commandments in line with the Oral Torah's instructions as well as Midrashic interpretation.[88] To counter these doubts, attention was typically given to the works of Samuel da Silva and Rabbi Moses Raphael d'Aguilar that defended the Oral Law against the challenges of Uriel da Costa. Other treatises such as Rabbi Immanuel Aboab's *Nomologia* written in 1629 and Rabbi David Nieto's *Kuzari ha-Sheni* authored in 1714 were also produced to counter doubt with regards to the veracity of the oral tradition. The issue was also a concern in Bordeaux as late as 1755 and 1777-1778 as recorded by Rabbi Hayyim Yosef David Azulai from the land of Israel. He traveled to the area as an

---

wealth, honors, even family- and return to God. Then He will have mercy upon them." Ibid., 376.

[86] Ibid.

[87] "When people who find themselves in a difficult situation remember a far more serious one from which they have been saved and enabled to escape, the current problem seems like nothing to them, and they are thankful to God that they have escaped from the other. For example, the 'children of Israel' who have left Portugal, though they live here in conditions of severe economic hardship that make even the provision of food a burden, nevertheless accept it all cheerfully, giving thanks to God for having saved them from the terrible suffering and the fearful oppression they experienced in the place they left. For when they were back there, they used to say, 'If only we could escape from this place, we would be content to eat grass.' So it was with Moses: though he was living in the house of his father-in-law, dependent on others, earning his keep with difficulty as a shepherd, when he thought of the place from which God had saved him he rendered praise and thanks." Ibid., 380.

[88] Albert van der Heide, "The Role of the Bible in the Amsterdam Portuguese Sephardi Milieu," Studia Rosenthaliana, Vol. 35, No. 2 (2001): 241.

emissary only to find very open discussions about the rejection of the Oral Law.[89]

The issue was not new to the community. In previous years, a notable member of the *Bet Jacob* synagogue, David Farrar, was accused of espousing unorthodox views. While the veracity or legitimacy of the Oral law does not appear to have been a source of contention, he did apparently reject particular Midrashic and Kabbalistic interpretations. Part of this may have stemmed from the Conversos' Christian past that emphasized a scientific approach to biblical interpretation derived from medieval Jewish thought and emerging Christian scholarship.[90] The tension that grew out of this situation led to various members leaving and creating a new synagogue in Amsterdam named *Bet Israel* with Rabbi Joseph Pardo at its head. The matter was taken to the rabbinic court in Venice. Rabbi Leon of Modena noted in Farrar's defense that "…if he interprets some of our sages' unreasonable words literally or interprets in a different way from Rashi or the early commentators, this is the way of an expositor or student of the Torah." The most important issue, was that "…all of us should observe it (i.e. the Torah) in every detail in a uniform manner and not one this way and the other that way, otherwise Israel will not be one nation."[91]

The concerns over deviations from traditional rabbinic practice and belief were intense, as the stakes were high.[92] Any rejection or

---

[89] Miriam Bodian, "Hebrews of the Portuguese Nation: The Ambiguous Boundaries of Self-Definition," Jewish Social Studies, New Series, Vol. 15, No. 1, Sephardi Identities (2008): 73.

[90] Albert van der Heide, "The Role of the Bible in the Amsterdam Portuguese Sephardi Milieu," Studia Rosenthaliana, Vol. 35, No. 2 (2001): 241.

[91] Yosef Kaplan, "The Portuguese Jews in Amsterdam: From Forced Conversion to a Return to Judaism," *Studia Rosenthaliana* XV, No. 1 (1981): 50. David Farrar appears to have been a conundrum of sorts for the rabbis. Rabbi Leon of Modena described him as "donning phylacteries and wearing a fringed garment almost every day and not drinking any impure wine since his coming to take refuge in God and strictly fulfilling the sages' decrees which many of those circumcised from birth and teachers of the Torah in our provinces take lightly and observe in a permissive manner." Ibid. 51.

[92] Miriam Bodian, *Hebrews of the Portuguese Nation* (Bloomington: Indiana University Press, 1997), 49.

perceived dismissal of what the rabbis considered traditional was problematic. This was because many Conversos were skeptical about the Judaism they encountered upon their escape from Spain and Portugal.[93]

Rabbi Morteira saw doubt regarding the Oral Law and the authority of the sages as a spiritual blemish and sickness of the soul. Interpreting Leviticus 13:10, which discusses *Tazria* (skin afflictions), Rabbi Morteira derived three spiritual diseases that characterized the challenges the fragile community of Amsterdam faced.

> "Thus...three kinds of heretics [*kofrim*] who diverge from the path of faith of God's Torah. They are the ones mentioned at the beginning of the *parashah* [in Lev. 13.2]. The first are the philosophers, who follow the path of logical deduction, deriving from it what they apprehended and nothing else...The second are those who accept the divine Torah, and have commandments and deeds intended for the service of God, but whose Teaching has been falsified, attributed to God although it is not [from God]...The third are those from among the children of Israel, who boast that they observe the Torah of our rabbi Moses, but who diverge from some of its principles and roots, such as the Karaites and those like them."[94]

Morteira struggled with all three types of heresy in and around his community. The identity of philosophers is evident, but their numbers were always small. Christianity in its Protestant form presented a greater threat to the Jewish fidelity of former Conversos since the classical theological points of objection were lessened to a degree with the elimination of statues and many Catholic rituals.

---

[93] Miriam Bodian, "Hebrews of the Portuguese Nation: The Ambiguous Boundaries of Self-Definition," Jewish Social Studies, New Series, Vol. 15, No. 1, Sephardi Identities (2008): 75-76.

[94] Daniel Frank and Matt Goldish, eds. *Rabbinic Culture and Its Critics: Jewish Authority, Dissent, and Heresy in the Medieval and Early Modern Times* (Detroit: Wayne State University Press: 2007), 316-317.

The third category was the most problematic since many Conversos struggled with the authority of the Oral Torah. Morteira likened those who doubted the veracity of the Oral Torah to Korah, who led a rebellion against Moses and the Karaites who rejected the rabbinic tradition.[95] The doubters of the Oral Torah just like Korah and his followers subverted rabbinic practices. There were those like Uriel da Costa, who claimed that the Oral Torah had been invented by rabbis. But the concern was not limited to a few voices. Morteira noted:

> "As for all those who arose from among the Jewish people to dispute the Jewish religion, they did not dare to dispute about the Written Law. Had they done this, they would have left the category of the Jewish people and would no longer have been considered as part of our nation; thus no one would have paid them any heed. Rather, when they sought to introduce contention and strife, they did so regarding the words of tradition and the interpretation of the Law that was given orally, for this is the most vulnerable part, having no support in a written record. They, therefore, thought they could destroy the Torah through the breach of this wall, for certainly without the Oral Law, the Written Law would be sundered into a thousand Torahs according to the large number of opinions, and everyone make of it whatever he wanted."[96]

The doubters of the Oral Torah slandered the rabbis and students of the Torah. Like Korah they waged war against Moses and Aaron and proclaimed, "All the community are holy, all of them and the LORD is in their midst. Why then do you raise yourselves up to lord it over us?" [Num. 16:3]"[97] While acknowledging the serious nature of the challenge these doubters posed, Morteira related that this struggle was not unique to his generation. Harboring

---

[95] Ibid., 319.
[96] Ibid., 321.
[97] Ibid., 324.

doubts about the immortality of the soul, divine reward and punishment, the authenticity of the Oral Torah, and the authority of the rabbis resulted in spiritual if not physical destruction (i.e. Uriel da Costa's suicide). While it may have been natural for former Conversos, given their past, to contest the veracity of the Oral Torah, challenging the tradition was an ever-present danger that confronted the Jewish people.[98]

## Conversos Who Failed to Return to Judaism

Rabbi Morteira questioned the pure Jewish descent of those who remained behind in "the lands of idolatry". The challenge to their Jewish identity did not lie in their halakhic status, but rather in their spiritual ancestry. In a homily given in 1622 or 1623 and subsequently published in his work titled, *Givat Sha'ul*, Rabbi Morteira wrote:

> "Those who are truly of the children of Israel never cease, day or night, from returning to the estate that they inherited from their ancestors, paying no heed to the dangers or tribulations that might occur to them. And those who have been forgotten, why they are from that element mixed into [the Jewish people]. For God, who knows all hidden things, purified our dross and removed our slag (cf. Isa 1:25) so that we might return to our original condition."[99]

Rabbi Morteira reassured those who had escaped the Peninsula or other regions where they suffered persecution that their efforts reflected their true loyalty to Judaism and their actual lineage from biblical Israel. He noted that during the time of the Hasmoneans, John Hyrcanus forced scores of Edomites to convert to Judaism.

---

[98] Ibid., 326- 327.
[99] Marc Saperstein, "Christianity, Christians, and 'New Christians' in the Sermons of Saul Levi Morteira," Hebrew Union College Annual, Vol. 70/71, One Hundred Twenty-Fifth Anniversary (1999-2000): 356.

These forced converts were injurious to the welfare of the Jewish people and the Talmud (Yebamot 47b) referred to them as boils on the skin. While these events happened long before, the deleterious effects of such converts remained a real issue in the present. Rabbi Morteira stated:

> "For God separated out all of those who became assimilated among them during the Second Temple period, in that they were the Jews who accepted the new religion [Christianity] and were removed from the rest. Therefore, this is one of the reasons why this nation is called Edom, as R. Isaac Abravanel explained in chapter 34 of Isaiah. And those who were assimilated among the Gentiles in their exile became estranged from their brothers and alien to their mother's children, so that they were set aside for evil from all the tribes of Israel (cf. Deut 29:20)."[100]

The picture of the Edomites as forced converts to Judaism and the subsequent adoption of Christianity by many of them was a striking comparison to the Iberian Jews who had adopted Christianity. The forced conversion of the Edomites to Judaism resulted in weak ties to the Jewish people and Judaism. This made many of them vulnerable to heresy; consequently many adopted the teachings of the early Christian movement. Not all the descendants of the Edomites had converted to Christianity. Many had remained as Jews, but their offspring had similarly succumbed by adopting Christianity.

Unlike other forced converts that had fled and had now joined openly Jewish communities, those individuals refused to leave and had striven to assimilate among non-Jews. Their actions could only identify them as the descendants of the Edomites. Morteira adopt-

---

[100] Ibid., 357.

ed a type of genetic determinism similar to what Christians had argued about Conversos and their propensity to Judaize.[101]

Rabbi Morteira argued that there were several categories of individuals who failed to leave the Peninsula. One group was those who were concerned over losing their fortunes in any attempted escape. Rabbi Morteira compared this decision to the choice made by Jacob's sons in not staying in the land of Canaan when they journeyed there from Egypt to bury Jacob. They returned to Egypt; Morteira argued because life was more comfortable for them. Hence he wrote:

> "We have seen this very same phenomenon, because of our sins, in those who thinking of their need for sustenance, assimilate in a land that is not theirs and worship idols. They make vows to God that as soon as they accumulate a little wealth; they will leave that land and go to serve the true God. But when wealth comes to them, they forget their vows, and their good fortune makes them rebellious. So it has always been."[102]

This theme appears several times in Morteira's writings. Just like Esau, Conversos, who refused to leave the lands of idolatry were selling their birthright.[103]

Rabbi Morteira also condemned those who were unwilling to leave the Peninsula due to fear of Inquisitional prosecution. He

---

[101] Ibid., 357.

[102] Ibid., 358.

[103] Ibid., 359. Rabbi Morteira wrote that the sins of Esau were related in order,"...to teach all those who are similar to Esau, those who, because of physical sustenance and bodily pleasures spurn the Eternal and His service, bury their offspring among the Gentiles, destroy their souls and lose their portion in the resurrection of the dead. They do not trust that God will provide them with food without transgressing His word. Yet this is all done to no avail, for they spurn their birthright after experiencing wealth and tranquility, and they are embarrassed over it, although it is the highest birthright of all. In this regard they are similar to Esau, and their inheritance will be like his, as the Bible says, I hate Esau (Malachi1:3)."

considered these Conversos as trapped between two realms. They were reluctant to observe the commandments out of fear. They were also hesitant to embrace Christianity because they did not have faith in its tenets.[104] Rabbi Morteira related that:

> "It is as Rabbi Isaac Abravanel interpreted: it speaks about the conversos, who have become like masses (*hamon*) of the Gentiles. They do not observe God's Law *because of fear,* and they do not observe the idolatrous law because they do not believe in it. Their portion is worse than that of the original idolaters, for they merely remained the same as believers in their idols. But those who believe in God and know Him: their sin is too great to bear (cf. Gen 4:13).
>
> About them, God said that he would do something He has never done, the like of which He would never do again (cf. Ezek. 5:9). That is the judgment of the Inquisition, something unprecedented, and never to be replicated as the experts know. What will result from it? *Assuredly fathers shall devour their children* (Ezek 5:10), meaning not the devouring of food in hunger but as in the verse, *They have devoured Jacob* (Ps 79:7), referring to destruction. Thus the fathers, in order to appear like the others before the Gentiles, will destroy their children by making them priests and nuns, cutting off their line of descent, destroying and annihilating them. *And children will devour and destroy their parents* (ibid.) by informing on them before the judges, as has occurred in many cases, so that the fire devoured them. And *because of this fear,* they will be dispersed in every direction. That is why the prophet concluded, *I will scatter all your survivors in every direction* (ibid.)"[105]

## Conclusions

---

[104] Ibid., 359.
[105] Ibid., 359-360.

The Conversos who maintained their identity despite being cut off from openly practicing Jewish communities for generations faced difficult challenges. They had to decide whether the risk of escaping the Peninsula or other lands they inhabited was worth the physical and financial risks for their families. They found the Jewish communities in the new lands they journeyed to supportive and embracing as long as they returned to Judaism.

While many of them maintained knowledge of certain Jewish practices, those who did journey to other lands were confronted with the task of adopting a lifestyle and identity that had often been theoretical at best. The experiences and education that had often given them social or financial success were often obstacles. The former Conversos, who were able to surmount all these issues and successfully embrace Jewish life, were nevertheless still tied to their past and the challenges that came from having lived as Christians. Jewish attitudes towards Conversos reflected an awareness of these difficulties and the rabbis and communities that Conversos joined attempted to cajole as well as chastise Conversos to return to Judaism and leave their past behind.

CHAPTER 7

# Modern Day Conversos

The Portuguese Inquisition ended its activities in 1821. The Spanish Inquisition ended its reign in 1834. The Inquisition's focus on Judaizing had, however, dissipated centuries before. Despite this, as late as the end of the 18<sup>th</sup> century, several new members of the Spanish and Portuguese congregation in London pointed to Inquisitional harassment as the reason for their recent departure to England. The last recorded cases of former Conversos leaving the Peninsula for England were Isaac Lopes Simões and David Pereira, who were circumcised in 1791.

From there, the story of the descendants of Conversos continuing to practice Jewish rites sounds like a mystery novel. An English Jew, who had lived in Lisbon during his youth, recorded that in 1819 two Portuguese men had attended Shabbat services in a Jewish home. They had reached Lisbon from Tras-os-Montes in the northeastern corner of the country and asked when Yom Kippur was observed. The account continues with the story of a Polish Jew named Samuel, who spent time with several Converso families. These families told Samuel that they never revealed their secret religion to their children until they were mature. They related that it was even customary for a young man from these families to enter the priesthood, to act as the confessor for them.

[1]

In 1917, a Polish Jew M. Samuel Schwarz, visited Belmonte, Portugal. He was introduced to a group of Conversos, but they were doubtful about his Jewish identity. They had no knowledge of Jewish communities outside Portugal. The fact that Mr. Schwarz could not recite any of the traditional Portuguese prayers they were familiar with only added to their incredulity. When he recited the Shema and came to the word Adonai, the matriarch of the group covered her eyes with her hands and confirmed Schwarz was a Jew because he knew the name of God. The Judaism of these Conversos was extremely limited. They rejected the messianic claims of Jesus and the saints of the Catholic Church. They met at regular intervals for prayer. They were endogamous. They observed elements of the Sabbath, Passover, Yom Kippur, and the Fast of Esther. The holidays were often delayed by one or two days to avoid prying eyes. On Friday night, some of them lit candles and hid them inside a pitcher. A few isolated Hebrew words survived in their prayers.

In 1924, the Jews of Lisbon contacted the Rabbinate in Jerusalem regarding the descendants of Conversos. A Portuguese Marranos Committee was formed in London under the joint auspices of the Alliance Israelite Universelle, the Anglo-Jewish Association, and the Spanish and Portuguese community in London. The congregation of Oporto was established. The community was supported by Baron Edmond de Rothschild of Paris and the Kadoorie family of Shanghai. A synagogue and school were built on the outskirts of Oporto with the goal of educating descendants of Conversos.[2]

## The Modern Period

From there the story of Crypto-Jews fell mostly silent. The recent phenomena of Crypto-Jews arose with Stanley Hordes, the

---

[1] Cecil Roth, *A History of the Marranos* (New York: Meridian Books, Inc., 1959), 136.
[2] Ibid., 139.

author of the work titled, *To the End of the Earth: A History of the Crypto-Jews of New Mexico. He and* Rabbi Joshua Stampfer founded the Society for Crypto Judaic Studies. The Society for Crypto-Judaic Studies was established in 1991 with the purpose of providing a forum for research, support, testimonials, and information on Crypto-Judaism. Hordes' doctoral dissertation centered on the original Spanish and Portuguese settlers of New Mexico and their Converso origins.[3]

Hordes served as the state historian of New Mexico and as a professor at the University of New Mexico. Hordes' interest in Crypto-Judaism was initiated by visits from locals who reported what they believed to be Jewish practices by their neighbors or themselves. Hordes was told certain families lit candles on Friday nights.[4] He was unclear why people related this information and thought it normal given the practice of many Catholic women to light candles. Hordes was also contacted by others who revealed that they or others did not eat pork. The continuing stories led Hordes to question whether Jewish customs and even Jewish consciousness had survived among the descendants of the Conversos who had settled in New Mexico.[5] Following the Mexican Inquisition's spree of activity in the 17th century, the remaining Conversos in New Spain are believed to have been assimilated into the larger Hispanic culture. Arnold Wiznitzer thought that the entire crypto-Jewish community in Mexico was destroyed by the end of the

---

[3] For an extensive review of the story of Luis Carvajal y de la Cueva, Luis de Carvajal el mozo, Gaspar Castaño de Sosa, Juan de Oñate, and many others Conversos in Mexico and New Mexico see Stanley Hordes *To the End of the Earth: A History of the Crypto-Jews of New Mexico. For a brief review see* City of Albuquerque "Conversos & Crypto-Jews" accessed April 1, 2015, https://goo.gl/U7eomW

[4] The most extensively reported crypto-Jewish practice that is non-biblical in origin is Friday night candle lighting. Schulamith Halevy argues that rabbinic practices serve as compelling evidence of ongoing Jewish tradition among the descendants of the Conversos. Schulamith C. Halevy and Nachum Dershowitz, "Obscure Practices among New World Anusim," Proceedings of the Conferencia Internacional de Investigacion de la Asociacion Latinoamericana de Estudios Judaicos November 1995, https://goo.gl/qNJkNW

[5] Wyatt Orme, "'Crypto-Jews' In the Southwest Find Faith in a Shrouded Legacy," Code Switch February 19, 2014, accessed March 25, 2015, https://goo.gl/uz1CbY

seventeenth century.⁶ Seymour Liebman concluded Crypto-Jews disappeared in the eighteenth century.⁷

After additional research and extensive interviews, Hordes found that the people providing him with anecdotal evidence of Jewish practices were potentially the descendants of Conversos who settled in the area centuries before. These individuals represented a broad continuum with respect to Jewish identity. Some had no consciousness of Jewish identity and did not retain Jewish practices. They did, however, have a bloodline, a name, or a predisposition towards genetic diseases typically associated with Jewish populations.⁸ At the other extreme were those whose grandmothers lit candles on Friday nights, who observed the Sabbath on Saturday in some form, who refrained from eating pork, or who circumcised their sons before it was medically customary. For Hordes, the genetic and genealogical research offered historical evidence that Crypto-Jewish practices had been passed down.

Hordes' views were challenged by individuals like Judith Neulander a folklorist and Case Western Reserve University lecturer. Neulander argued that Hispanics were possibly inventing a fictional Crypto-Jewish identity that was likely influenced by Christian Sabbatarian groups.⁹ She argued that the appearance of

---

⁶ Arnold Wiznitzer, "Crypto-Jews in Mexico During the Sixteenth Century," American Jewish Historical Quarterly 51 (1962): 168-214.

⁷ Seymour Leibman, *The Jews in New Spain* (Miami:University of Miami, 1970), 303.

⁸ As an example, Hordes points to the name Rael in New Mexico. He notes that the name goes back to one Jewish family in southeastern Spain that had converted in the 1480s.

⁹ Barbara Ferry and Debbie Nathan, "Mistaken Identity? The Case of New Mexico's "Hidden Jews," The Atlantic December 2000, accessed April 1, 2015 https://goo.gl/1GhPfQ In an interesting twist to Neulander's theory that Protestant sects affected those claiming Crypto-Jewish ancestry, sociologist Tomás Atencio suggests that the descendants of Crypto-Jews may have been early adherents to Protestantism in New Mexico. Access to the Hebrew bible may have been a key reason that the descendants of Conversos adopted Protestantism. City of Albuquerque "Conversos & Crypto-Jews" accessed April 1, 2015, http://www.cabq.gov/humanrights/public-information-and-education/diversity-booklets/jewish-american-heritage/conversos-crypto-jews

six-pointed stars on tombstones or reported kosher practices were insufficient to verify Jewish identity.[10] Many of those traditions, she contended, could be derived from separatist sects of Seventh-day Adventists, whose practices were notably more Hebraic than those of normative Protestant denominations.[11] Neulander also argued that Hispanics were looking to distance themselves from Native American or African ancestry. Hordes rejected this view since these individuals were identifying with a community still subject to anti-Semitism in various quarters of Latin American Catholic society.[12]

Hordes continued to interview individuals in New Mexico who reported vestiges of Jewish practices. He compared their family names with the birth, baptismal, marriage, death, and burial

---

[10] The Church of San Felipe de Neri in Old Town Albuquerque was renovated around the turn of the 20th century. During this century, artisans fashioned six-pointed stars in the arch over the altar. The "stars of David" were interpreted decades later as symbolizing Jewish faith. In the parish church on the plaza images of the biblical figures like Aaron, Moses, Samson, and David were included near the main altar. The inclusion of these figures is unique among New Mexican colonial churches. Above the entrance to St. Francis Cathedral, the Tetragrammaton in Hebrew letters is inscribed within a triangle. Whether Archbishop Jean Baptiste Lamy included this in honor of his friendship with the Jewish community of Santa Fe, which contributed to the construction of the cathedral is unclear. Ibid.

[11] Wyatt Orme, "'Crypto-Jews' In the Southwest Find Faith in a Shrouded Legacy," Code Switch February 19, 2014, accessed March 25, 2015, http://www.npr.org/blogs/codeswitch/2014/02/19/275862633/crypto-jews-in-the-southwest-find-faith-in-a-shrouded-legacy

[12] According to Aviva Ben-Ur, the evidence for Jewish identity transmitted uninterruptedly beyond the eighteenth century is slight. The notable exceptions are the descendants of Conversos who are endogamous. Examples of these are the descendants of Conversos in Belmonte, Portugal near the turn of the 20th century. Another example is the Chuetas of Majorca. Aviva points to the challenges in the testimonials of individuals claiming Crypto-Jewish backgrounds. Ben-Ur describes the case of a woman from a New Mexico. The woman wrote about the ostracism she felt as a Protestant. Her extended family was predominately Catholic. She later reinterpreted her childhood experience as a consequence of her crypto-Jewish backgrounds. Ben-Ur relates Seth Kunin's explanation that such changes do not reflect an invention of memory, but instead represent a move towards a strong Crypto-Jewish identity. Ben-Ur relates Kunin's view that all cultures undergo constant redefinition and recreation. The challenge of this, Aviva Ben-Ur, argues is that any attempt to demonstrate the authenticity of modern-day Crypto-Judaism is circular. Aviva Ben-Ur Review of Seth Daniel Kunin's Juggling Identities: Identity and Authenticity among the Crypto Jews https://goo.gl/NWDYDz

records archived in the state. He compared these results to Inquisition documents from Mexico, Spain, and Portugal. Hordes established genealogical links between several of these individuals and those in Inquisitional records. In subsequent years, the topic of continued Crypto-Jewish identity has grown tremendously with dozens of articles and stories in major American newspapers, academic journals, and various Jewish publications including *Shofar*, *Hadassah*, and *The Forward*.

## Modern Day Crypto Jews

In the last 25 years, the phenomenon of modern day Crypto-Judaism has been attested by many families. While there are countless stories, the following are intended to provide some examples. Many share common elements.

One such tale is that of Daniel Yocum. Yocum was raised in Albuquerque's Atrisco Valley as a Catholic. The men of his family gathered each Friday night as part of a secret society of Catholic *flagellants*. The men covered the wooden images of the saints, lit candles, and conducted what Yocum described as an altered Sabbath service. They also read from a handwritten Book of Psalms.

As a child, Yocum believed these acts were merely Catholic rituals particular to rural New Mexico. As an adult, Yocum became convinced of their Jewish origin. He began to live openly as a Jew and attended synagogue, observed kashrut, read the weekly Torah portion, and wore a head covering.

The existence of these practices was confirmed by Perry Peña, Daniel Yocum's college roommate, who related that his grandmother lit candles on Friday. His grandparents attended church on Saturday instead of Sunday. His family used biblical names including Abrana, Adonais, Ezekiel, Isaac, Eva, Eliasim, and Moises.¹³ Perry's ancestors slaughtered animals by slitting their throats, drained the blood, removed the sciatic nerve, and salted the meat. They never ate pork, rabbit, or shellfish.¹⁴ Peña's family also swept dust into the middle of a room.¹⁵ They burned their fingernail trimmings and hair clippings in the hope of preventing miscarriages. This is a common practice among many families with Converso backgrounds. Peña's family also buried their loved ones within a day of death. They mourned them for a year. In contrast to many families claiming a Crypto-Jewish background, the Peña family did not cover the mirrors in the homes of the deceased. New mothers did not abstain from marital intimacy for forty days.¹⁶

Another individual claiming a Crypto-Jewish background is Sonya Loya. She was raised Catholic and later became involved in Pentecostal churches. Like other persons claiming a Crypto-Jewish background, her first foray into Judaism was through Messianic

---

¹³ In Sandoval County, in Northern New Mexico there is a tombstone of a World War II veteran. The name of the man, who was born in 1921, is Adonay P. Gutierrez. Eli Rosenblatt, "Picturing Today's Conversos," Forward April 2008, Accessed March 25, 2015, https://goo.gl/WpkWvk

¹⁴ According to Richard Santos, chicken is slaughtered in a special way in the regions encompassing Nuevo Leon, Tamaulipas, Coahuila, and parts of Texas. They are slaughtered by either wringing the neck by hand or by severing the head with only one stroke of a sharp knife. The blood is drained from the chicken into a basin. The fowl is then placed in hot water to remove the remaining blood. This method is the same Crypto-Jews practiced in the 17th century. Anne DeSola Cardoza, "Texas Mexican Secret Spanish Jews Today," accessed on April 1, 2015, https://goo.gl/zeAMf6 *See also* Schulamith C. Halevy and Nachum Dershowitz, "Obscure Practices among New World Anusim," Proceedings of the Conferencia Internacional de Investigacion de la Asociacion Latinoamericana de Estudios Judaicos November 1995, https://goo.gl/so3tC3

¹⁵ According to Schulamith C. Halevy, the descendants of *anusim* often sweep floors towards the middle of the room. This practice was observed by Portuguese Conversos according to Rabbi Moshe Hagiz approximately two hundred years after the Expulsion. Ibid.

¹⁶ Theodore Ross, "Shalom on the Range: In search of the American Crypto-Jew" Harper's December 2009, Accessed March 27, 2015, https://goo.gl/ajFz72 Some women abstained from marital relations and did not attend Church for forty days after giving birth. This practice was based on an interpretation of Leviticus 12:4 which was the subject of argument among rabbis of the medieval period. Schulamith C. Halevy and Nachum Dershowitz, "Obscure Practices among New World Anusim," Proceedings of the Conferencia Internacional de Investigacion de la Asociacion Latinoamericana de Estudios Judaicos November 1995, https://goo.gl/so3tC3

Jewish groups near Santa Fe. She experienced her first Sabbath service there and saw Hispanics wearing yarmulkes and reading Hebrew. This led her to a spiritual trek that culminated in her conversion to Judaism.[17] It was only later that Sonya Loya's father related that his family members made him promise to keep their Jewish past secret. Her father's uncles served in World War II and saw the concentration camps. They told Loya's mother that it was still not safe to be a Jew.[18] Sonya's research led her to a DNA test that showed her father possessed a Cohen gene.[19]

Loya relates that her grandmother had an altar facing east. She prayed three times daily with a shawl over her head. This same grandmother routinely checked eggs for spots of blood. The descendants of some Conversos are meticulous in avoiding blood to the point of discarding eggs with blood spots.[20] She requested that when she died, her feet face east. Loya continued her research and found other Jewish Loyas. She even learned of a Loya Synagogue in Tiberias in northern Israel. There were also rabbis with the Loya

---

[17] Wyatt Orme, "'Crypto-Jews' In the Southwest Find Faith in a Shrouded Legacy," Code Switch February 19, 2014, accessed March 25, 2015, https://goo.gl/dMVsdc

[18] Paul Foer and Chananette Pascal Cohen, "For Hispanic 'Crypto-Jews,' lawsuits may follow religious rediscovery," JNS October 2012, accessed March 25, 2015, https://goo.gl/RjxhxC

[19] Jeff Wheelright, "The 'Secret Jews' of San Luis Valley," Smithsonian Magazine 2008, accessed March 25, 2015, https://goo.gl/kjcKdW Another aspect of DNA testing is found in the arena of genetic illnesses. In 2001, two Hispanic women with breast cancer were linked to a genetic mutation found primarily in Jews from Central or Eastern Europe. In comparing DNA samples from Jews around the world, scientists discovered the origins of the 185delAG mutation. Approximately 2,000 years ago, an ancient Israelite's DNA underwent this mutation. Because Jews often married other Jews, the 185delAG mutation gained a strong foothold. Approximately one out of a hundred Jews carries this gene variant. For Stanley Hordes the mutation's presence among Hispanics provides additional confirmation of the Jewish origins of certain Hispanic families.

[20] Schulamith C. Halevy and Nachum Dershowitz, "Obscure Practices among New World Anusim," Proceedings of the Conferencia Internacional de Investigacion de la Asociacion Latinoamericana de Estudios Judaicos November 1995, https://goo.gl/FX548k

family name and Jewish Loyas in Portugal, Israel, Morocco, Bulgaria and Turkey.²¹

Loya's passion for Judaism extends to others in an almost evangelical manner. She created a learning center to teach Hebrew and basic Judaism. The majority of her students are members of various evangelical Christian sects including the Seventh-day Adventists or the Church of God Seventh Day. Others are members of Messianic Jewish congregations with varying levels of adherence to traditional Jewish observances.

Some descendants of Conversos became aware of their Jewish past more directly. Keith Chaves was told he was a Jew when he was 13 years old by his great grandmother. His grandmother kept a special knife used for slaughtering animals. His grandmother slit the animal's throat in one motion and found other approaches repulsive. Keith Chaves now attends an Orthodox synagogue in Albuquerque.

A Catholic priest from Albuquerque named William Sanchez provides an example of the continued fusion of religious beliefs from Christianity and Judaism that exists for many descendants of Conversos. Sanchez maintains a menorah in his church's sanctuary. He blows a *shofar on* Ash Wednesday. He wears a Star of David. He refers to God as *Yahweh* in his sermons in an attempt to emphasize the Jewish background of the Bible. As a boy, Father William Sanchez's Catholic family spun tops on Christmas, avoided pork and spoke of their family past in medieval Spain.²² Father Sanchez's claim to Jewishness is based on a DNA test that revealed the presence of a Y-chromosome marker called the Cohen Modal Haplotype. The chromosome is claimed only to be held by descendants of the Aaronic priesthood. Sanchez caused a

---

²¹ Paul Foer and Chananette Pascal Cohen, "For Hispanic 'Crypto-Jews,' lawsuits may follow religious rediscovery," JNS October 2012, accessed March 25, 2015, https://goo.gl/MwTKxe

²² David Kelly, DNA Clears the Fog Over Latino Links to Judaism in New Mexico," December 2004, accessed on March 25, 2015, https://goo.gl/vGK5Ej

stir with some local Catholics by declaring himself as genetically Jewish.[23] A Semitic finding on this test is not necessarily definitive. It can theoretically also apply to non-Jews.[24] Father Sanchez sees no clash between Judaism and Christianity. In a manner that echoes the dual identity of many present-day descendants of Conversos, Sanchez states, "Some of us believe we can practice rituals of crypto-Judaism and still be good Catholics."[25] Sanchez remarks that "Being Sephardic and Catholic began as a means of survival centuries ago; today they have both survived and coexist."[26]

Elisea Garcia is similar to Father Sanchez in attempting to meld her Jewish and Christian identity. Garcia is a Catholic but attends synagogue services as well.[27] For Garcia, this gives her what she describes as a complete concept of God. When she was growing up, Garcia's family enjoyed a big dinner on Friday nights with candles. Her grandmother slaughtered animals and then examined them inside for any sign of a defect. On Saturdays, work was

---

[23] Jeff Wheelright, "The 'Secret Jews' of San Luis Valley," Smithsonian Magazine 2008, accessed March 25, 2015, https://goo.gl/kjcKdW

[24] Michael Hammer, a research professor at the University of Arizona and an expert on Jewish genetics, said that fewer than 1% of non-Jews possessed the male-specific "Cohanim marker" (which in itself is not necessarily endemic to all Jews, but is prevalent among Jews claiming descent from hereditary priests), and 30 of 78 Latinos tested in New Mexico were found to be carriers. DNA testing of Hispanic populations also revealed between 10% and 15% of men living in New Mexico, south Texas and northern Mexico have a Y chromosome that traces back to the Middle East. Am I Jewish? "Crypto Jews" accessed March 25, 2015, http://www.amijewish.info/w/crypto-jews/

[25] Jeff Wheelright, "The 'Secret Jews' of San Luis Valley," Smithsonian Magazine 2008, accessed March 25, 2015, https://goo.gl/kjcKdW

[26] Eli Rosenblatt, "Picturing Today's Conversos," Forward April 2008, Accessed March 25, 2015, https://goo.gl/WpkWvk

[27] Cary Herz, the author of *New Mexico's Crypto-Jews: Image and Memory*, contends that even today Crypto Jews are sometimes wary about their acceptance in New Mexico's predominantly largely Ashkenazic Jewish community. Jews from Central and Eastern Europe settled in the American Southwest around the turn of the century. "Some anusim attend synagogues in Santa Fe, but many also still attend churches." Herz continues by noting that "… there are people who don't feel welcome all the time, but Nahalat Shalom, a Jewish-Renewal congregation in Albuquerque, has held Shabbat services in Spanish as a way to reach out." Eli Rosenblatt, "Picturing Today's Conversos," Forward April 02, 2008, Accessed March 25, 2015, https://goo.gl/WpkWvk

prohibited to the extent that she was not even allowed to wash her hair. When her grandmother passed, Elisea found a menorah hidden in her room.[28]

For other descendants of Crypto-Jews, physical objects handed down through the generations are also markers of Jewish identity. Ruth Ruiz Reed relates that an amulet was passed down through the women of her family for generations. She was unaware of what it was until it was identified as the tablets with the Ten Commandments etched in Hebrew. Ruth Ruiz Reed relates that her grandfather told certain ceremonies his father performed at night in his room. He also read the Old Testament. Neither pork nor shellfish was served in Reed's home.[29]

## Brazilian Crypto-Jews

The phenomenon of Crypto-Judaism extends well beyond Mexico and the American Southwest. Individuals throughout South America have revealed what they believe to be Crypto-Jewish ancestry. For example, Helio Cordeiro describes his grandfather as a Crypto-Jew from Braganza, Portugal. His family avoided pork, observed the Sabbath, did not go to church, celebrated some biblical holidays, and slaughtered their meat in a unique manner.

Convinced of his Jewish background, Helio attempted to embrace Judaism officially, but several Brazilian Orthodox rabbis questioned the authenticity of his Crypto-Jewish claims and refused to accept him as a Jew. They maintained that he had to undergo a formal conversion. Disappointed by what he considered a rude reception, Helio was warmly received by liberal Rabbi Henry Sobel of Sao Paulo. Rabbi Sobel directed a ceremony of return and Cordeiro was accepted by Brazil's Reform Jewish community.

---

[28] David Kelly, DNA Clears the Fog Over Latino Links to Judaism in New Mexico," December 2004, accessed on March 25, 2015, https://goo.gl/Scc24r

[29] "The Crypto-Jews: An Ancient Heritage Comes Alive Again," Southwest Jewish History Volume 2, no. 1. Fall 1993. accessed on https://goo.gl/RtJUBx

Cordeiro, much like Sonya Loya, felt a mission to educate other Brazilians about Crypto-Jewish history. He formed an organization focused on the study of Crypto-Judaism. The organization named SHEMA trained leaders who led workshops for those interested in learning about and returning to Judaism. The workshops have been held in ten cities, and more than 2000 people have attended.

Gilvanci ben Shmuel Portillo is another Brazilian with Crypto-Jewish claims. Portillo recounts that his grandmother spoke what he characterized as a strange language. Portillo's family was also endogamous. His family used Christian Bibles but cut out the New Testament. His father attended church but never mentioned Jesus. His father began prayers with the phrase "Blessed are you God of Abraham, Isaac, and Jacob." His family lit candles on Friday nights. When his grandmother left a cemetery, she washed and changed her clothes. Boys were circumcised, and a celebration was held on the eighth day. Portillo recounts that his grandmother had a statue of the Madonna. As was customary, she kissed the Madonna's foot. Portillo once saw her take a little box out of it while cleaning it. Portillo's family accepted their Jewish ancestry. Portillo's brother joined the Chabad movement. Portillo recounts that many Brazilian Jews reject the Jewish claims of Crypto-Jews. Since he already sees himself as Jewish, Portillo's father refuses to convert if this is the requirement for official acceptance.

Another Brazilian claiming Crypto-Jewish ancestry is Joao Madeiros. He embraced Judaism, but several rabbis rejected his return and argued that a formal conversion was needed. In response, Madeiros assembled other former descendants of Conversos, and they established a synagogue. Madeiros claimed that his synagogue follows what he termed Iberian Judaism. This spurred controversy since Madeiros does not follow traditional Halakhah in many cases. His Shabbat services do not follow traditional forms. Madeiros' group is viewed as rejecting legitimate rabbinic authority. To justify his approach, Madeiros claims he is a Jew in the same manner that Moses was a Jew. "I am a returned Jew as was Moshe Rabenu.

Moshe had experiences outside of Judaism; he was raised an Egyptian. He came back."

For Madeiros, the issue is centered on the reception he initially received from the Jewish community. Madeiros claims that "Rules of law should not prevent one from following the law."[30] Madeiros is bitter about the rabbi's frosty attitude when he first visited a synagogue. After introducing himself as a descendant of Portuguese Crypto-Jews, the rabbi, Madeiros states, ignored him while his assistant motioned contemptuously. Madeiros contends, "That's been the mentality to this day. Since then, I constantly argue with rabbis who refuse to accept us."[31]

In the middle of the night, David de Andrada and his grandfather ventured out to the sidewalk in front of their home. His grandfather read stories from the Hebrew Bible to him. Through these stories, De Andrada learned about the Patriarch Abraham and the Twelve Tribes who were subjugated in Egypt. Only outside the home, was the New Testament read. De Andrada was raised in a village in northern Brazil. He never heard the word Jew until he was 19 years old. His family only ate ham and pork in the presence of others. At home, though, they kept a different diet.

Luciano Olivera from Campina Grande was unaware of his ancestors' Jewish background. His family, however, was called pigs (Marranos) by their neighbors. When he was 19, his aunt related how his great-grandfather's family would dress in their finest clothes once a week. When the stars appeared, they locked their doors and prayed in a language other than Portuguese. Luciano eventually found his great-grandmother's birth certificate. The document contains the Portuguese word for pig. Luciano's encounter with his past has not led to a warm reception by the

---

[30] Arthur Benveniste, "Finding Our Lost Brothers and Sisters: The Crypto Jews of Brazil," Western States Jewish History Volume XXiX No. 3 (1997). https://goo.gl/rrL2Kd

[31] Avner Hopstein, "The Crypto-Jews of Brazil," Y Net News October 06, 2006, accessed on March 31, 2015, https://goo.gl/s9yvuf

Jewish communities of Sao Paolo and Rio de Janeiro. Various rabbis in these cities have rejected the Jewish status of individuals like Luciano. Luciano considers the requirement to convert demeaning and believes that doing so is a betrayal of his ancestors. Luciano is active in helping other descendants of Crypto-Jews undergo circumcision. Unable to marry in the established Jewish community, Luciano views his family's practice of marrying a cousin as an option.[32]

## Crypto-Jews from Cuba

While most descendants of Crypto-Jews are not told verbally about their past, at the age of eight George Albo's mother and father told him that he was a Jew. He was not to forget that, and he was not to repeat it. For years, his identity remained a secret. Albo eventually embraced his Jewish identity openly and eventually led *Los Caminos de Israel,* an organization focused on reaching out to the descendants of Conversos. Albo embraced Orthodox Judaism in 1997.

Roberto Gonzalez was born in Havana Cuba in a seemingly typical Catholic home. His father related to him that they were Jewish. Their family had fled from the Canary Islands to Cuba. Gonzalez eventually left Cuba and the Catholic Church. He moved to Florida. He spent years in various Pentecostal and Baptist churches. After his father had died, Gonzalez's stepmother gave him a Star of David that belonged to him. Gonzalez left the Church and ventured into Messianic Jewish circles. He combined faith in Jesus with some Jewish traditions. He grew increasingly concerned by the stress on Jesus in Messianic circles. Gonzalez eventually left the Messianic movement and started conversion classes at Temple Beth Tov, a Conservative synagogue in Miami.[33]

---

[32] Ibid.

[33] Even among Jews describing themselves as Messianic, the subject of Crypto-Jews has become a contentious one. Messianic Jews from Ashkenazi backgrounds have purportedly discriminated against them perhaps fearing they undermine their own contested legitimacy. As one Joe Moraz, a friend of Perry Peña, described "They didn't give them

He converted and eventually served as the president of the synagogue.

Mariano Moshe Otero's family is also Cuban. He was baptized a Catholic but was raised as a Southern Baptist. He later joined a Pentecostal church and was eventually ordained as a minister with the Assemblies of God. Otero's spiritual journey did not end there. He embraced his Jewish background in 1991. Otero's father told him their family was descended from the kings of Israel. Otero has led conversion classes since his embrace of Judaism.[34]

## The Crypto-Jews in Mallorca (Majorca)

Among those claiming to be the descendants of Conversos, those with the strongest claims are found in places like the island of Mallorca, where the Conversos and their offspring were called *Chuetas* or *Xuetas*. Because marrying a *Chueta* was frowned upon, they maintained an endogamous community.[35] Joan Punyet Miró is one such individual. His last name is a known *chueto* name. The extent of endogamy diminished the variety of family names. Though there are estimated to total approximately 20,000, only 15 or so family names exist.[36] Because of the high endogamy, this community has the highest possibility of being accepted as Jewish without conversion.[37]

---

an opportunity to really come into their fullness." Theodore Ross, "Shalom on the Range: In search of the American Crypto-Jew" Harper's December 2009, Accessed March 27, 2015, http://harpers.org/archive/2009/12/shalom-on-the-range/

[34] Alexandra Alter, "'Secret Jews' of the Spanish Inquisition" August 2005, Accessed March 30, 2015, https://goo.gl/pn6uk8

[35] "B'nei Anusim," Be'chol Lashon, Accessed on April 3, 2015, https://goo.gl/Ks8Apa

[36] Sarah Wildman, "Mallorca's Jews Get Their Due: Spanish Island's Community Alive and Thriving," Forward, April 2012, accessed March 27, 2015. https://goo.gl/gCd56c

[37] "B'nei Anusim," Be'chol Lashon, Accessed on April 3, 2015, https://goo.gl/Ks8Apa

The chairman of the Beit Din Tzedek in Bnei Brak, Rabbi Nissim Karelitz, has related that members of the *chueto* population of Mallorca can officially reclaim their Jewish identity. Their unique separation from the rest of Spanish and Mallorcan society preserved their Jewishness. Rabbi Nissan ben Avraham was born Nicoals Aquilo, in Palma in 1957. He has been at the vanguard of driving for official recognition of the Chuetas' Jewishness. At the age of 10, his mother informed him that he was a descendant of Conversos. At 21, he immigrated to Israel. He converted to Judaism. He became a rabbi and joined the outreach organization *Shavei Israel*. In December 2010, he was sent as a representative to Mallorca. In a historic event, Rabbi Nissan ben Avraham became the first Spanish-born descendant of Conversos to serve as a rabbi in Spain.[38]

## The Crypto-Jews of Portugal

Joao Santos discovered his Jewish background when he found what he described as typical Jewish candlesticks handed down through his family. Joao Santos wears a kippah and a Star of David. He rejects the need to convert and is confident that he is already Jewish. This is a sentiment expressed by many other Crypto-Jewish descendants.

For those seeking formal recognition as Jews, assistance has been extended to them by the aforementioned *Shavei Israel*. The organization based in Jerusalem is focused on strengthening the connection between the Jewish people and those it considers lost Jews. A permanent representative is stationed in Portugal, and dozens of Crypto-Jewish descendants in Portugal have embraced Judaism with their assistance. One success story is that of Jose Ferrao Filipe. Filipe is the leader of the Jewish community in Porto. Filipe heads a Jewish community formally recognized by

---

[38] Sarah Wildman, "Mallorca's Jews Get Their Due: Spanish Island's Community Alive and Thriving," Forward, April 2012, accessed March 27, 2015 https://goo.gl/gCd56c

Israel's Chief Rabbinate. The community was established following the conversion of Filipe and 16 other Crypto-Jewish descendants.[39]

Filipe describes the conversion process long and hard. Filipe saw it as a battle to prove that he and his fellow congregants are part of the Jewish people. That fact is resented by many. Paulo Vitorino, a Crypto-Jewish descendant from Lisbon, understands the need to receive the Chief Rabbinate's endorsement. He resents it, though, since he believes that the descendants of Conversos do not need to become Jewish. Paulo, his wife, and five children underwent Orthodox conversion in 2004, with assistance from Shavei Israel. As of 2009, the Chief Rabbinate had not yet recognized the 2004 conversion, despite the fact that it was approved by Lisbon's chief rabbi.[40]

## Rabbis Supporting Crypto-Jewish Outreach

The various individuals who have returned or embraced Judaism have not been without the support of an eclectic group of rabbis. While most American rabbis are often unfamiliar with the Crypto-Jewish aspects of Sephardic history, a handful of rabbis has become actively involved in helping the descendants of Conversos return to Judaism.

Rabbi Joshua Stampfer is one of these important rabbis. He helped create the Society for Crypto-Judaic Studies and the Association of Crypto-Jews. Rabbi Stampfer was also involved with supporting Joseph (Yosef) Garcia, a descendant of Conversos, and now a rabbi focused on Crypto-Jewish outreach. Raised in Panama as a Catholic, Rabbi Yosef Garcia was 32 years old when he learned of his Jewish background. Garcia had even been an altar boy. Garcia's great uncle related the family history. Garcia did not know anyone who was Jewish and was

---

[39] Cnaan Lipshiz, "Secret No More," Shavei Israel November 09, 2009, accessed on March 25, 2015, https://goo.gl/tgqTJ1
[40] Ibid.

ignorant of Judaism. After a long process of study, Garcia embraced Judaism and established a small synagogue of other individuals with Crypto-Jewish backgrounds. Garcia later recalled his grandmother lighting candles every Friday night and singing songs in a language he believed to have been Hebrew."[41] His work was recognized by Rabbi Zalman Shachter-Shalomi, the founder of the Jewish Renewal movement. Shalomi granted Garcia *smicha*, and through the former's endorsement, Garcia joined the rabbinical council of Phoenix. Despite accusations that Garcia was once a messianic Jew, Stampfer and Shalomi stood firm in the support for him. In 2004, Garcia co-founded the Association of Crypto-Jews of the Americas whose focus is on helping Crypto-Jews return to Judaism. Rabbi Garcia in cooperation with Rabbi Yitzchak Cohen and Rabbi David Rosenberg hold a ceremony of return. They stress this process as being an alternative to conversion, though they require some components that are typically connected with conversions.[42]

Congregation B'nai Zion in El Paso headed by Rabbi Stephen Leon also reaches out to Hispanics from Crypto-Jewish backgrounds. Rabbi Leon moved to El Paso from New Jersey in 1986. He quickly received visits and calls from people who claimed Jewish ancestry or practices.[43] Rabbi Leon has converted approximately two hundred individuals from Crypto-Jewish backgrounds. Leon

---

[41] Stuart Thornton, "Hidden History: Rabbi Explains the Identity of the Crypto-Jews," accessed on March 25, 2015, https://goo.gl/yR8f4q

[42] According to the Association of Crypto Jews, the return process requires that the applicant have attended a synagogue, where available, at least 3 out of 4 Sabbaths a month. The applicant must not work or spend money on the Sabbath. Participation is required for all major holidays. 10% of their monthly income must be given to the sons of Levi. The applicant must participate in ongoing Torah, Kashrut, and Jewish History classes. A male must be circumcised or undergo *Hatafat Dam Brit* if they circumcision. They must also undergo the *mikveh* and give unspecified financial offerings. Their knowledge of Judaism is reviewed by the Bet Din and they must give reasons why they believe they are of Jewish descent. "Ceremony of Return," Association of Crypto-Jews, accessed April 7, 2015, http://www.cryptojew.org/about_us.html

[43] Paul Foer and Chananette Pascal Cohen, "For Hispanic 'Crypto-Jews,' lawsuits may follow religious rediscovery," JNS October 2012, accessed March 25, 2015, https://goo.gl/r7Ysg7

views these people as returning but uses conversion to improve their chances for *aliyah*. Adding to the excitement as well as controversy are Rabbi Leon's estimates that 10 to 15 percent of the Hispanic community in El Paso- Ciudad Juarez have Jewish ancestors and do not know it. Rabbi Leon has related that "American Jews have helped Jews from the Soviet Union, Ethiopia, and Syria, and it's time to help our internal 'hidden' Jews." In 2009, the Conservative Jewish movement adopted his resolution to welcome the descendants of *anusim*. They also voted to honor the anguish of Spanish Jews under the Inquisition as part of Tisha B'Av observances.[44]

In August 2014, Rabbi Leon opened the Anusim Center in El Paso at the site of the former Holocaust Museum. While the center is partly a museum, its principal purpose is to assist descendants of Conversos in returning to Judaism. The center features information on the Inquisition, provides an environment to hear the stories of Crypto-Jews and helps individuals interested in converting. Rabbi Leon's contrasts his center with the Center for Hispanic-Jewish Relations at Texas A&M, directed by Reform Rabbi Peter Tarlow. Rabbi Tarlow also has conducted outreach to descendants of Crypto-Jews in South America and hosts a yearly Crypto-Jewish symposium at Texas A&M. While the latter is focused on historical information, Leon's center includes outreach to crypto-Jews and counseling. Perhaps the most contentious aspect of Rabbi Leon's vision is his view that the descendants of *anusim* could form a counterweight to the non-Jewish demographic problems in the state of Israel.

In Mexico, Crypto-Jewish outreach was primarily undertaken by Conservative Rabbi Samuel Lerer, who passed away in 2004. Rabbi Lerer devoted years to helping Mexicans who believed they were descended from Spanish and Portuguese Jews. He undertook this mission despite an established Mexican Jewish community that is largely insular and rejects conversion. Lerer claimed to have

---

[44] Ibid.

converted as many as 3,000 people. Most of them were from Veracruz, Venta Prieta, and Puebla. Approximately 500 of them have moved to Israel.

When Lerer arrived in Mexico, he learned about Mexicans who claimed Jewish ancestry. Lerer met with Catholics who had family customs they were not able to explain. Rabbi Lerer was eventually invited to Veracruz to give a presentation on Judaism. This presentation led to weekly classes. Rabbi Lerer converted the first group of people from Veracruz a few years later. He visited regularly and continued to teach and perform conversions, weddings, and other services. The Mexican Jewish community was not enthusiastic about Rabbi Lerer's work. It was quick to deny any linkage between these individuals and the original Conversos who settled in Mexico. "From a historical perspective, there is not a relation between these people and the Jews who came to Mexico with Cortes," Mauricio Lulka, the Executive Director of the Central Committee of the Jewish Community noted.[45] Following Rabbi Lerer's death, the community in Vera Cruz dissolved.

Conservative Rabbi David Kunin has argued that the requirements set by many rabbis for the descendants of Conversos are ironic. The demand for the descendants of Conversos to provide ketubot or other documents to prove their Jewish identity is almost impossible. For Rabbi Kunin, since Conversos maintained their identity orally and by custom, to require such records is effectively a punishment since any written material was in the hands of the oppressors. To resolve this, Rabbi Kunin proposed that education be the determining factor for accepting the descendants of Conversos back into the Jewish community. Extensive genealogical investigation should not be undertaken. Males should undergo circumcision or hatafat dam brit, but Kunin argues that conversion should not be required.[46]

---

[45] "Obituary Samuel Lerer, an American Rabbi Who Converted Mexicans, Dies at 89," February 9, 2004, accessed March 25, 2015, https://goo.gl/aFXgBq

[46] David A Kunin, "Welcoming Back the Anusim: A Halakhic Teshuvah" 2009.

Perhaps the most controversial support regarding *anusim* was extended by the late Rabbi Aharon Soloveitchik of the Brisk Yeshiva. In 1994, Rabbi Soloveitchik signed an ambiguous letter through the efforts of Schulamit Halevy that simultaneously confirmed the Jewish status of the descendants of *anusim* while requiring their conversion for full standing. Rabbi Soloveitchik opined that the male descendants of anusim should be counted in a *minyan* and given *aliyot* for the Torah. If they wished to marry a Jewess, however, they were to convert by undergoing circumcision or *hatafat* dam brit and immersion (without the blessing). As amazing as such a statement was in extending acknowledgment of Crypto-Jews, its convoluted nature only added another layer of complexity as to how the descendants of *anusim* should be treated. Rabbi Soloveitchik's position was in contrast to the view of Rabbi Mordechai Eliahu, a former chief Sephardic rabbi of Israel. In 1994, Rabbi Mordechai Eliahu stressed that the descendants of *anusim* should be welcomed with kindness. A certificate of return should be provided to *anusim* after completing the same requirements for conversion because of the length of time that had passed since the initial conversions.[47]

The Israeli organization most widely known for its efforts to reach out to "lost Jews" is Shavei Israel. Its founder, Michael Freund sees the growing interest and return of the descendants of Conversos as a positive development in strengthening support for Israel.[48] While helping the descendants of Conversos, the organization has also focused on various groups such as the descendants of Jews in China, the *Bnei Menashe* of India, and others.[49] Rabbi

---

[47] Rabbi Simcha Green of Yeshiva University has worked with the descendants of Conversos wishing to return to Judaism. He estimates that only 10 percent of those who discover their background decide to embrace Judaism. Whether this is based on the reception they receive or the requirements they are made to undergo is unclear. Rabbi Green sees the return of the descendants of Conversos as something positive. Simcha Green, "Welcoming Anusim Back into the Family," December 8th, 2010, accessed on March 25, 2015, https://goo.gl/RJ5j2M

[48] Cnaan Lipshiz, "Secret No More," Shavei Israel November 09, 2009, accessed on March 25, 2015, https://goo.gl/tgqTJ1

[49] *Name Your Roots* was formed in Israel by a group of academics who hope to help facilitate research into Converso family names and customs. Ronit Treatman, "Queen

Avraham Amitai of Shavei Yisrael was sent to Recife. He serves as Recife's rabbi. Rabbi Avraham Amitai contends that he accepts a person who can prove that he or she has Jewish roots for several generations as a descendent of the Jewish people. Consequently, his goal is to bring them back without a full conversion.[50] Orthodox Rabbi Manny Viñas is from a Cuban background and is a descendant of Conversos. Viñas moved to Miami where his family returned to Judaism. Viñas now focuses his efforts on reaching out to Jews of color, not only those who are descendants of Conversos.

On the more progressive spectrum of Judaism, there are individuals like Rabbi Henry Sobel. Sobel was born in Portugal but was raised in the United States. He served as a rabbi in Brazil until 2007. For years, he received multiple inquiries from people who believed that they were descended from Conversos and were interested in returning to Judaism. If they did have documents, Rabbi Sobel performed a ceremony of return. In other cases, he considered each situation. He then decided whether a ceremony of return or conversions were appropriate.[51] Rabbi Cukierkorn, who was raised in Sao Paulo, has also been instrumental in the return of many crypto-Jewish descendants to Judaism. The latter has been particularly active in distance conversions. In the United States, the Conservative Rabbi Juan Mejia originally from Colombia and from Crypto-Jewish backgrounds has reached out to Crypto-Jews though his principal focus has been directed toward the established Jewish community. Rabbi Manuel Armon, an Argentinian, became the rabbi of the Conservative synagogue Temple Beth Tov in Florida in 1998. He notes that many Latin American families have joined the synagogue since his tenure. Most of them claim to be the descendants of *anusim*. They were drawn to the ongo-

---

Esther: Patron Saint," The Times of Israel, March 16, 2014, accessed on April 2, 2015, https://goo.gl/UQkbkG

[50] Avner Hopstein, "The Crypto-Jews of Brazil," Y Net News October 06, 2006, accessed on March 31, 2015, http://www.ynetnews.com/articles/0,7340,L-3319972,00.html

[51] Arthur Benveniste, "Finding Our Lost Brothers and Sisters: The Crypto Jews of Brazil," Western States Jewish History 1997 Volume XXiX No. 3 https://goo.gl/7e1mft

ing conversion classes offered through the synagogue.[52] Rabbi Jules Harlow has also been active in Portugal. As part of the Masorti movement, Rabbi Harlow has reached out to the descendants of Anusim. He leads Kehilah Beit Israel where the descendants of Anusim make up a substantial portion of his community.[53]

## The Challenges of Conversos Today

Aside from groups like the *Chuetas* of Mallorca, most individuals claiming a Converso background face challenges in approaching the Jewish community. Part of this is related to the cultural, economic, and social distinctions that exist between the dominant Jewish communities and the backgrounds of most Hispanics. This is particularly pronounced in Latin American countries where adopting a different religion is much less common and less socially acceptable. Hispanics in the United States face a much more open society that allows for shifts in religious beliefs, but still, encounter some issues that often present challenges to their consideration of Judaism.

Many people who come to believe they are descendants of Anusim do so through tangential means and lack concrete evidence of their Jewish backgrounds. Many arrive at this conclusion by studying last names purported to be Sephardic in origin. The availability of this information on the internet has led many people to believe that a name is a sufficient pointer of a Crypto-Jewish background. DNA testing has also materialized as a way of discovering Sephardic identity. According to *Be'chol Lashon*, other people are attracted to Jews and Judaism. This attraction is explained by assuming a Crypto-Jewish background even if any other evidence is not readily available.[54] This tendency is only compounded by the pervasive attention to the State of Israel and

---

[52] Alexandra Alter, "'Secret Jews' of the Spanish Inquisition" August 06, 2005, Accessed March 30, 2015, https://goo.gl/pn6uk8

[53] "Portugal, " Jewish Virtual Library, accessed on July 28, 2015, http://www.jewishvirtuallibrary.org/jsource/vjw/Portugal.html

[54] "B'nei Anusim," Be'chol Lashon, Accessed on April 3, 2015, https://goo.gl/Ks8Apa

the ease of available information on the internet about Crypto-Judaism.[55] Another factor potentially leading to individuals claiming Crypto-Jewish backgrounds is the proliferation of Messianic Jewish groups. Some groups have even merged age-old theories of the ten Lost Tribes and conflated this with Crypto-Jewish claims.

There are, however, various factors that do not adequately address the increase in the rise of Crypto-Jewish claims. Anti-Semitism remains an active component of Latin American culture. Claiming Jewishness is not an attractive identity to assume or embrace. The existence of largely isolated Jewish communities in Latin America only serves to reinforce the separation and sense of otherness. Despite the existence of some evangelical groups with seeming affinities towards Jewishness, the extent of Jewish identity or culture that is tolerated is often limited. This is because these groups also maintain traditional Pauline views on Judaism and "the Law."

Individuals claiming Jewish ancestry are not necessarily supported by their families and even meet with significant aversion and resistance to such suggestions. The persons wishing to restore or assume their place among the Jewish people face challenges similar to that of any convert. The problem is increased, however by the heartfelt conviction that they are already members of the Jewish people and should not be blocked or made to pass through difficult steps to officially rejoin. In this manner, the circumstances that created the Converso class in the 14$^{th}$ and 15$^{th}$ centuries and the Inquisitions charged with resolving Judaizing among them continues to affect the lives of their descendants, real or imagined.

---

[55] Ibid.

CHAPTER 8

# The Crypto-Jewish Controversy

Anna D'Abrera in her work *The Tribunal of Zaragoza and Crypto-Judaism* provides an excellent analysis of the major controversies surrounding the documents of the Inquisition as well as the scholarly support for and against the phenomena of Crypto-Judaism. D'Abrera begins her review by explaining a major challenge that researchers face regarding Inquisitional archives. The tribunal's records are incomplete. As early as 1820, in the decade following the Napoleonic invasion of Spain, the court archives in Galicia, Logrono, and Valladolid had vanished. Those of Valencia, Mallorca, and Seville were also heavily compromised. The records of the Central Council of the Inquisition known as the *Suprema* were better preserved. Other collections including those of Toledo, Cuenca, Ciudad Real, Valencia, and Zaragoza conserved elements of their collections intact.[1]

In summary, many records are no longer available, and incomplete facts are always an issue that any researcher must confront. The lack of intact records has not prevented wide-ranging views on the veracity of Inquisitional documents from being adopted.

### Early Studies on the Inquisition

---

[1] Anna Ysabel D'Abrera, *The Tribunal of Zaragoza and Crypto-Judaism 1484-1515* (Turnhout: Brepols Publishers, 2008), 9-10.

Several studies on the Inquisition were published in the initial years of the 19th century. One of the first was written by Juan Antonio Llorente. Llorente was employed by the Holy Office and had unfettered access to tribunal records. His work titled *Historia Critica de la Inquisicion en España* (1822) argued that greed was the motivating factor behind the work of the Inquisition.[2]

Despite Llorente's belief in the ulterior motives of the Inquisition, he along with other historians including Marcelino Menendez Pelayo who authored *Historia de Los Heterdoxos Españoles* (1880), and Henry Charles Lea, who wrote *A History of the Inquisition of Spain* (1887), believed that significant Crypto-Jewish activity did in exist in the 15th century. From the Church's perspective, this provided the theological justification for the creation of the Inquisition.[3] Such objections notwithstanding, Llorente's views on the ulterior motives of the Inquisition have morphed and resurfaced in contemporary scholarship.[4]

## The 20th Century

The study of Conversos in the 19th century was focused on Inquisitional documents. In 1932 in the Hebrew article titled, *Anusei Sefarad u'portugal be-sifrut ha-teshuvot* Simcha Assaf drew attention to halakhic literature as a source for understanding the Converso experience. A more extensive collection or rabbinic responsa was published by H. J. Zimmels the same year. His work was published in German and was titled *Die Marranen in der Rabbinischen Literatur.* This book focused on rabbinic responsa dating from the late 14th century until the 18th century. These two works were largely free of controversy and presented material that had largely been neglected in considering the history of Conversos. Cecil Roth's well-known book titled *History of the Marranos* was also published in 1932 and provided a historical narrative of Conversos and Crypto-Jews in

---

[2] Ibid., 10-11.
[3] Ibid., 12.
[4] Anna Ysabel D'Abrera, *The Tribunal of Zaragoza and Crypto-Judaism 1484-1515* (Turnhout: Brepols Publishers, 2008), 11.

perhaps a somewhat romanticized manner. Cecil Roth's work was broad in its depiction of Judaizing among Conversos and was based on the premise that Inquisitional testimonies were largely accurate.

## The Controversy Begins

The continuing Jewish identity of Conversos and the veracity of the Inquisitional process as an accurate depiction of Converso Judaizing were challenged in the 1960s. A scholarly debate regarding the real religious perspectives of Conversos, the motivations for the establishment of the Inquisition, and the reasons for the decision to expel the Jews of Spain, has ensued since. Whether Conversos maintained Jewish practice and identity is the primary issue of contention between the views of Yitzhak Baer and Benzion Netanyahu and the various scholars that align with each of them. Yitzhak Baer saw Conversos as forced converts and considered their descendants in the 15$^{th}$ century as remaining faithful to Jewish identity to the best of their ability. Benzion Netanyahu while allowing for the possibility that the pogroms of 1391 produced legitimately forced converts, believed that most conversions were voluntary. According to Netanyahu, by the time of the establishment of the Inquisition, most Conversos were sincere Christians. The critical area of contention between these two views of Converso identity lies to a great part, in how the vast archives of the Inquisition are perceived.

## The Perspective of Yitzhak Baer

Yitzhak Baer related his view of the ongoing ties between Jews and Conversos in the second volume of his work, *History of the Jews in Christian Spain*. He states the following:

> "Conversos and Jews were one people, united by bonds of religion, destiny, and messianic hope, which in Spain took on a unique coloration typical of the people and the country…The confession and testimonies contained in these records (of the Inquisition) breathe a nostalgic yearning for

the national homeland, both earthly and heavenly- a yearning for all things, great and small, sanctified by the national tradition, and for something even greater, which had created the people and maintained in life."[5]

Haim Beinart, Baer's student and the author of *Conversos on Trial: The Inquisition in Ciudad Real* (1981) believed that Jews and Conversos shared a common destiny, which included persecution, violence, expulsion, and martyrdom. As D'Abrera describes, Baer and Beinart believed wholeheartedly that the available records represented irrefutable evidence of the Conversos continuing adherence to Judaism.[6] For Jews, Conversos remained Jews. Then day contemporary historians such as Rabbi Yitzhak Arama and Rabbi Shlomo ibn Verga rightly understood this fact according to Beinart. For Beinart, Conversos, who returned to Judaism or even expressed their desire to do so, could expect to be welcome without reservation by their Jewish compatriots everywhere. The relationship between Jews and their Converso brethren was clear cut and required little elaboration.

A cadre of academics including David Gitlitz in his *Secrecy and Deceit: The Religion of Crypto-Jews* (1996), Michael Alpert in his *Crypto-Judaism and the Spanish Inquisition* (2001), Janet Jill Jacobs in her work titled *Hidden Heritage: The Legacy of the Crypto-Jews* (2002) and *Renee Levine* Melammed in her work titled *Heretics or Daughters of Israel?: The Crypto-Jewish Women of Castile* (1999) among others have operated on the premise that while caution must always be used when Inquisitional documents, they do document real occurrences of Crypto-Judaism among Conversos. While more nuanced, this perspective generally supports the positions of Baer and Beinart.

## The Challenge of Benzion Netanyahu

---

[5] Yitzhak Baer, *A History of the Jews in Christian Spain: Volume 2* (Philadelphia: Jewish Publication Society, 1961), 424-425.
[6] Anna Ysabel D'Abrera, *The Tribunal of Zaragoza and Crypto-Judaism 1484-1515* (Turnhout: Brepols Publishers, 2008), 12.

While Yitzhak Baer and Haim Beinart accepted the Inquisitional records as reliable sources, Benzion Netanyahu, claimed that the Inquisitional records were unreliable at best, and in the case of Norman Roth, outright fiction. The belief that the Inquisitional records were legitimate representations of Converso proclivity towards retaining Jewish practice was first challenged by Benzion Netanyahu in his work titled *The Marranos of Spain: From the Late 14th to the Early 16th Century, According to Contemporary Hebrew Sources* (1966). He further developed this theme in subsequent works. He was joined by scholars such as Henry Kamen in his work titled *The Spanish Inquisition: A Historical Revision* (1965) and by António José Saraiva in his book titled *The Marrano Factory: The Portuguese Inquisition and Its New Christians 1536-1765* (1969). Many years later, Norman Roth authored the work titled *Conversos, Inquisition, and the Expulsion of the Jews from Spain* (1995) which also supported Netanyahu's claims.

Netanyahu's perspective relies on two fundamental assumptions. The first is that the Inquisition's goal was not the eradication of Judaizing among Conversos, but rather the destruction of this social-economic class as a whole. The second premise is that since the overwhelming majority of Conversos were sincere Christians, Inquisitional charges must necessary be false. Netanyahu summarized his view as follows:

> "Marrano Christianization had been steadily advancing for three generations (from 1391 on), so that at the beginning of the 1480s, when the Spanish Inquisition was established, virtually all Jewish authorities in Spain and elsewhere regarded the mass of the Marranos as renegades-that is as apostates or Gentiles. By any of these definitions they were Christians, and in no way Judaizers or crypto-Jews."[7]

The tribunals were, therefore, unreliable and for Norman Roth, Jewish practices often reappear in various trials not because they

---

[7] Benzion Netanyahu, *The Marranos of Spain: From the Late 14th to the Early 16th Century, According to Contemporary Hebrew Sources* (Ithaca: Cornell University Press, 1999), xviii.

represent common elements of Jewish faith that Conversos would naturally have continued to maintain, but rather because the Inquisition was incapable of conjuring up better false charges. Roth unequivocally states:

> "There is no doubt whatever that in the overwhelming majority, nearly all of these accusations are totally false."[8]

Netanyahu was willing to admit rare cases of Crypto-Judaism. But even then, he blamed the Inquisition for the resurgence of Judaic practices among Conversos. Any vestiges of Jewish identity "would have, in all likelihood, soon faded into nothingness, had not the process of assimilation been violently interfered with by the repellent and bewildering actions of the Inquisitional and that thus, it was due to the Inquisition itself that the dying Marranism in Spain was given a new lease on life."[9]

With the ability to fabricate any charge against any individual, the destruction of the Converso social-economic class was an easy goal. The destruction of the Conversos according to Benzion Netanyahu was anti-Semitic in nature. He pointed to the purity of blood laws that were increasingly adopted in the 15th and 16th centuries as proof that ancestry and not practice was the principal issue. Both Netanyahu and Roth saw anti-Semitism as the actual motivation for the Inquisition.[10]

## The Problems with Netanyahu's Thesis

Yitzhak Baer, despite his overall disagreement with Netanyahu, was willing to recognize the multi-layered nature of the Inquisitional procedure and its susceptibility to an agenda other than sup-

---

[8] Norman Roth, *Conversos, Inquisition, and the Expulsion of the Jews from Spain* (Madison: University of Wisconsin Press, 1995), 40.

[9] Benzion Netanyahu, *The Marranos of Spain: From the Late 14th to the Early 16th Century, According to Contemporary Hebrew Sources* (Ithaca: Cornell University Press, 1999), 3.

[10] Anna Ysabel D'Abrera, *The Tribunal of Zaragoza and Crypto-Judaism 1484-1515* (Turnhout: Brepols Publishers, 2008), 14.

pressing Judaizing by Conversos. Regarding the differences between certain tribunals, Baer stated:

> "The Inquisition had usually taken pains, according to their rights to proceed in accordance with the rules of law and justice, demonstrating facts which were unquestionably correct and refraining from malicious libels. Now, however, they began to conducting a trial, from beginning to end on the basis of the vile slanders which emanated solely from the imaginations of medieval anti-Semites."[11]

Baer was capable of assessing individual tribunals instead of applying a blanket charge to all of them.[12] He was willing to see the differences in how each court related to those on trial. In the case of the court at Valencia, for example, Baer saw a more measured if not lenient approach in its prosecution of Conversos.[13] This was in comparison to the court at Ciudad Real, which he saw as intent on destroying Conversos regardless of their culpability. This tribunal exhibited a relative laxity in its procedural process. Baer believed this betrayed its ulterior motives.[14] Albert Sicroff argued that Netanyahu was focused on one of two extremes of Converso life.

> "Netanyahu has chosen to emphasize only one of the two poles between which Jewish opinion oscillated on the Marrano question, that which castigated the Marranos as apostates who were becoming increasingly assimilated in Christian society."[15]

---

[11] Yitzhak Baer, *A History of the Jews in Christian Spain Volume 2* (Philadelphia: Jewish Publication Society, 1961), 398.

[12] Anna Ysabel D'Abrera, *The Tribunal of Zaragoza and Crypto-Judaism 1484-1515* (Turnhout: Brepols Publishers, 2008), 15.

[13] Yitzhak Baer, *A History of the Jews in Christian Spain: Volume 2* (Philadelphia: Jewish Publication Society, 1961), 334.

[14] Ibid., 292.

[15] Martha G. Krow-Lucal, "Marginalizing History: Observations on the Origins of the Inquisition in Fifteenth-Century Spain by B. Netanyahu." Judaism Volume 46 (1997): 48.

The inherent challenge with Netanyahu's position is as Martha Krow-Lucal notes, his sweeping generalizations about enormous heterogeneous groups. Netanyahu believed that there were almost no Judaizers among Conversos. The problem, however, lies in the fact that the evidence of Crypto-Jewish tradition in Inquisitional records was buttressed by the stream of Converso refugees to Jewish communities in North Africa, Europe, and the Ottoman Empire.[16]

## Greed as the Principal Motivator

If Judaizing was not the actual motivation for the Inquisition then a possible motivator was greed. While confiscation of property could indeed prove lucrative depending on the individual on trial, one point that appears to counter such motivation is the extent to which the tribunals meticulously recorded their work. If confiscation were the only aim, the purpose or benefit of such detailed trial accounts seems dubious.

In short, if economic gain were the only concern, a much more efficient way to seize such wealth could certainly have been arranged. Martha Krow-Lucal also argues for the Inquisition's genuine alarm over Crypto-Judaism and its willingness to forgo financial gain to prove a point. As an example, she points to the case of the Converso Pedro Onofre Cortes, who owned a piece of land in Majorca which he used as a garden. The garden was frequented by other Conversos to celebrate Jewish holidays. He was arrested in 1679 and his property confiscated. His garden was seized, plowed under, and sowed with salt. A plaque was placed in the middle of the old garden that read as follows:

> "Year 1679 this garden was demolished and sowed with salt by order of the Inquisition because the Law of Moses

---

[16] Ibid., 48.

was taught in it. None may break or take away this stone at any time, under pain of excommunication."[17]

The sign remained posted until the nineteenth century. For Martha Krow-Lucal, this is proof that there were more pressing issues at stake for the Inquisition than just seizing property. Krow-Lucal notes that,

> "If the Inquisition had simply been interested in economic gain, it could have taken the land for its own use, or rented it out. To destroy for generations a fertile piece of land- on an island!- by sowing it with salt is a strong symbolic statement that indicates another type of concern."[18]

## Rabbinic Responsa

Netanyahu also viewed rabbinic responsa as the real arbiter of the ongoing or better yet lack of ongoing Jewish observances by the Conversos. For Netanyahu, after 1391, Conversos should be considered as voluntary converts and no longer as forced converts. Rabbinic responsa according to Netanyahu showed a gradual shift from an open embrace of Conversos as Jews to an increasing doubt as to their level of observance. Since he interpreted the responsa as not supporting the image of the masses of Conversos as faithful adherence to Judaism, the Inquisition's records were worthless.

Netanyahu pointed to the opinions of rabbis like Shlomo Duran, who characterized Conversos as entirely ignorant of Judaism and Jewish observance. Netanyahu also appealed to the testimony of the Relator Fernan Diaz de Toledo and his characterization of the Conversos as ignorant of Judaism.[19] While

---

[17] Angela Selke, *Los Chuetas y La Inquisicion* (Madrid: Taurus, 1972), 81.
[18] Martha G. Krow-Lucal, "Marginalizing History: Observations on the Origins of the Inquisition in Fifteenth-Century Spain by B. Netanyahu." Judaism Volume 46 (1997): 57.
[19] Benzion Netanyahu, *Origins of the Inquisition in Fifteenth-Century Spain* (New York: Random House, 1995), 411.

Netanyahu pointed to certain responsa as proof that Conversos were sincere converts after 1391, Baer pointed to other rabbis that corroborated Crypto-Jewish practice.[20] Interestingly, Krow-Lucal notes out that no matter what the status of either Duran or Diaz, their testimony is, in fact, problematic. Krow-Lucal writes that,

> "The fact that both men were highly respectable and leaders of their communities says nothing about their direct knowledge of the practices of Conversos in the Peninsula; indeed, the fact that both were men of high position argues against their knowing a great deal about what the lower-class people in various locales were doing."[21]

Another serious problem lies in what individual responsum say, and whether in fact it as a whole reflects a general trend. As Dorottya Zsom notes, Netanyahu often introduces statements from responsa without even presenting the question under consideration.[22] Furthermore as Krow-Lucal relates, rabbinic responsa discusses the legal status of Conversos as a response to their level of observance and not to what any individual or group may have believed. Arguably, Netanyahu reaches questionable conclusions due to a superficial interpretation of the texts. At times Netanyahu refers to a part of a supporting statement while ignoring any contradicting information.[23] When, for example, Netanyahu relates the decision of Rabbi Simeon ben Ẓemaḥ Duran that the death of a convert should not be mourned by his Jewish relatives, he fails to note that this responsum (Simeon b. Ẓemaḥ Duran: 2:139) also distinguishes between three types of converts.[24] In this case, two of

---

[20] Ibid., 14.

[21] Martha G. Krow-Lucal, "Marginalizing History: Observations on the Origins of the Inquisition in Fifteenth-Century Spain by B. Netanyahu." Judaism Volume 46 (1997): 53.

[22] Dorottya Zsom, *Conversos in the Responsa of Sephardic Halakhic Authorities in the 15th Century* (PhD diss., Eotvos Lorand University, 2011), 10.

[23] Ibid., 12.

[24] Benzion Netanyahu, *The Marranos of Spain: From the Late 14th to the Early 16th Century, According to Contemporary Hebrew Sources* (Ithaca: Cornell University Press, 1999), 42.

them should be mourned while the third class should not.[25] Netanyahu's oversimplification leads unwittingly to a distortion of the complexity of Converso life.[26]

When reviewing literature produced by Conversos, Netanyahu also believed it to represent their religious views adequately. How or why Conversos would present themselves as other than good and faithful Christians is unclear.[27] Netanyahu seems to recognize this in part when addressing the necessity of maintaining certain levels of Christian observance but automatically assumes that many Conversos would have taken advantage of the situation.

> "Since most Jews sympathized with the forced convert's plight, they would usually give him the benefit of the doubt when they saw him violate Jewish law; they tended to assume that on such occasions, he considered it perilous to expose his Jewishness. It was course natural that many a convert took advantage of this prevailing Jewish attitude and permitted himself to be rather lax in the fulfillment of the Commandments. He knew that his failure to act like a Jew would be excused not only by his fellow converts but also by most Jews, who 'understood' his predicament and trusted his judgment as to what he could or not do as a forced convert. On the other hand, he could not expect such 'understanding' from Christians should they find him violating Christian law or custom."[28]

The difficulties of generalizing about what Conversos thought and acted should be clear then. No universal statement can be

---

[25] Dorottya Zsom, *Conversos in the Responsa of Sephardic Halakhic Authorities in the 15th Century* (PhD diss., Eotvos Lorand University, 2011), 12.

[26] Martha G. Krow-Lucal, "Marginalizing History: Observations on the Origins of the Inquisition in Fifteenth-Century Spain by B. Netanyahu." Judaism Volume 46 (1997):49.

[27] Ibid. 50.

[28] Benzion Netanyahu, *Origins of the Inquisition in Fifteenth-Century Spain* (New York: Random House, 1995), 208.

easily applied.[29] In dealing with the Conversos, Yosef Haim Yerushalmi proposed a different approach to understanding their dilemma.

> "We must not approach the problem [of 'Marranism] with preconceived notions as to what constitutes 'Jewishness' nor, least at of all, with legalistic definitions. Rather than superimpose external criteria which derive from traditional Jewish life and behavior, thereby ignoring the genuine peculiarities of the Converso position, we should…confine ourselves to the inductive method."[30]

Hence, Netanyahu's aim of definitively determining the Jewish status of Conversos is inherently problematic as this was never addressed by the rabbis as a distinct subject but only in relationship to particular acts nor presents the complicated nature of the halakhic process and of the ability of rabbis to deal with circumstances on an individual basis.[31]

In the end, the unacceptability of dismissing the majority of the Inquisitional documents as trustworthy is apparent. With regards to the Inquisitional records, Yosef Haim Yerushalmi states:

> "To view the Inquisitors as involved in what amounts to a universal conspiracy of fabrication is to ignore the mentality of men of a bygone day and to flatter them with Machiavellian intentions and capabilities beyond their reach."[32]

---

[29] Martha G. Krow-Lucal, "Marginalizing History: Observations on the Origins of the Inquisition in Fifteenth-Century Spain by B. Netanyahu." Judaism Volume 46 (1997): 52.

[30] Y. H. Yerushalmi, *From Spanish Court to Italian Ghetto. Isaac Cardoso: A Study in Seventeenth Century Marranism and Jewish Apologetics,* (New York & London: Columbia University Press, 1971), 31.

[31] Benzion Netanyahu, *The Marranos of Spain: From the Late 14th to the Early 16th Century, According to Contemporary Hebrew Sources* (Ithaca: Cornell University Press, 1999), 22.

[32] Yosef Hayim Yerushalmi *From Spanish Court to Italian Ghetto: Isaac Cardoso; a Study in Seventeenth-century Marranism and Jewish Apologetics* (New York: Columbia University Press, 1971), 24.

As D'Abrera relates, the complexity of actually carrying out such a conspiracy would necessitate the organization and orchestration of the Supreme Council, something for which evidence simply does not exist. The countless number of witnesses, interrogations, and confessions cannot be explained away without supporting evidence to the contrary.[33] D'Abrera explains:

> "Netanyahu is of the opinion that any conclusions previously arrived at by scholars researching the Inquisition have been erroneous precisely because they have mistakenly chosen to consult its records. He believes that his fellow historians have been duped, themselves becoming victims of a vast conspiracy which took place among the Old Christians five hundred years ago."[34]

Hateful and destructive as it was, the individuals who led the Inquisition appear for all purposes to be genuinely and radically faithful to their religious agenda. While monetary benefits may have added energy to the motivation, we need not assume that they would have detracted from the commitment of the Inquisitors. The symbolic idea of the wealth of the evil being appropriated by the faithful would certainly be in concert with what the Inquisitors envisioned as a holy mission. Stephen Haliczer writes:

> "I cannot accept [the] interpretation of the role of Valencia's inquisitors as the docile clients and servants of the Inquisitor-Generals who appointed them. Once in Valencia, the inquisitors were far from the reproving eye of the inquisitor-general or Suprema, and each man tended to interpret for himself the role of provincial inquisitor…the Inquisition in Valencia was founded at a supreme moment of religious fanaticism and strong centralization."[35]

---

[33] Anna Ysabel D'Abrera, *The Tribunal of Zaragoza and Crypto-Judaism 1484-1515* (Turnhout: Brepols Publishers, 2008), 19.

[34] Ibid., 18.

[35] Stephen Haliczer, *Inquisition and Society in the Kingdom of Valencia, 1478-1834* (Berkley: University of California Press, 1990), 6.

## Conclusion

So then having reviewed the perspectives and the two principal schools of thought, what avenue should be taken? There is no question that the both the Inquisitional documents and rabbinic responsa should be consulted when formulating a picture of Converso life in Spain and Portugal as well throughout the empires of both. The romantic notion of all Conversos as Crypto-Jews in mass should not be held, but neither should the view that most just became faithful Christians be assumed either. When the tribunal records show a consistent pattern of observances such as lighting candles, eating kosher food, celebrating Jewish holidays, etc. they should not be taken as reflective of the inability of the Inquisition to invent a better list of made up observances. Like any community facing assimilation, whether coerced or voluntary, Jewish practice and belief will often be reduced to some common elements. The Conversos should not be treated as a class but as individuals whose circumstances varied and whose responses to outside pressure and their Jewish identity would have naturally merited different responses. Some entire Jewish quarters were destroyed and left some Converso communities alone even in the 15th century. These communities had limited reinforcement of their already stressed Jewish identity.

# Conclusions

In the end, the unequivocal rejection of the Inquisitional records as reliable sources of information by Netanyahu and Roth has led to a reconsideration of the sources in a more focused manner. This fact has led subsequent scholars to appreciate the complex religious continuum that existed among Conversos and a realization that the extreme positions of Conversos as either wholly Crypto-Jews on the one hand or as devout Christians on the other is to be rejected.

The history of Conversos is immediately relevant to individuals throughout the United States, Latin America, Spain, and Portugal who in the present day claim or trace Converso lineage as a result of genealogical investigation, DNA testing, or Crypto-Jewish practices and beliefs that were passed down through their families over the generations. Several thousand individuals who claim Converso ancestry have acted to reintegrate themselves into the Jewish community in some form or fashion. As significant and emotionally stirring as this may be, the subject of Conversos is quite pertinent to the broader world of contemporary Judaism and the situation of American Jewry more specifically. The reasons are manifold.

A study of the Converso experience raises a number of fundamental questions regarding core issues concerning "Jewishness" and Judaism. The questions are often interwoven with other matters. The first is related to a question relating to the identity of the Conversos. Were the Conversos Jewish? Whether one answers in the affirmative or not, either answer requires us to investigate the ever-challenging question of who is a Jew. Did the Conversos practice Judaism after their conversion to Christianity? This issue, in turn, must lead us to ask what exactly constitutes Judaism, and whether can one remain a member of one faith while participating in another or at least mixing elements from outside traditions. The Converso phenomenon also leads us to consider how Judaism differs from Christianity and what delineations cannot be crossed. That being said, what is the status of Jews who convert to other religions with respect to Jewish law? May they serve as witnesses to a *ketubah* (i.e. a marriage contract), to a *get* (i.e. a divorce document), may they be counted in a *minyan* (i.e. a prayer quorum), etc.? Does their inclusion in the former matters depend on some measure of effort and a cognizant connection to Jewish identity? To render it in Orthodox Jewish parlance, is *Kedushat Yisrael*, the spiritual state of being a Jew as a member of the spiritual community of Judaism, terminated when a person alienates themselves from the Jewish People if they no longer identify with them in any form or fashion?

[1] Does Jewish identity extend to their children? What about if alienation is through no fault of their own?

If these questions are not relevant enough, we may further consider the common occurrence of intermarriages in present day America. How will the children of such marriages that often incorporate both religious traditions be perceived? How are children assimilated into non-Jewish religions to be treated? How are converts to Christianity, Buddhism, and Hinduism to be approached if they desire to return to Jewish practice? Should Jewish converts to other religions be granted citizenship in the State of Israel? These are some of the many questions that arise when discussing the Converso experience. While these issues require their own extensive research, understanding the issues

---

[1] Aharon Lichtenstein, "Brother Daniel and Jewish Fraternity." *Leaves of Faith: The World of Jewish Living* (Jersey City, NJ: Ktav, 2004), 67.

Conversos faced provides a valuable measure of context for discussing such relevant present day problems.

## Forced Conversions in Spain and Beyond

The phenomenon of forced conversions was not limited to the Iberian Peninsula, nor was it a new experience in the 14$^{th}$-16$^{th}$ centuries. Similar periods of mass conversions were experienced by Jewish communities in Spain in the 5$^{th}$ and 7$^{th}$ centuries of the Common Era as well as by Jewish communities in North Africa, Yemen, and Spain in the 12$^{th}$ century.

Beyond the Iberian Peninsula, forced conversions also occurred in other Jewish communities. Forced conversions took place among Mashhadi Jews in Iran in 1839. When faced with violence and the deaths of numerous members of their community, they acceded to conversion to Islam. For almost a century, they practiced Judaism secretly until the rise of a new government allowed most to flee and openly return to Judaism. The comparison to Iberian Jews is evident.[2] While the forced conversions of Mashhadi Jews is no longer an active area of inquiry, other cases of coerced conversions are.

Ethiopian Jewry is one such example. Ethiopian Jewry experienced confronted forced conversions in 1862. Many Ethiopian Jews converted to Christianity for a variety of reasons, some of which parallel the Converso experience. Some converted because of threats made by Emperor Theodorus II, while others converted because of a severe famine that had devastated the country from 1888-1892. Yet others succumbed to intense Christian missionary activity, and others still converted to survive the severe economic pressure that derived from the inability of Jews to own land. These Ethiopian converts were referred to as

---

[2] Joseph Wolff, *Narrative of a Mission to Bokhara, in the Years 1843-1845, to Ascertain the Fate of Colonel Stoddart and Captain Connolly*, 2$^{nd}$ ed. London 1845, II 173, and I 241, respectively..

*Falash Mura*. The *Falash Mura* like many Spanish and Portuguese Conversos in the 15th century continued to live as a separate social caste. They were not fully assimilated into the dominant Christian society. The *Falash Mura* lived in distinct villages, practiced endogamy- a practice similar to Converso custom, continued to observe the Sabbath, and maintained relations with their Jewish family members and their eligibility to immigrate to Israel has been discussed of late.

## The Moriscos: Crypto-Muslims

The importance of understanding the Converso experience also applies to the case of the Moriscos. Confronted with the option of leaving their homes or converting, many Iberian Muslims converted to Christianity. Their strong cultural and linguistic connections helped foster a sustainable point of identification even beyond the discriminatory attitudes often adopted by Spanish society towards them. Like Jewish Conversos, Moriscos would also face Inquisitional prosecution, though at a much lower rate. In the end, they remained sufficiently distinct to be regarded as a threat and would be expelled in 1609 in a manner which echoed the expulsion of Spanish Jews more than a century earlier. The comparison between Moriscos and Conversos has been increasingly studied of late. Understanding the Converso experience provides a better vantage point for appreciating the circumstances of Muslim converts to Christianity as well as the thought process behind the Spanish authorities which orchestrated their persecution and eventual expulsion.

## The Converso Experience and Rabbinic Authority

The relevance of the Converso experience is of additional significance beyond those topics already described. Along with the aforementioned issues of identity, the nature of rabbinic authority and the ability of individual rabbis to issue decisions relative to their own situations and their own communities are of particular importance given the increasing trend toward centralization and uniformity in Orthodox Jewish circles. The Converso experience generated questions to distinguished rabbis regarding how Conversos should be treated on a whole host of Jewish issues. The rabbis receiving the inquiries responded with far-reaching impact and sometimes with more immediate concerns in mind. The decisions were at times contradictory which shows that the ability of each rabbi to act independently was important.

In the present day, what once lay under the purview of the local rabbi and his community has increasingly been redefined and limited, however. This is particularly noteworthy in the relatively recent changes that have taken place as a result of the conversion to Judaism controversy in and outside of the State of Israel. Orthodox conversions have been overturned while the orthodox rabbinates of various countries (i.e., Great Britain, France, etc. have rejected the validity of conversions performed under the purview of the chief rabbinate of Israel as well as each other's conversions). This does not of course even entail the issues confronting non-orthodox conversions. The subject of Conversos with all the assumptions and biases held regarding whether they truly converted under duress or converted due to the collapse of commitment to Jewish values reveals a complexity and perhaps political considerations that mirror the challenges of Jewish life throughout the ages. It is worth noting that painting a picture of rabbinic authority as a reflection of general Jewish attitudes can give distorted pictures of Jewish life which contradict the most nuanced realities that were experienced by both individuals and the communities they interacted with. This is especially characteristic at the family level. All in all, the Converso experience provides valuable information for understanding the complex world of 21$^{st}$ century Jewry.

# Glossary of Frequently Used Terms

**Arabic (**Ar**); Hebrew (**Heb**); Spanish (**Sp**)**

**Agunah (**Heb**) – A** previously married woman unable to remarry due to the lack of a Jewish divorce document.

**Aljama (**Ar**)** - A term used in official documents in Iberian kingdoms to label the self-governing communities of Moors and Jews living under Christian rule in the Iberian Peninsula.

**Alcalde Mayor (**Sp**)** - A local, administrative, and judicial official.

**Alguacil (**Sp**)** - A Spanish term referring a judge or the governor of a town or fortress. The aguacils of higher importance were referred to as Aguaciles Mayores.

**Anusim (**Heb**)** - A term referring to forced converts. It is a category of Jews in Jewish law who were converted forcibly to another religion.

**Beit Din (**Heb**)** - A Jewish court of law. A Beit Din traditionally consists of three observant Jewish men, capable of deciding Jewish legal matters.

**Cohen (**Heb**)** - A Hebrew term referring to a Jew descended from the Aaronic priesthood.

**Converso (Sp)** - A Jew or Muslim, who converted to Catholicism in Spain or Portugal during the 14th and 15th centuries, or one of their descendants.

**Convivencia (Sp)** - The period of Spanish history from the Muslim Umayyad conquest of Hispania in the early eighth century and which continued for several hundred years. It typically connotes peaceful coexistence between Muslims, Christians, and Jews.

**Corregidor (Sp)** - A local, administrative and judicial official in Spain.

**Cortes (Sp)** - A Spanish parliament in which prelates, nobles, and commoners participated.

**Dhimmis (Ar)** - The name applied by the Muslim conquerors to indigenous non-Muslim populations (i.e. Christians, Jews, etc.) who surrendered to Muslim control.

**Geonim (Heb)** - The heads of the two great Babylonian, Talmudic Academies of Sura and Pumbedita.

**Get (Heb)** - A Jewish divorce document.

**Haliza (Heb)** - The procedure for the *yavam* to forgo marriage and release the widow to remarry whomever she wished.

**Hildago (Sp)** - A member of the Spanish or Portuguese nobility.

**Iggeret Hashamad (Heb)** - The Epistle Concerning Apostasy written by Moses ben Maimon in which he discusses what constitutes sanctification or desecration of God's Name and the acceptance of forcibly converted Jews to Islam

**Infante (Sp)** - A Spanish title given to the sons and daughters (infantas) of the king in the various Christian Iberian kingdoms.

**Karaites** - A Jewish movement characterized by the recognition of the Hebrew Scriptures as its sole supreme legal authority as opposed to rabbinic Judaism, which considers the Oral Torah, to provide authoritative interpretations of the Torah.

**Karet** (Heb) - Spiritual excision from the Jewish people.

**Kashrut** (Heb) - Jewish religious dietary laws derived from the Written and Oral Laws.

**Ketubah** (Heb) - A Jewish wedding contract.

**Las Siete Partidas** (Sp) - A Castilian law code compiled during the reign of King Alfonso X of Castile (1252–1284). It was intended to establish a uniform body of legislation for the kingdom.

**Limpieza de Sangre** (Sp) – A phrase meaning "purity of blood." It referred to those who were regarded as pure "Old Christians," without Muslim or Jewish ancestors.

**Levirate Marriage** - A case in which the husband had died and his wife remained childless, and the brother in law was to marry the widow by biblical law.

**Levir/Yavam** (Heb) - The brother in law, bound to perform a levirate marriage.

**Mahamad** (Heb) – The governing board of each Spanish and Portuguese Jewish communities established in Western European cities.

**Marrano** (Spanish) - A derogatory term meaning swine or pig. It was often used to designate Conversos who Judaized.

**Matzah** (Heb) – Unleavened bread eaten during Passover.

**Mikveh** (Heb) - A ritual bath used for the purpose of ritual immersion in Judaism.

**Mishnah** (Heb) - The first major written redaction of Jewish oral traditions known as the Oral Torah. Together with the Gemara, it forms the Talmud.

**Mitzvot** (Heb) - The commandments of the Written and Oral Law.

**Mohel** (Heb) – A Jewish person trained to perform circumcision.

**New Christian** – Another term used for Conversos to distinguish them from Old Christians. Old Christians were Christians prior to 1391 and did not have Jewish or Muslim heritage. The term was often used in Portugal. For the sake of simplicity, the term Converso is used throughout this work.

**Niddah** (Heb) - A term which refers to a woman during her menstrual cycle. It also relates to a woman who has menstruated and not completed the requirement of immersion in a mikveh (ritual bath) before resuming marital relations with her husband.

**Noahides**- Refers to non-Jews observing the Seven Noahide Laws which include moral and ethical aspects.

**Oral Law** - Rabbinic Judaism maintains that the Torah was revealed in Written and Oral form. The written text is comprised of the "Books of Moses," The Oral Torah provides the interpretation and implementation of the commandments outlined in the Written Torah.

**Shulchan Aruch** (Heb) - literally the "Set table"; the principal code of Jewish law written in the $16^{th}$ century.

**Talmud** (Heb) - A central text of Rabbinic Judaism composed of the Mishnah and its commentary, the Gemara.

**Talit** (Heb) - A Jewish prayer shawl. The tallit is donned during the morning prayers or all the services of Yom Kippur.

**Tefillin** (Heb) - Small black leather boxes containing scrolls of parchment. The scrolls inscribed with verses from the Torah. They are worn by religious Jews during weekday morning prayers.

**Terumah** (Heb) - A food item given to a priest, as a gift.

**Tosefta** (Heb) - A compilation of the Jewish oral law from the late 2nd-century period, the period of the Mishnah.

**Tosafot** (Heb) - Medieval commentaries on the Talmud.

**Tzitzit** (Heb) – Ritual fringes worn on a four cornered garment or on a Tallit in accordance with Numbers 15:37-40.

**Zohar** (Heb) - The principle book of Jewish mysticism.

# Bibliography

Abrera, Anna Ysabel D. *The Tribunal of Zaragoza and Crypto-Judaism, 1484-1515.* Turnhout, Belgium: Brepols, 2008.

Adler, Cyrus, and Isidore Singer. "Inquisition." Jewish Encyclopedia. 1906. Accessed June 9, 2015. http://www.jewishencyclopedia.com/articles/8122-inquisition.

Adler, Cyrus, and Isidore Singer. "Apostasy and Apostates from Judaism." Jewish Encyclopedia. 1906. Accessed June 9, 2015. http://www.jewishencyclopedia.com/articles/1654-apostasy-and-apostates-from-judaism.

"Al-Taqiyya, Dissimulation Part 1." Al Islam. Accessed June 2, 2015. http://www.al-islam.org/shiite-encyclopedia-ahlul-bayt-dilp-team/al-taqiyya-dissimulation-part-1.

Albert, Bat-Sheva. "Isidore of Seville: His Attitude Towards Judaism and His Impact on Early Medieval Canon Law." *The Jewish Quarterly Review* 80, no. 3-4 (1990): 207-20.

Alfassa, Shelomo. *The Sephardic 'Anousim': The Forcibly Converted Jews of Spain and Portugal.* New York: ISLC, 2010.

Alpert, Michael. *Crypto-judaism and the Spanish Inquisition.* Basingstoke, Hampshire: Palgrave, 2001.

Alter, Alexandra. "'Secret Jews' of the Spanish Inquisition." Derkeiler. August 6, 2005. Accessed March 30, 2015. http://newsgroups.derkeiler.com/Archive/Soc/soc.culture.cuba/2005-08/msg00977.html.

Altmann, Alexander. "Eternality of Punishment: A Theological Controversy within the Amsterdam Rabbinate in the Thirties of the Seventeenth Century." *Proceedings of the American Academy for Jewish Research* 40 (1972): 1-88.

Amital, Yehuda. "A Torah Perspective on the Status of Secular Jews Today." The Israel Koschitzky Virtual Beit Midrash. Accessed January 13, 2015. http://etzion.org.il/vbm/english/alei/2-2chilo.htm.

Amran, Rica. "Judíos Y Conversos En Las Crónicas De Los Reyes De Castilla (desde Finales Del Siglo XIV Hasta La Expulsión)." *Espacio, Tiempo Y Forma* Serie III, no. 9 (1996): 257-76.

Antine, Nissan. "Responsa Relating to the Conversos." Lecture, from Beth Sholom and Talmud Torah, Potomac, January 1, 2010.

Antonio Escudero, José. "Luis Vives Y La Inquisicion." *Revista De La Inquisición : Intolerancia Y Derechos Humanos* 13 (2009): 11-24.

Assis, Yom Tov. "The Jews of the Maghreb and Sepharad: A Case Study of Inter-communal Cultural Relations through the Ages." *El Prezente* 2 (2008): 11-30.

Baer, Yitzhak. *A History of the Jews in Christian Spain*. Vol. II. Philadelphia: Jewish Publication Society of America, 1961.

Barnai, Jacob. "Christian Messianism and the Portuguese Marranos: The Emergence of Sabbateanism in Smyrna." *Jew History Jewish History* 7, no. 2 (1993): 119-26.

Baron, Salo W. *A Social and Religious History of the Jews*. Vol. IV. Philadelphia: Jewish Publication Society, 1957.

Baron, Salo W. *A Social and Religious History of the Jews*. Vol. IX. New York: Columbia University Press, 1965.

Baron, Salo W. *A Social and Religious History of the Jews*. Vol. X. Philadelphia: Jewish Publication Society, 1965.

Baron, Salo W. *A Social and Religious History of the Jews*. Vol. XI. Philadelphia: Jewish Publication Society, 1967.

Baron, Salo W. *A Social and Religious History of the Jews*. Vol. XIII. Philadelphia: Jewish Publication Society, 1969.

Baxter Wolf, Kenneth. "Sentencia-Estatuto De Toledo, 1449." Texts in Translation. 2008. Accessed June 2, 2015. https://sites.google.com/site/canilup/toledo1449.

Beinart, Haim, and Yael Guiladi. *Conversos on Trial: The Inquisition in Ciudad Real*. Jerusalem: Magnes Press, Hebrew University, 1981.

Beinart, Haim. *The Expulsion of the Jews from Spain*. Oxford: Littman Library of Jewish Civilization, 2002.

Ben-Sasson, Menahem. "On the Jewish Identity of Forced Converts: A Study of Forced Conversion in the Almohade Period." *Pe'amim* 42 (1990): 16-37.

Ben-Shalom, Ram. "Between Official and Private Dispute: The Case of Christian Spain and Provence in the Late Middle Ages." *AJS Review* 27, no. 1, 23-71.

Ben-Shalom, Ram. "The Converso as Subversive: Jewish Traditions or Christian Libel?" *Journal of Jewish Studies* 50, no. 2 (1999): 259-83.

Ben-Shalom, Ram. "The Typology of the Converso in Isaac Abravanel's Biblical Exegesis." *Jew History Jewish History* 23, no. 3 (2009): 281-92.

Ben-Ur, Aviva. ""Fakelore" or Historically Overlooked Sub-Ethnic Group?" HNet Humanities and Social Sciences Online. 2010. Accessed June 9, 2015. http://www.h-net.org/reviews/showrev.php?id=29438.

Benveniste, Arthur. "Finding Our Lost Brothers and Sisters: The Crypto Jews of Brazil." *Western States Jewish History* 29, no. 3 (1997): 103-09.

Benveniste, Henriette-Rika. "On the Language of Conversion: Visigothic Spain Revisited." *Historein* 6 (2006): 72-87.

Berenbaum, Michael, and Fred Skolnik eds. "Isaac Ben Sheshet Perfet." *Encyclopedia Judaica*. 2nd ed. Vol. 10. Detroit: Macmillan, 2007.

Bermúdez Vázquez, Manuel. "Intuiciones De Criptojudaísmo En El "Quod Nihil Scitur" De Francisco Sánchez." *Revista Internacional De Filosofía* 13 (2008): 285-94.

Bermúdez Vázquez, Manuel. "La Influencia Del Pensamiento Judeo-cristiano En Michel De Montaigne, Giordano Bruno Y Francisco Sánchez." *Ámbitos* 23 (2010): 19-27.
Bodian, Miriam. "Hebrews of the Portuguese Nation: The Ambiguous Boundaries of Self-Definition." *Jewish Social Studies* 15, no. 1 (2008): 66-80.
Bodian, Miriam. *Hebrews of the Portuguese Nation: Conversos and Community in Early Modern Amsterdam*. Bloomington: Indiana University Press, 1997.
"B'nei Anusim." Be'chol Lashon. Accessed June 9, 2015. http://www.bechollashon.org/projects/spanish/anusim.php.
Carpenter, Dwayne. "From Al-Burak to Alboraycos: The Art of Transformation on the Eve of the Expulsion." In *Jews and Conversos at the Time of the Expulsion*. Jerusalem: Zalman Shazar for Jewish History, 1999.
Carvajal, Luis De, and Seymour B. Liebman. *The Enlightened; the Writings of Luis De Carvajal, El Mozo*. Coral Gables, Fla.: University of Miami Press, 1967.
Carvalho, Joaquim. *Religion and Power in Europe: Conflict and Convergence*. Pisa: PLUS-Pisa University Press, 2007.
Chazan, Robert. *European Jewry and the First Crusade*. Berkeley: University of California Press, 1987.
Cohen, Jeremy. "Between Martyrdom and Apostasy: Doubt and Self-definition in Twelfth-century Ashkenaz." *Journal of Medieval and Early Modern Studies* 29, no. 3 (1999): 431-71.
Cohen, Mark R. *Under Crescent and Cross: The Jews in the Middle Ages*. Princeton, N.J.: Princeton University Press, 1994.
Cohen, Shaye J. D. *The Beginnings of Jewishness Boundaries, Varieties, Uncertainties*. Berkeley: University of California Press, 1999.
"Conversos & Crypto-Jews." City of Albuquerque. Accessed June 9, 2015. http://www.cabq.gov/humanrights/public-information-and-education/diversity-booklets/jewish-american-heritage/conversos-crypto-jews.
"Crypto Jews." Am I Jewish? Accessed March 25, 2015. http://www.amijewish.info/w/crypto-jews/.
Cutler, Allan Harris, and Helen Elmquist Cutler. *The Jew as Ally of the Muslim: Medieval Roots of Anti-Semitism*. Notre Dame, Ind.: University of Notre Dame Press, 1986.
Davidson, Herbert A. *Moses Maimonides: The Man and His Works*. Oxford: Oxford University Press, 2005.
Dorff, Elliot N., and Arthur I. Rosett. *A Living Tree the Roots and Growth of Jewish Law*. Albany, N.Y.: the State University of New York Press, 1988.
Faur, Jose. *In the Shadow of History Jews and Conversos at the Dawn of Modernity*. Albany, N.Y.: the State University of New York Press, 1992.
Faur, José. "Four Classes of Conversos." *Revue Des Études Juives* 149, no. 1-2 (1990): 113-24.

Faur, José. "Anti-Maimonidean Demons." *Review of Rabbinic Judaism* 6 (2003): 3-52.
Ferry, Barbara, and Debbie Nathan. "Mistaken Identity? The Case of New Mexico's "Hidden Jews." The Atlantic. December 1, 2000. Accessed April 1, 2015. http://www.theatlantic.com/magazine/archive/2000/12/mistaken-identity-the-case-of-new-mexicos-hidden-jews/378454/ I.
Ferziger, Adam S. "Between 'Ashkenazi' and Sepharad: An Early Modern German Rabbinic Response to Religious Pluralism in the Spanish-Portuguese Community." *Studia Rosenthaliana* 35, no. 1 (2001): 7-22.
Fishman, Talya. "The Jewishness of the Conversos." Lecture, Early Modern Workshop: Jewish History Resources, January 1, 2004.
Foer, Paul, and Chananette Pascal Cohen. "For Hispanic 'Crypto-Jews,' Lawsuits May Follow Religious Rediscovery." JNS. October 29, 2012. Accessed March 25, 2015. http://www.jns.org/latest-articles/2012/10/29/for-hispanic-crypto-jews-lawsuits-may-follow-religious-redis.html#.VXdW0dLBzGd.
Fram, Edward. "Perception and Reception of Repentant Apostates in Medieval Ashkenaz and Premodern Poland." *AJS Review* 21, no. 2 (1996): 299-339.
Frank, Daniel, and Matt Goldfish. *Rabbinic Culture and Its Critics: Jewish Authority, Dissent, and Heresy in the Medieval and Early Modern Times.* Detroit: Wayne State University, 2007.
Friedenwald, Harry. "Montaigne's Relation to Judaism and the Jews." *The Jewish Quarterly Review* 31, no. 2 (1940): 141-48.
Furst, Rachel. "Captivity, Conversion, and Communal Identity: Sexual Angst and Religious Crisis in Frankfurt, 1241." *Jew History Jewish History* 22, no. 1-2 (2008): 179-221.
Gampel, Benjamin R. "The 'Identity' of Sephardim of Medieval Christian Iberia." *Jewish Social Studies* 8, no. 2/3 (2002): 133-38.
Gerber, Jane S. *The Jews of Spain.* New York: The Free Press, 1992.
Gilman, Stephen. *The Spain of Fernando De Rojas; the Intellectual and Social Landscape of La Celestina.* Princeton, N.J.: Princeton University Press, 1972.
Gitlitz, David M. *Secrecy and Deceit: The Religion of the Crypto-Jews.* Philadelphia: Jewish Publication Society, 1996.
Goldish, Matt. *The Sabbatean Prophets.* Cambridge, Mass.: Harvard University Press, 2004.
Golinkin, David. "How Can Apostates Such as the Falash Mura Return to Judaism?" *Responsa in a Moment* 1, no. 5 (2007). Accessed June 9, 2015. http://www.schechter.edu/responsa.aspx?ID=30.
Gomez-Hortiguela Amillo, Angel. "La Vida Sine Querella De Juan Luis Vives." *EHumanista* 26 (2014): 345-56.
Grayzel, Solomon. "The Beginnings of Exclusion." *The Jewish Quarterly Review* 61, no. 1 (1970): 15-26.

Grayzel, Solomon. *The Church and the Jews in the XIIIth Century.* New York: Hermon, 1966.
Green, Simcha. "Welcoming Anusim Back Into The Family." The Jewish Press. August 22, 2012. Accessed March 25, 2015. http://www.jewishpress.com/indepth/opinions/welcoming-anusim-back-into-the-family/2010/12/08/0/?print.
Green, Toby. *The Reign of Fear.* London: Macmillan: 2007.
Guerson, Alexandra. "Seeking Remission: Jewish Conversion in the Crown of Aragon, C.1378–1391." *Jewish History* 24, no. 1 (2010): 33-52.
Gutwirth, Eleazar. "The Jews in 15th Century Castilian Chronicles." *The Jewish Quarterly Review* 74, no. 4 (1984): 379-96.
Halevy, Schulamith C., and Nachum Dershowitz. "Obscure Practices among New World Anusim." *Proceedings of the Conferencia Internacional De Investigacion De La Asociacion Latinoamericana De Estudios Judaicos*, 1995. Accessed June 9, 2015.
Haliczer, Stephen. "Conversos Y Judíos En Tiempos De La Expulsión : Un Análisis Crítico De Investigación Y Análisis." *Revistas Espacio, Tiempo Y Forma* Serie III (1993): 287-300.
"Jewish History Sourcebook: The Jews of Spain and the Visigothic Code, 654-681 CE." Fordham University. 1998. Accessed June 2, 2015. http://legacy.fordham.edu/halsall/jewish/jews-visigothic1.asp.
Halperin, David J. trans. Abraham Miguel Cardozo; Selected Writings. New York: Paulist Press, 2001.
Hayim Sofer, Yitshaq BenTsvi Ben Naftali. *Sefer Shu "T Ha-Radbaz Mi-Ktav Yad.* Benei Brak, 1975.
Hershman, A.M. *Rabbi Isaac Bar Sheshet Perfet and His Times.* New York, N.Y.: Jewish Theological Seminary, 1943.
Hinojosa Montalvo, José. "Los Judios En La España Medieval: De La Tolerancia a La Expulsión." In *Los Marginados En El Mundo Medieval Y Moderno.*, 25-41. Almería: Instituto De Estudios Almerienses, 1998.
Hochbaum, Jerry. "Who Is a Jew: A Sociological Perspective." *Tradition* 13/14, no. 4/1 (1973): 35-41.
Hopstein, Avner. "The Crypto-Jews of Brazil." Y Net News. October 26, 2006. Accessed March 31, 2015. http://www.ynetnews.com/articles/0,7340,L-3319972,00.html.
Hordes, Stanley M. *To the End of the Earth: A History of the Crypto-Jews of New Mexico.* New York: Columbia University Press, 2005.
Idel, Moshe. *Messianic Mystics.* New Haven: Yale University Press, 1998.
Ingram, Kevin. *Secret Lives, Public Lies the Conversos and Socio-religious Nonconformism in the Spanish Golden Age.* San Diego, California: UC San Diego Electronic Theses and Dissertations, 2006.
Ingram, Kevin, ed. *The Conversos and Moriscos in Late Medieval Spain and beyond.* Vol. 2. Leiden: Brill, 2012.

Israel, Jonathan. "Sephardic Immigration into the Dutch Republic, 1595-1672." *Studia Rosenthaliana* 23 (1989): 45-53.

Israel, Jonathan. "Spain and the Dutch Sephardim, 1609-1660." *Studia Rosenthaliana* 12, no. 1/2 (1978): 1-61.

Jacobs, Louis. "Attitudes towards Christianity in the Halakhah." Louis Jacobs. 2005. Accessed June 1, 2015. http://louisjacobs.org/articles/attitudes-towards-christianity-in-the-halakhah/?highlight=Attitudes towards Christianity.

Jocz, Jakob. *The Jewish People and Jesus Christ; a Study in the Relationship between the Jewish People and Jesus Christ*. London: S.P.C.K., 1949.

JOSPIC -J Staff "A List of 134 Books Containing Marrano, Converso, Crypto Jew, Secret Jew, Hidden Jew, New Christian, or Anusim in the Title or Subtitle: Changes in Usage Over 86 Years." *Journal of Spanish, Portuguese, and Italian Crypto-Jews*, 2011, 149-55.

Juster, J. *Les Juifs Dans L'Empire Romain*. Vol. II. Paris: P. Geunther, 1914.

Kaplan, Yosef. "The Portuguese Jews in Amsterdam: From Forced Conversion to a Return to Judaism." *Studia Rosenthaliana* 15, no. 1 (1981): 37-51.

Kaplan, Yosef. "The Jewish Profile of the Spanish-Portuguese Community of London during the Seventeenth Century." *Judaism* 41, no. 3 (1992): 229-40.

Kaplan, Yosef. "Wayward New Christians and Stubborn New Jews: The Shaping of a Jewish Identity." *Jewish History* 8, no. 1-2 (1994): 27-41.

Katz, Jacob. *Exclusiveness and Tolerance; Studies in Jewish-gentile Relations in Medieval and Modern Times*. West Orange: Behrman House, 1961.

Katz, Jacob. *Halakhah Ve-Qabbalah*. Jerusalem: Magnes Press, 1984.

Katz, Solomon. *The Jews in the Visigothic and Frankish Kingdoms of Spain and Gaul*. New York: Kraus, 1970.

Kedourie, Elie. *Spain and the Jews: The Sephardi Experience: 1492 and after*. London: Thames and Hudson, 1992.

Kelly, David. "DNA Clears the Fog Over Latino Links to Judaism in New Mexico." Los Angeles Times. December 5, 2004. Accessed March 25, 2015. http://articles.latimes.com/2004/dec/05/nation/na-heritage5.

Krow-Lucal, Martha G. "Marginalizing History: Observations on the Origins of the Inquisition in Fifteenth-century Spain by B. Netanyahu." *Judaism*, 1997, 47-62.

Kunin, David A. "Welcoming Back the Anusim: A Halakhic Teshuvah." Sephardim Hope. July 9, 2009. Accessed June 10, 2015. http://sephardimhope.net/index.php?view=article&catid=36:articles&id=62:welcoming-back-the-anusim-a-halakhic-teshuvah&format=pdf&option=com_content&Itemid=69.

Lavender, Abraham D. "The Secret Jews (Neofiti) of Sicily: Religious and Social Status Before and After the Inquisition." *Journal of Spanish, Portuguese, and Italian Crypto-Jews* 3 (2011): 119-33.

Lawrance, Jeremy. "Alegoría Y Apocalipsis En "El Alboraique"" *Revista De Poética Medieval* 11 (2003): 11-39.
Lazar, Moshe. *The Jews of Spain and the Expulsion of 1492*. Lancaster, Calif.: Labyrinthos, 1997.
Lea, Henry Charles. "Ferrand Martinez and the Massacres of 1391." *The American Historical Review* 1, no. 2 (1896): 209-19.
Leibman, Seymour. *The Jews in New Spain*. Miami: University of Miami, 1970.
Lent, Dani. "Analysis of the Israeli High Courts: Jewish Apostates and the Law of Return." Kol Hamevaser. 2010. Accessed June 1, 2015. http://www.kolhamevaser.com/2010/09/analysis-of-the-israeli-high-court-jewish-apostates-and-the-law-of-return/.
Lewis, Bernard. *The Jews of Islam*. Princeton, N.J.: Princeton University Press, 1984.
Lichenstein, Aharon. *Brother Daniel and Jewish Fraternity, Leaves of Faith: The World of Jewish Living*. Jersey City: Ktav, 2004.
Lieberman, Julia R. "Sermons and the Construct of a Jewish Identity: The Hamburg Sephardic Community in the 1620s." *Jewish Studies Quarterly* 10, no. 1 (2003): 49-72.
Liebman, Seymour B. *The Jews in New Spain; Faith, Flame, and the Inquisition*, Coral Gables, Fla.: University of Miami Press, 1970.
Liebman, Seymour B. *New World Jewry, 1493-1825: Requiem for the Forgotten*. New York: Ktav Pub. House, 1982.
Linder, Amnon. *The Jews in Roman Imperial Legislation*. Detroit, Mich.: Wayne State University Press, 1987.
Lindo, E.H. *The Jews of Spain and Portugal*. London: Longman, Brown, Green, & Longmans, 1848.
Lipshiz, Cnaan. "Secret No More." Shavei Israel. November 9, 2009. Accessed March 25, 2015. http://www.shavei.org/communities/bnei_anousim/articles-bnei_anousim/secret-no-more/?lang=en.
Llobet Portella, Josep Maria. "Los Conversos Según La Documentación Local De Cervera (1338-1501)." *Revista De La Facultad De Geografía E Historia* 4 (1989): 335-49.
Maimonides, Moses, and Abraham S. Halkin. *Crisis and Leadership: Epistles of Maimonides*. Philadelphia: Jewish Publication Society of America, 1985.
Marcus, Jacob Rader. *The Jew in the Medieval World: A Source Book, 315-1791*. Cincinnati: Union of American Hebrew Congregations, 1938.
Margaliot, Reuben. *Sefer Ḥasidim*. Jerusalem: Mosad Ha-Rav Kook, 1956.
"Marranos, Conversos & New Christians." Jewish Virtual Library. Accessed June 1, 2015. https://www.jewishvirtuallibrary.org/jsource/Judaism/Marranos.html.
Martin, J. J. "Marranos and Nicodemites in Sixteenth-Century Venice." *Journal of Medieval and Early Modern Studies* 41, no. 3 (2011): 577-99.

Mentzer, Raymond A. "Marranos of Southern France in the Early Sixteenth Century." *The Jewish Quarterly Review* 72, no. 4 (1982): 303-11.

Metzger, David, ed. *Sheelot U-Teshuvot Le-rabbenu Ha-gadol Marana Ve-rabbana Harav Yizhak Bar Sheshet*. Jerusalem: Makhon Or HaMizrah, 1993.

Meyers, Charles, and Norman Simms eds. *Troubled Souls: Conversos, Crypto-Jews, and Other Confused Jewish Intellectuals from the Fourteenth through the Eighteenth Century*. Hamilton: Outrigger Publishers, 2001.

Meyerson, Mark D. "Aragonese and Catalan Jewish Converts at the Time of the Expulsion." *Jewish History*, 1992, 131-49.

Meyerson, Mark D. *A Jewish Renaissance in Fifteenth-century Spain*. Princeton: Princeton University Press, 2004.

Montalvo, Jose. *The Jews of the Kingdom of Valencia: From Persecution to Expulsion, 1391-1492*. Jerusalem: Magnes Press, Hebrew University, 1993.

Nelson, Zalman. "Is a Jew Who Converts Still Jewish?" Chabad. Accessed June 2, 2015. http://www.chabad.org/library/article_cdo/aid/1269075/jewish/Is-a-Jew-Who-Converts-Still-Jewish.htm.

Netanyahu, B. "Americo Castro and His View of the Origins of the Pureza De Sangre." *Proceedings of the American Academy for Jewish Research* 46/47, no. Jubilee Volume (1928-29 / 1978-79) (1979): 397-457.

Netanyahu, B. *The Origins of the Inquisition in Fifteenth Century Spain*. New York: Random House, 1995.

Netanyahu, B. *The Marranos of Spain: From the Late 14th to the Early 16th Century, According to Contemporary Hebrew Sources*. 3rd ed. Ithaca, N.Y.: Cornell University Press, 1999.

Nirenberg, David. "Conversion, Sex, And Segregation: Jews And Christians In Medieval Spain." *The American Historical Review* 107, no. 4 (2002): 1065-093.

Nirenberg, David. *Anti-Judaism: The Western Tradition*. New York: W. W. Norton &, 2013.

Nissimi, Hilda. "Religious Conversion, Covert Defiance and Social Identity: A Comparative View." *Numen* 51, no. 4 (2004): 367-406.

"Obituary Samuel Lerer, an American Rabbi Who Converted Mexicans, Dies at 89." Jewish Telegraph Agency. February 9, 2004. Accessed March 25, 2015. http://www.jta.org/2004/02/09/archive/obituary-samuel-lerer-an-american-rabbi-who-converted-mexicans-dies-at-89.

Oeltjen, Natalie. *Crisis and Regeneration: The Conversos of Majorca, 1391-1416*. Toronto: University of Toronto, 2012.

Orme, Wyatt. "Crypto-Jews' In the Southwest Find Faith in a Shrouded Legacy." Code Switch Frontiers of Race, Culture, and Ethnicity. February 19, 2014. Accessed March 25, 2015. http://www.npr.org/sections/codeswitch/2014/02/19/275862633/crypto-jews-in-the-southwest-find-faith-in-a-shrouded-legacy.

Parello, Vincent. "La Apologética Antijudía De Juan Luis Vives (1543)." *Melanges De La Casa De Velazquez* 38, no. 2 (2008): 171-87.

Perez, Joseph, and Lysa Hochroth. *History of a Tragedy: The Expulsion of the Jews from Spain.* Chicago: University of Illinois Press, 1993.

Perlmann, Moshe. "Apostasy." Jewish Virtual Library. 2008. Accessed June 2, 2015.
http://www.jewishvirtuallibrary.org/jsource/judaica/ejud_0002_0002_0_01188.html.

Popkin, Richard H. *The History of Scepticism from Erasmus to Spinoza.* Rev. and Expanded ed. Berkeley: University of California Press, 1979.

"Portugal." Jewish Virtual Library, accessed on July 28, 2015,
http://www.jewishvirtuallibrary.org/jsource/vjw/Portugal.html

Quesada Morillas, Yolanda. "La Expulsion De Los Judios Andaluces a Finales Del Siglo XV Y Su Prohibicion De Pase a Indias." *Actas Del I Congreso Internacional Sobre Migraciones En Andalucia*, 2011, 2099-106.

Rábade Obrado, María Del Pilar. "La Instrucción Cristiana De Los Conversos En La Castilla Del Siglo XV." *En La España Medieval* 22 (1999): 369-93.

Raphael, Amia. "Goldsmiths and Silversmiths." Jewish Virtual Library, accessed on July 31, 2015.
http://www.jewishvirtuallibrary.org/jsource/judaica/ejud_0002_0007_0_07579.html.

Rosenblatt, Eli. "Picturing Today's Conversos." The Forward. April 1, 2008. Accessed March 25, 2015.
http://forward.com/culture/13079/picturing-today-s-conversos-01595/.

Rosenbloom, Noah H. "Menasseh Ben Israel and the Eternality of Punishment Issue." *Proceedings of the American Academy for Jewish Research* 60 (1994): 241-62.

Rosenstock, Bruce. "Abraham Miguel Cardoso's Messianism: A Reappraisal." *AJS Review* 23, no. 1 (1998): 63-104.

Ross, Theodore. "Shalom on the Range: In Search of the American Crypto-Jew." Harpers. December 1, 2009. Accessed March 27, 2015.
http://harpers.org/archive/2009/12/shalom-on-the-range/.

Roth, Cecil. *A History of the Marranos.* Philadelphia: Jewish Publication Society of America, 1947.

Roth, Cecil. *The Spanish Inquisition.* New York: WW. Norton and Company, 1964.

Roth, Norman. "Anti-Converso Riots of the Fifteenth Century, Pulgar, and the Inquisition." *En La España Medieval* 15 (1992): 367-94.

Roth, Norman. *Jews, Visigoths, and Muslims in Medieval Spain: Cooperation and Conflict.* Leiden: E.J. Brill, 1994.

Roth, Norman. *Conversos, Inquisition, and the Expulsion of the Jews from Spain.* Madison, Wis.: University of Wisconsin Press, 1995.

Ruderman, David B. *Jewish Thought and Scientific Discovery in Early Modern Europe.* Detroit, Michigan: Wayne State University, 2001.
Sachar, Howard Morley. *Farewell España: The World of the Sephardim Remembered.* New York: Knopf, 1995.
Salomon, H.P. "New Light on the Portuguese Inquisition: The Second Reply to the Archbishop of Cranganor." *Studia Rosenthaliana* 5, no. 2 (1971): 178-86.
Sanchez, Francisco, and Douglas F.S. Thomson. *That Nothing Is Known.* Edited by Elaine Limbrick. Cambridge: Cambridge University Press, 1988.
Saperstein, Marc. "Christianity, Christians, and 'New Christians' in the Sermons of Saul Levi Morteira." *Hebrew Union College Annual* 70/71:329-84.
Saperstein, Marc. "Saul Levi Morteira's Treatise on the Immortality of the Soul." *Studia Rosenthaliana* 25, no. 2 (1991): 131-48.
Schiffman, Lawrence H. *Who Was a Jew?: Rabbinic and Halakhic Perspectives on the Jewish-Christian Schism.* Hoboken, N.J.: Ktav Pub. House, 1985.
Scholberg, Kenneth R. "Minorities in Medieval Castilian Literature." *Hispania* 37, no. 2 (1954): 203-09.
Scholem, Gershom. *The Messianic Idea in Judaism: And Other Essays on Jewish Spirituality.* New York: Schocken Books, 1972.
Selke, Angela. *Los Chuetas Y La Inquisicion.* Madrid: Taurus, 1972.
Shatzmiller, Joseph. "Converts and Judaizers in the Early Fourteenth Century." *Harvard Theological Review* 74, no. 1 (1981): 63-77.
Sherwin, Byron L. *Faith Finding Meaning: A Theology of Judaism.* Oxford: Oxford University Press, 2009.
Singer, Isidore, and Cyrus Adler, eds. "Spain." *Jewish Encyclopedia.* 1906.
Spinoza, Benedictus De, and Dagobert D. Runes. *The Ethics Of Spinoza: The Road to Inner Freedom.* Secaucus: Citadel, 1976.
Stern, Sacha. *Jewish Identity in Early Rabbinic Writings.* New York: Brill, 1994.
Stillman, Norman A. *The Jews of Arab Lands: A History and Source Book.* Philadelphia: Jewish Publication Society of America, 1979.
Suarez Bilbao, Fernando. "Cristianos Contra Judios y Conversos." Lecture, from Universidad Rey Juan Carlos, Madrid, January 1, 2004.
Swetschinski, Daniel M. "Kinship and Commerce: The Foundations of Portuguese Jewish Life in Seventeenth-Century Holland." *Studia Rosenthaliana* 15, no. 1 (1981): 52-74.
Synan, Edward A. *The Popes and the Jews in the Middle Ages.* New York: Macmillan, 1965.
Szajkowski, Zosa. "Trade Relations of Marranos in France with the Iberian Peninsula in the Sixteenth and Seventeenth Centuries." *The Jewish Quarterly Review* 50, no. 1 (1959): 69-78.
Thornton, Stuart. "Hidden History: Rabbi Explains the Identity of the Crypto-Jews." National Geographic. Accessed March 25, 2015. http://www.nationalgeographic.com/hidden-history/.

Touger, Eliyahu. "Avodah Kochavim - Chapter Two." Chabad. Accessed June 9, 2015. http://www.chabad.org/library/article_cdo/aid/912360/jewish/Avodah-Kochavim-Chapter-Two.htm.

Touger, Eliyahu. "Ma'achalot Assurot - Chapter 17." Chabad. Accessed June 9, 2015. http://www.chabad.org/library/article_cdo/aid/968273/jewish/Maachalot-Assurot-Chapter-17.htm.

Touger, Eliyahu. "Gerushin - Chapter Three." Chabad. Accessed June 9, 2015. http://www.chabad.org/library/article_cdo/aid/957708/jewish/Gerushin-Chapter-Three.htm.

Touger, Eliyahu. "Yibbum VChalitzah - Chapter One." Chabad. Accessed June 9, 2015. http://www.chabad.org/library/article_cdo/aid/960619/jewish/Yibbum-vChalitzah-Chapter-One.htm.

Treatman, Ronit. "Queen Esther: Patron Saint of Crypto-Jews." The Times of Israel. March 16, 2014. Accessed April 2, 2015. http://www.timesofisrael.com/queen-esther-patron-saint-of-crypto-jews/.

Usque, Samuel, and Martin Cohen. *Consolations for the Tribulations of Israel (Consolacam as Tribulacoens De Israel)*. Philadelphia: Jewish Publication Society of America, 1977.

Utterback, Kristine T. ""Conversi" Revert: Voluntary and Forced Return to Judaism in the Early Fourteenth Century." *Church History* 64, no. 1 (1995): 16-28.

Wakefield, Walter L. *Heresy, Crusade, and Inquisition in Southern France, 1100-1250*. Berkeley: University of California Press, 1974.

Wheelwright, Jeff. "The 'Secret Jews' of San Luis Valley." Smithsonian Magazine. 2008. Accessed March 25, 2015. http://www.smithsonianmag.com/science-nature/the-secret-jews-of-san-luis-valley-11765512/?no-ist.

Wildman, Sarah. "Mallorca's Jews Get Their Due: Spanish Island's Community Alive and Thriving." The Forward. April 13, 2012. Accessed March 27, 2015. http://forward.com/articles/154649/mallorcas-jews-get-their-due/?p=all#ixzz3TLpkmfSl.

Wiznitzer, Arnold. "Crypto-Jews in Mexico during the Sixteenth Century." *American Jewish Historical Quarterly* 51, no. 3 (1962): 168-214.

Yerushalmi, Yosef. "The Re-education of the Marranos in the Seventeenth Century." Scribd. 1980. Accessed June 2, 2015. http://www.scribd.com/doc/63071643/Re-Education-of-the-Marranos-by-Yosef-Yerushalmi#scribd.

Yerushalmi, Yosef Hayim. "The Inquisition and the Jews of France in the Time of Bernard Gui." *Harvard Theological Review* 63, no. 3 (1970): 317-76.

Yerushalmi, Yosef Hayim. *From Spanish Court to Italian Ghetto; Isaac Cardoso; a Study in Seventeenth-century Marranism and Jewish Apologetics.* New York: Columbia University Press, 1971.

Yovel, Yirmiyahu. "Converso Dualities In The First Generation: The Cancioneros." *Jewish Social Studies: History, Culture, and Society* 4, no. 3 (1998): 1-28.

Zeitlin, S. "Mumar and Meshumad." *The Jewish Quarterly Review* 54, no. 1 (1963): 84-86.

Zeldes, Nadia. "Legal Status of Jewish Converts to Christianity in Southern Italy and Provence." *California Italian Studies,* 1, no. 1 (2010). Accessed June 2, 2015. http://escholarship.org/uc/item/91z342hv.

Zohar, Zvi. "The Sephardic Tradition-Creative Responses to Modernity." Lecture, January 1, 2010.

Zsom, Dora. "Uncircumcised Converts in Sephardi Responsa from the Fifteenth and Sixteenth Centuries." *Iberoamerica Global* 1, no. 3 (2008): 159-71.

Zsom, Dora. "The Return of the Conversos to Judaism in the Ottoman Empire and North-Africa." *Hispania Judaica* 7 (2010): 335-47.

Zsom, Dora. "Converts in the Responsa of R. David Ibn Avi Zimra: An Analysis of the Texts." *Hispania Judaica* 6 (2008): 267-92.

Zsom, Dora. "The Levirate Marriage of Converts in the Responsa of Some Sephardic Authorities." *Kut* 3 (2008): 96-113.

De Covarrubias Horozco, Sebastian. "Tesoro De La Lengua Castellana O Española." Universidad De Sevilla-Fondo Antiguo. Accessed June 2, 2015. http://fondosdigitales.us.es/fondos/libros/765/1119/tesoro-de-la-lengua-castellana-o-espanola/.

De Salazar Acha, Jaime. "La Limpieza De Sangre." *Revista De La Inquisicion* 1 (1991): 289-308.

De Spinoza, Benedict, and R.H.M Elwes. *A Theologico-Political Treatise.* New York: Dover, 1951.

DeSola Cardoza, Anne. "Texas Mexican Secret Spanish Jews Today." Sefarad. Accessed June 9, 2015. http://sefarad.org/lm/011/texas.html.

Ldez, Andre, and Manuel Moreno. *Memorias Del Reinado De Los Reyes Católicos,.* Madrid: [Real Academia De La Historia], 1962.

# Index

Abd al-Mu'min, 19
Abdallah ibn Tumart, 19
Abraham Benveniste, 41, 43
Abraham ibn Daud, 19
Abraham Israel Pereyra, 9, 133, 134, 137, 138, 157
Abraham Miguel Cardozo, 10, 144, 145, 146, 147, 148, 149, 150, 151, 152, 154, 156, 157, 269
Abraham Seneor, 43, 47
Alfonso de Aguilar, 81
Alfonso de Espina, 87
Alfonso de Fuentelsaz, 65
Al-Ḥakim, 17
Almeria, 32
Almohades, 3, 6, 19, 20
Almoravides, 18, 19
Al-Mu'tamid, 18
Alonso de Carrillo, 92
Alonso de Cartagena, 76, 77, 122, 127
Alonso de Espina, 7, 44, 87, 88, 89, 90, 91
Alonso de Mella, 75
Alonso de Palencia, 78, 81
Alonso Manrique, 127
Al-Razi, 14, 15
*Alumbrado*, 54
Alvaro da Costa, 128
Alvaro de Luna, 41, 71
Alvaro Dinis, 142
Alzira, 29
Andalusia, 19, 28, 45, 46, 47, 63, 82

Andres Bernaldez, 48, 69, 70, 79, 92
Antonio Fernandes Carvajal, 131
Antonio Ferreira, 131
*Apology for Sebonde*, 174
Archbishop Alphonso Carrillo, 84
Arias Diaz, 73
Augstin Coronel Chacon, 132
*Avodah Zarah*, 95, 97
Balearic Islands, 13
Barcelona, 21, 29, 31, 33, 61, 105, 189
Bartolome Mendez Trancoso, 132
Baruch Spinoza, 11, 128, 142, 166, 176, 179, 181, 184
Basques, 75
Benzion Netanyahu, 4, 6, 196, 243, 244, 245, 246, 249, 250, 251
Bernard of Clairvaux, 61
Bertrand du Guesclin, 23
*Birkat Hamazon*, 113
Bonafonat de Sant Feliu, 29
Borriana, 29
*Breviarium*, 56
Canary Islands, 132, 231
Cardinal Pedro Gonzalez de Mendoza, 63
Castello, 29
Castile, 4, 8, 18, 21, 22, 23, 24, 26, 28, 29, 31, 32, 33, 34, 37, 38, 41, 42, 43, 44, 46, 48, 49, 51, 53, 57, 58, 60, 64, 71, 75, 79, 88, 92, 93, 94, 120, 121, 203, 244, 261

Catherine of Aragon, 125
Catholics, 6, 9, 227, 236
Charles I, 54
Charles V, 54, 125
Christianity, 3, 4, 6, 7, 8, 10, 14, 15, 16, 22, 30, 31, 32, 33, 34, 35, 38, 42, 45, 48, 50, 54, 56, 57, 58, 59, 61, 62, 63, 64, 65, 66, 67, 72, 75, 77, 89, 97, 98, 99, 100, 101, 103, 104, 105, 113, 114, 116, 118, 120, 121, 122, 123, 125, 126, 127, 132, 134, 139, 140,146, 149, 150, 156, 158, 161, 163, 166, 170, 174, 176, 178, 181, 183, 184, 187, 196, 202, 208, 209, 213, 215, 217, 226, 254, 255, 256, 257, 270, 276, 278
Christians, 5, 6, 7, 13, 14, 15, 16, 17, 20, 24, 25, 27, 31, 32, 34, 37, 39, 40, 41, 44, 45, 46, 48, 50, 51, 56, 57, 59, 60, 61, 62, 64, 65, 66, 67, 68, 69, 70, 72, 74, 75, 76, 77, 79, 82, 83, 84, 86, 88, 89, 93, 100, 103, 104, 108, 110, 111, 118, 127, 129, 130, 132, 143, 150, 159, 171, 172, 183, 187, 199, 200, 202, 208, 209, 215, 216, 218, 243, 245, 250, 252, 254, 260, 262, 273, 276
Ciudad Real, 5, 28, 73, 74, 75, 80, 81, 89, 91, 92, 241, 244, 247, 265
Clara Fuster, 187, 189
Comunero Revolt, 54
*Constitutio Pro Iudaeis*, 58
Conversos, v, 3, 4, 5, 6, 7, 8, 9, 10, 11, 12, 17, 22, 29, 30, 32, 33, 34, 35, 38, 39, 42, 43, 44, 45, 46, 47, 48, 51, 52, 53, 54, 56, 60, 61, 62, 63, 64, 65, 66, 67, 68, 69, 70, 71, 72, 73, 74, 75, 76, 77, 78, 79, 80, 81, 82, 83, 84, 85, 87, 88, 89, 91, 92, 93, 94, 95, 100, 108, 109, 110, 111, 112, 113, 114, 115, 116, 118, 119, 120, 122, 124, 128, 129, 130, 131, 133, 134, 135, 136, 137, 139, 140, 142, 143, 144, 145, 153, 155, 157, 158, 159, 160, 161, 162, 163, 164, 165, 166, 168, 169, 170, 171, 172, 173, 174, 175, 176, 177, 178, 179, 180, 183, 184, 185, 186, 187, 188, 189, 190, 191, 192, 193, 194, 195, 196, 197, 198, 199, 200, 201, 202, 203, 204, 205, 206, 207, 208, 209, 210, 211, 212, 213, 214, 216, 217, 218, 219, 220, 221, 222, 223, 224, 226, 227, 228, 229, 231, 232, 233, 234, 235, 236, 237, 238, 239, 242, 243, 244, 245, 246, 247, 248, 249, 250, 251, 252, 254, 255, 256, 257, 258, 261, 262, 265, 266, 267, 268, 269, 270, 272, 273, 274, 275, 276, 278
Córdoba, 5, 13, 16, 17, 18, 19, 21, 27, 28, 32, 36, 46, 81, 82, 85, 115, 116
Council of Elvira, 13
Council of Trent, 59
Cristobal Mendez, 130
Cuenca del Duero, 29
Daniel Levi de Barrios, 129, 134
Daniel Ribera, 176
David el Rau, 187
David Farhi, 203
David Farrar, 141, 211, 212
David Gabay, 132
*dhimmi*, 18
Dom Ferdinand of Portugal, 24
Duarte Enriques Alvares, 132
Eastern Roman Empire, 13

Edict of Expulsion, 8, 64, 90
Egica, 16
*El Alboraique*, 7, 66, 69, 91, 186, 187, 271
Eliahu de Lima, 132
Esteban de Ares Fonseca, 131
Etienne de la *Boétie*, 173
Even Thomas de Rojas, 132
Extremadura, 46
Eyquem de Montaigne, 170
Fernando de Antequera, 33, 37
Fernando de la Torre, 80
Ferrant Martinez, 25, 26, 32
Fourth Toledo Council, 76
Francesc Castellar, 119
Francesc Sagarriga, 30
Francisco Lopes Capadosse, 129
Francisco Sanchez, 11, 160, 161, 162, 163, 169, 170, 171, 174, 180
Francisco Tomas de Miranda, 132
Gabriel da Costa, 132, 176
Geonim, 98, 146, 260
Geronimo de Santa Fe, 7, 35, 38, 122
Girona, 29, 190
Gonzalo Alonso de Siles, 73
Gonzalo Garcia dei Santa Maria, 122
Granada, 13, 16, 18, 19, 21, 23, 27, 32, 46, 47, 65, 71, 75
Guadalajara, 39
Guillem Ramon Splugues, 8, 117
Henry de Trastamara, 22, 23
Henry Méchoulan, 135
Henry of Trastámara, 6
Hernando de Talavera, 63
Hernando del Pulgar, 35, 46, 82
Howard Sachar, 31, 37
Illescas, 36
Inquisition, 4, 5, 7, 9, 12, 17, 31, 44, 45, 47, 48, 49, 53, 54, 63, 64, 71, 72, 74, 75, 76, 77, 81, 82, 83, 88, 89, 90, 91, 92, 93, 94, 114, 116, 117, 118, 119, 120, 124, 125, 130, 132, 133, 134, 138, 160, 169, 174, 188, 191, 198, 203, 209, 210, 217, 219, 221, 223, 232, 235, 236, 239, 241, 242, 243, 244, 245, 246, 247, 248, 249, 250, 252, 253, 264, 265, 271, 272, 273, 275, 277, 278
*Instrucción del Relator*, 83
Isaac Abravanel, 11, 43, 46, 48, 149, 158, 159, 160, 215, 217, 266
Isaac de Azevedo, 132
Isaac La Peyrère, 11, 160, 166
Isaac Orobio de Castro, 9, 138, 140, 161, 168
Isaac Xamblell, 187
Islam, 6, 17, 18, 19, 20, 21, 45, 75, 97, 98, 99, 125, 137, 148, 149, 153, 256, 260, 264, 272
Jacob Adzoni, 187
Jacob Facan, 187
Jews, i, 3, 4, 5, 6, 7, 8, 9, 10, 11, 13, 14, 15, 16, 17, 18, 19, 20, 21, 22, 23, 24, 25, 26, 27, 28, 29, 30, 31, 32, 33, 34, 35, 36, 38, 39, 40, 41, 42, 43, 44, 45, 46, 47, 48, 49, 50, 51, 52, 56, 57, 58, 59, 60, 61, 62, 63, 64, 65, 66, 67, 68, 69, 70, 71, 72, 73, 74, 75, 76, 77, 78, 79, 80, 81, 82, 83, 84, 85, 86, 87, 88, 91, 92, 93, 95, 97, 98, 99, 100, 101, 102, 104, 107, 108, 109, 110, 111, 112, 113, 115, 116, 118, 119, 120, 121, 122, 123, 127, 128, 129, 130, 131, 132, 134, 135, 136, 137, 139, 141, 143, 144, 145, 153, 155, 159, 160, 161, 162, 163, 164, 165,

166, 167, 168, 169, 170, 171,
172, 173, 174, 175, 176, 177,
178, 182, 184, 185, 186, 187,
188, 189, 190, 194, 195, 196,
197, 198, 199, 200, 201, 203,
204, 205, 207, 208, 210, 212,
215, 216, 220, 221, 222, 223,
224, 225, 226, 227, 228, 229,
230, 231, 232, 233, 234, 235,
236, 237, 238, 239, 240, 242,
243, 244, 245, 246, 247, 248,
250, 252, 254, 255, 256, 257,
259, 260, 262, 264, 265, 266,
267, 268, 269, 270, 271, 272,
273, 274, 275, 276, 277, 278,
279, 288

Joaõ Mocho, 51

Jonah Gabay, 132

Joseph Albo, 39, 40

Joshua Lorqui, 10, 121, 122

Juan de Mella, 75

Juan de Prado, 139, 142, 166, 176

Juan de Torquemada, 74

Juan de Villanueva, 169

Juan Fernández Pacheco, 43

Juan Poeta, 114, 115

Judaism, i, 3, 4, 5, 9, 11, 12, 13,
14, 15, 16, 21, 31, 34, 35, 40,
42, 45, 54, 56, 57, 58, 59, 62,
63, 64, 65, 66, 70, 71, 75, 76,
87, 88, 95, 98, 100, 102, 103,
104, 105, 106, 107, 109, 111,
112, 117, 119, 120, 123, 124,
125, 126, 128, 129, 130, 131,
132, 133, 134, 135, 136, 137,
138, 139, 140, 141, 142, 145,
146, 148, 154, 157, 158, 161,
162, 166, 171, 172, 173, 174,
175, 176, 177, 178, 182, 183,
184, 185, 186, 187, 190, 191,
192, 193, 194, 195, 196, 197,
200, 201, 202, 203, 204, 205,
208, 210, 212, 214, 215, 218,
220, 221, 223, 225, 226, 227,
228, 229, 231, 232, 233, 234,
235, 236, 237, 238, 239, 240,
241, 242, 244, 245, 246, 247,
248, 249, 250, 251, 254, 256,
257, 260, 261, 262, 264, 267,
268, 269, 271, 273, 274, 276,
277, 278, 288

Judaizing, 3, 5, 7, 9, 42, 44, 45,
47, 50, 53, 66, 68, 72, 77, 82,
93, 116, 118, 124, 125, 127,
140, 162, 170, 176, 191, 219,
240, 242, 243, 245, 246, 247

King Alaric II, 56

King Alfonso X, 57, 261

King Enrique IV, 44, 74, 76, 77,
79, 80, 82, 88, 91

King Ferdinand, 21, 35, 39, 40,
44, 47, 48, 50, 64, 80, 86, 92,
93, 94, 160

King Ferdinand I, 21, 40

King Henry II, 23, 25, 161

King Henry III, 26, 32, 37

King James I, 59

King John I, 24, 25, 26, 38, 121

King John II, 36, 46, 49, 112

King Juan II, 41, 42, 71, 74, 76,
77, 93

King Louis VII, 57

King Manuel, 49, 50, 51, 52

King Marti, 67

King Pedro I, 22

Kingdom of Navarre, 4, 22

*La Certeza del Camino*, 135

*Las Excelencias y Calumnias de los
Hebreos*, 148

*Las Siete Partidas*, 57, 261

León, 29

*Limpieza de Sangre*, 49, 83, 85, 86,
116, 188, 261

Lisbon, 5, 24, 46, 50, 51, 52, 131,
219, 220, 233

Lliria, 29
Lope de Barrientos, 74
Lorca, 36
Lucena, 17, 18, 19, 21
Luis Salvador, 124
Luis Vives Valeriola, 124
*Mahamad*, 129, 131, 137, 138, 145, 178, 194, 203, 261
Maimonides, 20, 98, 100, 101, 106, 122, 142, 163, 164, 179, 180, 190, 191, 193, 198, 267, 272
Majorca, 21, 22, 29, 30, 38, 60, 61, 190, 192, 223, 232, 248, 274
Malaga, 16, 32
Manuel Carvalho, 128
Marcos Garcia de Mora, 78
Maria da Costa, 176
María del Pilar Rábade Obrado, 63
*Marranos*, 5, 14, 22, 26, 29, 30, 32, 34, 35, 42, 130, 140, 145, 148, 149, 151, 194, 196, 202, 219, 220, 230, 242, 244, 245, 246, 247, 249, 251, 265, 272, 273, 275, 276, 278
Martin V, 40
*matzah*, 187
Mayer Pacagon, 169
Meir Melamed, 43
Michel de Montaigne, 11, 160, 162, 169, 170, 171, 174
Miranda de Ebro, 22
Mohammed, 19, 60
Morvedre, 28, 112, 117, 118, 119, 187, 188
Murcia, 28, 36
Nathan of Gaza, 148, 149
New Christians, 3, 34, 42, 52, 53, 67, 69, 76, 80, 93, 129, 130, 132, 133, 158, 199, 201, 202, 208, 209, 215, 245, 271, 272, 276
Nicolas Donin, 59
Ocaña, 36
Old Christians, 5, 6, 7, 42, 44, 51, 52, 60, 61, 64, 66, 67, 68, 70, 71, 72, 75, 79, 80, 82, 86, 110, 118, 119, 188, 252, 261, 262
Omayyad Caliphate, 21
Order of Calatrava, 73
Paris Disputation, 59
Pedro de Arbues, 124
Pedro de Cordova, 82
Pedro de la Caballeria, 8
Pedro Fernandez de Solis, 63
Pedro Sarmiento, 71, 74
*Pirke Avot*, 144, 163
Plaza de Zocodover, 71
Pope Alexander VII, 169
Pope Benedict XIII, 35, 38, 121, 123
Pope Gregory IX, 59
Pope Innocent III, 57, 58
Pope Leo X, 85
Pope Nicholas V, 84
Portugal, 3, 4, 12, 24, 29, 38, 46, 48, 49, 50, 51, 53, 75, 128, 129, 131, 138, 140, 161, 170, 173, 175, 176, 177, 195, 210, 211, 212, 220, 223, 226, 228, 233, 238, 239, 252, 254, 260, 262, 264, 272, 274
*Praeadamitae*, 167
Prince Marti, 27
Prince of Condé, 167, 169
Queen Isabella, 35, 44, 45, 50, 64, 86, 92, 93, 94, 115
*Quod nihil scitur*, 161, 162, 163
Rabbi Asher ben Yehiel, 28
Rabbi Benjamin Zev, 197
Rabbi David ibn Avi Zimra, 193

Rabbi Gershom ben Judah Me'or ha-Golah, 103
Rabbi Hasdai ibn Crescas, 27
Rabbi Hayyim Yosef David Azulai, 211
Rabbi Immanuel Aboab, 133, 143, 203, 211
Rabbi Isaac Aboab, 11, 199, 204, 207
Rabbi Joseph ben Joshua ben Meir, 36
Rabbi Joseph Caro, 106, 196
Rabbi Joseph Orabuena, 121
Rabbi Joseph Pardo, 212
Rabbi Judah Loew, 107, 210
Rabbi Menachem Meiri of Perpignan, 100
Rabbi Menasseh ben Israel, 134
Rabbi Moses ben Nachman, 59
Rabbi Moses Raphael D'Aguilar, 199, 200
Rabbi Moshe Gaon, 102
Rabbi Nissim Gerundi, 31
Rabbi Saadia ben Maimon ibn Danan, 195
Rabbi Saul Levi Morteira, 11, 202, 204
Rabbi Shlomo ben Shimon Duran, 106
Rabbi Simeon ben Shlomo Duran, 194, 195, 196
Rabbi Simeon ben Zemah Duran, 192, 193, 198
Rabbi Solomon Alami, 37
Rabbi Solomon ben Aderet, 105, 193
Rabbi Solomon ben Isaac, 101, 103
Rabbi Solomon Luria, 107
Rabbi Yehudah heHasid, 104
Rabbi Yitzhak ben Avraham, 105

Rabbi Yom Tov ben Avraham Ishbili, 105
Ramon Llull, 58
Rav Amram Gaon, 103
Rav Hai Gaon, 104
Reccared, 14
Recceswinth, 16
*Refundición de la Cronica de 1344*, 84
Richard Simon, 166
Rua Nova, 24, 51
Ruy Perez, 25
Salamo Caporta, 187, 188
Samuel Abulafia, 43
Samuel Nayas, 46
Samuel Primo, 145, 148
Samuel Yahya, 9, 142
Santo Tomás de Aquino, 85
Sara Athias, 131
Saragossa, 13, 15, 35, 38, 39, 112, 113, 124
Second Council of Nicaea, 57
Segovia, 23, 29, 35, 38, 43, 74, 87
*Sentencia-Estatuto*, 72, 73, 265
Seville, 13, 14, 15, 16, 19, 21, 25, 26, 27, 32, 44, 45, 46, 53, 82, 85, 87, 91, 94, 127, 138, 241, 264
Shaltiel Bonafos, 70
Shulchan Aruch, 10, 104, 106, 142, 196, 262
Sisebut, 14, 15, 16
Sisenand, 15
Solomon Franco, 128, 132
Solomon Ha-Levi, 10, 120, 122
St. Isidore, 14, 91
St. Thomas, 49, 51
Swinthila, 15
Talmud, 39, 40, 41, 59, 95, 96, 97, 98, 99, 100, 106, 107, 122, 124, 192, 197, 198, 215, 261, 262, 263, 265
Theodosian code, 56

Thomas Rodriguez-Pereyra, 133
Toledo, 5, 13, 14, 15, 16, 21, 22, 23, 28, 35, 36, 45, 56, 70, 71, 72, 73, 74, 75, 76, 77, 78, 79, 80, 83, 84, 85, 86, 90, 91, 92, 94, 116, 130, 203, 241, 249, 265
Tortosa Disputation, 6, 7, 38, 112, 115, 123, 124
Uriel da Costa, 11, 141, 160, 176, 180, 211, 213, 214
Valencia, 21, 28, 33, 39, 60, 61, 69, 93, 111, 118, 124, 188, 189, 241, 246, 252, 273
Valladolid, 23, 36, 41, 86, 114, 241
Vicente Ferrer, 28, 35, 36, 38, 68, 123
Vicente Mut, 30
Vidal Astori, 43

Visigoths, 3, 6, 13, 14, 15, 275
Western Roman Empire, 13
Xativa, 29, 118
Yitzhak ben Shmuel, 103
Yusuf ibn Tashfin, 19
Zallaka, 19
Zamora, 36, 75
Zohar, 10, 142, 143, 150, 263, 278
Zoroastrians, 17
child, 9, 14
contrary, 8
dreams, 3
foundation, 2
inferred, 10
Malocchio, 8
psychical, 4
satisfactory, 1
spinach, 9
unravelled, 3

# ABOUT THE AUTHOR

Juan Marcos Bejarano Gutierrez is a graduate of the University of Texas at Dallas where he earned a bachelor of science in electrical engineering. He works full time as an engineer but has devoted much of his time to Jewish studies. He studied at the Siegal College of Judaic Studies in Cleveland and received a Master of Arts Degree in Judaic Studies. He completed his doctoral studies at the Spertus Institute in Chicago in 2015. He studied at the American Seminary for Contemporary Judaism and received rabbinic ordination in 2011 from Yeshiva Mesilat Yesharim.

Juan Marcos Bejarano Gutierrez was a board member of the Society for Crypto-Judaic Studies from 2011-2013. He has published various articles in *HaLapid*, *The Journal for Spanish, Portuguese, and Italian Crypto-Jews*, and *Apuntes-Theological Reflections from a Hispanic-Latino Context*, and is the author of *What is Kosher?* and *What is Jewish Prayer?* and *Who is a Jew?* He is currently the director of the B'nai Anusim Center for Education at CryptoJewishEducation.com.

Printed in Poland
by Amazon Fulfillment
Poland Sp. z o.o., Wrocław